Mastering Criminal Procedure
Volume 1
The Investigative Stage

Peter J. Henning
PROFESSOR OF LAW
WAYNE STATE UNIVERSITY LAW SCHOOL

Andrew Taslitz
PROFESSOR OF LAW
HOWARD UNIVERSITY SCHOOL OF LAW

Margaret L. Paris
DEAN
UNIVERSITY OF OREGON SCHOOL OF LAW

Cynthia E. Jones
PROFESSOR OF LAW
AMERICAN UNIVERSITY, WASHINGTON COLLEGE OF LAW

Ellen S. Podgor
PROFESSOR OF LAW
STETSON UNIVERSITY COLLEGE OF LAW

CAROLINA ACADEMIC PRESS
Durham, North Carolina

Library of Congress Cataloging in Publication Data

Mastering criminal procedure. Vol. 1, The investigative stage / Peter J. Henning ... [et al.].
    p. cm. -- (Carolina Academic Press mastering series)
    ISBN 978-1-59460-350-1 (alk. paper)
    1. Criminal procedure--United States. I. Henning, Peter J. II. Title: Investigative stage. III. Series.

KF9619.85.M378 2010
345.73'05--dc22

                                    2009046263

Carolina Academic Press
700 Kent Street
Durham, NC 27701
Telephone (919) 489-7486
Fax (919) 493-5668
www.cap-press.com

Printed in the United States of America

To Durstan and Ruth McDonald.
Peter J. Henning

To my wife, Patty, who makes life worthwhile;
my sister, Ellen, who taught me to read and write in the first place;
and my students, who give me more than I can ever say.
Andrew Taslitz

To Shel, who makes everything possible.
Margaret L. Paris

To the memory of my wonderful mother, Ernestine C. Jones (1932-2004),
who continues to motivate and inspire me.
Cynthia E. Jones

To all my students.
Ellen S. Podgor

Contents

Table of Cases

Series Editor's Foreword

The Carolina Academic Press Mastering Series is designed to provide you with a tool that will enable you to easily and efficiently "master" the substance and content of law school courses. Throughout the series, the focus is on quality writing that makes legal concepts understandable. As a result, the series is designed to be easy to read and is not unduly cluttered with footnotes or cites to secondary sources.

In order to facilitate student mastery of topics, the Mastering Series includes a number of pedagogical features designed to improve learning and retention. At the beginning of each chapter, you will find a "Roadmap" that tells you about the chapter and provides you with a sense of the material that you will cover. A "Checkpoint" at the end of each chapter encourages you to stop and review the key concepts, reiterating what you have learned. Throughout the book, key terms are explained and emphasized. Finally, a "Master Checklist" at the end of each book reinforces what you have learned and helps you identify any areas that need review or further study.

We hope that you will enjoy studying with, and learning from, the Mastering Series.

Russell L. Weaver
Professor of Law & Distinguished University Scholar
University of Louisville, Louis D. Brandeis School of Law

Preface

It is difficult to synthesize all of criminal procedure in two volumes. One finds state and federal differences in procedure, and systems that constantly change as a result of new statutes, rules, and court interpretations. The authors hope that this overview of criminal procedure will offer students an accessible study guide in understanding this important subject. The book, however, is not intended to serve as a guide for resolving a specific problem or case.

This Volume One covers the major issues in criminal procedure that relate to the Fourth, Fifth, and Sixth Amendment rights provided in the U.S. Constitution and also covers entrapment. Volume Two examines procedure issues from the bail through the jail process and also considers post-conviction matters. Because the law is not stagnant, it is important to note in using these books that one needs to look to updates that may modify the existing law.

There are many to thank:

- Professor Peter J. Henning thanks his assistant, Olive Hyman, who makes it all work, and the research assistance of Bob Rogosich (Wayne State University Law School Class of 2011).

- Professor Andrew Tasltiz thanks his wife, Patricia V. Sun, Esq., and his dogs, Odo and B'lanna, for their support, patience, love, and feedback on early drafts of several chapters (trust me—the dogs can give you a look that says, "Oh, come on! You can do better than that!"); his research assistants, Melissa Bancroft, Jasmine Modoor, Jeanne Laurenceau, Natasha Williams, and Cassandra Thomas, for their excellent work; his secretary, Gay Kirsch, for her outstanding production skills; and his co-authors, criminal procedure geeks all, albeit with warm hearts and an instinctive way of knowing just how to make me smile.

- Dean Margaret L. Paris thanks her co-authors, who always inspire.

- Professor Cynthia E. Jones thanks her wonderful deans fellows, Molly Bruder, Rebecca Walters, Brandi Taylor, and Shari D'Andrade, for their research assistance , and her Criminal Procedure students—past, present and future—at the American University, Washington College of Law

- Professor Ellen S. Podgor thanks Gordon J. Kirsch, Shannon Mullins, Stetson University College of Law, and her incredible co-authors.

Peter J. Henning
Andrew Taslitz
Margaret L. Paris
Cynthia E. Jones
Ellen S. Podgor

January 2010

Mastering Criminal Procedure
Volume 1

Chapter 1

Introduction

Roadmap

- The content of the Fourth, Fifth, Sixth, Eighth, and Fourteenth Amendments to the United States Constitution
- The steps in a criminal prosecution, including investigation, arrest, preliminary arraignment, filing of the complaint, bail-setting, preliminary hearing, grand jury hearing, indictment, information, pre-trial motion hearings (including to suppress evidence), arraignment, guilty plea, trial, post-trial motions, sentencing, appeals, and post-conviction proceedings
- The data sources for interpreting the Constitution and the methods for doing so

---

The law of criminal procedure is principally embodied in the Fourth, Fifth, Sixth, Eighth, and Fourteenth Amendments to the United States Constitution. The United States Supreme Court cases interpreting these provisions delineate the minimal scope of protection afforded to individuals charged with a crime or involved in some way in its investigation, while correspondingly imposing limits on the government's ability to investigate, arrest, detain, prosecute, and punish individuals for criminal charges. Greater protection is sometimes provided by analogous state constitutional provisions. Those provisions nevertheless involve similar concepts, text, and doctrine to those under the federal Constitution, so the latter serves as our model in much of the discussion in this volume.

Accordingly, Volume One of *Mastering Criminal Procedure* will focus on the rules of constitutional criminal procedure that govern police investigation of crime, primarily those derived from the Fourth (governing search and seizure), Fifth (the portion reciting the privilege against self-incrimination), Sixth (the portion guaranteeing an accused the right to counsel), and Fourteenth (the due process and equal protection clauses) Amendments. However, these same provisions govern the conduct of various other state actors—from elementary school teachers to occupational safety and health investigators—that can lead to the discovery of evidence of crime, so these other state actors will be considered as well.

Furthermore, it is not only the courts that engage in constitutional reasoning. Legislatures and executive branch personnel are also bound by the Con-

3

stitution and rely in part on lawyers' advice to determine what the constitution requires. These other branches engage in ongoing conversations with the judiciary and the People about what constitutional law is or should be. Legislatures likewise sometimes act to expand rights where they see the judiciary taking a cramped view of the constitution, or the legislature may act to reign in an Executive that oversteps its bounds. Consequently, Volume One will also touch on the most important federal statutory provisions and court rules that govern police investigation, though the volume's primary emphasis is on constitutional law.

Volume Two shifts the focus from the police to lawyers, that is, to prosecutors and defense counsel, emphasizing their role in investigating crime, preparing cases for trial, trying those cases or plea-bargaining them, and, if there is a conviction, preparing for and engaging in sentencing hearings and appeals. Although Volume Two will also emphasize the federal Constitution, it will also consider federal statutes, executive orders and policies, and various guidelines (such as the federal sentencing guidelines) that are of great everyday relevance to the practicing criminal lawyer doing what he or she can to make the accused's constitutional rights real while meeting the state's obligation to protect the safety and security of the People and to do justice.

This Chapter briefly outlines the text of the relevant federal constitutional provisions to be discussed here, concisely summarizes the various stages of a criminal prosecution to provide context for understanding the doctrines to follow, and briefly reviews the process of constitutional interpretation.

I. Federal Constitutional Provisions on Criminal Procedure

A. The Fourth Amendment

The right of the people to be secure in their persons, houses, papers, and effects, against unreasonable searches and seizures, shall not be violated, and no Warrants shall issue, but upon probable cause, supported by Oath or affirmation, and particularly describing the place to be searched, and the persons or things to be seized.

B. The Fifth Amendment

No person Shall be held to answer for a capital, or otherwise infamous crime, unless on a presentment or indictment of a Grand Jury, except in cases arising in the land or naval forces, or in the Militia, when in actual service in the time of War or public danger; nor shall any person be subject for the same offense to be twice put in jeopardy of life or limb; *nor shall be compelled in any criminal case to be a witness against himself,* nor be deprived of life, liberty, or property without due process of law; nor shall private property be taken for public use, without just compensation.

C. The Sixth Amendment

In all criminal prosecutions, the accused shall enjoy the right to a speedy and public trial, by an impartial jury of the State and district wherein the crime shall have been committed, which district shall have been previously ascertained by law, and to be informed of the nature and cause of the accusation; to be confronted with the witnesses against him; to have compulsory process for obtaining witness in his or her favor, and *to have the Assistance of Counsel for his defense.*

D. The Eighth Amendment

Excessive bail shall not be required, nor excessive fines imposed, nor cruel and unusual punishments inflicted.

E. The Fourteenth Amendment

No State shall make or enforce any law which shall abridge the privileges or immunities of citizens of the United States; *nor shall any State deprive any person of life, liberty, or property, without due process of law; nor deny to any person within this jurisdiction the equal protection of the laws.*

II. Stages of the Criminal Adjudication Process

The criminal procedure provisions of the Constitution collectively ensure that the criminal adjudication process is fair and untainted by government overreaching. As discussed below, some of the rights guaranteed by the Constitution apply throughout the various stages of the criminal adjudication process.

A. Initial Pre-Arrest Investigation

The criminal adjudication process usually begins when there has been a report of a criminal act. At this stage the police have to make two determinations: (1) whether a crime has been committed, and (2) who committed the crime (who "did it"). If a law enforcement officer personally witnesses the criminal conduct (*i.e.*, undercover drug buy, traffic violation, purse snatching, disorderly conduct), both of these determinations are generally resolved without further investigation. More commonly, however, police officers learn of criminal behavior after the crime has been completed and the perpetrator has escaped. Police may arrive at the scene of the purported crime in response to an emergency "911" call from a victim or eyewitness, and the police have to make a determination of what crime, if any, occurred. If there has been a crime committed, the next phase of the investigation, "solving the crime," involves collecting evidence to identify the perpetrator and to prove legal guilt.

In other instances, however, the process begins with an independent investigation by police or by prosecutors, and sometimes both, to determine whether a crime has been committed and by whom rather than in response to a victim's report of a crime. Or, the state may have reason to believe that a crime *will be* committed in the near future, but it has not yet occurred. In those instances, most of the investigative techniques are the same as with criminal cases that begin with a victim or eyewitness's report of a completed or attempted crime. The differences between cases starting with a victim's report versus those starting with prosecutor or police investigation of possible crimes thus primarily involve the order in which the investigation proceeds and the various stages of the prosecution occur rather than differences in the nature of those events. One important difference in chronological order is that state-initiated investigations, unlike complainant or eyewitness-initiated ones, often begin with an investigatory agency or grand jury investigation, perhaps followed by a later arrest, whereas victim or eyewitness-report cases may involve some investigation but arrest *precedes* grand jury or prosecutor action rather than following it.

In the course of a criminal investigation by law enforcement officers, there are a wide array of "evidence-gathering" practices that can be used to identify and locate the perpetrator of a crime. Some investigative practices are constitutionally permissible because the government does not seek to collect information directly from a specific suspect or witness nor to examine the suspect's personal belongings to find incriminating evidence. These investigative techniques include collecting physical evidence left at the crime scene, interviewing victims and eyewitnesses to get the details of the crime and descriptions of the perpetrator, canvassing the area to locate people who might have seen or heard things that could be useful in solving the crime, and gathering background information on potential suspects using the police database of criminal records.

Other investigative practices are constitutionally regulated because they involve the collection of evidence directly from a person suspected of, or a witness to, criminal activity. As such, these government investigative practices must comply with the restrictions imposed by the Fourth, Fifth, and Sixth Amendments. One constitutionally regulated investigative technique that could potentially run afoul of the Fourth Amendment protection against "unreasonable searches and seizures" is searching individuals and their personal belongings (pockets, purses, briefcases) to determine if they are in possession of incriminating evidence (e.g., the victim's credit cards, bloody gloves, marked money). Likewise, the Fifth Amendment protection against compelled self-incrimination is implicated when law enforcement officers interrogate a suspect held in custody in an attempt to elicit a confession. Interrogations must also occur in a fair manner consistent with due process and, for "post-indictment" interrogations, while respecting the Sixth Amendment right to counsel. Finally, law enforcement must comply with the Fifth and Fourteenth Amendment Due Process Clauses and the Sixth Amendment right to counsel if, for example, they seek to require a suspect to appear before eyewitnesses or to present the suspect's image to witnesses (*i.e.*, to present a line up, one-on-one "show up" identification, or photo array).

While these investigative practices are not flatly prohibited by the Constitution, the Supreme Court has interpreted these constitutional provisions to permit such techniques only if they are: (1) conducted in a fair manner, as due process requires, and, (2) for lineups and show-ups occurring after formal adversarial proceedings have begun, if counsel is present or the right to counsel has been knowingly, voluntarily, and intelligently waived. These rules are explored in great detail in the Chapters that follow.

B. Arrest

The next step in the criminal adjudication process is the arrest. Arrests usually involve the police officer taking physical control of an individual (by force, if necessary). The arrestee is usually handcuffed, placed in a police vehicle, and transported to the police station for processing. An arrest may be made with or without a warrant if made on the street, but the Fourth Amendment demands that the police have probable cause before making an arrest. Probable cause requires the government to accumulate sufficient facts to establish a fair probability that a crime has been committed and that a specific person committed the crime. Absent exigent circumstances, an arrest in a home must generally be done pursuant to an arrest warrant. Arrest warrants authorize seizures of a person, while search warrants authorize searches and seizures of tangible or intangible objects, which can include computer data and electronic files.

C. Booking

Upon arrival at the police station following an arrest, the arrestee undergoes a series of administrative procedures, commonly referred to as "booking." At this stage, police officers collect background information from the arrestee (*i.e.*, address, date of birth, place of employment), and conduct a criminal background check to determine whether the arrestee has a criminal history and outstanding arrest warrants. The booking process also includes the completion of police reports and the fingerprinting and photographing of the arrestee.

In addition, the investigation of the crime frequently continues after the arrest. Police are allowed to search the individual pursuant to a lawful arrest and the area in which he might reach to destroy evidence or grab weapons at the time of his arrest. The police also might question the arrestee about the crime to obtain incriminating statements, but must still comply with the limitations imposed by the Fifth Amendment protection against compelled self-incrimination. Indeed, police may use most of the investigative techniques after arrest that they could have used before it, although some of the constitutional rules governing how and when they do so may change.

Post-booking, the arrestee is usually placed in some form of holding cell until the police reports are reviewed by senior police officials and delivered to the prosecutor. The prosecutor must then review the information collected by the police and determine whether to file criminal charges against the defendant and what charges to pursue. While the police have the power to make arrests, the prosecutor — not the police officer — has the sole discretion to determine whether the defendant will be prosecuted at all and, if so, what charges the defendant will face.

D. Initial Court Appearance

Usually within 48 hours of the arrest, the arrestee will appear before a judicial officer for the initial court appearance, also often known as the "preliminary arraignment." At this court proceeding, the government notifies the court of its intention to open a criminal case against the arrestee, and the criminal adjudication process is thus formally initiated. The arrestee now becomes the defendant. This formal distinction has practical consequences, triggering certain rights, such as the Sixth Amendment right to counsel, that do not apply during the pre-charge phase of the process.

Three significant events occur at this stage of the process. First, at the initial court appearance, or shortly thereafter, indigent defendants are provided with legal representation. The Sixth Amendment provides that the accused is entitled to "the Assistance of Counsel." Accordingly, the court will appoint a lawyer to represent the defendant throughout the remainder of the case. The Supreme Court has, moreover, interpreted this right to be not merely to the presence of counsel but to his or her *effective* assistance, though the Court's standard for "effectiveness" is, in the view of some critics, quite low.

Second, the prosecutor will file a charging document (commonly a criminal "complaint") that sets forth the nature of the charges and the date and location of the alleged offenses. If the crime is minor, generally meaning a misdemeanor, a trial date or date to accept a plea will be scheduled, though the precise chronology may vary among jurisdictions. For more serious charges, generally meaning felonies, intermediate steps will occur before a date is set for trial or plea. In federal prosecutions, the Fifth Amendment mandates that felony and capital charges be presented to a grand jury (discussed below) before the defendant is formally charged. While this requirement is not constitutionally mandated in state court proceedings, some states nonetheless require a grand jury indictment for some or all criminal charges. In these indictment jurisdictions, the charging document presented at the initial court appearance (the complaint) simply provides the defendant with notice of the charges the government intends to pursue before the grand jury. The case may proceed further only if the grand jury indicts. If the indictment is waived, or in jurisdictions using preliminary hearings rather than indictments for most criminal prosecutions, the case may proceed only if the court issues an "information," a second charging document replacing the complaint (further details on the indicting versus the information-issuing alternatives follow shortly).

Finally, the judicial officer (usually a magistrate judge) will make a determination whether the defendant will be released pending trial, given a monetary bond (bail) that often imposes conditions of release, or held in jail until the trial date. Many factors affect this determination, including the defendant's prior criminal history, whether there is a risk that the defendant will abscond or flee the jurisdiction and not return for trial, and the seriousness of the underlying offense. If the defendant was arrested without a warrant, before the court can permit the continued detention of the defendant the judge must make an initial determination, based solely on the contents of the charging document, whether the government's evidence establishes probable cause. If not, the defendant must be released. If the judge allows the defendant to be released on a monetary bond (bail), the Eighth Amendment prohibits the court from imposing "excessive" bail.

E. Preliminary Hearing

In felony cases, after the initial court appearance, the defendant is usually entitled to a preliminary hearing. This hearing is generally held approximately two weeks after the initial court appearance. The purpose of this hearing is, depending upon the standard in each jurisdiction, either to establish probable cause to proceed on each of the charges or to make out a prima facie case of those charges. However, this determination is not made based solely on the content of the complaint. The government must present some evidence in support of those charges. What kind of evidence it must present will vary with each jurisdiction's rules and with the tactical judgments of the prosecutor.

For example, many jurisdictions require live witness testimony, though the full panoply of trial evidence rules may not apply. Witness credibility is generally not formally in issue, and the defense does not present its own case, an option it will have at trial. Nevertheless, defense counsel may hope that challenging a witness's credibility, if permitted by the court, will influence the judge's decision whether to hold the case for trial (*i.e.*, to find sufficient evidence to proceed to trial). Defense counsel might also question prosecution witnesses to show that there is not probable cause for some or all the charges, even if the witness is telling the truth. Furthermore, defense counsel might question prosecution witnesses as a form of pretrial discovery. Although using the preliminary hearing as a discovery tool is usually not recognized formally as a purpose of the preliminary hearing, many judges permit defense counsel some leeway concerning discovery because of the limited discovery usually available to the defense even at later stages of the prosecution—limited at least in comparison to the relatively wide-ranging discussion allowed in civil cases.

The judicial officer has the authority to dismiss some or all the charges if the court finds that the government evidence does not establish probable cause. In this way, the preliminary hearing potentially serves as a check on the discretionary authority of the prosecutor and vests the court with the power to prevent a "rush to judgment" by an over-zealous district attorney. More commonly, however, the prosecution has little difficulty meeting the probable cause standard, and the preliminary hearing has very little lasting impact on the case.

F. Grand Jury

The grand jury is another check on the power of the government to prosecute individuals accused of criminal conduct. Because a grand jury indictment is not constitutionally mandated for state criminal prosecutions, most also allow prosecutors to initiate felony prosecutions based solely on a criminal complaint (for misdemeanor cases) or an information (for felony cases). For federal felony charges, however, the Fifth Amendment mandates that the government secure an indictment by a grand jury. Eighteen states and the District of Columbia follow this process. In other jurisdictions, a grand jury indictment is required only for an enumerated list of the most serious felony charges or not at all. Even in jurisdictions rarely, if ever, requiring *indicting* grand juries, legislation authorizes prosecutors, at least under certain circumstances, to turn to *investigating* grand juries. An indicting grand jury decides whether there is probable cause to take some or all of the charges in a criminal complaint to trial. But an investigating grand jury initially has no one to indict. Instead, the grand jury investigates whether any crime has been committed at all and, if it has, who committed the crime.

The advantage for the prosecutor is that a grand jury can issue subpoenas for persons to testify as witnesses and for documents or other physical evidence, a power that the prosecutor alone generally lacks. Moreover, in many jurisdictions grand jury proceedings are secret, making it easier to investigate without the prosecutor's tipping off witnesses to what other witnesses have said. A prosecutor who lacks sufficient evidence to indict a particular individual or even to arrest him and proceed to a preliminary hearing thus embraces the investigating grand jury as an alternative.

Grand Jurors are selected among the citizens in the jurisdiction to hear the government's evidence and determine whether the government has sufficient evidence to require a defendant to stand trial on the charges. If the grand jury believes the government's evidence is sufficient, they can issue an indictment or a "true bill" authorizing the government to proceed on the criminal charges. The grand jury only hears the government's evidence of guilt and the defendant does not have the right to appear before the grand jury or present evidence. Not even the trial judge is present when the prosecution presents its case to the grand jury. Moreover, the rules of evidence are greatly relaxed, in some jurisdictions so much so that an indictment may be obtained purely upon hearsay, the lead detective, for example, simply reading the police reports into the record. As a result, although the grand jury has the power to refuse to indict, or to indict on lesser charges, grand juries almost always return an indictment on all of the charges presented by the government.

G. Arraignment

After an indictment is returned by the grand jury, it becomes the official charging instrument. The government must then file the indictment with the court. Thereafter, the defendant is scheduled for an arraignment. Similarly, if only a preliminary hearing is used, a decision to hold the case for trial results in issuance of an information, which is also followed by arraignment. The purpose of the arraignment is to give the defendant formal notice of the charges prior to trial, a right guaranteed by the Sixth Amendment. The defendant also enters a formal plea (guilty or not guilty) to the charges at the arraignment. Although many cases are resolved by a guilty plea, if the defendant pleads not guilty, the case will continue and the judge will schedule a trial date.

H. Pretrial Litigation

After the arraignment, a great deal of work on the case takes place outside of the courtroom. Defense counsel is required to conduct a thorough investigation of the case, including: visiting the crime scene, collecting police reports, inspecting the tangible government evidence, and interviewing witnesses. The defense can also file written motions to suppress tangible evidence, statements, or pretrial identifications that the government intends to introduce at trial. Commonly, the defense motions to suppress are based on allegations that the government obtained evidence by violating the defendant's constitutional rights. As a result, the defendant seeks the remedy of suppression of the evidence. The court usually holds a pretrial suppression hearing wherein the government has the opportunity to establish that the defendant's constitutional rights were not violated.

After the conclusion of the hearing, the court will rule on the admissibility of the evidence. If the evidence is excluded, the government may lack sufficient evidence to prove the charges, and the case will be dismissed. More commonly, however, the court finds no constitutional violation and the evidence is deemed properly admissible. In other instances the court does suppress *some* evidence, but there is sufficient remaining admissible evidence to enable the case to go to trial, though the prosecution will have the handicap of relying on a smaller body of evidence in its favor.

I. Trial

The overwhelming majority of criminal cases (over 90%) are resolved with a plea agreement between the prosecution and the defense. The government agrees to reduce the charges, and the defendant agrees to waive his right to a trial and admit to criminal violations. Commonly, plea agreements either spare the defendant incarceration or reduce the length of a prison term. If, however, the defendant opts to go to trial on the criminal charges, there are several constitutional provisions—principally embodied in the Fifth and Sixth Amendments—designed to ensure the defendant receives a fair trial.

In a criminal trial, the government has the burden of proving guilt beyond a reasonable doubt. If the government cannot prove guilt beyond a reasonable doubt, the fact-finder (judge or jury) is required to return a verdict of not guilty. The Supreme Court has repeatedly held that the presumption of innocence and the burden of proof, though not expressly enumerated in the Constitution, are protected rights essential to our system of justice. In addition, the Sixth Amendment Confrontation Clause secures the right to confront (and the opportunity to cross-examine) government witnesses at trial. If the defendant elects to present evidence at trial, the Sixth Amendment Compulsory Process Clause ensures that the defendant will be allowed to subpoena witnesses and evidence needed to mount a defense. Finally, if the defendant is acquitted at trial, the Fifth Amendment Double Jeopardy Clause prevents the government from instituting a re-trial of the defendant in the same jurisdiction on the same charges.

J. Sentencing

If the defendant is found guilty at trial, in most jurisdictions, the judge then imposes a sentence hearing. At that hearing, both the prosecution and the defense are entitled to present evidence. The prosecution will often seek to emphasize the seriousness of the crime, the unlikelihood of rehabilitating the defendant, the need for a severe sentence to deter other would-be offenders, and the defendant's lack of remorse, among other factors. The defense will argue just the opposite. Sentencing is as important an event as a trial because it may determine whether a defendant is free to pursue his life's goals or must instead face incarceration and, if incarcerated, for what length of time.

Even if not incarcerated, a sentenced defendant may be required to comply with conditions for avoiding confinement, such as successfully completing a drug rehabilitation program, a job-training program, a high school graduate equivalency diploma, an anger management course, or public service while also avoiding involvement in further crime. Although the rules of evidence at sentencing are usually minimal, lawyers on both sides must thus make tactical judgments about what live witnesses to call and what evidence to present. Defense attorneys may also work to place their clients in rehabilitative programs well in advance of sentencing, hoping to garner favorable progress reports to show that the defendant is well on his way to reform. Probation officers also usually prepare a report for the court [or sentencing judge] about the case, including the defendant's life experiences and character and a recommended sentence, and mental health services might also prepare a report. Counsel often can have significant input in seeking to tilt these reports one way or another. Furthermore, sentencing often involves complex legal issues that counsel must research, often requiring briefing.

Although state statutes establish the permissible range of sentences — the maximum and minimum sentences — that can be imposed by the court, judges still have enormous flexibility in determining the exact sentence imposed in each case. Moreover, many jurisdictions have sentencing guidelines that at least presumptively require a sentence within a fairly narrow range based upon the severity of the current charge and the defendant's prior criminal record. However, what range the defendant's case fits in can vary based upon a variety of facts whose presence or absence the parties may contest. Moreover, even within the narrow guidelines range, there may be some room for judicial discretion in choosing precisely where within that range to sentence the defendant. Some guidelines jurisdictions are mandatory, meaning the judge must follow the guidelines. However, the federal Constitution has been interpreted to require that juries find certain facts on which the sentence in a mandatory guidelines jurisdiction depends. Other jurisdictions have advisory guidelines, permitting the sentencing court to deviate up or down from the guidelines for good reasons adequately stated on the record. In such jurisdictions, the constitution does not mandate any jury involvement. A criminal sentence may include incarceration for a term of years, supervised probation, or a monetary fine, among other options. The wide latitude that courts enjoy in crafting an appropriate sentence is tempered by the Eighth Amendment prohibition against "excessive fines" and "cruel and unusual" punishment.

Sentencing should not be thought of solely as something relevant at the end of the criminal process. Plea negotiations, for example, turn in part on the likely sentence after conviction. A prosecutor risking an acquittal or a lesser sentence than he or she could obtain if all cards fall his or her way has an incentive to accept a plea for less than the maximum likely sentence. Correspondingly, however, a defendant likely to be convicted and face a harsh sentence after trial has an incentive to plead guilty in exchange for a prosecutorial recommendation of a less-than-maximum-likely-sentence.

K. Appeals

The Double Jeopardy Clause generally prohibits the government from appealing a verdict of not guilty. Most criminal appeals, therefore, are filed by criminal defendants who have been found guilty at trial and seek a reversal of the conviction based on legal errors at trial. To secure a reversal, the defendant must establish either that no reasonable jury should have been able to find all the elements of each crime beyond a reasonable doubt (an "insufficiency of the evidence" claim) or that the trial court committed legal errors that rendered the verdict unfair. Commonly, such alleged legal errors include the trial court's giving erroneous jury instructions that misstated the law or misled or confused the jury, or the judge wrongly admitting inculpatory evidence.

An appellate court finding insufficient evidence will reverse the conviction, and the case ends. The Double Jeopardy Clause in such cases prohibits a re-trial. An appellate court finding trial error will still vacate the conviction, but the prosecution generally remains free (absent proof of some extreme forms of prosecutorial misconduct) to re-try the defendant before another jury. The re-trial must, however, include the corrected jury instructions and exclude any improperly admitted evidence from the first trial. Convictions are very rarely reversed on appeal. In fact, even in cases where DNA evidence exonerated the defendant, earlier appeals challenging the conviction had often been unsuccessful.

L. Post-Conviction Remedies

In addition to the state appellate process, defendants can also petition the federal court for a writ of habeas corpus to seek relief from a conviction based on certain alleged constitutional violations. Access to federal court usually turns first on an exhaustion of state remedies, so most states have their own post-conviction statutory processes. Probably the most commonly asserted claim in post-conviction cases is that prior defense attorneys were constitutionally ineffective.

The right of prisoners to file federal collateral appeals has been significantly curtailed by Congress in recent years. In response to the proliferation of DNA exonerations, however, many states now have innocence protection statutes that allow prisoners to petition the court for post-conviction DNA testing to prove their actual innocence. To date, over 230 innocent people have been exonerated by DNA testing.

III. A Brief Word on the Process of Constitutional Interpretation

Although this book focuses on the relevant doctrine and its meaning and application, that doctrine is crafted by the courts' interpreting the relevant constitutional provisions. That process of interpretation matters for several reasons.

First, the Supreme Court sometimes reverses itself, particularly in close decisions and with a changing line-up of Justices. Second, it can sometimes be argued that a client's situation does not fit into any existing doctrinal rule, leading to creation of a new rule, which, in turn, requires turning back to first principles of constitutional interpretation. Third, state constitutions can provide more, though never less, protection than the federal Constitution. An advocate can, therefore, sometimes argue in state court that a federal constitutional doctrinal rule should be supplemented by a stronger state constitutional rule. Once again, that often requires interpreting a constitution, albeit now a state constitution, using first principles. Accordingly, it is worth reviewing the process of constitutional interpretation. One concise, helpful way to do this is to view constitutional interpretation as an evidentiary question: What evidence is there to support a particular argument as to the Constitution's meaning and its application to a particular case?

There are seven sources of evidence to which courts look to determine the (or a) constitution's meaning:

A. Text

All constitutional interpretation starts with the text of the Constitution. Some "textualists" argue that, whenever possible, that is also where interpretation should end. Such an approach is easy for provisions that are quite specific, for example, specifying the minimum age required to be a candidate for President. But other provisions, particularly those concerning criminal procedure, use broad, sweeping language that is far from self-defining. Thus the Fourth Amendment prohibits "unreasonable" searches and seizures, but what does "unreasonable" mean? The Supreme Court has often suggested that it is self-evident that it means the state is barred from conducting searches where individual interests outweigh the state's interests. But even if this suggestion is correct, that balancing process leaves wide room for debate about what is reasonable in any particular case or class of cases. Yet the text is not meaningless either. It makes clear that not all searches and seizures are barred, and it focuses debate on the meaning of a particular word—"unreasonable"—as the locus of debate.

B. Intent of the Framers, Ratifiers, and the "People"

Some "originalists" insist that, whenever possible, the "original intent" of the framers of the relevant constitutional provision should control, meaning what they subjectively intended the provision to mean. But evidence of intent is often sparse, and it can be hard to divine a single intent where many of the framers had different views on the provision's meaning. Other originalists seek to solve this problem by looking to not the original intent of the framers but the original "meaning" that the words would have had to informed readers at the time of the framing. But this too raises problems concerning whether we had adequate evidence of that meaning, how such evidence should be interpreted, and how to handle evidence of conflicting understandings. Moreover, whose views as readers should count: the drafters of dictionaries of the time? All Americans eligible to vote (a small percentage of the population in 1789, the date of the ratification of the Constitution and 1791), the date of the ratification of the Bill of Rights? All literate Americans?

A second source of debate over whose intentions or understandings should control turns on the distinction among framers, ratifiers, and the "People." The "framers" were those who wrote the relevant constitutional provision. For the original constitution, that meant the members of the Constitutional Convention meeting in Philadelphia, Pennsylvania. For the Bill of Rights, that meant Congress. But the original Constitution and the Bill of Rights lacked the force of law until ratified by a sufficient number of state conventions. Other interpreters therefore look to the state ratifying conventions, though often the intentions and understandings differed among the various state conventions. Yet the state conventions consisted of representatives of the People. Still other theorists argue, accordingly, that we must look to broader history to determine the likely intentions or understandings of the People themselves.

One further relevant debate concerns time. The Fourteenth Amendment was ratified in 1868. The Court has read that Amendment as applying or "incorporating" most of the Bill of Rights, and all of its provisions discussed in this volume, to the states. If that is so, then should not the intentions or understandings of the framers, ratifiers or People in 1868, rather than 1791, control? Should the 1868 intentions or understandings be read as consistent with those of 1791 whenever possible, or should 1868 be viewed as a radical break with the past? Even if this last question is answered in favor of radicalism, must not the 1791 intentions and understandings still be examined if we are fully to understand those of 1868?

Finally, originalists debate the degree of specificity at which intentions or understandings should be divined. Some emphasize the most specific intentions or understandings. Taken literally, that leads to a very limited scope of the Constitution to adapt to changing times. Thus the Fourth Amendment could not have been intended by its framers to protect against electronic wiretapping because such things did not exist in 1791 or 1868. A more common variant of high-specificity uses the specific intentions for purposes of analogy rather than absolute control. "Eavesdropping," under this approach, was a practice known to the framers, yet neither the text nor the history of the Fourth Amendment in 1791 or 1868 reveals an intention to prohibit governmental eavesdropping. Because wiretapping is but a modern version of eavesdropping, argue these theorists, wiretapping is also not prohibited by the Fourth Amendment. Still other originalists, however, look to a more general, higher level intention of the framers. Under this view, the framers chose the broad language of "unreasonable" searches and seizures precisely because they knew they could not anticipate every relevant violation of the People's liberties. One relevant liberty they meant to protect was privacy, though they used other words at that time to describe what we modernly label as "private." Because wiretapping is a highly intrusive government invasion of privacy, it should, therefore, be governed by Fourth Amendment strictures. This conclusion would hold even if we analogize wiretapping to eavesdropping and even if the framers specifically did not at that time intend to bar eavesdropping.

C. Constitutional Structure

There are two forms of structural constitutional reasoning: text-based and institution-based structures. A text-based approach reads the Constitution holistically to find patterns revealed by the interconnections among various provisions read as a whole. Thus a Justice might see in the Fourth Amendment's protection against unreasonable searches and seizures, the Fifth Amendment's protections against revealing the contents of one's mind (the privilege against self-incrimination), the First Amendment's protection of free speech as often including (as interpreted by the courts) shielding of organizations from revealing their membership lists to the government, and other provisions a series of "penumbras" that create a more general right to privacy. Yet the word "privacy" does not itself appear anywhere in the Constitution. An institution-based approach, by contrast, looks for themes not only in the text but in the institutions the text creates. For example, Professor Akhil Amar contends that the emphasis on jury-related rights in the criminal procedure provisions of the Bill of Rights—rights to a jury trial, to confrontation of witnesses at that trial, to compulsory process for defense witnesses at that trial, and for that trial's speedy and public nature—reveal a theme of concern with monitoring governmental abuses and promoting populist justice through the institution of the jury. Accordingly, Amar finds that the primary structural remedy for violations of the Fourth Amendment should be civil jury trials for damages, though the Fourth Amendment read in isolation never mentions juries. Both approaches may look to history, but they do so only in search of these underlying themes.

D. Precedent

This data source is a familiar one and requires little commentary. Once the Court has interpreted a constitutional provision to have a particular meaning in a specific case, that case becomes precedent in future cases, as the doctrine of *stare decisis* requires. At the same time, *stare decisis* has less force in constitutional litigation, so the Court may sometimes prove more willing to overrule cases in this area than in non-constitutional ones. Even given that a precedent is not overruled, however, advocates frequently argue that their case is factually distinguishable and should be governed by a different, more favorable line of precedent or require an entirely new rule for a new class of cases.

E. Evidence of American Customs, Traditions, and Practices

Due process has been defined as protecting "fundamental fairness" as understood in a system of "ordered liberty" that defines our "Anglo-American system of justice." The Court has read the Fourteenth Amendment's Due Process Clause as applying the Bill of Rights provisions relevant here to the states (the original 1791 Bill of Rights applied only to the federal government). Consequently, logic arguably suggests that those provisions must be read in light of the specifically *American* conceptions of justice and ordered liberty—not America as it exists at any one point in time but rather American themes of justice cutting across, and evolving over, many periods of time. Accordingly, American customs, traditions, and practices matter. The primary difference between an originalist approach and a customs-based one is that the former looks to one or two or, at most, three specific moments in time (1789, 1791, 1868), while the latter looks to the broad sweep of American history.

Perhaps, for example, governmental eavesdropping was not a significant concern in 1791 or 1868 but became an increasingly important concern of the People, including as manifested in legislation, jury verdicts, court decisions, public protests, newspapers, and fiction, from World War I until today. That development might be seen as rooted in a still-older tradition of privacy protection dating back to 1791. But that tradition evolved as the People better came to understand eavesdropping as a danger to privacy, an understanding embedded in customs and practices. Finally, is there a real difference among the three terms, "customs," "traditions," and "practices"? The courts often use the terms interchangeably and without clear definition. Theorists often debate whether there are semantic differences and whether they matter. But those debates are less important than simply understanding that the terms connote attention to evolving but long-standing behaviors and ideas of the populace across significant spans of time. How much time is required, what to do when different sub-groups seem to embrace different traditions, how to interpret behaviors as revealing one tradition or another are also, however, all subject to dispute, so the customs-based approach, like all the others, is no cure-all.

F. Contemporary Morality and Attitudes

The difference between this data source and the one just discussed above is that the focus here is on modern attitudes—those embraced *today*—rather than at any time in the past. Thus the Fourth Amendment applies only when there has been a "search" or a "seizure." The Court defines a "search" as an invasion of a "reasonable expectation of privacy." Some writers interpret this phrase to state an empirical question: What privacy expectations, if any, do most Americans expect to have? Under this view, as at least one study has revealed, most Americans today believe they have a substantial privacy interest in the content of their bank accounts. Yet the Court has held to the contrary. This result may be because the Court too often relies on its own intuition rather than on empirical data to determine what expectations Americans hold. But the result might also suggest that the Court means something other than, "What do most Americans actually think" when it refers to "reasonable" expectations of privacy. Indeed, in the view of many commentators, the Court is simply inconsistent: sometimes it relies on actual expectations, sometimes it considers those expectations as but one factor in the analysis, still other times it ignores actual expectations entirely. Moreover, it often seems to include a strong normative component—what underlying constitutional *values* require finding one expectation reasonable, another not.

G. Considerations of Practicality and Prudence

Courts often consider the real-world impact of certain constitutional rules—their likely effect on persons, groups, and institutions—in deciding whether to adopt those rules. The modern Court has repeatedly insisted that the purpose of the exclusionary rule in the Fourth Amendment context is to deter wrongful police behavior. But whether, and to what extent, applying exclusion to a particular class of seized evidence will or will not significantly deter the police is an empirical question too. Often times social science is available on such empirical matters, though Justices are sometimes selective about when they pay attention to social science and how much weight they give it, and sometimes the social science conflicts. That leaves Justices with their intuitions, analogies, ideologies, logic, and informed speculation. On the questions of when the exclusionary rule has a police deterrent effect and how significant it is the Justices simply reach different conclusions.

Individual Justices frequently claim to embrace a philosophy that focuses entirely on one or two of these data sources, while other Justices openly consider them all in a pragmatic process of weighing and sifting the evidence. Other Justices openly consider all data sources but favoring giving some more weight than others, at least under certain circumstances. Many theorists and social scientists agree, however, that no matter what the Justices claim to be doing, they in fact give some consideration to all these data sources, sometimes considering some in one case, others in a different case, all of them in a third case, often without conscious awareness of their choice or, if aware, careful justification for it. An advocate must thus be ready to consider the relevance to his or her argument of each of these data sources, recognizing too that some might be more persuasive to certain Justices, while other data sources might persuade remaining hold-outs.

The differences among Justices in considering and weighing these data sources will become evident in the Chapters that follow, often especially visible in concurring and dissenting opinions. Awareness of these data sources can also be of enormous value in understanding, distinguishing, and critiquing majority opinions. We begin this journey in the next Chapter, where we start our discussion of the constitutional provision that, among those covered in this volume, has led to the most voluminous and complex body of precedent: the Fourth Amendment.

Checkpoints

- The Fourth Amendment prohibits unreasonable searches and seizures; the Fifth Amendment compelled self-incrimination; the Sixth Amendment denial of the right to counsel; the Eighth Amendment cruel and unusual punishments and excessive bail; and the Fifth and Fourteenth Amendments denial of a fair trial.

- Most criminal cases start with an arrest, followed by booking (photographing, fingerprinting, and other processing procedures) and a preliminary arraignment at which bail, if any, is set, counsel is appointed for the indigent, the suspect is informed of the charges against him, and the judge makes a determination, assuming the truth of the complaint, of whether there is probable cause to proceed with any or all the charges.

Checkpoints *continued*

- Next steps involve in most jurisdictions a preliminary hearing in felony cases (misdemeanors usually skip this step) at which evidence, generally including some testimony, is taken to determine whether there is probable cause to proceed on any or all of the charges to trial; if the judge finds that there is, an "information" is issued, replacing the complaint as a charging document. The preliminary hearing is an adversarial proceeding in which both prosecutors and defense counsel participate, though no affirmative defense evidence is usually allowed.

- Other jurisdictions often proceed alternatively or additionally by a grand jury, which also decides the probable cause question, though most grand jury hearings occur in secrecy and in the presence only of the prosecutor, the grand jury, and each witness (one-at-a-time). If a grand jury finds probable cause, it issues an indictment.

- If a prosecutor initially lacks probable cause to arrest, the prosecutor may in many jurisdictions start the case with a grand jury, which has the power to subpoena witnesses, and those witnesses may create the probable cause needed for indictment and arrest.

- After information or indictment, there will be pre-trial motion hearings, including to suppress evidence allegedly obtained in violation of the Constitution, and an arraignment at which the defendant may plead guilty or not guilty. If he pleads guilty, depending upon the case and the jurisdiction, he might do so at that time or at a later date set for taking his plea, usually as the result of plea-bargaining. If he pleads not guilty, the case will proceed to trial, unless a plea agreement is reached between arraignment and trial.

- If convicted at trial, the defendant will proceed to a sentencing hearing and may file motions to overturn the conviction, or for a new trial, or for re-sentencing. Thereafter, he may appeal and, if his appeals fail, may proceed to post-conviction or collateral proceedings, in which one of the most common claims is that he must be heard anew because all his earlier lawyers provided the ineffective assistance of counsel, contrary to the guarantees of the Sixth Amendment.

- Most constitutional criminal procedure provisions are broad and ambiguous, requiring them to be interpreted. The courts generally turn to the following data sources to interpret these provisions:
    - text;
    - intentions of the framers and ratifiers;
    - constitutional structure (themes revealed across textual provisions or in the institutions created by the text);
    - precedent;
    - American customs, traditions, and practices;
    - contemporary morality and attitudes;
    - considerations of practicality and prudence

Chapter 2

When Does the Fourth Amendment Apply?

Roadmap

- The Scope of the Fourth Amendment
- The Requirement of "government action" against "the people"
- The *Katz* "Reasonable Expectation of Privacy" test
- What government investigative techniques constitute a "search" or "seizure"
- Government investigative activity beyond the reach of the Fourth Amendment

---

I. Introduction

In order to prosecute criminal conduct, the government, acting through law enforcement officers, must conduct an investigation and gather sufficient incriminating evidence to present at trial to prove guilt. There are, however, constitutional restraints on the extent to which the government can engage in these investigative or "evidence-gathering" practices. Specifically, the Fourth Amendment prohibits the government from engaging in "unreasonable searches and seizures" in gathering evidence. In criminal cases where the government has collected incriminating evidence on or near the defendant, or among the defendant's possessions, the defense frequently seeks to prohibit the government from using the evidence at trial by filing a motion to suppress (or exclude) the evidence. The basis for the defense motion is an assertion that the government acquired the evidence by engaging in an unreasonable search or seizure in violation of the defendant's Fourth Amendment rights. That is, the defense will challenge the authority of the police to engage in the investigative conduct that led them to the discovery of the evidence.

If the court finds that the government violated the Fourth Amendment, the trial judge can grant the defense motion to suppress and prohibit the government from using the evidence at trial. The exclusion of "constitutionally tainted" evidence could effectively result in the dismissal of all criminal charges if the government does not have sufficient "constitutionally acquired" evidence to prove guilt. Thus, the threshold question to be asked in analyzing the government's conduct under the under Fourth Amendment is: *"Did the government engage in an unreasonable search and seizure to obtain the evidence to be used against the defendant at trial?"* The answer to this question requires an understanding of the purpose and scope of the Fourth Amendment.

II. The Purpose of the Fourth Amendment

The Fourth Amendment to the United States Constitution states:

> *The right of the people to be secure in their persons, houses, papers, and effects, against unreasonable searches and seizures, shall not be violated, and no Warrants shall issue, but upon probable cause, supported by Oath or affirmation, and particularly describing the place to be searched, and the persons or things to be seized.*

The Fourth Amendment seeks to balance the right of citizens to be free from government interference in their personal lives with the authority of the government to protect public safety by investigating crimes and collecting evidence of criminal activity. These interests can collide when the government has reason to believe that incriminating evidence is located in a private place, like inside a purse, in the trunk of a car, or in the bedroom closet of a private residence. The Fourth Amendment governs whether and under what circumstances the government can go into these private locations and retrieve evidence. Supreme Court cases interpreting the Fourth Amendment have acknowledged the vital importance of the privacy rights of citizens and defined the extent to which these rights must yield to the government's superior public safety function. The Court has tried to strike this balance by establishing a set of rules to act as a restraint on the government's power to engage in criminal investigative practices that are unduly or unreasonably intrusive into the private lives of citizens.

It is important to emphasize that invasion of reasonable privacy expectations — searches — are not the Fourth Amendment's sole trigger. Government seizures of persons or things likewise implicate the Amendment's protections. We will briefly discuss the seizures shortly as a way of setting the stage for much of the rest of this book, but the nature of seizures is discussed in far more depth in Chapter 3. Here our focus is on privacy.

III. The Scope of the Fourth Amendment

The Fourth Amendment does not restrict every government investigative practice that yields incriminating evidence. Three conditions must exist to trigger the protections of the Fourth Amendment: government action, against "the people," and investigative activity that constitutes a "search" or "seizure."

A. Government Action

As stated above, the Fourth Amendment acts as a restraint on *government* conduct, both state and federal. While most searches and seizures are conducted by law enforcement officers working for the government, the Supreme Court has held that non-law enforcement government employees, like public school officials and government agencies, must also comply with the rights guaranteed by the Fourth Amendment. *New Jersey v. T.L.O.*, 469 U.S. 325 (1985) (public school employees conducting search of student's purse).

The protections of the Fourth Amendment are not implicated when non-government, private actors find and deliver evidence to the government. *United States v. Jacobsen*, 466 U.S. 109 (1984). While there may be a private cause of action against these individuals, their conduct is not covered by the Fourth Amendment unless they were acting at the behest of the government. If the discovery of the evidence is truly the result of an independent private search, there is no constitutional bar to the government's use of the evidence in a criminal trial. *Burdeau v. McDowell*, 256 U.S. 465 (1921). The government cannot, however, circumvent the Fourth Amendment by recruiting or "deputizing" private actors to do indirectly what the Fourth Amendment prohibits the government from doing directly. *United States v. Walther*, 652 F.2d 788 (9th Cir. 1981) (airline employee acting as an agent of the government when he routinely searched luggage with the government's tacit approval).

B. The "People"

The language of the Fourth Amendment expressly provides protection for "the people" against government action. The Supreme Court has held that "the people" refers to the "national community" of persons who have developed a sufficient connection with the United States to be considered part of the U.S. community. Accordingly, in *United States v. Verdugo-Urquidez*, 494 U.S. 259 (1990), the Court held that when U.S. government agents are in a foreign country conducting searches and seizures of property owned by nonresident aliens, the Fourth Amendment does not apply.

C. What Government Conduct Constitutes a Fourth Amendment Search

In order for investigative action by "the government" against "the people" to fall within the scope of the Fourth Amendment, the government conduct must constitute a "search" or a "seizure." If the government conduct falls within the definition of a "search" or "seizure," the Fourth Amendment commands that the government conduct be reasonable. Generally, at least in theory, if not always in practice, government searches and seizures are presumptively "unreasonable" if the government is not acting pursuant to a valid warrant issued by a magistrate. (See Chapter 3.) Alternatively, searches and seizures may be deemed reasonable if the government's actions fall within the scope of one of the exceptions to the warrant requirement. (See Chapters 4–11.) Even if an exception to the warrant requirement applies, however, a search or seizure may be unreasonable if it lacks adequate justification, usually meaning "probable cause" or "reasonable suspicion." On the other hand, as we will see in later chapters, sometimes courts find searches or seizures "reasonable" that lack any justification whatsoever, for example, random searches done without suspicion of any individual's wrongdoing. (See Chapter 11.) If, however, the government investigative conduct does not fit within the definition of a "search" or a "seizure," the Fourth Amendment does not apply and the government is free to engage in the conduct without first obtaining a warrant or otherwise complying with the reasonableness requirement.

1. What Is a "Search:" The Katz Test

In *Katz v. United States*, 389 U.S. 347 (1967), the government used an electronic listening device to intercept the telephone conversation Katz was having in a public telephone booth. The government maintained that there was no search or seizure because there was no physical intrusion into the booth and nothing tangible was actually seized when the agents overheard the conversation involving illegal gambling. The Court rejected these contentions and found that the government engages in a Fourth Amendment "search" whenever there is an intrusion into an area where an individual has reasonable and legitimate privacy interests. In his concurrence in *Katz*, Justice Harlan elucidated the Court's broad interpretation of the Fourth Amendment protection and articulated a two-prong test for determining whether government conduct constitutes a search. Justice Harlan stated that a search occurs when: (1) the citizen has manifested a subjective expectation of privacy in the area; and (2) the privacy interest is one society is prepared to recognize as reasonable. The Supreme Court later adopted Justice Harlan's two-prong test, commonly referred to as the "Katz test" or the *reasonable expectation of privacy*" standard. Each prong of the *Katz* test is critical to an understanding of the type of conduct included and excluded from the scope of the Fourth Amendment.

a. Subjective Expectation of Privacy

The first prong of the *Katz* test focuses on whether the individual has manifested a desire to keep private the information uncovered by the government investigation. If the defendant has taken reasonable measures to protect this item from public exposure, then the first prong of the *Katz* test is met. Conversely, if the information is openly accessible to any member of the public, the individual has not manifested a subjective expectation that the information would remain private. For example, an individual speaking on a cellular phone out in public where anyone in the vicinity can overhear the conversation likely has not manifested a subjective expectation that the phone conversation will remain private. Likewise, in *Florida v. Jimeno*, 500 U.S. 248 (1991), there was no Fourth Amendment violation when the police overheard the defendant speaking loudly on an open public telephone about a drug transaction.

Courts have also found no subjective expectation of privacy when an individual abandons her property. Abandonment has been found when an individual knowingly and purposely discards an item in a public place, *United States v. Wilson*, 36 F.3d 205 (1st Cir. 1994), where an individual walks away and leaves his or her property in a public place, *United States v. Thomas*, 864 F.2d 843 (D.C. Cir. 1989), or expressly denies ownership of the item, *United States v. Sanders*, 196 F.3d 910 (8th Cir. 1999).

b. Reasonable Expectations of Privacy

Even when the individual has taken steps to keep matters private, such desires for privacy may not be deemed reasonable. The second prong of the *Katz* test involves an assessment of whether it is reasonable for an individual to expect that certain matters will remain private, or whether society is prepared to honor the individual's subjective wishes to keep certain information private. The Court has consistently exempted the acquisition of personal characteristics or "external" information from the definition of a search. The Court has reasoned that unless a person chooses to live in complete isolation from society, during the normal course of public interaction with strangers one necessarily discloses information about themselves like appearance and facial characteristics. Thus, the police do not engage in a Fourth Amendment search by taking a person's photo while out in public, *United States v. Holland*, 438 F.2d 887 (6th Cir. 1971), collecting a handwriting sample, *United States v. Mara*,

410 U.S. 19 (1973), or obtaining a voice exemplar, *United States v. Dionisio*, 410 U.S. 1 (1973).

The Court has, however, never clearly explained how it decides what expectations are "reasonable." Is the question whether most Americans would see the expectation as justifiable under the circumstances? If yes, social science on American perceptions of privacy or other evidence of American attitudes (history, contemporary practices, statutory law, among other sources) toward privacy should control. Alternatively, if the question is not what most Americans do expect but rather what they should have a right to expect, then majority attitudes might be relevant, but would not control. Rather, the question would be one of constitutional values, a normative or moral question about what we as a polity want our citizens to expect. But that inquiry requires a clear statement of exactly what values the Fourth Amendment was designed to serve. The Court has often simply spoken in generalities on this question, though commentators have each argued for their favorite value, from restraining officer discretion, to protecting individual autonomy (freedom of choice in how to live one's life), to encouraging diversity, dissent, and non-conformity (this last trio of values requiring privacy to avoid social pressure to conform).

Given this uncertainty, practicing lawyers are usually forced to rely first and foremost on analogy to other cases, prosecutors relying on cases finding no reasonable expectation of privacy, defense attorneys relying on cases holding just the opposite. Although the categories of cases discussed below are organized by who or what is purportedly being searched or by what means, the cases reveal several factors that the Court considers in determining whether privacy expectations are reasonable. The key factors include: (1) location, *i.e.*, in a home, car, or public street; (2) "assumption of risk," or whether an individual revealed information to a third party who then shared that information with the police; (3) the nature of the property interests, for example, as owner versus visitor; (4) social custom, such as whether casual guests are treated by their hosts as if the guests had privacy expectations in the home; (5) past practices and expectations between or among the persons involved or as recognized in American history; (6) legality (or illegality) and intimacy of the activities occurring; and (7) vantage point, for example, whether from a helicopter or the street. But a sharp advocate will also look for evidence of majority attitudes, where it is available, and will make values-based arguments, though rooting them in traditional sources of constitutional interpretation, for example, by arguing that those values were embraced by the Framers, embodied in the scope of constitutional history, reflected in American traditions and practices or implicit in well-respected precedent.

One final introductory point must be noted. Although the Court generally examines both subjective and objective (*i.e.*, reasonable) expectations of privacy, the objective reasonableness inquiry is generally more important and sometimes the sole inquiry. The reason for this is to prevent the government from eliminating any real Fourth Amendment protection by simply declaring that no one under certain circumstances, or perhaps under all circumstances, should in the future expect to be free from government surveillance, for the government plans to ramp up its observation of its people to become ever-present. As the Court in *Smith v. Maryland*, 442 U.S. 735 (1979) put it:

> [I]f the Government were suddenly to announce on nationwide television that all homes henceforth would be subject to warrantless entry, individuals thereafter might not in fact entertain any actual expectation of privacy regarding their homes, papers, and effects. Similarly, if a refugee from a totalitarian country, unaware of this nation's traditions, erroneously assumed that police were continuously monitoring his telephone conversations, a subjective expectation of privacy regarding the contents of his calls might be lacking as well.

2. Invasion of Reasonable Expectations of Privacy

While the literal text of the Fourth Amendment protects "persons, houses, papers and effects" from unreasonable government searches and seizures, these items have not received co-equal protection under the Fourth Amendment. The Court in *Katz* famously stated that the Fourth Amendment "protects people, not places." Post-*Katz*, however, the Court has provided far more protection to individuals seeking to shield their homes from government intervention than is accorded to those seeking to prevent government intrusions outside the home. The Court has also been willing at times to give zero protection to the privacy expectations involved in examining one's person. It is important to stress that there must be *no reasonable expectation of privacy whatsoever* to render an invasion of purported privacy interests a "non-search." As will we will see throughout the material covered in this volume, when a small privacy interest is weighed against a purportedly larger state interest in crime-prevention, the Court becomes willing to find a search "reasonable."

a. The Home

The Court has consistently found that an individual's reasonable expectation of privacy is greatest in the home where intimate, personal activity most often occurs. Therefore, the Court places the greatest restrictions on the government's authority to enter a private residence to engage in investigative activities. As discussed more fully in Chapter 3, searches and seizures inside the home generally require that police obtain a warrant in advance from a judicial officer. The same Fourth Amendment protection afforded to an individual's residence is likewise extended to other dwelling places, including hotel rooms, *Stoner v. California*, 376 U.S. 483 (1964), rental property, *Chapman v. United States*, 365 U.S. 610 (1961), and also protects the privacy rights of overnight guests in the home of a third party, *Minnesota v. Olson*, 495 U.S. 91 (1990). The Court has held, however, that the heightened level of privacy accorded to one's dwelling place is not applicable to casual visitors in the home of a third-party, *Minnesota v. Carter*, 525 U.S. 83 (1998), or to prison cells, *Hudson v. Palmer*, 468 U.S. 517 (1984), or motor homes, *California v. Carney*, 471 U.S. 386 (1985) (privacy protection afforded to motor homes turns on "whether the vehicle is readily mobile or instead, for instance, elevated on blocks, whether the vehicle is licensed, whether it is connected to utilities, and whether it has convenient access to a public road").

b. The Curtilage

The reasonable expectation of privacy that individuals have in their homes also extends to the "curtilage" area immediately surrounding the dwelling. In *Oliver v. United States*, 466 U.S. 170 (1984), the Court reasoned that, like the home, the curtilage area is also the site of intimate personal activity and should be treated as part of the home. In *United States v. Dunn*, 480 U.S. 294 (1987), the Court listed four factors to be considered in determining whether an area of private property falls within the protected curtilage area, or within the "open field," the area of the property where an individual has no expectation of privacy. The factors that must be considered under the *Dunn* test are: (1) the proximity of the area to the home; (2) whether the area is enclosed with the house; (3) the nature of the use of the property in that area; and (4) the steps taken by the property owner to keep the area private. (See discussion of "open fields" below.) The curtilage generally includes any fenced-in area that abuts home, as well as porches and decks connected to the dwelling. Thus, the government must have a warrant before conducting a search of the curtilage area of a property or prior to entering the curtilage area in order to see and hear what is happening inside the home. *Olivera v. State*, 315 So. 2d 487 (Fla. Dist. Ct. App. 1975) (officers entered yard and overheard incriminating conversation through rear bedroom window).

c. Searches of "Persons"

As discussed in more detail in Chapter 6, the Court recognizes that people have a reasonable expectation of privacy in their own bodies, which precludes the government from randomly subjecting people to searches of their person. The Court has stated that subjecting an individual to such searches of their person is the kind of intrusive investigative practice that violates the core guarantees of basic human dignity and privacy protected by the Fourth Amendment. Such searches include the physical removal of tangible items concealed on one's person, as well the collection of bodily fluid and other information within a person's body. Courts have found that the government conducts a search by requiring an individual to open their mouth for inspection, *State v. Hardy*, 577 N.W.2d 212 (Minn. 1998), requiring government employees to provide a urine sample, *Skinner v. Ry. Labor Exec. Assoc.*, 489 U.S. 602 (1989), extracting a blood sample for alcohol intoxication analysis, *Schmerber v. California*, 384 U.S. 757 (1966), collecting fingernail scrapings, *Cupp v. Murphy*, 412 U.S. 291 (1973), and collecting breath samples for field sobriety tests, *Hulse v. State*, 961 P.2d 75 (Mont. 1988). As discussed more fully in Chapters 4 and 6, the government has much greater power under the Fourth Amendment to conduct these kinds of searches when an individual has been either placed under arrest, *United States v. Robinson*, 414 U.S. 218 (1973), or subject to temporary investigative detention, *Terry v. Ohio*, 392 U.S. 1 (1968).

d. Searches of "Papers and Effects"

The Court has broadly interpreted the "papers and effects" language of the Fourth Amendment to include all personal belongings. Generally, one has a reasonable expectation of privacy in personal items that are stored or concealed from public view. If the government seeks to investigate the nature of an item or discover its contents, such investigative action will likely constitute a Fourth Amendment search of "effects." As discussed more fully in Chapter 7, because an automobile is considered an "effect," the inspection of closed compartments of a car (trunk, glove compartment) constitutes a search. Likewise, if the government opens any closed container (*i.e.*, a purse, backpack, luggage, or briefcase), such conduct falls squarely within the definition of a search. In *Bond v. United States*, 529 U.S. 334 (2000), where officers squeezed and prodded the exterior of the luggage of bus passengers to determine the contents, the Court held that this conduct constituted a search of the luggage. Also, in *Arizona v. Hicks*, 480 U.S. 321 (1987), police officers conducted a search by merely moving stereo equipment to view the serial numbers.

3. "Non-Search" Investigative Techniques

Beyond the types of "searches" proscribed by the Fourth Amendment, the Court has excluded a wide range of police investigative activity from the definition of a search. In an effort to strike the delicate balance between the reasonable expectation of privacy of individuals and the government's legitimate law enforcement objectives, the Court has found that some specific investigative techniques are permissible because they are conducted in public and do not involve an intrusion into an area where an individual has a reasonable expectation of privacy. For example, the police commonly follow suspicious people and observe their movements in public or go to crime scenes to look for evidence left on the street by the perpetrator. These evidence-gathering techniques fall outside of the definition of a search because they do not involve exposing an individual's private information to government inspection.

The largest category of "non-search" government investigative practices fall under the broad umbrella of the Public Access Doctrine. The Supreme Court has held that if a member of the general public could lawfully engage in the same conduct used by the government to acquire the information then the government conduct is not a search within the scope of the Fourth Amendment.

a. Aerial Surveillance

In *California v. Ciraolo*, 476 U.S. 207 (1986), police used a low flying plane to fly one-thousand feet over defendant's property and observe a crop of marijuana plants not otherwise visible on the ground to members of the public. Even though the government was only able to see the contraband from the unique aerial vantage point, the Court held that the government's action in viewing the property from the plane was not a search because any member of the public could legally fly over the defendant's property and see the marijuana plants. Similarly, in *Florida v. Riley*, 488 U.S. 445 (1989), the Court found that the government's actions hovering 400 feet over the defendant's property in a helicopter was not a search. The Court rejected the defense's contention that no member of the public could legally conduct aerial surveillance over the property and ruled that the correct standard was whether the public would ordinarily have the ability to fly over property (or would legal restrictions prevent public access). The Court, per Justice O'Connor's concurrence, ruled that the burden is on the defendant to show that such public conduct does not occur on a regular basis.

b. Trash

In *California v. Greenwood*, 486 U.S. 35 (1988), the Court applied the public access rationale to searches of an individual's garbage left on the curb for sanitation pick-up. The Court ruled that there is no reasonable expectation of privacy in trash after it is left outside where any member of the public can access it, even if the trash is inside a closed, opaque container and local law (city ordinance) did not allow trash disposal other than by curbside pick-up. The Court stated that the question is not whether an individual has waived his privacy interest in the information contained in the trash, but whether the owner continued to have are reasonable expectation of privacy in the trash after placing it outside where stray animals, inquisitive neighbors, and all others could readily take and rummage through the contents of the bags. The Court concluded that, just as any member of the public could examine the contents of an individual's trash, the actions of the police in doing so was not an intrusion into an area where an individual retained a reasonable expectation of privacy.

c. Open Fields

The Fourth Amendment protection recognized for residential dwellings and the curtilage area does not extend to areas of private property beyond the curtilage, commonly referred to as "open fields." In *Hester v. United States*, 265 U.S. 57 (1924), the Court defined "open fields" as unoccupied or underdeveloped areas outside the curtilage. Although wooded areas are encompassed within the definition of open fields, the Court has long recognized that an area need not be "open" or a "field" to fall outside of the protection afforded to the curtilage area. *See Care v. United States*, 231 F.2d 22 (10th Cir. 1956) (cave containing illegal liquor still located 125 yards from house was an open field). In *Oliver v. United States*, 466 U.S. 170 (1984), the Court reasoned that any privacy interests the landowner might have in land outside the curtilage is not one society was prepared to recognize as reasonable because open fields are generally more accessible to the public, the property is far removed from the dwelling, and is not the likely site of the kind of intimate private activities protected by the Fourth Amendment.

d. Third Party Access

Closely related to the public access rationale is the Third Party Access Rule. The Court has held that there is no reasonable expectation of privacy in information knowingly made available to a third party. The Third Party Access Rule generally involves the government acquiring information from a private entity with whom the individual has a business relationship. While this information is not readily accessible to any member of public, the Court has stated that there is no reasonable expectation of privacy because the individual has already knowingly shared the information with a third party. *Smith v. Maryland*, 442 U.S. 735 (1979) (pen register device installed by police at telephone company allowing police to track telephone numbers called on the defendant's telephone); *United State v. Miller*, 425 U.S. 435 (1976) (government obtained defendant's financial records from bank). The third party access rational has more recently been used to allow government access to some information transmitted using modern technology, *United States v. Forrester*, 512 F.3d 500 (9th Cir. 2008) (computer surveillance techniques that reveal only to/from addresses of email messages and IP addresses of websites visited is not a search); *State v. Gubitosi*, 886 A.2d 1029 (N.H. 2005) (no reasonable expectation of privacy in cell phone records). Lower courts have found, however, that an individual has a reasonable expectation of privacy in the content of email messages that are not widely distributed.

e. Undercover Informants

A common investigative technique employed by the government to gather incriminating evidence — particularly in major narcotics and organized crime investigations — is the use of undercover informants. As trusted confidantes of the targeted suspect, undercover informants are in the unique position to engage the defendant in a voluntary conversation and elicit incriminating information that the government can use to prove guilt at trial. The Supreme Court has long held that the use of information gathered by informants in this manner does not violate the defendant's reasonable expectation of privacy. *Hoffa v. United States*, 385 U.S. 293 (1966) (The Fourth Amendment does not protect "a wrongdoer's misplaced belief that a person to whom he voluntarily confides his wrongdoing will not reveal it."). While criminals clearly have a subjective expectation that these "private" conversations will remain private, the Court has stated that this expectation of privacy is not one society is prepared to recognize as reasonable. The Court reasons that a defendant's "misplaced confidence" in a false friend does not translate into a reasonable expectation of privacy in the information voluntarily revealed. *United States v. White*, 401 U.S. 745 (1971).

In *Lewis v. United States*, 385 U.S. 206 (1966), the Court found that no different constitutional analysis applies when incriminating information is collected while the informant is inside the defendant's home. The *Lewis* Court stated that by conducting illicit business activities inside the home, the defendant's home became a "commercial center" with no greater privacy than retained by one who conducts business in a store or on the street. Likewise, in *Lopez v. United States*, 373 U.S. 427 (1963), the Court held that the use of a recording device by the undercover informant did not violate the defendant's expectations of privacy. The Court reasoned that the recording device was not "planted by means of an unlawful physical invasion of petitioner's premises under circumstances which would violate the Fourth Amendment. It was carried in and out by an agent who was there with the petitioner's assent, and it neither saw nor heard more than the agent himself." While the government's use of undercover informants to elicit incriminating statements from the defendant is not a violation of the defendant's Fourth Amendment rights, under certain circumstances, this investigative tactic could run afoul of the defendants Fifth or Sixth Amendment rights (see Chapters 14 and 15).

f. Sensory Enhancement Devices

Another line of "non-search" cases involves evidence-gathering activities conducted with the use of equipment or technology that allows the government to learn information that would not be detectable with the naked eye or perceptible using only the five human senses. As a general rule, the Court has only allowed the use of sensory enhancement technology that improves the government's ability to make public observations. *See, e.g., United States v. Lee*, 274 U.S. 559 (1972) (shining searchlight on motorboat to reveal contraband on deck); *United States v. Garner*, 907 F.2d 60 (8th Cir. 1990) (shining headlights onto exterior of property to expose marijuana plants); *State v. Curtin*, 332 S.E.2d 619 (W. Va. 1985) ("A flashlight merely provides at night what the sun does during the day."); *see also State v. Jackson*, 46 P.3d 257 (Wash. Ct. App. 2002) (use of GPS tracking device to monitor public movements not a search).

In *United States v. Knotts*, 460 U.S. 276 (1983), the Court held the use of an electronic beeper to track the movements of the defendant's car was not a search because the device simply allowed the police to more efficiently observe the defendant while he was in public, just as any member of the general public could do. Likewise, in *United States v. Karo*, 468 U.S. 705 (1984), the Court held that the police were permitted to secretly place a tracking device on merchandise prior to the defendant's purchase and use the device to track the defendant's movements through the public streets.

The Court has, however, placed some restrictions on the use of sensory enhancement devices when the government seeks to use advanced technology to conduct investigations inside the home. In *Kyllo v. United States*, 533 U.S. 27 (2001), to confirm their suspicions that the defendant was illegally growing marijuana in his home, police directed a heat-sensitive, thermal imaging device towards the defendant's residence. Because marijuana plants need intense heat to grow, the officers sought to determine whether there was an unusually high level of heat being generated from inside the home. The Court found that the government's conduct constituted a search because thermal imaging technology was not readily in use in the general public and the device allowed the government to learn information about what was transpiring inside the home, an area not subject to public view or access. *See also Karo*, 468 U.S. 705 (the use of a beeper to track movement of the defendant's property once inside the home violated the defendant's reasonable expectation of privacy).

g. Drug Detection

The Court's rationale behind the final category of "non-search" investigative activity is simple: there is no reasonable expectation of privacy in illegal contraband. Therefore, the Court has stated that the government's use of a narrowly tailored, minimally intrusive investigative techniques that can only detect the presence of contraband is not a search. The Court has, therefore, allowed the use of two such investigative techniques to detect illegal drugs: dog sniffs and chemical field tests.

i. Dog Sniffs

In *Unites States v. Place*, 462 U.S. 696 (1983), the Court found that subjecting luggage to an external examination by a canine specially trained to detect the smell of drugs (a "drug detection dog") does not constitute a search because the "sniff" does not reveal personal information beyond the presence of drugs. The Court reasoned that because there is no reasonable expectation of privacy in the possession of illegal drugs, dog sniffs do not constitute a "search" within the scope of the Fourth Amendment.

In *Illinois v. Caballes*, 543 U.S. 405 (2005), the Court upheld the use of a drug detection dog to inspect the exterior of a car during a routine traffic stop. Although the police did not have any reason to suspect the presence of drugs in the car, the Court upheld the use of the dog as a "reasonable" search. The Court recognized, however, that dog sniff detection can run afoul of the Fourth Amendment if the dog sniff necessitates that police hold or "seize" an individual in order to facilitate the dog sniff. In *Caballes*, the Court found that the dog sniff did not extend the duration of the routine traffic stop, but in *Place*, the Court found the defendant's luggage was held for an extended period of time solely to facilitate the dog sniff, resulting in a Fourth Amendment violation.

ii. Chemical Field Tests

In *United States v. Jacobsen*, 466 U.S. 109 (1984), the Court found that the use of a police-administered chemical field test to determine whether a suspicious-looking substance is an illegal drug is not a search because the test can only reveal the existence of illegal contraband. The Court again reasoned that an individual has no reasonable expectation of privacy in illegal contraband. While the Court acknowledged that using a small quantity of the drugs to conduct the field test is a Fourth Amendment "seizure" of that portion of the property, the Court found that the seizure was *de minimus* due to the small quantity of the substance needed for testing.

IV. The Scope of Fourth Amendment Seizures

The Supreme Court has defined the scope of government conduct that constitutes a Fourth Amendment "seizure." The Court has held that a seizure of property occurs when there is a meaningful interference with an individual's possessory interest in the item. *Soldal v. Cook County*, 506 U.S. 56 (1992). A seizure can be a physical taking of possessions or blocking access to personal belongings. In *Illinois v. McArthur*, 531 U.S. 326 (2001), the Court held that police refusal to allow the defendant to enter his residence until a search warrant was obtained constituted a seizure. In addition to the seizures of property, the Fourth Amendment also proscribes the seizure of one's person. As discussed in more detail in Chapter 3, an individual is seized when the government imposes a physical restraint which restricts an individual's freedom of movement, including persons arrested and individuals temporarily detained during an ongoing investigation of criminal activity. The Court has also recognized that even in the absence of physical restraint, a person is seized when there is a sufficient show of force by the government that would cause a reasonable person to believe she is not free to leave, *United States v. Mendenhall*, 446 U.S. 544 (1980), or terminate the encounter with the police, *Florida v. Bostick*, 501 U.S. 429 (1991).

V. The Reasonableness Requirement

When the government engages in investigative activity that falls within the scope of the Court's definition of a "search" or "seizure," such conduct does not violate the Fourth Amendment unless it is "unreasonable." The Court has used the Reasonableness Clause and the Warrant Clause of the Fourth Amendment to place specific restrictions on when the government can engage in searches and seizures and how such investigative activity must be conducted. As discussed more fully in the Chapters that follow, "unreasonable" searches and seizures generally fall into three categories:

(1) the government was required to obtain a warrant and either did not obtain a warrant in advance or the warrant was deemed defective (see Chapters 3–4);
(2) The government acted without a warrant, but its conduct was not justified under any of the recognized exceptions to the warrant re-

quirement (or exceeded the scope of its authority under one of the exceptions to the warrant requirement) (see Chapters 6–11); (3) the government conduct, though authorized by a valid warrant or properly within an exception to the warrant requirement, was excessive or extreme in the manner or method of execution, *see Tennessee v. Garner*, 471 U.S. 1 (1985) (use of deadly force to capture an unarmed fleeing felon) (See Chapters 3–4).

Checkpoints

- The conduct of private parties is not proscribed by the Fourth Amendment. The Fourth Amendment only governs the conduct of state and federal government actors (or those acting on behalf of the government).

- The Fourth Amendment restrains government "evidence gathering" techniques that constitute a "search" or a "seizure."

- A Fourth Amendment search occurs when government conduct intrudes into an area where an individual has a "reasonable expectation of privacy."

- Government investigative conduct that does not infringe upon an individual's reasonable expectation of privacy includes "public" observations and evidence-gathering techniques that do not involve going into the home or requiring an individual to expose private, personal, or intimate information that one has manifested an interest in keeping private.

- Examples of searches include any examination of the contents of one's pockets, looking inside one's luggage or other personal belongings, opening compartments of one's car or entering one's home to conduct investigative activities.

- Examples of "non-search" government activity that does not intrude on one's reasonable expectation of privacy include: (1) information readily available to the public under the Public Access Doctrine (trash, open fields, tracking devices); (2) information that has already been shared with a third party (records from telephone company, bank); (3) information voluntarily disclosed to undercover government informants; and (4) the use of non-intrusive investigative techniques that can only reveal the presence of contraband (dog sniffs, chemical field tests).

- A seizure occurs when the government takes control of one's property (either by physical possession or blocking access) or when the government restricts a person's freedom of movement by physical restraint or actions that would cause a reasonable person to feel she was unable to walk away or refuse the government's requests.

- Searches and seizures are generally only unreasonable if they are conducted without a warrant or do not fall within the scope of one of the exceptions to the warrant requirement.

Chapter 3

Warrants

I. The Warrant "Requirement"

The Fourth Amendment to the United States Constitution does not say when, if ever, the police or other state actors must obtain a warrant before searching or seizing persons or property. Rather, the amendment broadly declares, in its first clause, that, "The right of the people to be secure in their persons, houses, papers, and effects, against *unreasonable* searches and seizures, shall not be violated...." Reasonableness, therefore, is the only textual mandate, an interpretation often (though not always and not consistently) embraced by the Supreme Court.

The Court determines "reasonableness" by engaging in a process of "categorical balancing," meaning balancing state against individual interests to craft a rule adequately accommodating both interests to govern future cases of a similar category. There are, however, at least two questions that the Court answers each time that it crafts a new rule: (1) What level of justification, that is, of merited probability to believe a crime or other public wrong has been committed, is required?; and (2) Is a warrant authorizing the search and issued by a neutral and independent magistrate required, or may the police instead conduct the search or seizure without prior judicial authorization? Often, though again inconsistently, the Court states that, at least for searches or seizures aimed at finding evidence of crime, the presumptive answer to the first question is "probable cause" and to the second question is "yes, a warrant is required," absent the existence of a "well-recognized exception."

These well-recognized exceptions are many. They are ones earlier derived by categorical balancing. Perhaps the most commonly known exception is the "*Terry* stop," a brief seizure of the person for questioning, which, because of its brevity and the modest nature of the intrusion, requires only "reasonable suspicion," a level of probability below that of probable cause and which will be covered in more detail in Chapter 4. "Arrests," by contrast, are highly intrusive seizures of the person, a category requiring probable cause.

The Court did not create the "probable cause" idea, however, out of thin air, for the term appears in the second clause (the "Warrant Clause") of the Fourth Amendment and is qualified by the Amendment's third and final clause (the "Particularity Clause"): "[N]o Warrants shall issue, but upon probable cause, supported by Oath or affirmation, and particularly describing the place to be searched, and the persons or things to be seized." The Warrant Clause, unlike the Reasonableness Clause, does seem to state a clear, straightforward rule: *if* a warrant is required, it must be based on probable cause. This rule is indeed one usually (though again not always, as discussed in Chapter 11), followed by the Court. An understanding of warrants, therefore, must begin with analyzing the meaning of probable cause. Moreover, that analysis will prove important in other contexts as well because of the supposed presumptive probable cause requirement (a presumption often overcome, however) for all searches and seizures for evidence of criminal activity, even those searches and seizures permitted to be warrantless.

II. What Is Probable Cause?

A. Background and Definition

Unfortunately, there is no workable dictionary definition of probable cause nor a black-letter one. Its definition changes with the type of search (for example, for tangible things, such as drugs or weapons, versus intangible ones, such as conversations; by ordinary police observation versus observation enhanced by electronic or other technological means; for purposes of civil action versus criminal investigation versus protecting national security) and perhaps with the context (e.g., searches for drugs versus other sorts of items), though these differences are rarely explained, and even more rarely acknowledged, by the Court. Furthermore, probable cause is about more than simple probability, having quantitative, qualitative, temporal, and normative components. The discussion of probable cause in this Chapter assumes an ordinary search for physical evidence of crime or an ordinary seizure of a criminal suspect. Other types of searches and seizures will be briefly discussed, but only for comparison, although they will be analyzed in more detail in later Chapters.

The Court did articulate, in *Beck v. Ohio*, 379 U.S. 89 (1964), a working definition of probable cause as "whether, at the moment the arrest was made ... the facts and circumstances within their [the officers'] knowledge and of which they had reasonably trustworthy information were sufficient to warrant a prudent man in believing that the petitioner had committed or was committing an offense." Despite its ambiguity, this definition tells us several things about the nature of probable cause.

1. An Objective Concept

First, probable cause is an *objective*, not a subjective, issue. Ordinarily, therefore, what the officers actually believed the facts supporting the arrest to be or whether they believed that those facts established probable cause are irrelevant. What matters is whether a "prudent man," meaning a "reasonable police officer under the circumstances," would believe these facts and would, as a result, fairly believe he had probable cause. As in every area of the law, the reasonable man concept has two variants—a majoritarian one ("What would *most* people, or perhaps most officers, believe under the circumstances?") and a normative one (given the values that the Fourth Amendment and the probable cause concept are meant to serve, what *should* we as a society permit police to think and do under the circumstances?). The Court draws on both variants, sometimes one more than the other, generally without expressly saying when or why. But the latter variant (the normative one) makes clear that giving probable cause meaning in particular contexts requires knowing what purposes probable cause is meant to serve—purposes that may arguably include, for example, restraining governmental invasions of privacy, property, and locomotion absent strong justification for doing so; protecting the innocent; and minimizing harassment based on the exercise of other rights, such as the rights to free speech and association.

Reasonable man determinations also require deciding what circumstances should count as those in which the reasonable man (as opposed to the actual man) finds himself. Again, there are majoritarian and normative components to this question. Yet the Court has strongly suggested two circumstances that will generally be part of the reasonable officer's situation: he must be well-trained (which is not the same as perfectly trained), and he works in an institutional context, that is, for a police department rather than in isolation. The meaning of the well-trained officer is discussed in Chapter 12 on the exclusionary rule.

The institutional, collective nature of the reasonable police officer means that probable cause generally is judged based upon the department's knowledge, not only that of the officer executing the warrant. As the Court put it in *Whiteley v. Warden*, 401 U.S. 560, 568 (1971), "officers called upon to aid other officers in executing arrest warrants are entitled to assume that the officers requesting aid offered the magistrate the information requisite to support an independent judicial assessment of probable cause." . This emphatically does *not* mean that the arresting officer's actions are automatically constitutional if he *wrongly* believed that the officers or detectives requesting the arrest had probable cause. What *Whiteley* does mean is that an arresting officer acts appropriately, whether or not he personally had probable cause, if some officer within the chain of command had probable cause. Here are three illustrations (ignore, for the moment, whether a warrant is required):

> *Situation #1*: Officer A has probable cause to arrest the defendant and tells Officer B to do so. The arrest is valid.
> *Situation #2*: Officer A has no probable cause but tells Officer B to arrest the defendant. Unbeknownst to Officer A, Officer B has, however, independently obtained probable cause to arrest the defendant. The arrest is valid.
> *Situation #3*: Officer A tells Officer B to arrest the defendant when neither has probable cause to do so. Officer B arrests the defendant, not knowing that Officer C has, by independent investigation, obtained probable cause to arrest the defendant. The arrest is invalid. Officer C is outside the chain of command in this case, and neither A

nor B nor the police department as a whole should benefit from the happenstance of C's investigation.

There are practical reasons for this rule. Police operate as an institution. If only those officers individually having probable cause could act, the authorities would be severely hamstrung in combating crime. Suppose, for example, that one officer has probable cause to arrest a fleeing felon but does not know where he is, so he sends out an all-points radio bulletin describing the felon. If he personally had to do the arrest, the felon might well escape. On the other hand, if officers in the chain of command knowingly or just incompetently act without probable cause, we encourage police misconduct if they can simply gamble that someone in the department has probable cause.

In *Devenpeck v. Alford*, 543 U.S. 146 (2004), the Court emphasized the objective nature of probable cause, thus presumably excluding inquiry into the officer's state of mind. *Devenpeck* involved an arrest that the officer believed was justified for one crime but for which he in fact lacked probable cause, though he may have had probable cause to arrest for a completely different crime. More specifically, one officer investigating why Alford had stopped his car behind a disabled vehicle suspected that Alford had been impersonating a police officer, a crime in the State of Washington. That officer called his supervisor, Sergeant Gerald Devenpeck, to convey these suspicions, and Devenpeck arrived to investigate a short time later. While Devenpeck was questioning Alford, Devenpeck noticed that Alford had a tape recorder, with the operating buttons pressed to record, and, after further investigation, realized that Alford had been taping their conversation. Only then did Devenpeck arrest Alford, charging him with violation of the State's Privacy Act for taping a conversation without the other participant's (the officer's) consent and ticketing him for improperly flashing his headlights. The state trial court, however, later dismissed both charges. Importantly, a state Court of Appeals decision had held that conduct like Alford's was not in fact a State Privacy Act violation.

Alford brought suit in federal court under section 1983 for violation of his constitutional rights. The only part of the subsequent procedural history that matters here is that when the case reached the United States Court of Appeals for the Ninth Circuit, that court held that there was no probable cause to arrest under the Privacy Act because Alford's conduct did not in fact violate that Act as a matter of law. Nor, concluded the court, could probable cause be based on the charge of "impersonating an officer" because the facts giving rise to that charge were not "closely related" to the offense invoked by Devenpeck when he took Alford into custody.

The Supreme Court rejected both of the Ninth Circuit's conclusions. First, the Court considered Officer Devenpeck's belief that he had probable cause to arrest for the traffic violation irrelevant. What mattered was whether there were objective reasons that would allow a reasonable police officer to arrest for any crime under these circumstances, not necessarily the crime that Devenpeck believed occurred. This was so, explained the Court, because

"Evenhanded law enforcement is best achieved by the application of objective standards of conduct, rather than standards that depend upon the subjective state of mind of the officer."

Second, the Court rejected the "rule that the offense establishing probable cause must be 'closely related' to, and based on the same conduct as, the offense identified by the arresting officer at the time of arrest" because that rule "is inconsistent with ... precedent." Once again, the Court stressed the objective nature of probable cause and the risks created by an alternative, subjective approach:

> Such a rule makes the lawfulness of an arrest turn upon the motivation of the arresting officer — [thus] eliminating, as validating probable cause, facts that played no part in the officer's expressed subjective reason for making the arrest, and offenses that are not "closely related" to that subjective reason. [citations omitted]. This means that the constitutionality of an arrest under a given set of known facts will "vary from place to place and from time to time," *Whren, supra*, at 815, 116 S. Ct. 1769, depending on whether the arresting officer states the reason for the detention and, if so, whether he correctly identifies a general class of offense for which probable cause exists. An arrest made by a knowledgeable, veteran officer would be valid, whereas an arrest made by a rookie *in precisely the same circumstances* would not. We see no reason to ascribe to the Fourth Amendment such arbitrarily variable protection.

Another aspect of an objectively reasonable belief under the circumstance test is that it turns largely on the specific circumstances of each case, *i.e.* it is highly fact-sensitive. Thus, sometimes a single difference in the facts of one case versus another can distinguish them, creating probable cause in the first situation but not the second. Some appellate courts, including the Supreme Court, have gone so far, however, as to suggest that this extreme fact-sensitivity often renders analogy to the facts of similar cases irrelevant in determining probable cause.

Thus, in *Illinois v. Gates*, 462 U.S. 213 (1983), discussed in more detail shortly, the Court stressed that probable cause is a "fluid concept — turning on the assessment of probabilities in particular factual contexts—not readily, or even usefully, reduced to a neat set of legal rules." "One simple rule will not cover every situation," explained the Court, and magistrates should not, therefore, be "restricted in their findings of probable cause by an elaborate body of case law," in that case concerning when an informant's tip is sufficiently trustworthy.

Moreover, the *Gates* Court emphasized, the magistrate's case-specific judgment of probable cause is required to receive "great deference" from reviewing courts, and the probable cause concept itself must be sufficiently practical and informed by commonsense to allow its existence to be judged by non-lawyers, such as police officers. The *Gates* Court's approach, if taken literally, does not make the *facts* of similar precedent *always* irrelevant, but it does sharply limit their role, precedential facts being significant in resolving a current case only in extreme situations (though any guidelines articulated in precedent, and the rationales for those guidelines, would still play some role in most cases).

In practice, however, especially at the trial level, analogy to precedent proves important to giving the vague probable cause concept concrete meaning. It is helpful to the prosecution to argue that the court should find probable cause in a new case because the facts are similar to an earlier one in which the court found probable cause. Of course, the defense will seek to distinguish that case and argue that the new one is more similar to other precedent finding probable cause absent.

2. The Quantitative Component

The second aspect of the *Beck v. Ohio* probable cause definition is that the information of which the police are aware must be "sufficient"—that is, enough—to warrant a belief that criminal activity is afoot. The definition does not say how much is enough, but it does make clear that there is some quantitative element of probable cause, some level of certitude in the suspect's guilt, that is required. Nor does the definition say that the level of certitude is fixed at some specified degree of probability. But it is clear that the level of certitude matters, some levels of probable guilt being sufficient, others not.

3. The Qualitative Component

Third, *Beck* requires that probable cause be based on "reasonably trustworthy" information. Likely lies, hunches, random guesses, and unsupported opinions are inadequate. The sources of information must be of adequate quality, trustworthy enough, to justify conclusions supporting probable cause. The question of whether these information sources are sound enough is, once again, an objective one, in theory making the officers' personal beliefs in the evidence's trustworthiness irrelevant.

4. *The Temporal Component*

Fourth, *Beck* includes a temporal component to probable cause, noting that the objective belief can look backward, to whether a crime *has been* committed, or "present-ward," to whether a crime *is being* committed. These options are, of course, not exhaustive, for, as we will see when we discuss anticipatory warrants, the reasonable officer can also look forward, deciding whether there likely *will be* a crime in the future.

In much other case law, the Supreme Court also cautions against trial courts reviewing officers' actions with *hindsight bias* when the police end up not uncovering evidence. The question is what the officers reasonably could believe given the information available to them at the time of the search, *not* what they should have believed given what we learn at a later date. Making the latter, prohibited "later date" inference is known as "hindsight bias." Rephrased, just because an officer turns out to be wrong does not mean that he lacked probable cause in the first place.

The flip side of this point, albeit one too often ignored by the Court, is the risk that a court reviewing the adequacy of a warrantless search that *did* uncover evidence of crime will allow that knowledge to affect its judgment, thus finding probable cause with what it now knows when it would not earlier have found probable cause had the officers sought a warrant *before* searching. This effect may occur subconsciously but nevertheless poses a real risk of undermining the hindsight bias prohibition.

The details of all four of these lessons of the *Beck* definition are elaborated below.

B. Quantitative Requirements Redux

The phrase "probable cause" strikes many laypersons as meaning "more probable than not," something over 50% likelihood of guilt. There is indeed, according to some commentators, strong historical support for the more probable than not standard's having been the Framers' understanding of probable cause. Other commentators, however, argue that the history suggests a significantly lower level of probability, while still other authors insist that the history is too vague and contradictory to know what quantitative probability the Framers' intended.

If history gives no answer, perhaps legal practice will. But this proves to be elusive as well. A 1982 survey of judges found that they, on average, equated probable cause with a 44.52% likelihood of guilt. Professors LaFave and Israel, looking at case outcomes, argue that the lower courts distinguish between cases in which police are certain there is a crime, but not who did it, requiring for such cases something just *under* 50% probability, and cases where it is uncertain whether any crime has occurred at all, requiring for those latter cases *more than* 50% probability. The implicit reasons for this distinction are first, that too easily permitting police action where it is unclear whether there was a crime will too frequently interfere with innocent persons, and, second, once there is a known crime with a known victim, there is a need for prompt action lest the offender escape justice.

Further muddying the picture is the Court's use of new language to describe probable cause that it first employed in *Illinois v. Gates*, 462 U.S. 213 (1983). There, the Court began describing probable cause as a "substantial chance" of guilt or of finding evidence of a crime. This is a test that, in the view of some commentators, lessened the quantitative requirement to prove probable cause, a "chance" of something colloquially connoting a much lower likelihood of its occurring than does the "probability" of its being so.

Maryland v. Pringle, 540 U.S. 366 (2003), arguably confirms these commentators' fears of a lessening of the quantitative standard for probable cause. In *Pringle*, an officer stopped a car for speeding at about 3:00 a.m. Three occupants were in the car: the driver and owner; the front-seat passenger, Joseph Jermaine Pringle; and a back-seat passenger. When the driver, in response to the officer's request to produce his license and registration, opened the glove compartment, the officer saw inside it a large amount of rolled-up cash. When the computer check revealed no outstanding violations, the officer asked the driver to get out, issued him an oral warning, and a second patrol car arrived. The driver, responding to the officer's question on the point, denied having weapons or narcotics in the car and next consented to the search. That search uncovered $763 from the glove compartment and five glassine plastic baggies containing cocaine from behind the raised back-seat armrest — drugs that would not have been visible without the officer's having lowered that armrest.

The officer questioned all three men, telling them that he would arrest them all unless someone admitted to ownership of the drugs. None of the men admitted ownership of either the drugs or the money, and all three were arrested and taken to the police station. Later that morning, *Pringle* waived his *Miranda* rights and gave oral and written confessions that the cocaine was his and that he meant to sell it, though he denied that the other occupants knew anything about the drugs, and they were therefore released.

Pringle was convicted by a jury of possessing cocaine and of doing so with intent to distribute it. Maryland's substantive criminal law required proof that Pringle knew that the drugs were present and that he singly or jointly exercised dominion and control over them. There was no such proof because the drugs were hidden behind the armrest. Nor was there any evidence that Pringle, as a passenger, knew that there was a large quantity of money in the glove compartment *before the driver opened it* to retrieve the car's registration. Accordingly, the only evidence that Pringle possessed the drugs was that he was one of three occupants in a car containing contraband. But this was insufficient quantitative evidence that Pringle had engaged in wrongdoing to establish probable cause, or so the Court of Appeals of Maryland concluded. Likewise, that court saw the trial judge's logic in admitting the drugs into evidence as creating a slippery slope under which, for example, contraband found in a twelve-passenger van, rather than, as in *Pringle*, a three-passenger car, would justify arresting everyone until somebody confessed.

The Supreme Court reversed, rejecting the logic of the Court of Appeals of Maryland. In doing so, the Court stressed that the "probable cause standard is incapable of precise definition or quantification into percentages because it deals with probabilities and depends on the totality of the circumstances." Moreover, "the *quanta* ... of proof appropriate in ordinary judicial proceedings are inapplicable to the decision to issue a warrant.... Finely tuned standards such as proof beyond a reasonable doubt or by a preponderance of the evidence, useful in formal trials, have no place in the [probable-cause] decision." Rather, said the Court, it looks at all the events leading up to the arrest to decide whether, "viewed from the standpoint of an objectively reasonable police officer, [they] amount to probable cause." At the same time, the Court recognized that the "long-prevailing standard of probable cause protects citizens from rash and unreasonable interferences with privacy and from unfounded charges of crime, while giving fair leeway for enforcing the law in the community's protection." Moreover, emphasized the Court, as it earlier had in *Illinois v. Gates*, the probable cause concept is a "fluid," non-technical one, "turning on the assessment of probabilities in particular factual contexts — not readily, or even usefully, reduced to a neat set of legal rules."

Applying these standards to the case before it, the Court stressed the *accessibility* of the drugs to Pringle rather than their visibility. The cash was in a glove compartment "directly in front of Pringle," and five baggies of cocaine behind the armrest were "accessible to all three men," each of whom failed, when questioned, to offer any information about the ownership of the cocaine or the money. The Court also criticized the state appellate court's determination that "[m]oney, without more, is innocuous," complaining that the state court's "consideration of the money in isolation, rather than as a factor in the totality of the circumstances, is mistaken in light of our precedents." According, the Court concluded,

We think it an entirely reasonable inference from these facts that any or all three of the occupants had knowledge of, and exercised dominion and control over, the cocaine. Thus a reasonable officer could conclude that there was probable cause to believe Pringle committed the crime of possession of cocaine, either jointly or singly.

Note the disjunctive nature of the Court's conclusion — there was probable cause to believe *either* that Pringle jointly possessed the drugs *or* that he did so alone. The joint possession inference, however, seems inconsistent with Maryland state criminal law. Probable cause must relate to something, usually a particular crime rather than a generalized suspicion that some unspecified fishy thing is afoot. Where state-level police are involved, it is the state substantive criminal law that defines the elements of a crime. Under Maryland criminal law, joint possession of drugs could not be proven as an element unless the drugs were visible to all, which was not true in *Pringle*. The joint possession inference thus seems hard to defend.

That leaves the inference that Pringle alone possessed the drugs. At least one person in the car, of course, must have possessed the drugs, but there was no evidence (prior to his confession) that it was Pringle who was the possessor beyond his being one of three persons in a car where the drugs were found. But that means there was a one-third chance, a 33⅓% probability, that Pringle was the possessor. That level of suspicion seems more akin to the lesser quantity required to prove "reasonable suspicion," as lower court judges in a pre-*Pringle* survey and many commentators have agreed.

That leaves this question: after *Pringle*, what level of potential guilt is sufficient to establish probable cause? There is no definitive answer to this question, but a number of commentaries on the case suggest the following:

1. Probable cause still likely hovers somewhere around 50% likelihood of guilt, usually just a bit below 50%.
2. Probable cause is less than beyond a reasonable doubt and clear and convincing evidence, may be less than a preponderance of evidence, but is more than mere suspicion or reasonable suspicion.
3. Nevertheless, probable cause is a "fluid," that is, changeable, concept, so in appropriate cases, as in *Pringle*, the quantitative standard may drop considerably below 50% probable guilt, although it is unclear what those "appropriate cases" are.

Concerning this last point (probable cause's "fluidity"), it may be that the Court balances the severity of the crime against the intrusion on the individual to determine what level of probability it "appropriately" requires in a particular case, though it also may be that it will deviate downward only when state interests are ample. *Pringle* also might suggest that the Court considers drug cases, or at least possession with intent to distribute cases, "severe" crimes, tipping the balance to the state's side, thus reducing the quantum of evidence required to prove probable cause.

On the other hand, some commentators argue that *Pringle* implicitly stands for a much simpler proposition: the quantitative standard for probable cause has, in most cases, been significantly lowered to what used to be the reasonable suspicion standard, that is, about one-third likelihood of guilt in *all* cases. Thus, what can be said with certainty after *Pringle* is that uncertainty reigns.

C. Qualitative Requirements

It is insufficient to establish probable cause to show that the evidence on which it is based "adds up" to something around 50% likelihood of guilt. Case law also requires that the evidence relied upon be reasonable trustworthy. There is little trustworthiness problem if an officer personally observed the crime, such as an undercover officer might do in making a drug buy, at least absent evidence that the officer is lying. But mere unsubstantiated rumors will not do. Trustworthiness problems most often arise where the police rely on an informant. To understand the modern Supreme Court case law on informant trustworthiness, however, it is necessary first to understand the older, now-abandoned, "*Aguilar-Spinelli* test" that the Court applied until adopting in 1983 a new test in *Illinois v. Gates*, 462 U.S. 213 (1983).

1. Aguilar-Spinelli

The *Aguilar-Spinelli* test, as it came to be understood by the lower courts, was a two-pronged test. The first prong required that the informant's tip appear credible, that is, truthful. The second prong required that the tip appear reliable, meaning based upon good information with a solid basis rather than, for example, upon mere speculation or idle gossip. The test was one of admissibility: *both* prongs must have been met or the court would not consider the tip at all in determining whether there was probable cause. Either other independent evidence had to establish probable cause or any evidence resulting from the search or seizure would have been suppressed.

Neither prong could have been satisfied by conclusory assertions, such as, "I received a tip from a credible informant" or "the informant told me that narcotics were sold at this location." Instead, police must have provided specific, concrete information from which a magistrate deciding whether to issue a warrant, or a judge deciding whether to suppress evidence, could independently assess whether each prong had been met. Police could have bolstered tips by gathering corroborating facts that "permitted the suspicions engendered by the informer'[s] tip to ripen into a judgment that a crime was probably 'being committed.'" Even "innocent" facts could have corroborated tips, though logic suggests that such facts merited less weight than would ones inconsistent with innocence. Additionally, Justice White noted in his concurring opinion in *Spinelli* that an informant could base his opinion on hearsay, though there must have been "good reason for believing it—perhaps one of the usual grounds for crediting hearsay information."

Three key factors were considered relevant to meeting the *Aguilar-Spinelli* credibility prong: (1) whether the tip was against the informant's interest, such as by implicating him in crime; (2) whether the informant previously gave accurate tips; and (3) whether the informant had a reputation for truthfulness. For example, an informant who told the police that he bought drugs from John Lenin would be implicating the informant himself in a crime, something he would be unlikely to do if he were lying. Likewise, if the informant gave three prior tips, all of which turned out to be completely accurate, that track record would suggest that he is a truthful tipster, a conclusion that would also be supported if he were well-known in his community as a generally truthful person. A magistrate or suppression judge would be free to conclude from any of these circumstances that the credibility prong had been met. The harder cases occur when the circumstances are less clear or point in opposing directions. Thus a tipster may have given one completely accurate prior tip, one partially accurate one, and one completely inaccurate one, or his statement might be against his interest, yet he has a poor record of prior accuracy and a community reputation as a liar.

Three common factors relevant to the reliability prong were these: (1) whether the informant personally observed or participated in the activities reported in the tip; (2) whether the tip was so detailed that the informant must have had first-hand knowledge; and (3) whether the nature of the information contained in the tip, or the manner in which it was gathered, indicated that it could have come from personal knowledge or a highly reliable source.

Thus, if an informant bought drugs from John Lenin, the informant would have personally observed or participated in the reported crime. If, on the other hand, the informant did not mention his participation but gave a tip so detailed that he had to have a good basis, including facts with which only someone with correct information would be aware, that suggests that he either personally observed the crime, participated in it, or got his information from a reliable source. Of course, how much detail is enough or how unlikely it is that someone would have particular information without having a good basis for it are questions of degree that may be subject to dispute in a particular case.

Anonymous tips would be especially unlikely to survive the *Aguilar-Spinelli* test. If the judge has no idea who the tipster is, how can the judge determine whether or not he is a truthful informant? The credibility prong is thus missing for anonymous informants, and, under *Aguilar-Spinelli*, if one prong is unmet, the tip may not be considered in determining the existence of probable cause even if the other prong is very strong. Yet many tips essential to criminal investigations are anonymous. Worries about the per se exclusion of all anonymous tips ultimately led the Court to replace the *Aguilar-Spinelli* two-pronged test with the "totality of the circumstances" test articulated in *Illinois v. Gates*.

2. Gates

a. The *Gates* Test

Under the *Gates* test, the same inquiries are made as under *Aguilar-Spinelli*, but the "prongs" become merely considerations in a test of weight rather than admissibility. In other words, a weakness in one former "prong," or even its entire absence, can be made up by great strength in the other former "prong" or by powerful corroboration. In any event, even a weak tip is considered as among the "totality of the circumstances" relevant to probable cause, though a weak tip alone may be insufficiently weighty to carry the day. Thus, under *Gates*, an anonymous tip (one likely failing the *Aguilar-Spinelli* credibility prong) would still enter into the probable cause determination.

The *Gates* Court also refined the evidentiary trustworthiness analysis in several ways. First, it distinguished between ordinary and "predictive" corroboration. Ordinary corroboration confirms a past event. Predictive corroboration involves observing what was at the time the tip was made a predicted *future* event that actually came to pass. The *Gates* Court considered predictive corroboration the more impressive feat, meriting greater weight in the process.

Second, *Gates* declared a standard of review by appellate courts requiring deference to the magistrate's probable cause determination. Explained the Court:

> [W]e have repeatedly said that after-the-fact scrutiny by courts of the sufficiency of an affidavit should not take the form of de novo review. A magistrate's determination of probable cause should be paid great deference by reviewing courts. A grudging or negative attitude by reviewing courts toward warrants is inconsistent with the Fourth Amendment's strong preference for searches conducted pursuant to a

warrant; … courts should not invalidate warrants by interpreting affidavits in a hyper technical, rather than a common sense, manner.

The Court justified the non-technical, flexible, deferential *Gates* standard that replaced the *Aguilar-Spinelli* test on a number of grounds. Notably, the Court emphasized that search warrants can be issued by persons who are not even lawyers, in an "often hurried context" that can be inconsistent with complex, technical rules. Furthermore, if warrants are too difficult to obtain, police might circumvent them, perhaps by aggressively seeking warrantless consent searches, thus losing judicial oversight and the public's perception that it is at work. Moreover, maintained the Court, the rigid *Aguilar-Spinelli* test might unduly impede law enforcement in providing for the security of the individual and his property. *Gates* itself involved an anonymous handwritten letter sent to the Bloomington, Illinois, police department. The letter said that Sue Gates drives her car to Florida, loads it up with drugs, then her husband Lance flies down there, driving the car back home to Bloomington, while Sue flies back there. The letter predicted that on May 3 Sue would again drive to Florida, followed by Lance, who would return with the car loaded with over $100,000 in drugs. Furthermore, the letter identified Sue and Lance's home, said they already had over $100,000 in drugs in their basement and that they made their living by selling drugs, often bragging about it and having major drug dealers visit their home.

The tip was forwarded to a detective, whose independent investigations revealed the Gateses' address and that "L. Gates" had made a reservation for a May 5 plane from Chicago to West Palm Beach, Florida. Drug Enforcement Administration agents confirmed Lance Gates's arrival by plane in West Palm Beach, his entry to a motel room registered to Sue Gates, and his exit from it the next morning with a woman later identified as Sue, both individuals driving back in a car with Illinois plates on an interstate frequently traveled by the Chicago-bound. Based on an affidavit setting forth these facts and attaching the letter, the detective obtained a search warrant. When the Gateses arrived home, they were met by the Bloomingdale police, who searched their car, finding 350 pounds of marijuana in the trunk, then searching their home to find marijuana, weapons, and other contraband.

b. The Majority Opinion

Apparently recognizing that the tip could not survive the *Aguilar-Spinelli* test, the Supreme Court defended the totality of the circumstances alternative, finding that it was met under these circumstances. The Court found that the tip at least suggested the Gateses's involvement in drug trafficking, particularly given Florida's being "well-known as a source of narcotics trafficking." Furthermore, the brief overnight stay and quick return was "as suggestive of a pre-arranged drug run, as it is of an ordinary vacation trip." Moreover, the detective and DEA operatives confirmed the tip in major part, including powerful corroboration of the tipster's predictions. That the details verified were also consistent with innocent activity was irrelevant, said the Court, concluding that " 'seemingly innocent activity became suspicious in the light of the initial tip.' " Finally, the Court considered the tip to be highly detailed, referring to future actions not easily predicted and to travel plans of each of the Gateses that were of "a character likely obtained only from the Gateses themselves, or from someone familiar with their not entirely ordinary travel plans." Accordingly, the probable cause determination of the judge issuing the warrant had a "substantial basis," entitling it to great deference.

c. Stevens' Dissent

Justice Stevens, joined by Justice Brennan, dissented. It is useful here to summarize this dissent in some detail because Stevens drew very different inferences from the evidence before the Court. Those differences help in understanding the meaning of the majority's test.

Of greatest interest here is that Stevens disagreed that there was adequate corroboration of the tip. The tipster insisted that Sue Gates regularly drives a car to Florida to be loaded up with drugs, then *flies* back home immediately after dropping off the car. Yet Detective Mader's affidavit reported that Sue left the West Palm Beach area, *driving* northbound with Lance. This was no minor discrepancy, argued Stevens, for three reasons. First, the tip had suggested that the Gateses followed a schedule that always kept one of them at home, yet Mader's report showed both being absent from home at the same time. Presumably, at least one of the Gateses needed to be home at all times to protect the $100,000 worth of drugs that the informant said were already in their basement. An observed schedule permitting neither to be home thus called into question whether there were indeed drugs in the Gateses's home.

Second, the observed conduct was far less suspicious than the predicted conduct. Sue driving down for many hours only quickly to drive back is not ordinary behavior. But that in reality she was simply seen in Palm Beach with her car, joining up with her husband at a Holiday Inn, the couple then driving home together, was neither unusual nor probative of crime.

Third, the fact that the anonymous letter contained a material mistake undermines the reasonableness of relying on it as a basis for making a forcible entry into a private home. That the Gateses drove all night to get home, to be greeted by police who found nearly 400 pounds of marijuana in the Gateses's car, is irrelevant because those events occurred *after* the magistrate signed the warrant. No one knew who the informant was or what motivated him. Concluded Stevens, "[g]iven that the note's predictions were faulty in one significant respect, and were corroborated by nothing but innocent activity, I must surmise that the Court's evaluation of the warrant's validity has been colored by subsequent events."

That Stevens made different inferences than did the Justices in the majority arguably should not matter under the majority's rule. Because the majority rule requires deference to the magistrate's judgments, that reasonable judges might draw different inferences from the facts would not be enough to invalidate the magistrate's finding of probable cause. Moreover, the majority approach seems far more willing than Stevens's to find some discrepancies between a tip's predictions of future events and how they actually unfold to be "minor" or even irrelevant in light of more numerous or arguably more important consistencies. Stevens' final point, however—that events occurring after the warrant was issued are irrelevant to the warrant's validity—recites a rule that even the majority embraces, yet the majority did not seriously address Stevens's analysis on this point. One way to render the majority's approach on this point consist with the rule declaring post-warrant-issuance observations irrelevant is that the majority referred to such observations as a mere rhetorical flourish rather than as central to its holding. But that again suggests that the majority's approach is far more accepting of weaker evidence of probable cause than is Justice Stevens's. So understood, Stevens's challenge to the majority's application of its own rule might implicitly constitute a challenge to the rule itself.

Justice Brennan, in his own dissenting opinion, joined by Justice Marshall, did indeed challenge the wisdom of the majority's rule. Brennan challenged the accuracy of the Court's reading of its prior precedent. More important here, however, is that Brennan gave several very specific reasons for rejecting the majority's rule as unwise constitutional policy. First, Brennan considered the probable cause determination task more difficult when based upon informants' tips rather than solely police officer observations. In the latter case, magistrates need primarily to know only how the police acquired their information. But in the former case, that of informants, both the honesty of the informant and the reliability of the way in which he required that information matter. This greater complexity, said Justice Brennan, "suggests a need to structure the inquiry in an effort to insure greater accuracy." The *Aguilar-Spinelli* standards do just that, both by telling the police what information they must provide the magistrate and by telling the magistrate what conclusions he must make to find probable cause. Second, by encouraging police to gather and provide more information to the magistrate, *Aguilar-Spinelli* "assure[s] the magistrate's role as an independent arbiter of probable cause" rather than one merely deferring to police judgment.

Third, Brennan insisted that the *Aguilar-Spinelli* rule would not automatically invalidate all anonymous tips. To the contrary, said Brennan, a sufficiently detailed tip might establish both the veracity of the informant and the reliability of his basis of knowledge.

Fourth, Brennan likewise rejected the majority's belief that *Aguilar-Spinelli* was inconsistent with a "practical, non-technical" conception of probable cause. "Once a magistrate has determined that he has information before him," explained Brennan, "that he can reasonably say has been obtained in a reliable way by a credible person, he has ample room to use his common sense and to apply a practical, nontechnical conception of probable cause." Similarly, that non-lawyers must use the probable cause concept meant, in Brennan's view, that they need more, not less, guidance and structure. But that guidance was also not inconsistent with deference to a reviewing court that has followed the rules laid down by the Supreme Court.

Fifth, Brennan rejected any concern that the more structured *Aguilar-Spinelli* rules would discourage police from seeking warrants in the first place. The exceptions to the warrant requirement were, in his view, few and "jealously and carefully drawn" so that an officer choosing to arrest, search, or seize without a warrant would be taking a risky gamble on avoiding suppression of any evidence seized. Rather than take that gamble, said Brennan, police would still seek warrants whenever practicable.

Finally, Brennan rejected the majority's fear that *Aguilar-Spinelli* unduly interfered with prosecuting criminals and protecting public safety, a concern that, in any event, ignores societal interests in accurate probable cause judgments providing adequate assurances of being based on truthful and trustworthy evidence.

d. State Court Departures

Brennan's dissent has thus far not moved the Court to depart from the *Gates* rule. Yet Brennan's words have sometimes explicitly, sometimes implicitly, been taken to heart by state appellate courts. These courts have rejected the wisdom of the Court's shift to the totality of the circumstances test, finding *Aguilar-Spinelli* to survive under individual state constitutions (remember that state constitutions can always provide more, though never less, protection than the federal constitution). Said the New Mexico Supreme Court in *State v. Cordova*, 784 P.2d 30 (N.M. 1989), for example, in justifying its following just such an approach, and using words that sounded as if they were lifted directly from Justice Brennan's dissent:

> We simply do not believe this tradition [of *Aguilar-Spinelli*] to be
> one of unthinking rigidity or overly technical application of the [rel-

evant] principles.… Moreover, we believe these principles to be firmly rooted in the fundamental precepts of the constitutional requirement that no warrant issue without a written showing of probable cause before a detached and neutral magistrate. We are convinced that our rules, while providing a flexible, common sense framework, also provide structure for the very inquiry into whether probable cause has been demonstrated. The fact that "non-lawyers" are involved in drafting applications for search warrants underscores rather than obviates the need for such structure.

e. Conclusory Affidavits Probably Still Unacceptable

Gates does not alter the Court's opposition to warrants being issued based upon conclusory assertions. The Court is particularly wary of search warrant applications based upon standard form affidavits or, in the case of arrest, standard form criminal complaints. In *Giordenello v. United States*, 357 U.S. 480, (1958), the Court criticized such forms because they often mean that a magistrate cannot "assess independently the probability that the arrestee committed the crime charged." In 2001, in *Overton v. Ohio*, 534 U.S. 982 (2001), Ohio police allegedly used a form criminal complaint, with only the defendant's name and address inserted, to obtain a warrant for Overton's arrest, leading to the discovery of drugs. The trial court denied Overton's motion to suppress the drugs, and she was convicted, appealing on the grounds that the arrest warrant was not based on probable cause. The Ohio appellate courts denied relief, and the Supreme Court denied the subsequent petition for a writ of certiorari.

But, in an unusual written statement, Justice Breyer, joined by Justices Stevens, O'Connor, and Souter, stated that the Court should summarily have reversed Overton's conviction. Justice Breyer condemned the form criminal complaint as being so cursory as to undermine the ability of a neutral magistrate to exercise the "deliberate, impartial judgment of a judicial officer" that is needed for him to interpose himself "between the citizen and the police, to assess the weight and credibility of the information which the complaining officer adduces as probable cause." In addition to stating Overton's name, the date and name of the offense, and the statutory reference, the entire complaint said the following:

> The defendant, being the owner, lessee, or occupant of certain premises, did knowingly permit such premises to be used for the commission of a felony drug abuse offense, to wit: Desarie Overton, being the lessee, owner, or occupant of 620 Belmont, Toledo, Ohio 43607, knowingly permitted Cocaine, a Schedule Two controlled substance to be sold and possessed by the occupants, there, both being in vio-

lation of the Ohio Revised Code, a felony drug abuse offense. This offense occurred in Toledo, Lucas County, Ohio.

Justice Breyer described this complaint as doing no more than setting forth the relevant crime in general terms and asserting that Overton committed the crime. "But nowhere," emphasized Justice Breyer, does the complaint "indicate *how Detective Woodson knows, or why he believes, that Overton committed the crime.*" Accordingly, insisted Breyer, the case squarely fit within the principle that conclusory "affidavits or complaints of this kind do not provide sufficient support for the issuance of an arrest warrant."

f. Prosecutorial Ethics

Prosecutors must, as just suggested, be concerned with whether the police submitted affidavits to support the issuance of warrants based upon an adequate showing of probable cause. Prosecutors may also arguably have an ethical obligation, as part of their duty to "do justice," to make their own, independent judgment whether the police acted consistently with the constitution before using the fruits of warrants at a criminal trial. However, if a subordinate prosecutor concludes that there was a constitutional violation, but his superior disagrees, the subordinate's "whistleblowing" on his boss's efforts to silence his views by seeking retribution against him—perhaps by demoting him, cutting his salary, or firing him—will likely prove to be well within the boss's constitutional authority.

In *Garcetti v. Ceballos*, 547 U.S. 410 (2006), for example, Ceballos, a supervising district attorney, conducted an investigation that led him to believe that the police had obtained evidence pursuant to a warrant based upon serious misrepresentations in the supporting affidavit. When his superior proceeded with the prosecution in the face of his recommendation that the case be dismissed, Ceballos testified for the defense at a suppression hearing. He filed a lawsuit alleging violation of his First and Fourteenth Amendment rights when his superiors, in alleged retaliation for his efforts to speak out against an abuse of the warrant process, reassigned him to a different position and courthouse and denied him a promotion.

The Supreme Court reversed a Ninth Circuit decision that Ceballos had a viable cause of action, thus letting stand a district court's grant of summary judgment against Ceballos. Ceballos, said the Court, had no constitutional right to free speech protection because he spoke in his role as an employee of the prosecutor's office, *not* in his role as a private citizen. Accordingly, he could be subjected to discipline by his employer. A contrary rule, the Court insisted, would subject managerial discretion to judicial oversight, unduly interfering with management's ability to achieve its goals. Furthermore, there are ample statutory protections for whistleblowers.

Justices Stevens, Souter, and Breyer filed dissenting opinions. Justice Breyer's was of particular note. He emphasized that the speech in question was not just any employee's speech but that of a lawyer. The ethical canons governing lawyers obligate them to speak in certain instances. Prosecutors in particular are also constitutionally obligated to "learn of, to preserve, and to communicate with the defense about exculpatory and impeachment evidence in the government's possession." Where, as in Garcetti's case, there was such a constitutional and ethical obligation to speak, maintained Breyer, the government's managerial interest in forbidding that speech is diminished and must give way to the greater dictates of the constitution governing appropriate prosecutorial behavior.

D. Individualized Justice and Other Normative Concerns

The Supreme Court has repeatedly declared that probable cause is an individualized determination. *See* THOMAS K. CLANCY, THE FOURTH AMENDMENT: HISTORY AND INTERPRETATION 473–76, 518–19 (2008) (explaining and synthesizing the cases). There must be evidence, for example, that *this suspect* committed a crime, evidence based upon the suspect's *own* actions and character. It is not sufficient that the suspect falls into some group whose members are supposedly more likely to be criminals. Nor is it sufficient that he lives in a high crime area. Nor should one be condemned simply for associating with known criminals absent evidence of the suspect's own suspicious conduct. This principle seems to reflect a moral judgment that the state should not interfere with a person's privacy, property, or free movement unless there is serious reason to believe that his own actions cast suspicion on him. The principle of individualized justice also might embody a political judgment that only an individualization requirement adequately limits police officer discretion. Dragnet sweeps would thus be prohibited, like that in Oneonta, New York, in which a woman assaulted in her home described her attacker only as a young black male, so the police questioned every young black male in town.

But the individualized justice principle is easier to state than apply. All human reasoning involves some degree of generalization, some comparison of current circumstances to prior categories of experience. For example, to describe an assailant as "tall" is to say that his height was in the range of other males fitting into the group of men that you have learned to describe as "tall." The real question, therefore, is one of degree: How many generalizations are involved? How close are the inferences made to the "particularized" rather than the generalized end of an imagined spectrum of specificity? Lines must be drawn somewhere. The question is where.

Critics have argued that much of the Supreme Court's recent case law has come too close to the generalized end of the scale. The *Pringle* case, discussed earlier, is one example. Remember there, the Supreme Court found that an officer's finding cocaine hidden behind the upraised rear armrest of a car, combined with the refusal of the car's occupants to admit to who owned it and with the presence of a substantial amount of cash in the glove compartment, constituted probable cause to arrest all three men. Pringle had argued that the officers had no evidence against him other than his mere presence in the company of someone who possessed drugs, that is, that this was a mere "guilt by association" case. The Court, however, thought association with others *in a car* to be a critical fact, for no drug user would allow non-users to join him in a drive. In reaching this conclusion, the Court had to distinguish *Pringle* from other cases where it found the evidence of one person's consorting with others who might be guilty of wrongdoing insufficient alone to establish probable cause.

Pringle had relied in particular on *Ybarra v. Illinois*, 444 U.S. 85 (1979). In *Ybarra*, police executing a warrant to search a tavern and its bartender for evidence of possession of a controlled substance conducted pat down searches for all the customers present, including Ybarra, and seized six tinfoil packets containing heroin from a cigarette pack retrieved from Ybarra's pocket. The Court invalidated the search, stressing that it was based on insufficiently individualized suspicion as to Ybarra and noting that "[a] person's mere propinquity to others independently suspected of criminal activity does not, without more, give rise to probable cause to search that person." The *Pringle* Court distinguished *Ybarra* thus:

> This case is quite different from *Ybarra*. Pringle and his two companions were in a relatively small automobile, not a public tavern. In *Wyoming v. Houghton*, we noted that "a car passenger—unlike the unwitting tavern patron in *Ybarra*—will often be engaged in a common enterprise with the driver, and have the same interest in concealing the fruits or the evidence of their wrongdoing." Here we think it was reasonable for the officer to infer a common enterprise among the three men. The quantity of drugs and cash in the car indicated the likelihood of drug dealing, an enterprise to which a dealer would be unlikely to admit an innocent person with the potential to furnish evidence against him.

The *Pringle* Court also distinguished another case, *United States v. Di Re,* 22 U.S. 581 (1948). There, an informant had fingered one person, a Mr. Buttita, as about to sell the informant counterfeit gasoline ration coupons at a particular place. When a federal investigator arrived at that place, he saw not only Buttita but the informant and Mr. Di Re in a car in which the informant held in his hands counterfeit rationing coupons. The informant told the investigator that Buttita gave the informant the coupons, never mentioning Di Re's involvement. Nevertheless, the informant arrested and searched all three men. The *Di Re* Court concluded that the investigator lacked probable cause for Di Re's arrest because the informant had only identified Buttita as the seller. Emphasized that Court, "[a]ny inference that everyone on the scene of a crime is a party to it must disappear if the Government singles out the guilty person." But, by contrast, explained the *Pringle* Court, no such singling out had occurred in *Pringle* because none of the three men arrested there had singled out any other as owning the money or cocaine found by the police during a consensual search.

In another area of search and seizure law, to be discussed in more detail in Chapters 4 and 11, that involving "reasonable suspicion," the Court has also had to wrestle with individualized justice. Reasonable suspicion is a form of suspicion lower in quantity, and can be based on information lower in quality, than that necessary for probable cause. However, reasonable suspicion still must be *individualized* suspicion. Yet, although the Court says that neither flight from the police nor presence in a high crime area are sufficient for reasonable suspicion, both factors combined are adequate.

The Court has thus arguably held that *two* generalizations—no one would flee from the police unless guilty and persons in high crime areas are more likely than those in low crime areas to have committed a crime—together constitute individualized suspicion. Several dissenting Justices and a number of commentators have challenged whether such reasoning makes sense and whether either of these two generalizations is alone a fair one, as we will see. Indeed, at least one dissenting Justice has argued that it is *less* suspicious to flee the police in a high crime area, for residents of those areas have more reason to fear police abuse than do those in wealthier, safer locations.

Sometimes, without always acknowledging it, the Court entirely eliminates the individualized suspicion aspect of probable cause. The two primary areas where this has happened are for certain administrative searches and for Foreign Intelligence Surveillance Act warrants. One might question whether the generalized suspicion involved in the administrative and national security areas can fairly be called probable cause at all.

E. Temporal Components

1. Timing and Two Standards for Probable Cause

Hindsight bias is a well-known psychological phenomenon among social scientists. Simply put, it is the tendency to judge past events based upon our current knowledge of the surrounding circumstances and outcome of an action rather than based upon what the actor knew at the time. Hindsight bias often operates subconsciously, thus beyond conscious awareness or control. This bias can conflict with the black-letter law. Probable cause, for example, is supposed to be judged based upon the information available to the officer at the time of the search or seizure. Yet, because probable cause is an ambiguous concept, it can be hard for judges to comply with the law's mandate.

Suppose, for example, that the police conduct a warrantless search of a warehouse, finding a massive cache of explosives and written evidence suggesting that the explosives were about to be used to launch a terrorist attack on New York City. The defendants move to suppress the evidence on the ground that the search was done without probable cause. The law mandates that the judge at the suppression hearing must ignore the *results* of the search— namely, finding the explosives and written evidence. Instead, the judge must focus solely on what information the officers had *before* they entered the warehouse.

But the law is asking the judge to perform a difficult cognitive feat. Even if the judge's written or oral decision on the motion never mentions the outcome of the search, and even if he in good faith tries to ignore that outcome, his subconscious will not oblige. The hindsight bias will make it very hard for him to grant the motion, potentially freeing the terrorists to stalk the innocent once more. The warrant requirement averts this problem because the warrant judge must find probable cause as a *pre*-condition to signing the warrant. Furthermore, the warrant itself must be signed as a pre-condition for conducting the search. The warrant-issuing judge thus does not know what the police will find, so the hindsight bias cannot affect his judgment. It will be easier for him to choose not to sign the warrant because he concludes that probable cause is absent than it will be for the suppression judge—who knows what was eventually seized—to suppress evidence knowing that he is thereby helping to release truly dangerous criminals. Note an important corollary: in practice, even if not in theory, the quantitative and qualitative standards for probable cause, therefore, will be lower (easier to prove) for the suppression judge than for the warrant judge. *When* the probable cause determination is made will thus affect what probable cause actually means.

2. Anticipatory Warrants

Time plays a role in probable cause analysis in at least one other way. Most probable cause determinations use past events (a tip, police officer observations) to make informed guesses about past or current circumstances. A current circumstance might be that drugs will *now* be found at the suspect's home. A past circumstance, justifying arrest, might be that the suspect *yesterday* sold cocaine. But sometimes officers seek to predict events that have not yet occurred, such as that drugs *will arrive* at the suspect's home tomorrow or that he *will* make an illegal drug sale at the corner of Maine and New Hampshire streets next week. One common circumstance where this occurs is in seeking warrants for wiretaps, which by definition involve permission to overhear and record *future* telephone conversations. Wiretaps and other electronic surveillance mechanisms are discussed in Chapter 5. When seeking more routine, usually tangible, future-occurring evidence, however, the police seek an "anticipatory warrant."

Lower courts have generally found anticipatory warrants to be constitutional so long as there are strong guarantees that the "affiant's" (the person swearing to the truth of the allegations in the affidavit supporting probable cause that is submitted with the warrant application) predictions will come true. Many lower courts have accordingly required probable cause to believe that the contraband is on a "sure course" to its intended destination. These courts have also specified "triggering conditions"—post-warrant events that must come to pass before the signed anticipatory warrant may actually be executed, such as upon actually seeing a package, allegedly containing cocaine, with distinctive wrapping, arriving at a particular location at a specified time.

The Supreme Court recently weighed in on the constitutionality of anticipatory warrants and the standard for issuing them in *United States v. Grubbs*, 547 U.S. 90 (2006). There, federal officers obtained an anticipatory search warrant for Jeffrey Grubbs's home. The contraband sought was a videotape of child pornography that he had ordered from an undercover federal postal inspector via the internet. The supporting affidavit had indicated that the warrant was only to be executed upon a "controlled delivery" of contraband to the home. The warrant affidavit recited this triggering condition:

> [e]xecution of this search warrant will not occur unless and until the parcel has been received by a person(s) and has been physically taken into the residence.... At that time, and not before, this search warrant will be executed by me and other United States Postal inspectors, with appropriate assistance from other law enforcement officers in accord with this warrant's command.

The affidavit also contained attachments describing the items to be seized. These attachments were incorporated into the warrant, though the warrant made no reference to the affidavit itself. But the affidavit did mention the attachments as well:

> Based upon the foregoing facts, I respectfully submit there exists probable cause to believe that the items set forth in Attachment B to this affidavit and the search warrant will be found at [Grubbs' residence], which residence is further described at Attachment A.

Two days later, an undercover postal inspector delivered the package containing the videotape to Grubbs's home. Grubbs's wife signed for the package and took it unopened into her home. When Grubbs left home a few minutes later, police detained him, searching his home. A half hour into the search, the inspectors gave Grubbs a copy of the warrant that included the attachments but *not* the supporting affidavit containing the warrant's "triggering" condition.

Grubbs thereupon consented to being interrogated and admitted ordering the videotape. He was arrested, the videotape and other items were seized, and a grand jury indicted him on one count of "receiving a visual depiction of a minor engaged in sexually explicit conduct," a violation of 18 U.S.C. § 2252(a)(2). Grubbs moved to suppress the evidence, arguing that the warrant was invalid "because it failed to list a triggering condition." Grubbs's motion was denied by the district court; he pleaded guilty, reserving the right to appeal the denial.

The Supreme considered two challenges to the search warrant: (1) the "antecedent question" of whether anticipatory search warrants are "categorically unconstitutional" (failing to satisfy the Fourth Amendment requirements that "no Warrants shall issue, but upon probable cause") and (2) whether listing the "triggering condition" in the warrant is necessary to "'assure the individual whose property is searched or seized of the lawful authority of the executing officer, his need to search, and the limits of his power to search.'"

In discussing the first question, the Court determined that because probable cause "exists when 'there is a fair probability that contraband or evidence of a crime will be found in a particular place,'" and because this requirement necessarily "looks to whether evidence will be found when the search is conducted, all warrants are, in a sense, anticipatory." Granted, said the Court, with ordinary warrants police seek authority to search for what is already there. But the magistrate's determination in that ordinary case that there is probable cause for the search nevertheless "amounts to a prediction that the item will still be there when the warrant is executed." The anticipatory aspect of all warrants is even clearer, said the Court, with electronic surveillance. Accordingly, "[a]nticipatory warrants are … no different in principle from ordinary warrants." Moreover, anticipatory warrants:

> require the magistrate to determine (1) that it is now probable that (2) contraband, evidence of a crime, or a fugitive will be on the described premises (3) when the warrant is executed. It should be noted, however, that where the anticipatory warrant places a condition (other than the mere passage of time) upon its execution, the first of these determinations goes not merely to what will probably be found if the condition is met. (If that were the extent of the probability determination, an anticipatory warrant could be issued for every house in the country, authorizing search and seizure if contraband should be delivered—though for any single location there is no likelihood that contraband will be delivered). Rather, the probability determination for a conditioned anticipatory warrant looks also to the likelihood that the condition will occur, and thus that a proper object of seizure will be on the described premises.

Accordingly, the Court concluded that the validity of a conditioned anticipatory warrant turns on two prerequisites: first, that "there is a fair probability that contraband or evidence of a crime will be found in a particular place …" and, second, that there is probable cause to believe the triggering condition will occur.

Thus, "when an anticipatory warrant is issued, 'the fact that the contraband is not presently located at the place described in the warrant is immaterial, so long as there is probable cause to believe that it will be there when the search warrant is executed.'" Because the anticipatory warrant's affidavit explained that "execution of the search warrant will not occur unless and until the parcel [containing child pornography] has been received by a person(s) and has been physically taken into the residence," execution of the warrant before said triggering condition would give the government "no reason to believe the item described in the warrant could be found at the searched location; by definition, the triggering condition which establishes probable cause has not yet been satisfied when the warrant is issued." The Court found, however, that the magistrate judge had a substantial basis for concluding that the triggering condition would be satisfied (Grubbs's refusal of delivery of the videotape was deemed "unlikely" by the Court) and the government had probable cause to conduct the search of Grubbs's home, given that the warrant's triggering condition occurred prior to the search warrant's execution.

With respect to Grubbs's assertion that the anticipatory search warrant lacked sufficient particularity, thereby invalidating the government's search,

the Court determined that the Fourth Amendment "specifies only two matters that must be 'particularly described' in the warrant": "the place to be
searched" and "the persons or things to be seized." It does not address "un-
enumerated matters" such as "conditions precedent" to a warrant's execu-
tion.Regarding the government's "failure" to present either Grubbs or his wife
with a copy of the full warrant containing the triggering condition, the Court
noted that there is no such constitutional requirement of warrant presentment
in the Fourth Amendment's particularity provision.

F. Particularity

1. Particularity's Meaning

Submitting an affidavit adequate to support probable cause entitles the affiant to a warrant. But the warrant itself must comply with the Fourth Amendment's Particularity Clause, which requires that warrants "particularly describe[e]
the place to be searched, and the persons or things to be seized." The particularity requirement seeks to avoid the breadth of the "general warrants" used
by the British that so offended the pre-Revolutionary colonists. Particular warrants also limit police officer discretion, giving the police authority to search
only where and for what the magistrate approves. Moreover, the magistrate is
supposed to limit the warrant to only the places and things for which there is
probable cause to believe items that are contraband, fruits of crime, instrumentalities of crime, or evidence of crime will be found.

For example, if the police receive a credible tip with a reliable basis that a
sawed-off shotgun is at a particular person's house at 333 West 3rd Street in
Philadelphia, Pennsylvania, the warrant must authorize a search only for a
warrant for that type of rifle at that location. The warrant may not on that tip
alone authorize searching for other sorts of weapons, or for drugs, or for stolen
money. Moreover, the police may not search in dresser drawers too small to contain a shotgun or in wallets, cookie jars, or other small locations.

Whether a warrant is sufficiently particular is a fact-bound inquiry, a question of the reasonableness of the description in giving guidance to the police, adequately limiting their discretion and reflecting only what probable cause supports.
Furthermore, as the Supreme Court made clear in *Maryland v. Garrison*, 480
U.S. 79 (1987), the warrant is to be evaluated at the time it was issued and according
to the information that the officers disclosed, or should have disclosed, to the issuing judicial officer. The Court explained this test in the following manner:

> [w]e must judge the constitutionality of [law enforcement officers']
> conduct in light of the information available to them at the time they

acted. Those items of evidence that emerge after the warrant is issued have no bearing on whether or not a warrant was validly issued. Just as the discovery of contraband cannot validate a warrant when issued, so is it equally clear that the discovery of facts demonstrating that a valid warrant was unnecessarily broad does not retroactively invalidate the warrant. The validity of the warrant must be assessed on the basis of the information that the officers disclosed, or had a duty to discover and to disclose, to the issuing Magistrate.

Thus, suppose that the police get a warrant to search "a storage box on the topmost row of storage boxes at the train station for cocaine." If there are ten boxes in that row, the description is inadequate because it does not limit the police to the one mailbox for which probable cause to search exists, and they easily could have gone to the train station to determine how many boxes there were. Of course, if they did that and still had no information allowing them to know *which* mailbox had the cocaine, they would arguably lack the individualized suspicion that the Fourth Amendment generally requires. If the police knew from a tip that the cocaine was in box number 3 of the storage boxes at the train stain, and if there is only one box number 3, they would have the necessary individualized suspicion. But if the warrant itself was not limited to box number 3 or did not incorporate by reference an affidavit doing so, then the warrant would still be insufficiently particular to limit police discretion.

2. Residual Clauses

"Residual clauses"—generalized, catchall clauses at the end of a more specific warrant description—also typically raise particularity questions. *Andersen v. Maryland*, 427 U.S. 463 (1976), illustrates the problem. There, an attorney specializing in real estate settlements had represented to a purchaser that Lot 13T was free of liens and that title insurance was therefore unnecessary when he knew that there were in fact two outstanding liens on the property. The lienholders attempted to stop the sale by threatening to foreclose on the liens. When the purchaser confronted the attorney with this information, he issued, as an agent of a title insurance company, a title policy guaranteeing clear title.

The State's Attorney's Office's investigators, concluding that they had probable cause to believe that the attorney had committed the crime of false pretenses, obtained a warrant to search the attorney's law office and that of a corporation for which he was the sole shareholder. The warrant contained a long list of documents that could be seized "pertaining to sale, purchase, settlement and conveyance of lot 13, block T, Potomac Woods subdivisions, Montgomery County, Maryland ." At the end of this long list, the warrant concluded with the general statement that police could also seize "other fruits, instrumentalities and evidence of crime at this [time] unknown."

The searches of these two offices led to the seizure of a variety of files concerning lots other than, but in the same development as, Lot 13T. The attorney was charged with, and convicted of, the crime of false pretenses concerning Lot 13T. Some items seized had been suppressed at a pre-trial hearing on the ground that they were unconnected to the crime charged, but other items survived suppression, including some of those involving lots other than 13T. The trial judge concluded that these other items were "admissible to show a pattern of criminal conduct relevant to the charge concerning Lot 13T...." When the case reached the Supreme Court, the issue before it was whether the warrant description was so broad as to constitute a general warrant.

The defendant's argument was that the broadly unqualified phrase ending the warrant made it into a general one. As the Court explained, "[T]he problem [posed by the general warrant] is not that of intrusion per se, but a general, exploratory rummaging in a person's belongings." The particularity requirement "makes general searches ... impossible and prevents the seizure of one thing under a warrant describing another. As to what is to be taken, nothing is left to the discretion of the officer executing the warrant." The Court disagreed, however, with the assertion that *this warrant* was too general.

First, asserted the Court, the general phrase appeared at the end of a list of particulars, all of which, including the general phrase, were modified by the introductory phrase limited to the conveyance of Lot 13T. The warrant thus authorized seizure only of items relevant to the crime of false pretenses as to Lot 13T.

Second, however, why, given such a limitation, could the investigators nevertheless still seize items concerning other lots? The Court explained that the investigation concerned a complex real estate scheme and, "[l]ike a jigsaw puzzle, the whole "picture" of petitioner's false-pretense scheme with respect to Lot 13T could be shown only by placing in the proper place the many pieces of evidence that, taken singly, would show comparatively little." The specificity of the documents here, explained the Court, contrasted sharply with the absence of particularity in *Berger v. New York*, 388 U.S. 41, 58–59 (1967), where a state eavesdropping statute which authorized eavesdropping "without requiring belief that any particular offense has been or is being committed; nor that the 'property' sought, the conversations, be particularly described," was invalidated.

The Court's holding in *Andersen* might best be understood by reviewing some basic evidence law. Under Federal Rule of Evidence 404, evidence of a person's prior wrongful acts is not admissible to prove that he had a character making his current wrongful act more likely. But other wrongful acts can be admitted to show a common plan, scheme, or design, in effect, to show that the wrongful act charged was but one piece in a larger plan. Furthermore, under the "doctrine of objective chances," repeated prior misrepresentations, for example, made by this lawyer to other land purchasers, would give the lie to any claim that he did not *know* he had spoken untruths about Lot 13T. Rule 404 bars only using character to prove *acts*, not to prove mental states, such as knowledge. The Federal Rules of Evidence or state-level equivalents do not, of course, apply at suppression hearings. But this analysis clarifies why evidence that the attorney in *Anderson* lied to other lot purchasers would also be relevant to "the crime of false pretenses" "*as to Lot 13T.*"

3. Affidavit-Warrant Link

What happens if the warrant affidavit is sufficiently particular but the warrant itself is not? The Supreme Court recently suggested that unless the warrant expressly incorporates and appends the application, its silence violates the Fourth Amendment. In the situation giving rise to the Court's opinion in *Groh v. Ramirez*, 540 U.S. 551 (2004), Jeff Groh (a Special Agent for the Federal Bureau of Alcohol, Tobacco and Firearms) submitted an application for a warrant to search Mr. and Mrs. Joseph Ramirez's Montana ranch for "any automatic firearms or parts of automatic weapons, destructive devices to include but not limited to grenades, grenade launchers, rocket launchers, and any and all receipts pertaining to the purchase or manufacture of automatic weapons or explosive devices or launchers." The warrant itself did not specify these or any other items that law enforcement officers were authorized to seize. Instead, in the particularity portion of the warrant, Groh merely described the Ramirezes' residence. The warrant did not incorporate by reference the items identified in the application. Moreover, the application was not attached to the warrant when it was executed—indeed, it remained in court under seal.

Writing for a five-Justice majority, Justice Stevens held the warrant invalid, reiterating that "[t]he Fourth Amendment by its terms requires particularity *in the warrant*, not in the supporting documents." (emphasis added). The requirement serves a "high function":

> and that high function is not necessarily vindicated when some other document, somewhere, says something about the objects of the search, but the contents of that document are neither known to the person whose home is being searched nor available for her inspection. We do not say that the Fourth Amendment forbids a warrant from cross-refer-

encing other documents. Indeed, most Courts of Appeals have held that a court may construe a warrant with reference to a supporting application or affidavit if the warrant uses appropriate words of incorporation, and if the supporting document accompanies the warrant. But in this case the warrant did not incorporate other documents by reference, nor did either the affidavit or the application (which had been placed under seal) accompany the warrant.

The Court concluded that the warrant "did [not] make what fairly could be characterized as a mere technical mistake or typographical error." Instead, it was "so obviously deficient" that the Court had to regard the subsequent search as "warrantless."

Interestingly, Groh had conceded in the Supreme Court the invalidity of the warrant. Nevertheless, he urged the Court to evaluate the case based on the circumstances in which his search was carried out, rather than to decide it based simply on the presence or absence of a valid warrant. The search, he argued, was reasonable because it was "functionally equivalent to a search authorized by a valid warrant." Among the circumstances viewed by Groh as bearing on the search's reasonableness were (1) the Magistrate's determination that the application established probable cause, (2) the fact that during his execution of the warrant Groh told Mrs. Ramirez what he was looking for, and (3) the fact that Groh's search and seizure did not exceed the particulars contained in the application.

Justice Stevens rejected Groh's efforts to decouple the Fourth Amendment's warrant clause from its reasonableness clause. The Court's cases "have firmly established," he stated, "the basic principle of Fourth Amendment law that searches and seizures inside a home without a warrant are presumptively unreasonable." He explained further that this "presumptive rule against warrantless searches applies with equal force to searches whose only defect is a lack of particularity in the warrant."

Justice Stevens went further to explain that he saw no reason in this situation to deviate from the categorical rule:

> [U]nless the particular items described in the affidavit are also set forth in the warrant itself (or at least incorporated by reference, and the affidavit present at the search), there can be no written assurance that the Magistrate actually found probable cause to search for, and to seize, every item mentioned in the affidavit.... In this case, for example, it is at least theoretically possible that the Magistrate was satisfied that the search for weapons and explosives was justified by the showing in the affidavit, but not convinced that any evidentiary basis

existed for rummaging through respondents' files and papers for receipts pertaining to the purchase or manufacture of such items.

Furthermore, added Justice Stevens, the particularity requirement serves purposes in addition to preventing general searches. Notably, a particular warrant also "assures the individual whose property is searched and seized of the lawful authority of the executing officer, his need to search, and the limits of his power to search." *See Illinois v. Gates*, 462 U.S. 213 (1983) ("[P]ossession of a warrant by officers conducting an arrest or search greatly reduces the perception of unlawful or intrusive police conduct.").

In addition to the five justices who joined Justice Steven's opinion, two others agreed that the Fourth Amendment had been violated. Justices Thomas and Scalia, however, dissented from that holding. Both would decouple the warrant clause from the reasonableness clause and apply reasonableness balancing case-by-case rather than categorical balancing.

III. Executing the Warrant

A. Time, Place, and Manner

Rule 41 of the Federal Rules of Criminal Procedure provides in pertinent part:

The warrant must command the officer to:
(A) execute the warrant within a specified time no longer than 10 days;
(B) execute the warrant during the daytime, unless the judge for good cause expressly authorizes execution at another time; and
(C) return the warrant to the magistrate judge designated in the warrant.

In a later provision of the same rule, the term "daytime" is defined as "the hours between 6:00 a.m. to 10:00 p.m. according to local time."

These limitations are traditional common law ones, similar versions now codified in the laws of most jurisdictions. Whether they are constitutionally required is not entirely clear. The ten-day limit prevents officers from executing "stale" warrants—warrants that may no longer be supported by accurate facts. Although the Supreme Court has not addressed the issue of "stale" warrants, it has recognized that "stale" information cannot be used to establish probable cause. The daytime hours restriction also may have constitutional echoes in that it represents a balance between individual privacy interests (which, presumably, are heightened during nighttime hours) and government needs.

B. Knock and Announce

Many jurisdictions also require that officers "knock and announce" before entering premises pursuant to a search warrant. The federal statute, 18 U.S.C. § 3109, is illustrative:

> The officer may break open any outer or inner door or window of a house, or any part of a house, or anything therein, to execute a search warrant, if, after notice of his authority and purpose, he is refused admittance or when necessary to liberate himself or a person aiding him in the execution of the warrant.

The constitutional status of these "knock and announce" rules was in question for many years, but in *Wilson v. Arkansas*, 514 U.S. 927 (1995), the Court held that a "knock and announce" execution sometimes is constitutionally required. In so doing, Justice Thomas, writing for the Court, relied on history as an interpretive method, holding that the Fourth Amendment incorporates a common law requirement that police officers entering a home must knock and announce their identity and purpose before attempting to enter the home forcibly. Thomas's opinion stated, however, that the knock-and-announce procedure is not always constitutionally required: it may be reasonable to dispense with it if, for example, it would endanger officer safety or the preservation of evidence.

The Court faced that issue in *Richards v. Wisconsin*, 520 U.S. 385 (1997), when it reviewed whether a state can establish categorical exceptions to the knock-and-announce procedure, as did the state courts of Wisconsin when they determined that law enforcement officers need not knock and announce when executing warrants in felony drug investigations. In affirming that exception, the Wisconsin Supreme Court had reasoned that all felony drug crimes involve "an extremely high risk of serious if not deadly injury to the police as well as the potential for the disposal of drugs by the occupants prior to entry by the police." In *Richards*, the Court rejected Wisconsin's categorical approach and insisted that the reasonableness of a no-knock search must be determined on a case-by-case basis.

Writing for a unanimous Court, Justice Stevens observed that categorical exceptions over-generalize, because they may encompass situations that do not pose risks to officer safety or to the preservation of evidence. Moreover, the categorical approach "impermissibly insulates these cases from judicial review." Furthermore, the Court feared the slippery slope: "If a per se exception were allowed for each category of criminal investigation that included a consider-able—albeit hypothetical—risk of danger to officers, or destruction of evidence, the knock-and-announce element of the Fourth Amendment's reasonableness requirement would be meaningless." However, a probable cause standard would not give state interests appropriate weight. Consequently, the Court crafted this rule: to justify a no-knock entry, police must have reasonable suspicion that knocking and announcing their presence, under the circumstances, would be dangerous or futile, or that it would inhibit the effective investigation of the crime by, for example, allowing the destruction of evidence. The Court affirmed that the police officers who engaged in the particular no-knock entry at issue had acted with reasonable suspicion, because they had knocked and the suspect had slammed his door shut after observing their presence. At that point the officers could enter forcibly, said the Court, because they reasonably believed that the suspect was attempting to destroy evidence of drug activity.

The Court returned to the issue of no-knock entries a year later in *United States v. Ramirez*, 523 U.S. 65 (1998). Officers in that case had obtained a "no-knock warrant" after establishing reasonable suspicion to believe that "knocking and announcing their presence might be dangerous to themselves or to others." While executing the warrant, the officers broke through a garage window. The Ninth Circuit held that the entry violated the Fourth Amendment, stating that, "while a 'mild exigency' is sufficient to justify a no-knock entry that can be accomplished without the destruction of property, 'more specific inferences of exigency' are necessary when property is destroyed." The Supreme Court disagreed. Writing for a unanimous Court, Chief Justice Rehnquist pointed out that the reasonable suspicion standard announced in *Richards* "depends in no way on whether police must destroy property in order to enter." Rehnquist added, however, that:

> [t]his is not to say that the Fourth Amendment speaks not at all to the manner of executing a search warrant. The general touchstone of reasonableness which governs Fourth Amendment analysis governs the method of execution of the warrant. Excessive or unnecessary destruction of property in the course of a search may violate the Fourth Amendment, even though the entry itself is lawful and the fruits of the search not subject to suppression.

Reviewing the facts in *Ramirez*, the Court concluded that the officers had broken a single window "because they wished to discourage [any occupants] from rushing to the weapons that the informant had told them respondent might have kept there. Their conduct was clearly reasonable and we conclude that there was no Fourth Amendment violation." As it had in *Wilson*, the Court declined to elaborate on the exclusionary rule implications of no-knock entries and warrant executions that violate the Fourth Amendment, although in a footnote it indicated that the exclusionary rule might have applied in *Ramirez* if there had been a Fourth Amendment violation and if "there was sufficient causal relationship between the breaking of the window and the discovery of the gun to warrant suppression of the evidence."

In a follow-up to the Supreme Court's knock-and-announce cases, the Supreme Court of Pennsylvania, in *Commonwealth v. Martinelli*, 729 A.2d 628 (Pa. 1999), held that the purpose of its own state knock-and-announce rule can be achieved "only if the police officer awaits a response for a reasonable period of time after his announcement of identity, authority, and purpose." In the Pennsylvania case, detectives served a search warrant on Jean Martinelli's home. One of the detectives knocked, and when Mrs. Martinelli asked from within "who's there," the detective answered "Dave." The detective admitted that he responded in this fashion in order to get Mrs. Martinelli to open her door. When she opened her door part way, the detective pushed the door further open, walked in with his gun drawn, and announced his identity. The Pennsylvania court held that the knock-and-announce rule had been violated by the officer's failure to wait a reasonable time to permit Martinelli "to surrender her residence voluntarily," and it affirmed the suppression of evidence found during the search.

In *United States v. Banks*, 540 U.S. 31 (2003), the Supreme Court likewise faced the question of how long a period of time the police must wait after knocking and announcing before they may forcibly enter a residence. Agents arrived at Banks's two-bedroom apartment at 2:00 p.m. on a weekday afternoon to execute a search warrant for cocaine. Officers at the front door called out "police search warrant" and rapped hard enough on the door to be heard by officers at the back door. After waiting 15 to 20 seconds with no answer, and, given no indication whether anyone was home, the officers broke down the front door with a battering ram. Banks had been in the shower and did not hear the police knocking and was just exiting the shower as the police entered. Their search produced weapons, crack cocaine, and other evidence of drug dealing. Banks moved to suppress the evidence on the ground that the police waited an unreasonably short time before forcing entry, violating both the Fourth Amendment and the federal knock-and-announce statute.

The District Court denied the motion, and Banks pled guilty while reserving his right to challenge the search on appeal. The Ninth Circuit reversed, ordering suppression, after detailing a list of numerous factors to guide the reasonableness inquiry and dividing the possible knock-and-announce circumstances into four categories, each with its own test of reasonableness, placing the current case in category four, entries in which no exigent circumstances exist and in which forced entry by destruction of property is required. That category, the Circuit Court concluded, mandated an "explicit refusal of admittance or a lapse of an even more substantial amount of time" than for cases in the other three categories.

The United States Supreme Court reversed, rejecting the Ninth Circuit's categorical, multi-factor approach. Said the Court, "it is too hard to invent categories without giving short shrift to details that turn out to be important in a given instance, and without inflating marginal ones." Indeed, continued the Court, "no template is likely to produce sounder results than examining the totality of the circumstances in a given case." There was no evidence that the police knew that Banks was in the shower, and, given the risk that cocaine might be flushed down the toilet or otherwise disposed of quickly, the 15 to 20 second wait was appropriate, even without an express refusal of entry:

> On the record here, what matters is the opportunity to get rid of cocaine, which a prudent dealer will keep near a commode or kitchen sink. The significant circumstances include the arrival of the police during the day, when anyone inside would probably have been up and around, and the sufficiency of 15 to 20 seconds for getting to the bathroom or the kitchen to start flushing cocaine down the drain. That is, when circumstances are exigent because a pusher may be near the point of putting his drugs beyond reach, it is imminent disposal, not travel time to the entrance, that governs when the police may reasonably enter.... And 15 to 20 seconds does not seem an unrealistic guess about the time someone would need to get in a position to rid his quarters of cocaine.

In weighing the totality of these case-specific circumstances, the Court applied a reasonable suspicion test, in which the question was whether there was adequate evidence to establish reasonable suspicion of exigent circumstances that therefore required prompt entry. That test was analogous to the one used in determining whether the knock-and-announce requirement could be foregone entirely.

Thus the Court stressed that the usual, non-technical, flexible test for reasonable suspicion, which the Court articulated in its preceding term in *United States v. Arvizu*, 534 U.S. 266 (2002), applied:

> [W]e recently disapproved a framework for making reasonable suspicion determinations that attempted to reduce what the [Ninth] Circuit described as "troubling ... uncertainty" in reasonableness analysis, by "describ[ing] and clearly delimit[ing]" an officer's consideration of certain factors.... Here, as in *Arvizu*, the Court of Appeal's overlay of

a categorical scheme on the general reasonableness analysis threatens to distort the "totality of the circumstances" principle, by replacing a stress on revealing facts with [a] resort to pigeonholes.... Attention to cocaine rocks and pianos tells a lot about the chances of their respective disposal and its bearing on reasonable time. Instructions couched in terms like "significant amount of time," and "an even more substantial amount of time" ... tell very little.

Recently, in *Hudson v. Michigan*, 547 U.S. 586 (2006), the United States Supreme Court held that the exclusionary rule does not apply to violations of the knock-and-announce rule, or at least not where the violation is a failure to wait a sufficient amount of time after announcing their presence but before entering. The Court found that the social costs of applying the exclusionary rule in this context outweighed the social benefits. (A more detailed discussion of the case is in Chapter 12)

C. Treatment of Individuals during Warrant Executions

Suppose a large number of police officers burst into the law school cafeteria as you are sipping a beer. They are there to execute an arrest warrant for the cafeteria manager and a search warrant for the cafeteria itself. But they make you wait there for an hour on the floor, your hands behind your back, while they conduct the search authorized in the warrant, then frisk you and all your friends eating in the cafeteria before they let you leave. Is their treatment of you and your friends constitutional?

The answer is "probably not," but it depends on whether there were facts making the officers' actions objectively reasonable. The Supreme Court addressed similar, although less egregious facts, in *Ybarra v. Illinois*, 444 U.S. 85 (1979). That case involved the search of a tavern pursuant to a warrant that also directed the officers to search the tavern owner. While executing the warrant, the officers frisked the patrons, including Ybarra. The frisk of Ybarra revealed drugs. Ybarra was prosecuted for the drug possession and moved to suppress the evidence on the basis of the frisk, which he contended was illegal. The Supreme Court agreed. It explained, first, that the warrant to search the tavern and its owner did not give the officers authority to search anyone else on the premises. Second, although warrantless frisks are sometimes permissible under the rule of *Terry v. Ohio* (see Chapter 4), the frisk here was unconstitutional because there were no facts giving rise to a reasonable suspicion that Ybarra was involved in any criminal activity and was armed or dangerous.

These two pieces of the *Ybarra* holding are important. Recall that a warrant grants limited authority to law enforcement officers—they may search and seize only as the warrant directs them. A warrant to search a tavern and its owner does not convey the authority to search its patrons. Conversely, a warrant to search the tavern and "all individuals found on its premises" would be invalid for lack of particularity, unless there were unusual facts set forth in the affidavit that established probable cause to believe that "all individuals found on its premises" were involved in the criminal activity.

On the other hand, an entirely distinct doctrine (the "*Terry* rule") permits officers in all situations to frisk individuals for weapons if reasonable suspicion exists to believe that those individuals are armed and dangerous. This rule suggests that law enforcement activity may depend in part on whether the warrant execution takes place in a public setting or in private. In the public tavern setting, Ybarra's mere presence did not create reasonable suspicion to believe that he posed a danger to the officers. In more private settings, however, officers might have reason to believe that persons present during the execution of a search warrant might be dangerous. For example, an officer executing a search warrant on the secluded farm of an anti-government militia member might reasonably suspect that family members present during the search may pose a danger to the officer, because the family members might be involved in the illegal activities themselves or at least have such a close connection with the targeted individual as to try to harm the officers.

The Supreme Court has been especially solicitous of officer safety concerns that arise when warrants are executed in private places. For example, the Court held in *Maryland v. Buie*, 494 U.S. 325 (1990), that officers executing an arrest warrant in a private home may conduct a "protective sweep" for individuals who might be concealed on the premises if they are in areas immediately adjacent to the location of the arrest or if there is reasonable suspicion that they are present and might pose a danger to the officers. In another holding, in *Michigan v. Summers*, 452 U.S. 692 (1981), the Court has authorized the practice of temporarily detaining individuals who occupy a residence that is the subject of a search warrant, at least if the search is for contraband. The Court explained that in these circumstances, it is reasonable to detain the occupants, who might pose a danger of harm or of fleeing, and who might be able to assist the officers by opening locked containers and doors.

In some circumstances officers may handcuff home residents during search warrant executions. In *Muehler v. Mena*, 544 U.S. 93 (2005), the Supreme Court upheld against a Fourth Amendment claim the handcuffing of a woman during a two- to three-hour search of her residence. The Court analyzed the situation for its "objective reasonableness," a test that it had articulated in *Gra-*

ham v. Connor, 490 U.S. 386 (1989). The Court reasoned that law enforcement interests "in not only detaining, but using handcuffs, are at their maximum when, as here, a warrant authorizes a search for weapons and a wanted gang member resides on the premises." On the other hand, the individual's interests were less weighty because the restraint constituted a "minor intrusion." Justice Stevens disagreed with the majority's application of the *Graham* test, arguing that it did not give enough weight to the fact that the woman was very small, posed no flight risk to the two armed officers guarding her, and did not appear to be involved with the gang activity under investigation.

More recently, the Court upheld officers' ordering the occupants of a home at which a search warrant was being executed to stand nude before the officers for a limited period of time. In *Los Angeles County v. Rettele*, 550 U.S. 609 (2007), police investigating four African-American suspects in a fraud and identity-theft crime ring, one of which suspects had a registered nine-millimeter Glock handgun, obtained a valid search warrant to search two houses for the suspects and for documents and computer files, as well as searching the suspects themselves for these items. The affidavit filed in support of the warrant cited various sources to show that the suspects resided at one of the homes. These sources included Department of Motor Vehicle reports, mailing address lists, an outstanding warrant, and an internet telephone directory. What the affidavit did not say, and the affiant did not know, was that that house had been sold to Max Rettele, who had resided there for three months with his wife and seventeen-year-old son. The Retteles were White. When the officers executed the warrant and entered the bedroom with guns drawn, they ordered Retelle and his wife to get out of their bed and show their hands, but they protested that they were not wearing any clothes. When Rettele tried to put on sweatpants, they told him not to move. Both husband and wife stood up, while the wife unsuccessfully tried to cover herself with a sheet. After one or two minutes, Rettele was allowed to get a robe for his wife, and he was himself allowed to get dressed. Shortly thereafter, the police realized they had made a mistake, apologized, and left.

The Retteles filed a § 1983 civil suit alleging that the warrant was obtained in a reckless fashion and the search conducted in an unreasonable manner. The district court granted summary judgment for the defendants, finding the warrant and subsequent search reasonable and, in the alternative, that if any rights were violated, they were not clearly established ones, thus entitling the officers to qualified immunity. The Supreme Court sided with the district court's grant of summary judgment to the defendants. The Court concluded that the officers had no way of knowing whether the African-American suspects might be elsewhere in the house, and people of different races can work together, live together, and commit crime together. The police believed that an armed suspect might be present, giving them authority to secure the scene. Furthermore,

> The orders by the police to the occupants, in the context of this lawful search, were permissible, and perhaps necessary, to protect the safety of the deputies. Blankets and bedding can conceal a weapon, and one of the suspects was known to own a firearm, factors which underscore this point. The Constitution does not require an officer to ignore the possibility that an armed suspect may sleep with a weapon within reach. The reports are replete with accounts of suspects sleeping close to weapons.

Of course, added the Court, that does not mean that the police could unduly prolong their treatment of the Retteles, but they acted quickly here, allowing the Retteles to dress as soon as it was clear there was no threat. As for the harm done to the Retteles,

> The Fourth Amendment allows warrants to issue on probable cause, a standard well short of absolute certainty. Valid warrants will issue to search the innocent, and people like Rettele and Sadler unfortunately bear the cost. Officers executing search warrants on occasion enter a house when residents are engaged in private activity; and the resulting frustration, embarrassment, and humiliation may be real, as was true here. When officers execute a valid warrant and act in a reasonable manner to protect themselves from harm, however, the Fourth Amendment is not violated.

Given that the Court found no Fourth Amendment violation, the Court did not reach the qualified immunity question. Justice Souter would have denied the writ of certiorari, while Justices Stevens and Ginsburg merely concurred in the judgment.

Checkpoints

- Probable cause is an objective concept that does not turn on the subjective beliefs of any individual officer.

- Probable cause's quantitative meaning is unclear and seems to be in flux, but it is likely something just under 50 percent likelihood of guilt, though there are arguments that it is much lower or that the necessary percentage varies with the circumstances.

- Qualitatively, probable cause must be based on sufficiently trustworthy evidence. In the case of informants, the *Gates* "totality of the circumstances" test governs, requiring courts to examine evidence of the informant's credibility (truthfulness) and reliability (whether there is an adequate basis, for example, the informant's personal observations of the events), though a weakness on one of these factors can be made up by strength in the other.

- Probable cause must be based on individualized suspicion rather than solely upon generalizations.

- Warrants may be issued only upon an affidavit that is not conclusory but rather contains sufficient information to enable a magistrate to make an independent judgment of probable cause.

- Warrants must be sufficiently particular clearly to identify what or who is to be searched or seized and to limit undue police officer discretion.

- Officers executing a warrant at a residence must first knock, then announce their purpose, unless they have reasonable suspicion to believe on the specific facts of the case that knocking and announcing would endanger the officers or other persons or would permit the destruction of evidence, though violation of this rule will not result in suppression of the evidence as a remedy.

- Officers executing a search warrant at a place of business do not thereby automatically have reasonable suspicion to frisk patrons not mentioned in the warrant.

Chapter 4

Arrests with and without Warrants

Roadmap

- The definition of an "arrest"

- The requirement that all arrests be "reasonable"

- When arrests are required with an arrest warrant versus with a search warrant versus with no warrant at all

- The significance of a suspect's being an "overnight guest" in the home of a third party

- When, if ever, arrests may be made for minor offenses

- The definition of "exigent circumstances" and when they create an exception to any of the arrest rules

- "Reasonable suspicion warrants" for temporary detention for investigative purposes and whether they are constitutional

- The degree of non-deadly force that may be used to stop a fleeing suspect and in what circumstances

- When, if ever, deadly force may be used to stop a fleeing suspect, including the difference, if any, among felonies, misdemeanors, and other offenses

- A "Gerstein" probable cause hearing and when it must be held

- *Terry* stops and frisks based on reasonable suspicion of criminal activity

- The quality of the evidence of reasonable suspicion

I. The Requirement of Reasonableness

The rules for when an arrest warrant is needed are fairly simple. Like any other government action under the Fourth Amendment, arrests must be *reasonable*. The Supreme Court has dealt with various components of reasonableness in the context of arrests. Chief among these are (1) the seriousness of the offense for which an arrest is made; (2) the level of suspicion necessary; (3) the requirement of a warrant; (4) the use of force; and (5) the requirement of prompt arraignment for arrests done without a warrant. We will discuss each of these below.

A. Seriousness of Offense

The authority to arrest is given by statute, and each jurisdiction instructs law enforcement officers as to which offenses are arrestable. The Fourth Amendment, however, may, *in theory*, serve as a check on this authority, because jurisdictions may not authorize arrests if such intrusive invasions of individual liberty would be unreasonable given the jurisdiction's interests. For example, it may be argued that it is unreasonable under the Fourth Amendment for jurisdictions to authorize officers to arrest first-time parking offenders. Of course, arrests have long been considered reasonable for serious offenses, including felonies and breach-of-the-peace misdemeanors. In *Atwater v. City of Lago Vista*, 532 U.S. 318 (2001), however, the Court confirmed that the Fourth Amendment also permits arrests — even warrantless ones — for traffic misdemeanors committed in the officer's presence. In *Atwater*, a police officer arrested Gail Atwater for violating a Texas law mandating the use of seatbelts for children and passengers in the front seat. Texas punishes violations of this law with a maximum $50 fine. Atwater claimed that an arrest for such a minor offense constituted an unreasonable seizure. Justice Souter, writing for a 5-justice majority, disagreed. Basing his opinion on an analysis of conditions existing at the time the Fourth Amendment was drafted, Justice Souter found no reason to believe that the Framers would have viewed such an arrest as unreasonable. Moreover, the majority explained that its holding would create a bright-line rule and thus provide greater guidance to police and lower courts than Atwater's proposed rule, which would prohibit arrests "when conviction could not ultimately carry any jail time and when the government shows no compelling need for immediate detention."

The Court relied upon *Atwater* to reverse a Virginia Supreme Court determination that suppression of evidence obtained illegally under state law violated the Fourth Amendment. In *Virginia v. Moore*, 553 U.S. 164 (2008), the defendant was arrested for a citation-only offense. A search purportedly incident to arrest led to the discovery of cocaine. The defendant's motion to suppress was denied, and he was convicted of possession with intent to distribute cocaine. The Virginia Supreme Court reversed the defendant's conviction, given the officers' violation of Virginia's "citation only" law that prohibited arrest for this minor offense, and the lack of a Fourth Amendment "search incident to citation" exception. The Court, in a unanimous decision, reversed, finding that the arrest did not offend the Fourth Amendment, as governmental violations of state law do not thereby violate *federal* constitutional law, and any contrary rule would impose the harsh federal constitutional remedy of exclusion under the Fourth Amendment on a state that, while barring arrest, did not provide for such an extreme remedy when an arrest nevertheless takes place.

B. Level of Suspicion

Probable cause is always required for full-blown arrests, which are highly intrusive seizures of the person, as opposed to brief stops on the street. The distinction between arrests and brief stops is discussed later in this Chapter.

C. Warrant Requirement

The warrant requirement in the context of arrests and other seizures is governed by the location of the action. If the arrest is in a public place, the police can arrest without a warrant, so long as they have probable cause. Police also can seize contraband in a public place without a warrant. *Florida v. White*, 526 U.S. 559 (1999).

On the other hand, if the arrest or seizure takes place in a place protected by the Fourth Amendment, a warrant is required. For the arrest of a defendant in his home, an arrest warrant is all that is necessary, because it authorizes the intrusion on the defendant's liberty and privacy interests. *Payton v. New York*, 445 U.S. 573 (1980). If the arrest takes place in the home or premises of a third party, the police must also have a search warrant to protect the privacy expectations of that third party. *Steagald v. United States*, 451 U.S. 204 (1981). In such a situation, of course, the search warrant must be based on an affidavit establishing probable cause to believe that the defendant will be found in the home of the third party at the time of the search. Sometimes it is difficult to distinguish between a defendant's home and that of a third-party. The general rule is that the defendant's "home" includes any residence where the defendant is an overnight guest. *See Minnesota v. Olson*, 495 U.S. 91 (1990). A defendant's brief, temporary stay in a home — for example, having dinner, chatting, or sharing a few drinks — is not enough to treat that home as the defendant's. *See United States v. McNeal*, 955 F.2d 1067 (6th Cir. 1992).

The Court suggested in *dicta*, however, that it might consider permitting modestly extended seizures of a person from a home or from the street on less than probable cause, albeit under a narrow set of circumstances. In *Kaupp v. Texas*, 538 U.S. 626 (2003), the Court held that three police officers' awakening a 17-year-old boy in his bedroom at 3 a.m. with a flashlight, then bringing him hand-cuffed, shoeless, and in his boxer shorts to a police station in a police car, was a de facto "arrest," thus requiring probable cause. The Court explained: "[W]e have never sustained against Fourth Amendment challenge the involuntary re-moval of a suspect from his home to a police station and his detention there for investigative purposes ... absent probable cause or judicial authorization." Dropping a footnote at this point, and in the same breath, the Court contin-ued: "We have, however, left open the possibility that, under circumscribed procedure, a court might validly authorize a seizure on less than probable cause when the object is fingerprinting," citing *Hayes v. Florida*, 470 U.S. 811 (1985). In *Hayes*, the Court found the *warrantless* transport of a rape suspect to the stationhouse for fingerprinting on less than probable cause violative of the Fourth Amendment. But the Court noted that it did not necessarily bar rea-sonable suspicion detentions for fingerprinting where the judiciary authorized them by issuing a warrant, even though based on less than probable cause.

Sixteen years before *Hayes*, the Court had condemned as unconstitutional a roundup of 25 African-Americans for questioning and fingerprinting in an effort to identify a rapist. *See Davis v. Mississippi*, 394 U.S. 721 (1969). Again, however, the Court had noted that "because of the unique nature of the fin-gerprinting process, such detentions might, under narrowly defined circum-stances, be found to comply with the Fourth Amendment even though there is no probable cause in the traditional sense." The Court seems to be suggest-ing that certain sorts of seizures of the person are less intrusive than "arrests," thus requiring only reasonable suspicion, but are more intrusive than "stops," thus requiring judicial supervision via a warrant. The Court's repeatedly returning to this concept, albeit in *dicta*, over the course of 35 years suggests that it may be inviting a challenge on the fingerprint warrant issue.

The warrant requirement is excused in exigent circumstances, but the Court has not defined exigency in any great detail. In *Warden v. Hayden*, 387 U.S. 294 (1967). the Court had noted that the Fourth Amendment "does not re-quire police officers to delay in the course of an investigation if to do so would gravely endanger their lives or the lives of others." And in *Minnesota v. Olson*, 495 U.S. 91 (1990), the Court noted in dictum that warrants may be dispensed with if there is "hot pursuit of a fleeing felon, or imminent destruction of ev-idence, ... or the need to prevent a suspect's escape, or the risk of danger to the police or to other persons inside or outside the dwelling." The exigent cir-cumstances exception to the warrant requirement will be addressed in more de-tail later in this Chapter.

D. Use of Force

In making any arrest, with or without a warrant, the arresting officer may be required to use force if the suspect flees or resists. Because an arrest is a "seizure," the force used must be "reasonable," which the Court explained depends on:

> [a] careful balancing of the nature and quality of the intrusion on the individual's Fourth Amendment interests against the countervailing governmental interests at stake.... Our Fourth Amendment jurisprudence has long recognized that the right to make an arrest or investigatory stop necessarily carries with it the right to use some degree of physical coercion or threat to effect it.... [B]ecause [t]he test of reasonableness under the Fourth Amendment is not capable of precise definition or mechanical application, ... however, its proper application requires careful attention to the facts and circumstances of each particular case, including the severity of the crime at issue, whether the suspect poses an immediate threat to the safety of the officers or others, and whether he is actively resisting arrest or attempting to evade arrest by flight.

Graham v. Connor, 490 U.S. 386 (1989). Furthermore, the "reasonableness" of a particular use of force must be "judged from the perspective of a reasonable officer on the scene, rather than with the 20/20 vision of hindsight."

A more precise rule generally applies where police use deadly force. The deadly force rule was articulated in *Tennessee v. Garner*, 471 U.S. 1 (1985), where officers were dispatched to answer a "prowler inside call." One officer heard a door slam in the house identified by a neighbor as the one with the prowler and saw someone run across the backyard. Using a flashlight, the officer perceived a youth, apparently 17 or 18 years old, who appeared in height to be between 5'5" and 5'7". The officer asked the youth (who turned out to be Garner) to halt, but, when Garner tried to climb over a fence, the officer shot Garner, who later died from the gunshot wound. The officer was reasonably sure that Garner was unarmed but feared Garner's escape. Garner's father brought an action seeking damages for violation of Garner's constitutional rights. The Court held that the use of deadly force to prevent the escape of any suspect simply because the crime involved is a felony is unreasonable. However, explained the Court, deadly force may reasonably be used to prevent escape in one circumstance: where the officer has probable cause to believe that the suspect poses a threat of serious physical harm to himself or others. Such probable cause would be established, for example, if the suspect threatened the officer with a weapon or if the officer had probable cause to believe that the crime that the suspect committed involved the actual or threatened infliction of serious harm. However, where feasible, the officer must first warn the suspect before in fact using deadly force to halt his escape. The Court explained the rationale for its rule:

> It is not better that all felony suspects die than that they escape. Where the suspect poses no immediate threat to the officer and no threat to others, the harm resulting from failing to apprehend him does not justify the use of deadly force to do so. It is no doubt unfortunate when a suspect who is in sight escapes, but the fact that the police arrive a little late or are a little slower afoot does not always justify killing the suspect. A police officer may not seize an unarmed, nondangerous suspect by shooting him dead. The Tennessee statute is unconstitutional insofar as it authorized the use of deadly force against such fleeing suspects.

The Court rejected the argument that the common-law rule at the time the Fourth Amendment was adopted, allowing the use of whatever force was necessary to stop a fleeing felon, should control. "Because of sweeping change in the legal and technological context," concluded the Court, "reliance on the common-law rule in this case would be a mistaken literalism that ignores the purposes of a historical inquiry." Those changes were two-fold. First, at that time, most felonies were punishable by death, so killing a fleeing felon had no greater consequences than conviction. Second, the common-law rule developed when most weapons were so rudimentary that deadly force could be inflicted almost solely in a hand-to-hand struggle, placing the arresting officer at risk. Neither of these two facts hold true today.

Moreover, the long-term trend has been away from the common-law rule, which now holds in less than half the states. "This trend is more evident and impressive when viewed in light of the policies adopted by the police departments themselves. Overwhelmingly, these are more restrictive than the common-law rule." This suggests that abandoning the common law rule is unlikely to hamper law enforcement severely, particularly because there has been no suggestion that in states doing so crime has worsened. Similarly, there has been no indication that in states allowing use of deadly force only against dangerous suspects, the standard has been difficult for the police to apply. Accordingly, the balance tipped in favor of the Court's newly adopted rule, and, in applying that rule, the Court held that burglary is not an inherently violent crime and rarely involves physical violence. Given that there were no other indicators of Garner's dangerousness, the officer engaged in an unreasonable seizure in using deadly force to frustrate Garner's escape.

Also relevant to the amount of force police may use in making an arrest is *California v. Hodari D,* 499 U.S. 621 (1991), which held that a fleeing suspect has not been seized unless he stops, either because he is physically forced to do so or because he submits to an officer's show of authority. Similarly, if an officer shoots at an individual and misses, the Fourth Amendment does not apply because the person was not seized.

If a person is accidentally injured during the course of a high-speed police chase, the Fourth Amendment is inapplicable because the injury was not a result of government action "intentionally applied." The Court dealt with this situation in *County of Sacramento v. Lewis,* 523 U.S. 833 (1998), where it held that the Fourth Amendment did not apply to an action for damages under 42 U.S.C. § 1983, where the damages were caused by a high-speed police chase and ensuing vehicular crash. No search was involved, so the Fourth Amendment could apply only if the police chase itself, or in combination with the subsequent contact with the car, constituted a seizure. It did not. The Court explained as follows:

> We held in *California v. Hodari D.,* 499 U.S. 621 (1991), that a police pursuit in attempting to seize a person does not amount to a "seizure" within the meaning of the Fourth Amendment. And in *Brower v. County of Inyo,* 489 U.S. 593 (1989), we explained "that a Fourth Amendment seizure does not occur whenever there is a governmentally caused termination of an individual's freedom of movement (the innocent passerby), nor even whenever there is a governmentally caused and governmentally desired termination of an individual's freedom of movement (the fleeing felon), but only when there is a governmental termination of freedom of movement through means intentionally applied."

The Court had illustrated this last point in *Brower* by noting that no seizure would occur where a "pursuing police car sought to stop the suspect only by the show of authority represented by flashing lights and continuing pursuit," but accidentally stopped the suspect by crashing into him. But, concluded the *Lewis* Court, "[t]hat is exactly this case."

The *Lewis* Court went on to review plaintiff's claim that the police chase violated a different right—the Fourteenth Amendment substantive due process right against arbitrary action. Government action that "shocks the conscience" violates that right, but the Court in *Lewis* held that government action in the context of a high-speed police chase would have to be more than merely negligent or even "deliberately indifferent" in order to implicate the substantive due process right.

Instead, officers would have to be acting with a "purpose to cause harm" before resulting injuries would be redressible under the Fourteenth Amendment. The United States Court of Appeals for the Ninth Circuit has held that the "purpose to cause harm" requirement applies when innocent by-standers, as well as pursued suspects, sustain injuries. *Onossian v. Block*, 175 F.3d 1169 (9th Cir. 1999).

But may the police sometimes also use deadly force to pursue a fleeing *non-felon* whose conduct may nevertheless seriously endanger innocent bystanders? Under at least certain facts, "yes" appears to be the answer, as is shown by *Scott v. Harris*, 550 U.S. 372 (2007). There, the Court determined that a law enforcement official may, consistent with Fourth Amendment reasonableness, "take actions that place a fleeing motorist at risk of serious injury or death" in order to prevent that flight "from endangering the lives of innocent bystanders." There, a Georgia county deputy pursued Harris after Deputy Timothy Scott clocked Harris's vehicle speed at 73 mph, a violation of the 55 mph limit. The deputy activated his lights and siren and followed Harris, who did not stop. A six mile, ten minute long, high-speed chase ensued. It involved a number of law enforcement officers and ended when Scott "applied his push bumper to the rear of respondent's vehicle," causing it to veer off the road and crash at the bottom of an embankment.

The deputy received permission from his supervisor during the chase to employ a "Precision Intervention Technique" maneuver that would have resulted in the driver's vehicle spinning to a complete stop. The deputy decided, however, that the vehicle's speed made such a maneuver too dangerous. He chose instead to use the "push bumper" tactic, which caused the fleeing car to run off the road, careen down an embankment, and crash. As a result of injuries suffered in the crash, Harris was rendered a quadriplegic.

Harris filed suit under 42 U.S.C.S. Section 1983 alleging that Scott's "push bumper" use of force was excessive, violating the Fourth Amendment's proscription against unreasonable seizures. Scott did not contest that his termination of the chase by ramming Harris's car constituted a "seizure." Instead, Scott moved for summary judgment, based on qualified immunity.

The Court reversed, holding Scott's actions reasonable under the Fourth Amendment, even though he "placed [Harris] at risk of serious injury or death." Key to the Court's determination was videotaped evidence of the chase that utterly discredited Harris's version of the facts. The tape was so compelling, the Court refused to apply the normal standard of judicial review (Fed. Rule Civ. Proc. 56(c) requires that during a summary judgment motion, facts must be viewed in the light most favorable to the nonmoving party) — which requires reviewing courts to adopt Harris's version of the facts. Instead, the Court considered reliance upon Harris's version of events inappropriate:

[r]eading the lower court's opinion, one gets the impression that respondent, rather than fleeing from the police, was attempting to pass his driving test.... The videotape tells quite a different story. There we see respondent's vehicle racing down narrow, two-lane roads in the dead of night at speeds that are shockingly fast. We see it swerve around more than a dozen other cars, cross the double-yellow line, and force cars traveling in both directions to their respective shoulders to avoid being hit. We see it run multiple red lights and travel for considerable periods of time in the occasional center left-turn-only lane, chased by numerous police cars forced to engage in the same hazardous maneuvers just to keep up. Far from being the cautious and controlled driver the lower court depicts, what we see on the video more closely resembles a Hollywood-style car chase....

Additionally and given the videotape, the Court determined that it had to "slosh [its] way through the factbound morass of 'reasonableness,'" to determine whether Scott's ramming of Harris's car under the circumstances was constitutionally reasonable:

[s]o how does a court go about weighing the perhaps lesser probability of injuring or killing numerous bystanders against the perhaps larger probability of injuring or killing a single person? We think it appropriate in this process to take into account not only the number of lives at risk, but also their relative culpability. It was respondent, after all, who intentionally placed himself and the public in danger by unlawfully engaging in the reckless, high-speed flight that ultimately produced the choice between two evils that Scott confronted. Multiple police cars, with blue lights flashing and sirens blaring, had been chasing respondent for nearly 10 miles, but he ignored their warning to stop. By contrast, those who might have been harmed had Scott not taken the action he did were entirely innocent. We have little difficulty in concluding it was reasonable for Scott to take the action that he did.

Harris invoked the Court's *Garner* analysis and preconditions for using deadly force, claiming that the ramming was an unreasonable use of deadly force. The Court rejected his claim, stating that "*Garner* did not establish a magical on/off switch that triggers rigid preconditions whenever an officer's actions constitute deadly force." Instead, *Garner* represents only an application of the Fourth Amendment's reasonableness test to the use of a certain type of force in a certain type of situation. There, the use of deadly force was unreasonable; here, the Court determined that it did not matter: "[w]hether or not [the officer's] actions constituted application of 'deadly force,' all that matters is whether [his] actions were reasonable."

Under those circumstances, Scott's termination of the chase with the level of force employed was found to be reasonable. The lower court decision was reversed and Scott was entitled to summary judgment.

II. The Requirement of Prompt Arraignment

That a warrant*less* arrest may be reasonable does not mean that a defendant has no right to a judicial determination of probable cause. In *Gerstein v. Pugh*, 420 U.S. 103 (1975), the Court held that the officer's probable cause judgment justifies only "a brief period of detention to take the administrative steps incident to arrest." Once there is no longer a danger that the defendant will escape or commit further crimes, the Fourth Amendment requires a judicial determination of probable cause "promptly after arrest." This rule is clearly required for defendants in custody, although it may not apply to those promptly released, perhaps by posting bail. The probable cause hearing need not be adversarial but can instead be decided by a magistrate based upon hearsay and written testimony — in short, a procedure much like that for obtaining a warrant before arrest. A full-scale adversarial hearing may come much later, if a pre-trial suppression motion is filed, thus triggering a suppression hearing. It is important to stress that the *Gerstein* prompt probable cause-determination hearing rule *applies only to arrests done without a warrant*. Where an arrest is done pursuant to a warrant, the probable cause determination has already been made by a neutral and detached magistrate.

How "prompt" must a *Gerstein* hearing be? In *County of Riverside v. McLaughlin*, 500 U.S. 44 (1991), the Court held that a *Gerstein* hearing's taking place within 48 hours of arrest is presumptively reasonable. But a particular defendant may show that such a delay was done "for the purpose of gathering additional evidence to justify the arrest, a delay motivated by ill will against the arrested individual, or delay for delay's sake," thereby rendering the delay unreasonable. The Court further held that a post-48-hour *Gerstein* hearing is presumptively *un*reasonable, in which case "the burden shifts to the government to demonstrate the existence of a bona fide emergency or other extraordinary circumstance."

What is the consequence of a *Gerstein* violation? Presumably, if the state fails to provide a probable cause determination promptly and an arrestee complains (by filing a petition for habeas corpus, or through some other proceeding), the appropriate remedy is an immediate probable cause determination or, failing that, immediate release. The issue is more problematic, however, when the complaint occurs long after the violation—for example, in a motion to suppress evidence. Courts have not been consistent about whether evidence obtained in violation of *Gerstein* should be suppressed. (The Supreme Court has not yet determined the issue. In *Powell v. Nevada*, 511 U.S. 79 (1994), the Court declined to rule on it, stating that application of the exclusionary rule to *Gerstein* violations "remains an unresolved question."). The question comes up most frequently in the context of confessions taken in violation of the 48-hour period discussed in *County of Riverside v. McLaughlin*. At least one state court has held that the Fourth Amendment balancing test requires that such statements be suppressed, because

> [i]gnoring the requirements of *McLaughlin* is functionally the same as making warrantless searches or arrests when a warrant is required. In both situations, law enforcement officials act without necessary judicial guidance or objective good faith. The cost of applying the exclusionary sanction to a violation of *McLaughlin* is that evidence obtained as a result of the illegal detention will be suppressed. The benefit is the same as that gained from the application of the exclusionary rule to certain warrantless arrests. It will deter law enforcement officials from ignoring the Fourth Amendment mandate of a judicial determination of probable cause. Violations of *McLaughlin* can be easily avoided, and applying the exclusionary rule to evidence obtained as a result of the illegal detention will deter further violations.

State v. Huddleston, 924 S.W.2d 666 (Tenn. 1996).

III. *Terry* Stops (and Frisks)

Full-blown arrests occur when a person is handcuffed and brought down to the police station for booking as a pre-requisite to the formal start of criminal proceedings. But there are at least two other types of seizures: de facto arrests and stops, the latter often also known as "*Terry*" stops after the seminal case first recognizing them: *Terry v. Ohio*, 392 U.S. 1 (1968). Different rules govern each type of seizure.

De facto arrests require probable cause yet have practical consequences different from those of full-blown arrests, in that only full-blown arrests trigger the "search incident to arrest" exception discussed in Chapter 6. Stops, on the other hand, merely require reasonable suspicion. *Terry* stops are often paired with, or lead to, a special type of *search* - a *Terry* frisk -discussed below.

A. Seizures versus Voluntary Encounters

1. Defining Seizures

One first has to determine if there was a seizure. A seizure of the person occurs whenever, as a result of government action *intentionally applied*, a reasonable person would not feel free to leave, and her movement has in fact ceased, either because the government actor (usually a police officer) physically restrained her or because she submitted to an assertion of governmental authority. Roughly stated, a "seizure" of the person occurs whenever, as a result of government action, a reasonable person would not feel free to leave. But the full definition may sometimes be needed, and it is also important to recognize that the definition can change in certain circumstances, such as when persons are seized on public and similar forms of transportation, such as planes, trains, and buses.

2. A Comparison to Voluntary Encounters

A seizure of the person is distinguished from a "voluntary encounter." A voluntary encounter is a seizure's opposite, meaning that a reasonable person would indeed feel free to leave. The Supreme Court has clearly stated that mere contact with a single uniformed police officer is not alone sufficient to cause a reasonable person to feel that he or she is not free to leave. *United States v. Mendenhall*, 446 U.S. 544 (1980). Thus, if an officer approaches someone on the street and simply says, "Excuse me, sir, may I talk to you for a moment?," that would be a voluntary encounter because it would not alone constitute a seizure of the person. More is required for a seizure, but how much more turns on examining the totality of the circumstances. If that same officer pulled a gun, that would certainly constitute a seizure of the person. But there is no bright-line test. Common sense, precedent, and a close engagement with the facts of the particular case are the sole guides.

a. United States v. Mendenhall

In *United States v. Mendenhall*, 446 U.S. 544 (1980), the Court identified these non-exhaustive factors relevant to deciding on which line of the seizure/voluntary encounter distinction a particular case lies: (1) the threatening presence of several officers; (2) the display of weapons by an officer; (3) some physical touching of the person detained; and (4) the use of language or tone of voice indicating that compliance with the officer's request might be compelled. Although the Court's opinion in *Mendenhall* was fractured, a majority of the Court later approved its articulation of the standard. *Florida v. Royer*, 460 U.S. 491 (1983).

Sylvia Mendenhall had been approached by federal agents as she walked through an airport concourse. The agents identified themselves, requested her identification and airline ticket, and asked her some questions about herself. The Court did not answer definitively whether she had been seized because only two justices in the majority reached the issue, but those two justices concluded that no seizure occurred. The events occurred in public, and the agents were not wearing uniforms or displaying weapons. They did not summon Mendenhall to their presence but rather approached her and identified themselves. They also requested but did not demand to see her identification and ticket. This conduct was, in the two justices' opinion, insufficient to induce a reasonable person to believe that she would not be free to leave. Nor did it matter that the agents did not tell her that she could decline to cooperate.

It was likewise irrelevant that she seemingly acted contrary to her self-interest by answering questions. As these justices put it, "It may happen that a person makes statements to law enforcement officials that he later regrets, but the issue in such cases is not whether the statement was self-protective, but rather whether it was made voluntarily." Mendenhall's own perceptions also were irrelevant, the question simply being how a *reasonable person* would have perceived things. For these justices, "there was simply no objective reason to believe that she was not free to end the conversation in the concourse and proceed on her way."

b. Unresolved Issues After *Mendenhall*

The *Mendenhall* test involves the reasonable person "under the circumstances." But what circumstances count as part of those of the reasonable person? The Court has left this question vague, identifying only one circumstances that is always assumed: innocence. The test for the seizure of the person is thus to be made from the point of view of the reasonable innocent person. *Florida v. Bostick*, 501 U.S. 429 (1991). Yet the Court has never addressed whether race, age, ethnicity, gender, or a host of other circumstances should be part of the objective reasonable person's world. Lawyers and lower courts are left to struggle with these questions.

Nor has the Court explained whether the reasonable person's perspective in this context should be a majoritarian one ("How would most people perceive the situation?") or a normative one ("Given the values underlying the Fourth Amendment, how should we expect the reasonable person to perceive things?"). Lawyers must thus draw on everyday experience, analogy, constitutional values, and the various sources of evidence guiding constitutional interpretation summarized in Chapter 1 to frame their arguments.

3. The Special Case of Public Transportation

It is hard to apply the "free to leave" test to passengers on public transportation for a simple reason: a passenger on a moving train, bus, or plane, or on one that is stopped far from home, is already not free to leave, whether police are involved or not. For this reason, the Court modified the test in *Florida v. Bostick*, 501 U.S. 429 (1991), so that the analysis in these situations is whether a reasonable person would "feel free to decline" official requests "or otherwise terminate the encounter."

Bostick, a passenger on a bus from Miami to Atlanta, was approached during the bus's rest stop by two Florida officers replete with badges, insignia, and (in the case of one officer) weaponry. Although they had neither probable cause nor reasonable suspicion, the officers asked him to produce his ticket and identification, both of which matched and were immediately returned to him, and then explained that they were narcotics agents looking for illegal drugs. According to their later testimony, they asked Bostick for consent to search his luggage and advised him that he had the right to refuse, after which he consented. The search of his luggage revealed cocaine, which he unsuccessfully sought to suppress at trial on the ground that his consent was involuntary and had flowed from an illegal seizure of his person. The Court concluded that the appropriate test of seizure for someone in his situation was not whether a reasonable person would feel free to leave but rather whether such a person would "feel free to decline the officers' requests or otherwise terminate the encounter." The Court emphasized two facts as especially relevant to applying that test to Bostick's case before it: first, the fact that the officers had told him that he did not have to consent; second, that the officer carrying a gun in "the equivalent ... of a holster" never removed it from its pouch or "otherwise used [it] in a threatening manner." Nevertheless, the Court did not ultimately resolve the seizure question, remanding Bostick's appeal for further consideration.

In *United States v. Drayton*, 536 U.S. 194 (2002), the Court reiterated that "[e]ven when law enforcement officers have no basis for suspecting a particular individual, they may pose questions, ask for identification, and request consent to search luggage - provided they do not induce cooperation by coercive means." That the Court found no seizure in *Drayton* is significant, because it seemed to involve a stronger case for the defense than *Bostick*. Three plainclothes officers stepped onto Drayton's bus after passengers had reboarded from a rest stop. One knelt on the drivers' seat, facing the passengers, while the other two went to the rear of the bus. One of those two remained at the rear as the other made his way forward, questioning individual passengers about their travel plans and luggage in an attempt to match each passenger to a corresponding piece of luggage in the overhead racks. This officer approached both Drayton and Brown, who were seated next to each other, showed them his badge and explained he was conducting bus interdictions to deter the transport of drugs and weapons. Brown consented to a search of his luggage, which revealed no contraband, and then to a patdown of his person, during which the officer detected "hard objects similar to drug packages." The officer arrested and handcuffed Brown, escorting him from the bus. He then asked permission to check Drayton, who responded by lifting his hands eight inches above his legs. Lang's pat-down revealed similar packages, so he also arrested Drayton. A subsequent search revealed the men had concealed duct-taped plastic bundles of powder cocaine on their persons.

Drayton and Brown filed motions to suppress, and on appeal, the Eleventh Circuit held that reasonable bus passengers under the circumstances would not have felt free to leave. The Supreme Court disagreed, stressing that the officer had left the aisles free to permit exit, brandished no weapons, made no intimidating movements, spoke to passengers one-by-one in a quiet voice, used no threats, said or did nothing to suggest that passengers had to answer his questions, and issued no commands - all of which would signal to a reasonable passenger that he or she was free to terminate the encounter. Moreover, that one officer remained stationed at the front of the bus did not alter the analysis because he "did nothing to intimidate the passengers" and "said nothing to suggest that people could not exit and indeed he left the aisle clear."

Nor did Brown's arrest alter the nature of Drayton's encounter. The "arrest of one person does not mean that everyone around him has been seized by the police. If anything, Brown's arrest should have put Drayton on notice of the consequences of continuing the encounter by answering the officer's questions."Finally, the Court found no coercion in the general willingness of passengers to answer Lang's questions. Bus passengers do so, explained the Court, "not because of coercion but because the passengers know that their participation enhances their own safety and the safety of those around them." Justice Souter, joined by Justices Stevens and Ginsburg, dissented, interpreting the same facts as creating "an atmosphere of obligatory participation."

4. Successful Use of Physical Force or Suspect's Submission to Authority

The Court has stated that "[o]nly when the officer, by means of physical force or show of authority, has in some way restrained the liberty of the citizen may we conclude that a seizure has occurred." *Terry v. Ohio*, 392 U.S. 1 (1968). This requirement that an officer actually succeed in halting a suspect's movements matters in situations of "forced abandonment." Forced abandonment occurs when the police chase a suspect without having reasonable suspicion or probable cause to believe that he has committed a crime. If, during his flight, the suspect throws away drugs or contraband that were previously in his pants pocket, that arguably constitutes an "abandonment" of his privacy or possessory interest in the drugs, permitting the police to seize and search them.

In some states, like Massachusetts and New York, state constitutional equivalents to the Fourth Amendment would render this seizure invalid on the ground that the abandonment was "forced" by the chase - which, if it constituted a seizure of the person, would be illegal because of the lack of justification. *See Commonwealth v. Stoute,* 665 N.E. 2d 93 (1996); *People v. Martinez,* 80 N.Y. 2d 444 (N.Y. App. 1992). As the Massachussetts court explained, "a [p]ursuit that appears designed to effect a stop is no less intrusive than a stop itself" because it "infringes considerably on the person's freedom of action."

The Supreme Court's opposing approach is illustrated in *California v. Hodari D.,* 499 U.S. 621 (1991). Hodari, a juvenile, was being chased by a police officer when he threw a package to the ground. The package was found to contain cocaine, and during his prosecution he claimed that the cocaine was discovered during the course of an illegal seizure, arguing that the seizure took place when he *saw* the officer chasing him. The Court was not persuaded, holding that the word "seizure" in this context meant a "laying on of hands or application of physical force to restrain movement ... [as well as] submission to the assertion of authority." That the police officer neither grabbed Hodari nor got him to submit to his show of authority meant that Hodari had not been seized when he threw down the cocaine.

5. By Means Intentionally Applied

The requirement that cessation of a person's movement be achieved by means intentionally applied means that no seizure has occurred where an officer has lost control over his own movements, perhaps even due to his own negligence, that accidentally resulted in halting the suspect. This situation can occur when an officer engaged in a high speed chase loses control of his vehicle so that it swerves, crashes into the suspect's car, and stops its and its driver's movements. *See County of Sacramento v. Lewis,* 523 U.S. 833 (1998); *Brower v. County of Inyo,* 489 U.S. 593 (1989) (noting that there can be no seizure where a "pursuing police car sought to stop the suspect only by the show of authority represented by flashing lights and continuing pursuit" but accidentally stopped the suspect by crashing into him).

B. Stops versus *De Facto* Arrests

If the seizure of the person is minimally intrusive, it is a "stop." If it is significantly intrusive, it is a de facto arrest. The primary factors that the Court considers in distinguishing these two are the place and length of the detention. Thus in *United States v. Sharpe,* 470 U.S. 675, 687 (1985), the Court upheld a 20-minute detention as a *Terry* stop, emphasizing that during the detention officers were pursuing their investigation diligently and effectively. On the other hand, in *United States v. Place,* 462 U.S. 696 (1983), the detention of a suitcase (items may be "stopped") for ninety minutes was deemed too long. Its detention had "ripened" into a full-blown seizure and was no longer amenable to a *Terry* justification.

The place of detention has been addressed in several cases. In *Pennsylvania v. Mimms,* 434 U.S. 106 (1977), the Court created a bright-line rule permitting officers to order drivers out of their vehicles after *Terry* traffic stops as a matter of officer safety. Similarly, in *Maryland v. Wilson,* 519 U.S. 408 (1997), the Court held that passengers may be ordered out as well.

Detentions that move beyond the immediate vicinity of the stop are, however, likely to be considered de facto arrests. Thus the Court overturned a fifteen minute stop in *Florida v. Royer,* 460 U.S. 491 (1983), because Royer was taken from an airport concourse to an office about forty feet away. Suspects forcibly taken to police headquarters will also undoubtedly be viewed as having been arrested, *see Dunaway v. New York,* 442 U.S. 200 (1979), with the possible exception discussed earlier in this Chapter of court orders issued for brief detention for the purposes of identification (such as fingerprinting or DNA testing) based merely upon reasonable suspicion, a possibility mentioned by the Court only in dicta. In *Hayes v. Florida,* 470 U.S. 811 (1985), one of the cases containing such dicta, however, the Court held that a suspect had been arrested after he was picked up on reasonable suspicion of rape and taken to a stationhouse for fingerprinting. His pick-up was authorized neither by a warrant nor a court order.

In *Kaupp v. Texas,* 538 U.S. 626 (2003), the Court reaffirmed its rule that, with rare possible exceptions, forcible transport to police headquarters constitutes an arrest. The Court used the same factors that it identified in *Mendenhall* in deciding whether there was a seizure of the person in the first place. A seventeen-year-old boy was awakened in his bedroom at three a.m. by at least three police officers, handcuffed, escorted shoeless and in his underwear to a police car, and taken to the crime scene, after which he was driven to the sheriff's office and put in an interrogation room and questioned. The Court concluded that this detention was "in important respects indistinguishable from a traditional arrest," therefore requiring probable cause and a warrant.

On the other hand, in *Hiibel v. Sixth Judicial District of Nevada,* 542 U.S. 177 (2004), the Court found that Hiibel's encounter with police did not constitute an arrest. Hiibel had been in his car, talking with his daughter, when an officer (who had been dispatched to the location based upon a telephone call reporting a man assaulting a woman in a vehicle) approached, explained that he was investigating a report of a fight, and asked Hiibel his name. Hiibel refused to identify himself, even after the officer warned him that he could be arrested for his refusal. After eleven refusals, the officer arrested him pursuant to a Nevada statute making it a crime for anyone stopped upon reasonable suspicion to refuse to reveal his identity. Hiibel argued that compelling him by threat to answer questions about his identity was highly intrusive, going well beyond the scope of a proper *Terry* stop. (The implications of *Hiibel* for the privilege against self-incrimination are discussed in Chapter 14).

Precedent seemed to support Hiibel. In *Terry,* Justice White's concurring opinion had said that, "[o]f course, the person stopped is not obliged to answer, answers may not be compelled, and refusal to answer furnishes no basis for an arrest, though it may alert the officer to the need for continued observation." Later, in *Berkemer v. McCarty,* 468 U.S. 420 (1984), the Court declared that "an officer may ask the [*Terry*] detainee a moderate number of questions to determine his identity and try to obtain information confirming or dispelling the officer's suspicions. But the detainee is not obliged to respond." Even more recently, in *Illinois v. Wardlow,* 528 U.S. 119 (2000), the Court explained that allowing officers to stop and question a fleeing person is "quite consistent with the individual's right to go about his business or to stay put and remain silent in the face of police questioning."

The *Hiibel* Court declared, however, that these earlier statements meant only that the Fourth Amendment did not of its own force compel a suspect to answer. A statute could constitutionally compel the simple revelation of identity without increasing the intrusiveness of a *Terry* stop because it did not change the duration, location, or essential nature of the stop. Moreover, there were good reasons for officers to know the identity of those with whom they deal: permitting the officer to determine whether the suspect is wanted for another offense or has a record of violence or mental disorder; helping to clear a suspect quickly; and protecting the safety of the officer and any purported victims.

C. Sufficiency of the Evidence of Reasonable Suspicion

Once a seizure is identified as a stop, it must be justified by "reasonable suspicion"—a kind of "probable cause light." It differs from probable cause in two respects: first, it requires a lower degree of quantitative confidence in the suspect's guilt; second, that lower degree of confidence may be established by less trustworthy evidence than that required for probable cause. But there are still some quantitative and qualitative requirements. Moreover, reasonable suspicion, like probable cause, must still be particularized. The case law on probable cause is helpful in determining reasonable suspicion's meaning.

1. Quantum of Evidence

The quantitative degree of proof is uncertain, and, as with probable cause, the Court resists efforts to articulate that degree with precision. The Court has remarked that the level of suspicion is "considerably less than proof of wrongdoing by a preponderance of the evidence" and less than a "fair probability that contraband or evidence of a crime will be found." *United States v. Sokolow*, 490 U.S. 1 (1989).

a. *Terry v. Ohio*

Terry involved a police detective named Martin McFadden who, while patrolling downtown Cleveland in the afternoon, saw two men together taking up a post outside a store. One man would repeatedly walk some distance away, look in store windows, and then return to and confer with the other man. Next the other man would repeat the same ritual. After conferring with a third man and repeating this process five to six times over ten to twelve minutes, the two men started to walk in the direction of the third man, meeting up with him, at which point McFadden suspected that they were "casing a job, a stick-up." Accordingly, he stopped the three men. When one man mumbled in response to McFadden's inquiries, he spun around one of the men, Terry, patted the outside of his clothing, and in a pocket found a pistol. The Court found these facts sufficient to establish reasonable suspicion to believe that criminal activity was afoot (the standard for justifying a stop) and reasonable suspicion to believe that the men were armed and dangerous (the standard for justifying a frisk - a brief patdown of a person and his outer clothing for weapons).

b. *United States v. Arvizu*

Since *Terry*, the Court has emphasized that the sufficiency of the evidence question turns on the totality of the circumstances, purportedly rejecting any per se or rigid rules to dictate whether reasonable suspicion exists in certain categories of cases. Thus in *United States v. Arvizu*, 534 U.S. 266 (2002), it rejected an effort by the Ninth Circuit to define the precise weight to be given to certain factors taken in isolation from other factors. There, a border patrol agent had stopped a mini-van on an Arizona back road based upon a variety of facts. The Ninth Circuit held that facts consistent with innocence, such as the stopped van's suddenly slowing down upon encountering the border patrol agent's vehicle and its driver's failure to make eye contact with the agent while passing the agent's vehicle, were entitled to little or no weight. On the other hand, facts that *did* raise suspicions were highly general and did not contribute to raising suspicions *enough*. These insufficiently weighty facts included the prior use of the back road and minivans by drug smugglers and the fact that the minivan's travel coincided with a shift change among border patrol agents.

A unanimous Supreme Court refused to follow this "divide and conquer" strategy, concluding that a totality of the circumstances approach "allows officers to draw on their own experience and specialized training to make inferences from and deductions about the cumulative information available to them that might well elude an untrained person." *Arvizu* rejected the argument that some categories of evidence, such as slowing down, stiffening posture, and avoiding eye contact upon spotting a police vehicle, were always more consistent with innocence than guilt. "What might well be unremarkable in one instance," the Court explained, might be "quite unusual in another." Applying this deferential, flexible version of the totality of the circumstances approach, it found the stop properly based on reasonable suspicion.

c. The Standard of Review

The Court's deferential posture toward police in *Arvizu* might be confusing at first blush because it had earlier held that whether reasonable suspicion exists is a mixed question of law and fact justifying a non-deferential, de novo standard of review for appellate courts. *Ornelas v. United States*, 517 U.S. 690 (1996). The *Ornelas* Court distinguished between "historical facts" - "the events which occurred leading up to the stop or search" - and mixed questions of law and fact, primarily "the decision whether these historical facts, viewed from the standpoint of an objectively reasonable police officer, amount to reasonable suspicion or to probable cause." The former decision is reviewed deferentially, the latter de novo.

But this distinction between the clear error standard for historical facts and the de novo standard of review for mixed questions of law and fact is more complicated than at first appears. The *Ornelas* Court also said that reviewing courts should give "due weight to inferences drawn from [historical] facts by resident judges and local law enforcement officers," "due weight" sounding more like a call for deferential than de novo review. The Court might have been creating a third category of facts - "background facts," apparently meaning those facts that are seen through the lens of the officer's experience.

Background facts, noted the Court, are rarely the subject of explicit judicial findings, yet they inform the judge's assessment of the historical facts. "The background facts provide a context for the historical facts, and when seen together yield inferences that deserve deference." So understood, *Ornelas* would stand for the proposition that inferences based upon police expertise deserve deference, at least once the suppression judge finds the officer's testimony credible. However, the weight of all other inferences to be made from historical facts and the ultimate decision whether reasonable suspicion existed are reviewed de novo. If this reading is correct, then *Ornelas* and *Arvizu* are perfectly consistent.

An alternative reading of *Ornelas*, however, would be less generous to the majority, as was Justice Scalia in dissent, declaring the Court's opinion "not only wrong but contradictory." Finally, it is important to remember that the *Ornelas* standard applies only to appellate review of suppression motion rulings on warrantless searches and seizures based upon reasonable suspicion or probable cause. The Court has retained the deferential standard of review for magistrates' decisions to issue a warrant.

d. Bright-Line Tests?

Despite its claims to the contrary, the Court does seem to have adopted three bright-line sufficiency of the evidence rules about the quantity of evidence needed to prove reasonable suspicion: first, that mere presence in a high crime area is not enough to establish reasonable suspicion; second, that flight from the police alone is also insufficient; and third, that these two factors - flight from the police in a high crime area - when taken together are *sufficient.*.

In *Brown v. Texas,* 443 U.S. 47 (1979), patrol car officers spotted two men, one of them Brown, walking away from each other in an alley. The officers believed that the two men had been together or were about to meet until the patrol car appeared. They stopped and frisked Brown and asked him to explain what he was doing there. They later claimed that the situation "looked suspicious and we had never seen that subject in that area before." Furthermore, asserted the officers, the area had a "high incidence of drug traffic." The Court held that the officers' actions constituted a seizure and that they lacked reasonable suspicion for that seizure because the only concrete factor they articulated was that Brown had been present in a high-drug-use area. The Court emphasized that this single observation "is not a basis for concluding that ... [Brown] himself was engaged in criminal conduct."

In *Illinois v. Wardlow*, 528 U.S. 119 (2000), by contrast, the Court held that, in an "area of heavy narcotics trafficking," an individual's "unprovoked flight upon noticing the police" gave rise to reasonable suspicion. Police on a narcotics patrol had conducted a *Terry* stop of Wardlow after he looked in their direction and fled. The officers frisked him and found a gun, and he was later prosecuted and convicted for unlawful use of the weapon. The Illinois Supreme Court struck down the conviction, holding that sudden flight in a high crime area does not create reasonable suspicion. The Court disagreed. Although it conceded that presence in a high crime area was alone insufficient, such presence was "among the relevant contextual considerations in a *Terry* analysis." Nervous or evasive behavior was likewise relevant, with flight being the "consummate act of evasion." These two factors together - unprovoked flight while present in a high crime area - were sufficient to establish reasonable suspicion. Justice Stevens, joined by Justices Souter, Ginsburg, and Breyer, dissented on the grounds that it was unclear on the facts before them whether there even was flight and concluded that there can be sound reasons consistent with innocence for fleeing from the police in a high-crime area.

2. *Quality of Evidence*

As with probable cause, reasonable suspicion must be based upon sufficiently trustworthy evidence rather than conclusory assertions. Officers must identify with some specificity what evidence they relied on and must establish it as reliable. As the Court in *Terry* put it, "in justifying the particular intrusion the police officer must be able to point to specific and articulable facts which, taken together with rational inferences from those facts, reasonably warrant that intrusion." However, as the Court said in *Alabama v. White*, 492 U.S. 325, 330 (1990):

> Reasonable suspicion is a less demanding standard than probable cause not only in the sense that reasonable suspicion can be established with information that is different in quantity or content than that required to establish probable cause, but also in the sense that reasonable suspicion can arise from information that is less reliable than that required to show probable cause.

a. Informants' Tips

i. Alabama v. White

As in the probable cause area, most of the Court's reasonable suspicion cases addressing the trustworthiness of evidence have involved officers relying on tips. In *White,* for example, the Court upheld a stop based on an anonymous tip stating that Vanessa White "would be leaving 235-C Lynwood Terrace Apartments at a particular time in a brown Plymouth station wagon with the right taillight lens broken, that she would be going to Dobey's Motel, and that she would be in possession of about an ounce of cocaine inside a brown attaché case." The officers corroborated the fact that a brown Plymouth station wagon with a broken right taillight was parked at the apartments, and they observed White enter the station wagon (with nothing in her hands) and drive to a highway on which Dobey's Motel was located. They stopped her "just short" of the motel. The Court acknowledged that this was "a close case" but concluded that "when the officers stopped [White], the anonymous tip had been sufficiently corroborated to furnish reasonable suspicion that [she] was engaged in criminal activity."

ii. Florida v. J.L.

On the extreme end of the unreliable information scale, an anonymous tip that lacks all indicia of reliability does *not* satisfy the reasonable suspicion standard. In *Florida v. J.L.,* 529 U.S. 266 (2000), a unanimous Court held an anonymous tip that a person is carrying a gun to be insufficient, by itself, to justify a *Terry* stop and frisk. Police had received an anonymous tip informing them that "a young black male standing at a particular bus stop and wearing a plaid shirt" was carrying a gun. Arriving at the bus stop, police observed three black males, one of whom, J.L., was wearing a plaid shirt. The police noticed nothing suspicious about the individuals, but based on the tip stopped and frisked J.L., finding a gun. The Florida Supreme Court held the search invalid, and the Court agreed, comparing the paucity of details in the tip to the more detailed tip in *White.* The Court noted that *White* depended on the fact that the tipster accurately predicted future movements of the suspect. By contrast, the tip in *J.L.* lacked even those "moderate indicia of reliability." It cautioned, however, that its holding was fact-specific and would not necessarily apply if police were to receive an anonymous "man with a bomb" tip, or in situations — such as airports and schools — in which Fourth Amendment privacy is diminished.

iii. Adams v. Williams

The holding in *J.L.* also would not preclude a stop and frisk if police receive a "man with a gun tip" from a *known* informant. In *Adams v. Williams,* 407 U.S. 143 (1972), decided shortly after *Terry,* a police officer was told by an informant, who had given the officer information in the past, that a person seated in a nearby car was carrying narcotics and had a gun "at his waist." The officer approached the car and asked the driver to open the door. When the driver rolled down his window instead of opening the door, the officer reached into the car and immediately removed a gun from the driver's waistband. The Court treated the officer's actions as a frisk and found he had reasonable suspicion to believe that the driver was armed and dangerous, considering that the tip had come from a known informant who could have been subjected to an immediate arrest for false complaint if he had lied. Moreover, the seizure of the gun was proper given the officer's reasonable fear for his safety in a "high crime area" in the middle of the night. Said the Court, "the policeman's action in reaching to the spot where the gun was thought to be hidden constituted a limited intrusion designed to insure his safety, and we conclude that it was reasonable." That the intrusion was not based on the officer's personal observation was irrelevant:

> [S]ome tips, completely lacking in indicia of reliability, would either warrant no police response or require further investigation before a forcible stop of a suspect would be authorized. But in some situations—for example, when the victim of a street crime seeks immediate police aid and gives a description of his assailant, or when a credible informant warns of a specific impending crime—the subtleties of the hearsay rule should not thwart an appropriate police response.

Accordingly, the intrusion was reasonable, and the gun's presence established probable cause for an arrest.

b. Profiles

Another basis for suspicion can be a "profile." A profile is a list of characteristics believed to be shared by many persons engaged in a particular kind of criminal activity. The most famous profile is the "drug courier profile," a collection. of purported characteristics and behaviors displayed by those transporting or selling illegal drugs. The logic of a profile is simple. If, for example, seven behaviors and characteristics are common to drug smugglers, they may jointly constitute a profile. The police might argue that any particular individual fitting all seven elements of the profile is sufficiently suspicious of in fact being a smuggler as to justify stopping him.

In practice there are several flaws in this logic. First, particular individuals often fit only a few of the elements of a profile. How many (or few) must someone fit for the profile to be reliable? Second, few profiles are empirically validated, being the product of the officers' own perceptions of their individual and collective experience. Often these profiles are internally inconsistent, or different profiles are inconsistent with one another, such as one declaring "sloppy dressing" as suspicious while another asserting "smart dressing" to be suspicious. Justice Marshall noted in his dissent in *United States v. Sokolow,* 490 U.S. 1 (1989), that profiles have a "chameleon-like way of adapting to any particular set of observations." That chameleon-like quality arguably gives officers enormous discretion in the field. Third, profiles containing race as a factor raise the suspicion of either intentional racial bias or unjustified disparate racial impact.

The Court's approach to profiles is ambiguous. It has never squarely embraced, nor clearly rejected, the logic behind profiles. However, three points can be inferred from its holdings: (1) the fact that a person matches a profile *probably* does not, in and of itself, routinely give rise to reasonable suspicion; (2) officers (and reviewing courts) may rely in part on the cumulative law enforcement wisdom embodied in profiles when assessing the inferences that may be drawn from a person's conduct or attributes; and (3) the fact that a person matches a profile does not detract from the inferences that might reasonably be drawn.

In *Reid v. Georgia,* 448 U.S. 438 (1980), the Court found a profile inadequate to establish reasonable suspicion. There, a DEA agent saw two men walking in an airport terminal, each wearing similar shoulder bags. One occasionally looked back at the other, and the two then met up in the terminal main lobby, conferred briefly, and left together. The agent stopped the two men, identified himself and asked for their identification and tickets, which they produced. These items revealed that the men had spent only one day in Fort Lauderdale, Florida, before flying to Georgia. The agent thought the men seemed nervous and asked them to consent to a search of their bags and to re-enter the terminal. As they began to do so, Reid started to run, abandoning his shoulder bag that contained cocaine before being apprehended. Although the state trial court granted Reid's motion to suppress on the grounds that the agent lacked reasonable suspicion for the stop, the court of appeals reversed because Reid fit a DEA drug courier profile in a number of respects.

The Supreme Court reversed, viewing the profile as insufficiently particular to create reasonable suspicion. Other than one man occasionally looking back at the other, all the purportedly suspicious activities implicated "a very large category of presumably innocent travelers." Moreover, the agent's belief that the two men were attempting to conceal the fact that they were traveling together because of the way they walked through the airport one behind the other was more an "inchoate and unparticularized suspicion or hunch than a fair inference."

In later cases, the Court has appeared to be more willing to accept law enforcement assessments concerning the suspiciousness of certain behavior or characteristics. For example, in *United States v. Sokolow,* 490 U.S. 1 (1989), the Court upheld an airport stop that took place in circumstances not all that different from *Reid*. The government argued that the stop was justified because Sokolow was making a quick round trip to a drug "source city," had paid for his tickets in cash, had checked no baggage, and appeared nervous. These characteristics fit a drug courier profile, and the Court agreed that they combined to paint a suspicious picture—one that gave rise to reasonable suspicion to believe that Sokolow was trafficking in drugs. The Court stated that "the fact that these factors may be set forth in a 'profile' does not somehow detract from their evidentiary significance as seen by a trained agent."

The lesson of *Reid* and *Sokolow* appears to be that courts reviewing *Terry* stops cannot rely exclusively on the fact that an individual matched a profile, although they may defer to accumulated law enforcement experience, embodied in profiles, when they evaluate for themselves the suspiciousness of certain behaviors and characteristics that form the asserted basis for the stop.

D. *Terry* Frisks

A *Terry* frisk is a brief patdown of an individual's person and outer clothing for weapons. (There may also be a "frisk" of the passenger compartment of a vehicle, as is discussed in chapter 7). A frisk is a form of search, rather than seizure, of the person. As with seizures, however, there are various types of police searches of the person.

As explained in Chapter 2, a search occurs when the state has invaded a person's reasonable expectation of privacy. A full-blown search requires probable cause, but a minimally intrusive search of a person - involving the brief patdown for weapons just discussed - is a *Terry* "frisk" and can be based on reasonable suspicion. The sole purpose of the *Terry* frisk is protection of the officer and public. A frisking officer may not engage in movements designed to discover evidence of a crime instead of to uncover weapons. If an officer feels something that might be a weapon, he may remove it. But otherwise, after the frisk, he may proceed no further, with one exception (see Chapter 10's discussion of the "plain feel" exception).

All these and other matters concerning *Terry* frisks are addressed in more detail elsewhere in this text, including in Chapter 3 on warrants, Chapter 6 on searches of the person, Chapter 7 on cars, and Chapter 10 on plain view. Although *Terry* frisks often accompany stops, the right to stop someone does not automatically establish the right to frisk them. Each type of respective police action - the stop, then the frisk - requires a different type of reasonable suspicion. The stop is justified by reasonable suspicion that a person has engaged in, or is about to engage in, a crime. The shorthand term for this is reasonable suspicion to believe that criminal activity is "afoot." But that same person may be frisked only if there is reasonable suspicion to believe he or she is *armed and dangerous*. Although the Court used the phrase "armed and dangerous," it seems to assume danger from the mere fact that a suspect is armed.

For example, reasonable suspicion that a suspect is a forger does not automatically create reasonable suspicion that he is also armed and dangerous, because forgery ordinarily is not a crime involving weapons. Yet if the officer saw a knife handle protruding from the suspected forger's pocket, that would likely provide reasonable suspicion of danger, justifying the frisk. Correspondingly, it may be that some crimes are so inherently dangerous that a person reasonably suspected of such a crime may also be reasonably suspected of being armed and dangerous. That arguably was what happened in *Terry*, where the investigating officer suspected that a "stick up" - an armed robbery of a store clerk - was imminent.

The *Terry* Court crafted its reasonable suspicion rules and its stop/frisk distinction by weighing state against individual interests. Although it concluded that a stop is more than a "petty indignity," it also concluded that the need for effective crime control justified permitting that indignity on mere reasonable suspicion. Similarly, as to frisks, the Justices refused to "blind ourselves to the need for law enforcement officers to protect themselves and other prospective victims of violence in situations where they lack probable cause for an arrest." The Court conceded that a frisk can be an annoying, frightening, and even humiliating experience, thus justifying some measure of protection for the individual. But, given the officers' need to protect themselves and others, permitting a frisk based upon reasonable suspicion that the person is armed and dangerous properly balances the needs of the individual and the officers.

Checkpoints

- The Fourth Amendment does not flatly bar arrests for minor crimes, even for ordinary traffic offenses.

- That state law might bar arrests for certain minor crimes is irrelevant to whether the Fourth Amendment does so.

- Probable cause is generally required for a full-blown arrest—a highly intrusive seizure of the person.

- Moreover, if the arrest occurs on a public street, no arrest warrant is required.

- However, arresting a suspect in his own home requires a warrant, absent exigent circumstances.

- Arresting a suspect in a third party's residence requires a search warrant, based on probable cause to believe that the suspect will be in the third party's home at the time of the search, again, unless there are exigent circumstances.

Checkpoints *continued*

- Although the Court has never clearly defined "exigent circumstances," they include preventing imminent flight, destruction of evidence, or grave dangers to others' lives.

- For all practical purposes, a suspect obtains a home-like privacy interest in a third party's residence if the suspect is an overnight guest in the third party's home.

- The Supreme Court has suggested in *dicta* in several places that It may permit highly intrusive seizures of the person on less than probable cause in one circumstance: where a judicial officer authorizes the seizure (perhaps by warrant or by court order) solely for the purpose of prompt investigation (for example, by fingerprinting, photographing, placing in a lineup, or taking DNA samples from the suspect) based upon reasonable suspicion to believe that the suspect committed a crime.

- Officers may only use that force which is "reasonable" to effect an arrest or stop a fleeing suspect. What is reasonable is determined on a case-by-case basis weighing the state's need, the potential injury to any persons, including the officer, the suspect, and third parties.

- It is rarely reasonable, however, to use deadly force simply because the suspect is connected to a felony rather than to a misdemeanor or even lesser offense.

- However, deadly force may be used to stop a fleeing felon if the officer has probable cause to believe that the suspect poses a threat of serious physical harm to himself or to others. Where feasible, the officer must first warn the suspect before in fact using deadly force to halt his escape.

- Deadly force may sometimes be used to halt the flight of non-felons, even of mere traffic offenders, if their conduct endangers the lives of innocent bystanders, at least in the situation where a speeding, fleeing motorist created just such a danger.

- The Fourth Amendment applies only if there is a search or seizure, with the Court defining a seizure of a person as occurring only when a fleeing suspect has been physically restrained by law enforcement or submitted to the officer's show of authority by means "intentionally applied."

- Where a suspect is subjected to a warrantless arrest, he is entitled to a prompt probable cause hearing, also known as a *"Gerstein"* hearing. Such a hearing is based almost entirely on whether the facts alleged in the complaint establish probable cause, a fuller probable cause determination being reserved for a later suppression motion.

- In *County of Riverside v. McLaughlin*, the Court held that a *Gerstein* hearing's taking place within 48 hours of arrest is presumptively reasonable. But a particular defendant may show that such a delay was done "for the purpose of gathering additional evidence to justify the arrest, a delay motivated by ill will against the arrested individual, or delay for delay's sake," thereby rendering the delay unreasonable.

Checkpoints *continued*

- A "seizure" of the person occurs whenever a reasonable person would not feel free to leave as a result of government action.

- Factors relevant to finding a seizure are a threatening presence of officers, display of a weapon by an officer, a physical touching of the person detained, and language or tone of voice indicating compliance.

- Determination of whether a seizure had occurred is based on the totality of the circumstances based on a reasonable person's perception.

- For seizures on a means of public transportation, from which a person could not easily leave, the test is whether the person is free to decline an official request or otherwise terminate the encounter.

- A lengthy stop of a person may become a de facto arrest, for which probable cause is required.

- Reasonable suspicion for a *Terry* stop involves a lower degree of confidence in the suspect's guilt and can be based on less trustworthy evidence than for probable cause, but may not be based on an officer's hunch.

- Whether there is sufficient evidence to support a reasonable suspicion for a stop depends on the totality of the circumstances, including the source of the information and conduct by the person stopped, such as flight from an officer, although presence in a high-crime area alone is insufficient to justify a stop.

- In reviewing a lower court's finding that the officer had reasonable suspicion, the appellate court may give deference to an officer's expertise if the trial court found the testimony credible. The reviewing court should also give deference to the lower court's finding of historical facts but should otherwise review the decision whether those facts establish reasonable suspicion de novo.

- While a match to a profile of a typical person involved in criminal activity, such as a "drug courier profile," is probably not alone sufficient to establish reasonable suspicion, the facts in the profile will be considered on a case-by-case basis, along with any other facts, to determine whether there is reasonable suspicion, and the profile itself may be relevant evidence of officer experience.

- If there is a reasonable suspicion to support a stop, an officer can frisk a defendant, which involves a pat-down of the outer clothing of the person, only if the officer also has a reasonable suspicion that the person is armed and dangerous.

Chapter 5

Electronic Surveillance

Roadmap

- Fourth Amendment applicability to electronic surveillance
- Statutory restrictions and remedies:
  - The Wiretap Act and its amendments
  - FISA
  - The PATRIOT Act

Since the first decades of the 20th Century, law enforcement officials have made use of electronic technology to assist them in discovering criminal activity. As courts struggled to juxtapose constitutional principles with new technologies, it became clear that the Fourth Amendment applied in only a limited way to electronic surveillance. Stepping into the void, Congress became heavily involved in regulating electronic surveillance beginning in the 1930s, and it has been active in the arena ever since. Thus, limitations on electronic surveillance derive from statutory as well as constitutional provisions. This Chapter will discuss both of these sources of law.

I. Fourth Amendment Oversight of Surveillance

A. Threshold: Determining When the Fourth Amendment Applies

The Prohibition Era of the 1920s, which featured aggressive federal enforcement of the 18th Amendment's ban on the manufacture, sale, or transportation of alcohol, gave rise to the first of the United States Supreme Court's pronouncements on the constitutionality of electronic surveillance. In *Olmstead v. United States*, 277 U.S. 438 (1928), the Court reviewed the legality of a crude form of wiretapping accomplished by federal agents inserting small wires, or "taps," alongside telephone lines used by suspected members of a large alcohol importation ring. The agents were able to insert the taps outside of the suspects' residential and business premises, which enabled them to remain outside of those premises while they listened and took notes of the suspects' telephone conversations. The Court held that the taps did not violate the Fourth Amendment because the agents had not invaded the suspects' protected "places"—in other words, homes or businesses—and the conversations overheard were not "things" whose seizure was proscribed by the Constitution.

As discussed in Chapter 2, the Court later disavowed *Olmstead's* narrow, place-bound reading of the Fourth Amendment. In *Katz v. United States*, 389 U.S. 347 (1967), federal agents had avoided a physical trespass onto Katz's protected "places" when they installed a wiretap on the outside of a telephone booth that he used, but the Court nevertheless held that his Fourth Amendment rights had been violated. Emphasizing that the Fourth Amendment protects "people, not places," the Court articulated its important "reasonable expectation of privacy" test and, applying it to Katz's situation, found that the wiretap "intruded upon the privacy upon which [he] justifiably relied while using the telephone booth." *Katz* did not hold that electronic surveillance is unconstitutional per se, and in fact it contained dictum suggesting that properly conducted electronic surveillance could be constitutional.

Subsequent decisions from the Supreme Court narrowed the applicability of the Fourth Amendment in electronic surveillance contexts by expanding the circumstances in which people are found to have "forfeited" their reasonable expectations of privacy. As Chapter 2 details, people give up expectations of privacy when their activities (electronic bulletin board postings, for example) are observable by others, when they assume the risk of disclosing information (in an email, for example) to a potential "false friend," and when records of their activities are made and/or held by third parties (telephone companies and internet service providers, for example). In all of these situations, the Fourth Amendment would not apply. Instead, statutory provisions, and possibly contractual obligations, would form the only sources of limitation upon surveillance activities.

In other situations, though, the Fourth Amendment continues to have real force. The quintessential example is that of the content of telephone conversations. Unlike telephone records maintained by a telephone service provider, which might legally be obtained by the government without a warrant, and which would reveal numbers to and from which calls were made and taken, the actual words spoken during a telephone call are protected by the Fourth Amendment, unless those words were exchanged in an area in which they reasonably could be overheard. When law enforcement officials wish to listen into the content of telephone conversations, they must deal with the substance of the Fourth Amendment, as well as with statutory limitations.

B. The Substance of Fourth Amendment Protections

When it does apply to electronic surveillance, the Fourth Amendment imposes substantive limitations on law enforcement officials that arise out of its requirements of probable cause, particularity, and reasonable warrant execution. These have particular teeth in the arena of electronic surveillance, but they are subsumed within the requirements of the Wiretap Act, discussed below.

II. Statutory Regulation of Electronic Surveillance

A. Development of the Federal Statutory Framework

The original statute governing electronic surveillance was enacted in the wake of the Supreme Court's decision in *Olmstead*, which held that the Fourth Amendment did not apply to telephone taps effectuated without physical trespass upon protected places. Congress was troubled by the lack of restriction on law enforcement eavesdropping, and hence it declared in the Federal Communications Act of 1934 that no person "shall intercept any [wire] communication and divulge [it] ... to any person, ... and no person having received such intercepted communication ... shall divulge [it]."

In the 1960s, Congress broadened its coverage of eavesdropping, superseding the Federal Communications Act. Concerned about growing electronic surveillance, as well as about increased crime and greater social upheaval during that decade, it enacted the Omnibus Crime Control and Safe Streets Act of 1968. By that time, the Supreme Court had issued *Katz*, which expanded coverage of the Fourth Amendment to the contents of telephone conversations, and it had suggested that carefully crafted and monitored surveillance practices could satisfy the Fourth Amendment. In the Omnibus Crime legislation, Congress took up the Supreme Court's challenge and established a system of regulation over the interception of "aural" communications—in other words, those that can by overheard. These regulations are found in a portion of the Omnibus Crime bill commonly referred to as the Wiretap Act. Because it is based in the Commerce Clause, the Wiretap Act applies to all government actors, whether federal or state. And it covers private actors, creating the potential for individual criminal and civil liability. For these reasons, it applies to far more conduct than does the Fourth Amendment.

Congress acted again by amending the Wiretap Act in the Electronic Communications Privacy Act of 1986 [ECPA] and the Digital Telephony Act of 1994. These cover the interception of wire and electronic communications. As amended by these two laws, the Wiretap Act now governs everything from eavesdropping on person-to-person conversations to conducting surveillance of communications via telephone, cell phone, email, text messaging, and other devices. Having been broadened, the Wiretap Act now stands in a position to fulfill its dual purposes of protecting the privacy of communications and "delineating on a uniform basis" the circumstances under which courts may authorize the interception of communications. But while comprehensive, the Act remains, in the words of one court, "famous (if not infamous) for its lack of clarity." *Steve Jackson Games, Inc. v. United States Secret Service*, 36 F.3d 457 (5th Cir. 1994).

Two more legislative enactments warrant study. In 1978, Congress established a separate statutory framework to regulate surveillance by foreign intelligence gathering agencies. Known as the Foreign Intelligence and Surveillance Act [FISA], the statute governs domestic surveillance of foreign powers, their agents, and groups that engage in international terrorism. FISA makes electronic surveillance far easier, but it can be used only in those criminal investigations concerned with foreign intelligence gathering. In 2001, after the September 11th terrorist attacks, Congress quickly passed an act enlarging government surveillance powers. Formally titled the "Uniting and Strengthening America by Providing Appropriate Tools Required to Intercept and Obstruct Terrorism Act" [PATRIOT Act], this statute loosened some of the Wiretap Act's and FISA's restrictions.

B. Relationship Between Statutes and the Fourth Amendment

The lawyer faced with eavesdropping or surveillance activity must remember to analyze separately the Fourth Amendment and statutory issues. While federal statutory coverage might overlap with the Fourth Amendment, it sometimes goes beyond constitutional restrictions — notably because it may apply to private actors. Conversely, the statutory framework may leave unprotected situations that are covered by the Fourth Amendment. Hence, for each person affected by eavesdropping or surveillance, the lawyer must analyze (1) whether Fourth Amendment violations occurred; (2) whether a statute was violated; and (3) the appropriate remedy for each type of violation.

III. The Wiretap Act

Two characteristics of the Wiretap Act are particularly important: first, the Act creates a hierarchy of protections depending on the type of surveillance; second, where protections are highest, they exceed Fourth Amendment requirements by having more stringent jurisdictional and documentary requirements, as well as greater restrictions on the execution of intercepted orders. For this reason, when the government obtains what is known as a Title I intercept order under the Act, discussed below, it is not required to obtain a regular search warrant.

A. Title I: Highest Level of Protection

1. Types of Communications Covered by Title I

The Act's first section, known as Title I, contains the highest level of protection. Title I regulates the use of "any electronic, mechanical, or other device" to intentionally intercept oral, wire, and electronic communications.

- Oral communications—in other words, *face-to-face conversations*—are protected only if they consist of words uttered by persons "exhibiting" a reasonable expectation of privacy. In addition, in order to create the interstate commerce nexus necessary for federal jurisdiction, oral communications are protected only if the device used to intercept them has been sent through interstate or foreign commerce.
- Wire communications are those that transfer human voices from points of origin to points of reception by means (at least in part) of wires, cables, and "like connection[s]" that affect interstate or foreign commerce. Included within this definition are *telephone conversations* using landlines, cordless phone connections, cell phone networks, and Internet services that transmit voices.
- Electronic communications are those that do not transmit a human voice. They are defined as "transfers of signs, signals, writing, images, sounds, data, or intelligence of any nature transmitted in whole or in part by a wire, radio, electromagnetic, photoelectronic or photooptical system that affects interstate or foreign commerce." Examples of electronic communications are *emails, text messages, instant messages*, and other nonvocal communications using the Internet.

Title I regulates only the *contemporaneous* intentional interception of these three types of communications—in other words, the capture of communications while they are "in flight" or being transmitted. The Act makes an exception for voicemail messages, protecting them if they have been temporarily stored in an electronic system but not yet heard by the recipient. This exception, though, was eliminated when Congress passed the PATRIOT Act, as explained below.

The Wiretap Act has a few other exceptions. The most important one exempts communications in which one of the parties has given prior consent to being overheard. Because the consenting party may be someone "acting under color of law," an informant or undercover agent may call a suspect on the telephone and tape the conversation without implicating the Wiretap Act. Some states, though, have statutes forbidding interceptions unless all parties consent. In either event, suspects do not have Fourth Amendment claims in these situations, because by engaging in conversations, they assumed the risk of disclosure by other parties.

2. Requirements for Title I Intercept Orders

A communication protected by Title I may not be contemporaneously intercepted by a law enforcement official unless he or she first obtains an intercept order. This type of order requires a stringent showing beyond that required by the Fourth Amendment, and for that reason it has been called a "super search warrant." See Orin S. Kerr, *Internet Surveillance Law after the USA PATRIOT Act: The Big Brother That Isn't*, 97 NW. U. L. REV.. 607 (2003). The Wiretap Act imposes three categories of requirements on intercept orders: "jurisdictional" ones that limit the circumstances in which intercept orders may be obtained, documentary ones that regulate the content of applications and intercept orders, and rules that govern the execution of intercept orders.

a. Jurisdictional Requirements for the Intercept Order

The Wiretap Act imposes three jurisdictional thresholds upon intercept orders.

- *Seriousness of crime.* First, the crime for which the surveillance is sought must be a serious one. If the request is by a federal law enforcement agent, the list of applicable federal felonies is quite extensive. If the application is by a state agent, the crime must fall into the following list: "murder, kidnapping, gambling, robbery, bribery, extortion, or dealing in narcotic drugs, marihuana or other dangerous drugs, or other crime dangerous to life, limb, or property, and punishable by imprisonment for more than one year." In addition, the state must specifically authorize electronic surveillance for the crime involved.
- *Authorized applicant.* The second jurisdictional requirement is that a statutorily designated official must have approved the application for an intercept order. A police officer or low-level prosecutor, for example, may

not fall within the statutory definition and would have to obtain authorization from a designated official before applying for an intercept order.

- *Authorized issuer.* Finally, the application must be made to "a judge of competent jurisdiction." If a federal agent applies for an intercept order, the application must be considered by a federal judge with territorial jurisdiction over the point of interception, although the order may authorize interception anywhere within the United States if the surveillance will occur over a large area by use of a "mobile interception device." Applications by state agents must be made to those state court judges who are authorized by state statute to issue such orders.

b. Documentary Requirements for the Intercept Order

The Wiretap Act sets out documentary requirements for both the application and the intercept order itself. These requirements are lengthy, specific and more comprehensive than the requirements of a traditional warrant. Consistent with the Fourth Amendment, all applications must be made upon oath or affirmation; in addition, they must be in writing and state the applicant's authority to make such an application. The application must also include:

- The *particulars*: *i.e.*, a "full and complete statement of the facts," including details of the offense; a description of the "nature and location of the facilities" where the communication is to be intercepted; a description of the kind of communications sought to be intercepted; and the identity of all persons committing the offense and whose communications are to be intercepted;
- A statement of *necessity*: *i.e.*, a "full and complete statement as to whether or not other investigative procedures have been tried and failed or why they reasonably appear to be unlikely to succeed if tried or to be too dangerous"; and
- *Duration* of the intercept: *i.e.*, "a statement of the period of time for which the interception is required to be maintained."

Once an application is submitted to a judge of competent jurisdiction, the judge must determine the existence of probable cause as to the stated crime, as well as to the fact that communications concerning the offense will be intercepted, and that the point of interception will be used in the commission of the offense. The judge must also determine whether the government has satisfied its showing of necessity. The judge may issue an intercept order only if these determinations are made. Finally, when the judge issues the intercept order, he or she must ensure that the order contains all of the particulars mentioned above, as well as a *"minimization plan"* for reducing the impact of the interception on nonpertinent communications or on the privacy of people not involved in the offense.

c. Requirements Governing Execution of the Intercept Order

The last set of requirements imposed by Title I of the Wiretap Act relate to the execution of the intercept order. First, surveillance may be conducted only by the agency authorized by the order to intercept the communications. Moreover, the surveillance must satisfy the minimization plan. If possible, the intercepted communications must be recorded in a way that will prevent alteration. Once the communications have been intercepted or the order expires, surveillance must cease and any recordings made must be sealed and turned over to the issuing judge. Duplicates of the recordings may be made and used by law enforcement officers for investigative purposes.

The execution provisions also require that within a reasonable time, but not later than ninety days after expiration of the wiretap order, the issuing judge must serve persons named in the order with notice, including an inventory of intercepted matter; other overheard parties may be given inventory notice at the judge's discretion. In addition, both the issuing judge and the official authorizing the intercept application must provide the Administrative Office of the United States Court with a summary of each surveillance case. The Wiretap Act requires the Administrative Office of the United States Court to submit to Congress each April a "full and complete report" of the surveillance cases occurring over the past year.

3. *Remedies for Title I Violations*

Title I contains an exclusionary remedy for violations of certain of its provisions. The remedy protects only oral or wire communications, leaving electronic communications such as email out of its scope. Moreover, even with oral and wire communications, suppression is authorized only if:

- the intercept order was insufficient on its face;
- interception was not made in conformity with the intercept order; or
- the communication was otherwise unlawfully intercepted.

It is relatively easy to determine the presence of the first two grounds for suppression—namely, whether the intercept order was insufficient on its face or the execution noncompliant with the order. Much more difficult is determining whether, in the absence of one of those grounds, the communication was "unlawfully intercepted" so as to require suppression under the "catchall" provision.

The Supreme Court struggled with this issue for several years. Then, in *United States v. Donovan*, 429 U.S. 413 (1977), it held that an interception is "unlawful" only if it undermines the very purpose of the Wiretap Act, so that the exclusionary remedy is available only for violations of provisions that play "a central role" in the statutory framework. In *Donovan*, the Court refused to apply the exclusionary rule where the government's application, while identifying a number of persons about whom probable cause existed and whose communications would be intercepted, had failed to identify additional persons whose communications were likely to be intercepted. According to the Court, this failure in no way prevented the issuing court from identifying the sufficiency of particulars in the application, and thus it did not undermine the very purpose of the Act.

Other remedies created by Title I include civil damages and criminal prosecution of violators in certain circumstances. Neither of these is available, however, if the violator establishes "good faith reliance" on a court order or other reasonably official authorization.

B. Lower Protection for Stored Electronic Communications

Title II of the Wiretap Act, sometimes called the Stored Communications Act, governs communications in electronic storage, including stored email, voicemail, and subscriber records maintained by communications services providers. The government need not obtain a Title I intercept order for these stored communications. Instead, a court order based on probable cause will suffice in the case of communications that have been stored for 180 days or less.

For communications stored more than 180 days, the requirements are lower: a subpoena, which requires no showing of probable cause, is sufficient if the stored communications are in the hands of a third party (such as an Internet Service Provider). Of course, if stored communications are sought from a computer in which an individual has a reasonable expectation of privacy, then the search also must be accompanied by a warrant to search the computer. The Act does not provide an exclusionary remedy for violations of the stored communications provision. Thus, unless the Fourth Amendment was violated, these communications may be admitted in court even if their interception violated the Wiretap Act.

C. Lowest Protection for Pen Registers and Trap and Trace Devices

Title III of the Wiretap Act governs "pen registers" as well as "trap and trace" devices. Pen registers are records of outgoing calls from a particular telephone, while trap and trace devices capture the telephone numbers of incoming calls. Under Title III of the Wiretap Act (not surprisingly, called the "Pen Register Act"), the government can obtain pen registers and trap and trace records with court permission, which must be granted if the government certifies that the information is "relevant" to an investigation. There is no exclusionary remedy for violations of this part of the Wiretap Act.

IV. FISA

The government is granted considerably more leeway when it is investigating the activities of foreign powers than when it is engaging in traditional domestic criminal law enforcement. In part this leeway stems from the deference granted the executive branch in matters of foreign affairs by the legislative and judicial branches. FISA exemplifies this deference. It applies whenever federal law enforcement agents investigate foreign intelligence gathering within the borders of the United States. As will be discussed below, the PATRIOT Act has widened some of FISA's scope.

FISA enables the government to engage in some information gathering without judicial authorization. Even more significantly, where judicial oversight is necessary, a special court is invoked that operates in secret. This court is comprised of federal trial judges, and its orders are reviewed in secret by a special FISA court of appeals comprised of federal appellate judges. The FISA court is empowered to authorize surveillance without a showing of probable cause, so long as the government demonstrates that it is investigating a foreign power or an agent of a foreign power, including terrorist organizations. Information that the government gains through a FISA investigation may be shared with law enforcement officers working in traditional criminal law enforcement.

V. The PATRIOT Act

This long and complex document consists of amendments to other federal statutes. Some of those amendments affect criminal investigations.

A. Provisions Affecting Fourth Amendment Searches

One of the more controversial of the PATRIOT Act's provisions affects search warrants issued under traditional Fourth Amendment standards. As a result, the constitutionality of that provision remains in question. The provision endorses what are known as "sneak and peak" warrants—warrants that remain secret even after their execution. Recall that officers ordinarily must notify residents that a search warrant has been executed by leaving a copy of the warrant and an inventory of items seized. Under section 213 of the Act, the government can put off giving this sort of notice if a court finds that there is reasonable cause to believe that notice will create an "adverse result" in the form of danger to persons or evidence, or flight from the jurisdiction.

B. Provision Expanding Scope of FISA

The PATRIOT Act has expanded the numbers of investigations in which law enforcement officials can take advantage of FISA powers. Originally, FISA applied only where foreign intelligence gathering was "*the* purpose" of an investigation. The PATRIOT Act now permits the use of FISA powers in investigations for which foreign intelligence gathering is "*a* significant purpose." One federal trial court has declared this portion of the PATRIOT Act unconstitutional, see *Mayfield v. United States*, 504 F. Supp. 2d 1023 (D. Or. 2007), but that ruling has not been followed in other cases.

Under the PATRIOT Act, intelligence officials also may now share broadly the information they gather using FISA powers. The sharing of information need only "assist the official who is to receive that information in the performance of his official duties." Arguably, this information sharing provision, while making law enforcement more effective, provides incentives for agencies to use their aggressive FISA powers in order to help criminal investigators who otherwise must respect the more burdensome responsibilities of the Wiretap Act.

C. Provisions Affecting Wiretap Act

Most of the controversy surrounding the PATRIOT Act concerned changes it made to FISA. But it also affected statutory surveillance powers under the Wiretap Act. These changes can be summarized in the following categories:

- As written, Title I of the Wiretap Act protected voicemail messages not yet delivered to recipients. Under the PATRIOT Act, these are now treated under Title II like other communications in electronic storage. In other words, if such communications have been stored for 180 days or less, the government must obtain a warrant or order based on probable cause but need not obtain an intercept order. If the communications have been stored for more than 180 days, the government can intercept them with a subpoena.

- Warrants or orders for stored email communications now are effective nationwide, and not just in the jurisdiction in which they are issued. According to the government, this provision makes its work much more efficient, because Internet Service Providers [ISPs] often are located in places unconnected to the investigation. According to ISPs, however, nationwide jurisdiction makes it impossible in many cases for them to challenge intercept orders, because courts of issuance may be far from the ISPs and costs of the challenge prohibitive.

- The government now is entitled to greater information about ISP customers. Under Title II of the Wiretap Act, the government could obtain certain ISP records that fell within the definition of communications in electronic storage. These included customer names and addresses and duration of customers' accounts. The PATRIOT Act adds other records, including customer electronic aliases, times and duration of online sessions, and credit card and bank accounts with which customers pay their ISPs.

- Under the Wiretap Act, the government has access to pen registers and trap and trace devices upon a statement of relevance. The PATRIOT Act has added the Internet equivalent of these devices, so that the government now has access to email addressing data and routing information. In other words, the government can monitor to whom an individual is sending email, and from whom the individual receives email.

- Under the PATRIOT Act, courts with jurisdiction over an investigation can issue nationwide orders authorizing the release of pen registers, trap and trace records, and their Internet equivalents. Again, the government contends that it can fight crime more effectively with this nationwide jurisdictional provision; ISPs complain that they cannot meaningfully challenge (and thus monitor) the validity and execution of orders.

VI. Review Problem

A. Problem

Special Agent Park of the Federal Bureau of Investigation was investigating an interstate prostitution ring. One of her primary targets was Smith, the suspected ringleader. On April 15, an informant told her that in two days Smith and a confederate planned to transport something "big" from Seattle to Los Angeles. The informant did not know what was being transported or the identity of Smith's confederate. However, he did know that two minivans would be used for the operation and that Smith would be in one of them. The informant explained that he knew about the plans because he had been asked by Smith to supply Smith and the confederate with untraceable cell phones with which they would communicate during the operation.

Agent Park wanted to find out more about the nature of the operation, because if it involved the transportation of prostitutes, she wanted to catch the convoy en route to its drop-off point. On April 16 she filed an application for a Title I intercept order authorizing her to intercept cell phone calls to and from Smith and his confederate. In the supporting affidavit, she set forth detailed information regarding the imminence of the operation and the secretive nature that attends the illicit business of interstate prostitution. A United States District Court Judge for the Western District of Washington issued the order, and both of the cell phones were wiretapped before the informant delivered them to Smith.

Conversations on the cell phones were intercepted on April 17, and through them Agent Park found out that Smith and his confederate were en route with "the goods" as planned. She also learned through a conversation between Smith and an individual whom he called "Jake" that the men would transport 700 kilograms of heroin in the same vehicles back to Seattle after dropping off their cargo in Los Angeles. The conversation between Smith and Jake revealed the pick-up point for the heroin. Just before the vans reached the drop-off point, they were stopped and searched by federal agents, who took Smith, the confederate, and fifteen young women into custody. At the same time, federal agents in Los Angeles raided the heroin pick-up point, seizing the drugs and arresting Jake. The United States Attorney for the Southern District of California has charged Smith and Jake with various crimes, and each of them files a motion to suppress the intercepted conversations. What grounds should they allege for suppression?

B. Analysis

Although the facts are not sufficiently detailed to provide a complete analysis, they raise several questions under Title I of the Wiretap Act:

- *Type of crime*: Does the Wiretap Act's list of federal crimes include the interstate transportation of individuals for prostitution?

- *Authority*: Did Agent Park fall within the category of officials authorized by the Wiretap Act to request an intercept order? Was the federal judge in Seattle authorized to issue an intercept order that would cover interceptions outside of the Western District of Washington? Presumably, the application would have made a showing that "roving bugs" across a number of federal districts were required given the mobile nature of the criminal transaction.
- *Necessity*: Did Agent Park's affidavit contained a full and complete statement as to whether "traditional investigative techniques" were tried and failed or were proven inadequate to achieve investigation's objective? Although the problem does not reveal exactly what Agent Park wrote in her affidavit, it does say that her showing was a "detailed" one that explained the imminence of the operation and the secretive nature of the interstate prostitution business. This showing would have attempted to establish that grand juries, pen registers, trap-and-trace devices, and undercover agents would have been too time-consuming given the urgency of the situation, and that search warrants and physical surveillance would have been of little assistance because of the operation's mobile manner.
- *Minimization*: Did the application and intercept order contain a plan for minimizing intrusion into the privacy of others (such as Jake) not involved in the prostitution ring? If so, did execution of the intercept order violate the minimization plan by capturing Jake's conversations?

Checkpoints

- Instances of electronic surveillance must be analyzed under both the Fourth Amendment and federal statutes.

- The Fourth Amendment applies to communications made with a reasonable expectation of privacy, but privacy expectations are not reasonable where a person assumes the risk that another party to a conversation will disclose its contents, and that records in the hands of third parties will be revealed.

- Where it applies, the Fourth Amendment requires probable cause and a warrant to conduct electronic surveillance, but these are subsumed within the more stringent requirements of intercept orders under the Wiretap Act.

- Title I of the Wiretap Act provides a high level of protection to the contemporaneous interception of oral and wire communications. If the government wishes to engage in such a contemporaneous interception, it must obtain an intercept order.

- Intercept orders have special jurisdictional and documentary requirements, and they also are accompanied by rules governing their execution.

- Titles II and III of the Wiretap Act provide lower levels of protection to stored electronic communications, such as email, and to records, such as pen registers and trap and trace devices, held by telephone companies and other service providers.

- The government has much broader powers under FISA, applicable when it conducts domestic surveillance of persons involved in foreign intelligence gathering.

- The Patriot Act loosened restrictions on electronic surveillance under the Wiretap Act and FISA, and it also permits "sneak and peak" warrants.

Chapter 6

Searches of Persons

Roadmap

- Search of lawfully detained persons
- The limited scope of *Terry* frisks for weapons
- The broad scope of the search incident to arrest exception to warrant requirement
- Searches of personal belongings incident to arrest
- Inventory stationhouse searches

I. Introduction

As discussed in Chapter 2, people have a reasonable and legitimate privacy expectation in information contained on (or in) their body. Accordingly, if the government seeks to obtain evidence by conducting a search of a person, the government must either have a warrant or their conduct must be justified by an exception to the warrant requirement. Otherwise, searches of individuals may be deemed unreasonable and a violation of the Fourth Amendment. Although the government cannot conduct random "suspicionless" searches of persons they encounter during a criminal investigation, once the government has sufficient facts to link an individual to criminal activity, the Court has held that an individual's expectation of privacy in her person must yield to the government's superior interest in securing weapons and collecting any evidence concealed on the individual. Persons who may be subjected to searches of their person generally fall into three categories: (1) persons detained during an investigatory stop authorized by *Terry v. Ohio*; (2) motorists lawfully detained during a routine traffic stop; and (3) persons who have been placed under full custodial arrest.

II. *Terry* Searches

As discussed more fully in Chapter 4, under *Terry v. Ohio*, 392 U.S. 1 (1968), when the police have reasonable articulable suspicion that an individual is involved in on-going criminal activity and briefly detain the person to confirm or dispel their suspicions, they are permitted to conduct a limited "frisk" of the person's outer clothing to determine whether the individual is armed with a weapon that could be used to harm the officer. A *Terry* frisk or "pat down" search can only be conducted, however, if the officer has reasonable, articulable suspicion that the individual is armed. Moreover, a search of a *Terry* detainee is unreasonable if the officer goes beyond the authorized weapons search to try to find contraband or other evidence of criminal activity concealed on the individual.

III. Search Incident to Arrest Exception

When individuals are placed under arrest and taken into custody, the government can conduct a warrantless search of the arrestee, the personal belongings or "effects" in the arrestee's possession, and the immediate area within arm's reach of the arrestee at the time of the arrest. The justification for allowing warrantless searches of arrestees is to permit the police to immediately disarm the arrestee and prevent the destruction of incriminating evidence located on or near the arrestee. Another apparent justification for allowing searches of arrestees is the reduced expectation of privacy of those who have been lawfully arrested.

A. *Chimel v. California:* The "Grab-Reach" Rule

In *Chimel v. California*, 395 U.S. 752 (1969), the police arrested the defendant at his home pursuant to a valid arrest warrant. The police then conducted a search of the entire three-bedroom house and seized incriminating evidence in a room that was not in close proximity to where the defendant was placed under arrest. The defendant moved to suppress evidence on the grounds that the police did not have a warrant to search his home. While the Supreme Court had previously permitted such broad searches in *United States v. Rabinowitz*, 339 U.S. 56 (1950), the *Chimel* Court confined the scope of the search incident to arrest to: (1) a search of the arrestee; and (2) the physical area within the arrestee's immediate control, commonly referred to as the "grab-reach" area.

The *Chimel* Court found that it was reasonable for the arresting officer to search the person arrested in order to remove any weapons that might be used to resist arrest or effect an escape, and to seize any evidence on the arrestee in order to prevent its concealment or destruction. The Court reasoned that "a gun on a table or in a drawer in front of one who is arrested can be as dangerous to the arresting officer as one concealed in the clothing of the person arrested." The Court also stated that any further searches beyond the person of the arrestee should be confined to "the area into which an arrestee might reach in order to grab a weapon or evidentiary items." Searches beyond the immediate grab-reach area of the arrestee are beyond the limited scope of the search incident to arrest exception.

B. *United States v. Robinson:* The Automatic Search Rule

The holding in *Chimel* appeared to restrict the mission of the search incident to arrest to securing weapons and preventing evidence destruction. In *United States v. Robinson*, 414 U.S. 218 (1973), however, the Court clarified that the government's power to search arrestees extends well beyond a search for weapons and destructible evidence. In *Robinson*, the defendant was arrested for driving while having an expired driver's license. After being placed under arrest, the officer reached into the defendant's coat pocket and retrieved a crumbled cigarette packet which, upon inspection, revealed 14 capsules of heroin. The lower court held that retrieval of the package from Robinson's pocket and inspection of the contents exceeded the limited goal of securing weapons and preventing evidence destruction. The court reasoned that the officer had no basis for concluding the package in Robinson's coat was a weapon. The court also stated that there would have been no additional evidence related to the traffic offense on his person.

The Supreme Court held in *Robinson* that arrestees have no Fourth Amendment protection against searches of their person and their personal belongings, regardless of whether there is any reason to believe that the arrestee is armed or might be in possession of evidence related to the crime. The Court stated that "[a] custodial arrest of a suspect based on probable cause is a reasonable intrusion under the Fourth Amendment; that intrusion being lawful, a search incident to the arrest requires no additional justification." Thus, post-*Robinson*, police have an automatic right to conduct a "full-blown" search of all arrestees, including a search of their person, inspection of all personal belongings in their possession, and seizure of any incriminating evidence related or unrelated to the underlying arrest. As discussed in Chapter 7, the Supreme

Court has extended the automatic search incident to arrest rule to allow limited searches of automobiles incident to the arrest of motorists.

C. The Scope of the Search Incident to Arrest Exception

1. The Requirement of a Custodial Arrest

The search incident to arrest rule applies only when the police exercise their authority, with or without a warrant, to place an individual under custodial arrest. If state law gives the police officer the discretion to either issue a citation or place the individual under arrest, a "grab-reach" search can only be conducted if the officer elects to make a custodial arrest. There is no "search incident to citation" exception to the warrant requirement. *Knowles v. Iowa*, 525 U.S. 113 (1998). In *Robinson*, the Court recognized that "the danger to an officer is far greater in the case of the extended exposure which follows the taking of a suspect into custody and transporting him to the police station." By contrast, the *Knowles* Court found that "the threat to officer safety from issuing a traffic citation ... is a good deal less than in the case of a custodial arrest."

2. Probable Cause to Arrest

Just as there can be no search incident to citation, the Court will not allow the government to use evidence secured during a search incident to an arrest not supported by probable cause. As discussed in Chapter 4, in order for an arrest to be valid, the government must have probable cause to believe that the person has committed a crime. If the police lack the requisite facts to meet the probable cause standard, the arrest is not lawful and the proceeds of the search are subject to suppression under the exclusionary rule (see Chapter12). The Court has long held that "[a]n arrest may not be used as a pretext to search for evidence." *United States v. Lefkowitz*, 285 U.S. 452 (1932). Thus, the police must have probable cause before the arrest and independent of information obtained during the search. *Sibron v. New York*, 392 U.S. 40 (1968). While the actual arrest will usually precede the search of the arrestee, that sequence is not dictated by the Fourth Amendment. In *Rawlings v. Kentucky*, 448 U.S. 98 (1980), the Court held that as long as probable cause to arrest existed and the formal arrest "followed quickly on the heels of" the search of the suspect, the search is within the scope of the search incident to arrest rule.

In recent cases, the Court has made clear that probable cause — not state law — dictates whether an arrest and the accompanying search incident to that arrest is constitutional. In *Virginia v. Moore*, 553 U.S. 164 (2008), the Court upheld a search incident to arrest where the officers had probable cause to believe the arrestee was driving with a suspended license. While the Court acknowledged that state law only authorized the officer to issue a summons and did not authorize the officers to make a custodial arrest for this minor traffic infraction, the Court upheld the search. The Court reasoned that an arrest is "lawful" even if not authorized by state law as long as the arrest is based on probable cause.

Similarly, in *Atwater v. Lago Vista*, 532 U.S. 318 (2001), state law authorized officers to make full custodial arrests for very minor "fine only" traffic offenses. The Court found that an arrest for an extremely minor offense is not an "unreasonable seizure" of the defendant in violation of the Fourth Amendment as long as there is probable cause to arrest. Thus, *Moore* and *Atwater* have vastly expanded the scope of the government's power to conduct searches of people by allowing custodial arrests and accompanying "full blown" searches of individuals who have committed extremely minor, non-criminal traffic infractions.

3. Spatial Proximity: The Theoretical "Grab-Reach" Limitation

The "grab-reach" limitation articulated by the Court in *Chimel* has been very liberally construed by courts to include searches of the area within the immediate vicinity of the arrest, even when there is no physical possibility that the arrestee could secure a weapon or contraband. Since *Chimel*, lower courts have upheld searches conducted after the arrestee has been placed in handcuffs, after the arrestee has being removed from the room, and even after the arrestee is placed in the police car and transported to the police station. *United States v. McLaughlin*, 170 F.3d 889 (9th Cir. 1999); *United States v. Queen*, 847 F.2d 346 (7th Cir. 1988) (upholding search where arrestee was handcuffed and guarded by two armed officers before searching closet three feet away). Thus, the original justification of preventing the suspect from gaining access to weapons or destructible evidence has been largely abandoned by lower courts. As now interpreted by lower courts, incident to a lawful arrest, police are allowed to search any area in arm's reach of the location where the arrestee was taken into custody from which the arrestee could have "*theoretically*" obtained a weapon if the police had not restrained him and removed him from the scene of the crime. The rationale for this expansive interpretation seems to be that there is always the remote possibility that the arrestee might "break free" from custody and obtain a weapon to harm the officers and/or attempt to destroy incriminating evidence. This interpretation of the search incident to arrest power may be overbroad in light of the Court's recent ruling in *Arizona v. Gant*, 129 S. Ct. 1710 (2009), which significantly restricted the power of police to conduct car searches incident to the arrest of a motorist. (See Chapter 7.)

4. Temporal Proximity: When Is the Search "Incident to" the Arrest

The premise behind the search incident to arrest is the dual dangers of taking a person into custody and preventing access to nearby weapons and destructible evidence. In most cases when a custodial arrest is made, the issue of temporal proximity does not arise because the need to secure weapons and prevent evidence destruction dictates the need for a swift—almost simultaneous—on-the-scene search of the arrestee and personal effects in the arrestee's possession. In some cases, however, the police do not conduct the search of the arrestee right away. The Court has held that a search can be so remote in time and place from the original arrest that the two events become detached. In such cases, courts have held that the government must obtain a warrant to conduct a search of the arrestee's property. *Preston v. United States*, 376 U.S. 364 (1964) (warrantless searches of property seized at the time of an arrest cannot be justified as incident to the arrest if the search is "remote in time or place from the arrest").

IV. Searches of Personal "Effects"

An individual's personal effects are generally either on their person, in their clothing, or enclosed in some form of container (*i.e.*, luggage, purse, backpack). The Court allows searches of the personal belongings of an arrestee if the requirements of the search incident to arrest exception are met or, for arrestees subsequently confined at the stationhouse, the requirements of an inventory search are met.

A. Search of Personal Effects Incident to Arrest

Robinson makes clear that a search incident to arrest includes a search of personal belongings within the immediate possession of the arrestee. As the Court expressly stated in *Robinson*, the arresting officer's right to conduct a search of the arrestee is not dependent on the "*probability*" that evidence or weapons will be found. Thus, police officers are free to conduct a "suspicionless" search for any incriminating evidence that the arrestee happens to have among his or her personal belongings. Lower courts have found that the search incident to arrest exception includes bags, *United States v. Morales*, 923 F.2d 621 (8th Cir. 1991), luggage, *United States v. Talvolacci*, 895 F.2d 1423 (D.C. Cir. 1990), back packs, *People v. Boff*, 766 P.2d 646 (Colo. 1988), and even a wallet, *United States v. Passaro*, 624 F.2d 938 (9th Cir. 1980) (including photocopying papers contained in wallet). More recently, a court allowed officers to seize a cell phone, open it and retrieve the telephone numbers called and the text messages sent and received on the phone. *See United States v. Finley*, 477 F.3d 250 (5th Cir. 2007).

Pursuant to this broad authority, if the police arrest a suspect for drug possession, they can search through all items with the grab-reach area of the arrestee, even if their motivation is to search for child pornography, illegal gambling receipts, stolen credit cards, or any other evidence unrelated to the drug arrest. In this respect, the search incident to arrest gives the police broader authority than they have when conducting searches pursuant to a valid search warrant. As discussed in Chapter 4, a search warrant requires the police to state with specificity what they are looking for and restricts their search to those areas where the identified items could be located (*i.e.*, they cannot look for a gun inside a flat, sealed envelope).

Although the power to conduct warrantless searches of arrestees and their belongings is very broad, it is not limitless. Intrusive searches involving the collection of bodily fluids for drug or alcohol detection are generally beyond the scope of a search incident to arrest, absent extraordinary circumstances and demonstrated necessity. *Schmerber v. California*, 384 U.S. 757 (1966) (forced extraction of blood). Likewise, strip searches are well beyond the scope of a routine search incident to arrest. *Illinois v. Lafayette*, 462 U.S. 640 (1983) ("the interests supporting a search incident to arrest would hardly justify disrobing an arrestee on the street").

B. Post-Arrest Inventory Search

After an arrestee has been transported to the police station for the "booking" process, police departments routinely examine the contents of any bags and other personal items in the possession of the arrestee, especially if the arrestee will be jailed. While inventory searches are frequently employed by police in searching impounded vehicles (see Chapter 7), the Court has extended the inventory search exception to the warrantless removal and examination of an arrestee's personal possessions. *Illinois v. Lafayette*, 462 U.S. 640 (1983). The Supreme Court has stated that the individual's privacy interest in personal belongings is outweighed by the government's interest in: (1) preventing the introduction of contraband or weapons into the facility; (2) preventing the theft or careless handling of the arrestee's personal belongings by law enforcement staff; (3) deterring false claims of stolen property filed by arrestees against the police department; and (4) assisting police in verifying the identity of the arrestee. Inventory searches are only permitted when the police department has lawful possession of the property and when officers are acting pursuant to valid police department regulations that define the scope of such searches and provide adequate guidance and restrictions on the discretionary authority of an officer in conducting an inventory search.

In *Illinois v. Lafayette*, 462 U.S. 640 (1983), the defendant was placed under lawful custodial arrest and transported to the police stationhouse. At the time of his arrest, the defendant had in his possession a "purse-type shoulder bag." Upon arrival at the police station, officers removed the contents of the bag and found drugs concealed within a cigarette case. The Court found that it was reasonable for police officers to conduct a warrantless search of the defendant's bag "as part of the routine administrative procedure at a police stationhouse incident to booking and jailing the suspect." The Court stated that such searches were "an incidental administrative step following arrest and preceding incarceration." The Court also stated that "it is not 'unreasonable' for police, as part of the routine procedure incident to incarcerating an arrested person, to search any container or article in his possession, in accordance with established inventory procedures." The so-called "search incident to incarceration" or "stationhouse search" is a form of non-investigative, administrative search that does not require probable cause or a warrant, but must be conducted pursuant to the established administrative procedures of the police department.

Checkpoints

- Searches of persons are proscribed by the Fourth Amendment and are deemed unreasonable if not conducted pursuant to a warrant or an exception to the warrant requirement.

- Police are sometimes permitted to conduct searches of persons that the police have the lawful authority to seize, though the permissible scope of the search ("full blown" versus "pat down") will vary depending on whether the individual is subject to temporary investigative detention or is under arrest.

- Searches of persons during *Terry* stops are limited to a "frisk" for weapons when there is reasonable, articulable suspicion that the person is armed.

- Searches of persons incident to a lawful arrest are automatic and include a search for weapons and incriminating evidence on or within the grab-reach area of the arrestee or contained within the arrestee's personal possessions.

- If the police do not make a custodial arrest or if the arrest (with or without a warrant) is not supported by probable cause, the search incident to arrest exception to the warrant requirement does not apply.

- Searches of personal belongings in the possession of the arrestee at the time of arrest are included within the search incident to arrest exception.

- If the arrestee is to be jailed at the stationhouse, the police are also permitted to examine and inventory the arrestee's personal belongings in order to prevent theft, false claims and ensure dangerous items are not introduced into the facility. Inventory searches of personal belongings can only be conducted when the police have lawful possession of the property and are acting pursuant to valid police department regulations that define the scope of discretionary authority that can be exercised by the officer conducting the search.

Chapter 7

Searches of Cars

Roadmap

- Visual inspections and tracking of cars
- Automobile searches during non-custodial traffic stops
- Pretextual traffic stops and racial profiling
- Searches of automobiles incident to lawful custodial arrests of motorists
- The automobile exception to the warrant requirement
- Administrative Inventory searches of impounded automobiles

There are a myriad of circumstances that occur during the course of a criminal investigation that give police officers the lawful authority to conduct warrantless searches and seizures of automobiles. Whether the police pull a car over for a routine traffic stop or pursue a fleeing felon in a high-speed car chase, there are constitutional boundaries that govern the extent to which the police can search the occupants of a car, examine personal belongings in the vehicle, and examine other enclosed compartments in the automobile.

I. "Non-Search" Investigations of Vehicles

As with all other government investigative practices, the starting point of the Fourth Amendment analysis of car searches is whether the government conduct was in fact a "search" or a "seizure." As discussed in Chapters 2 and 3, there is a wide range of non-intrusive investigative practices that neither intrude into an area where an individual has a reasonable expectation of privacy nor involve any meaningful interference with an individual's possessory interests. Consequently, these techniques are not proscribed by the Fourth Amendment. Thus, in investigating vehicles, police officers can engage in many different investigative practices that do not involve entering the vehicle or conducting a physical examination of the contents of a car. These include following a car on a public street or placing a beeper or other tracking device on the vehicle. Also, because an individual does not have a reasonable expectation of privacy in information knowingly exposed to the public, the Fourth Amendment does not prohibit a police officer from peering inside the window of a parked car with the naked eye or with a flashlight. The Supreme Court has held that this level of vehicle investigation is not a "search" and is, therefore, outside of the scope of the Fourth Amendment.

II. Automobile Searches during Non-Custodial Traffic Stops

As discussed in Chapter 4, when police observe a traffic violation and order a car to pull over, the driver and all of the occupants of the vehicle are seized for purposes of the Fourth Amendment. *Brendlin v. California*, 551 U.S. 249 (2007). If the police have observed a traffic violation, the seizure is reasonable and the officer is permitted to lawfully detain the occupants for a reasonable period of time to process the traffic citation. This can include running a records check to determine whether driver has valid license and registration, determining whether the car is stolen, and investigating whether the driver has any outstanding warrants. As a general rule, however, police officers do not have the authority to conduct "full-blown" searches of the occupants or the vehicle during a routine traffic stop.

For non-custodial traffic violations where the police officer simply issues a ticket and allows the motorist to leave, police officers have limited authority to search the occupants and the vehicle. The Supreme Court has stated that the officer's authority during these non-custodial traffic stops is akin to the police authority to conduct limited investigative detentions under *Terry v. Ohio*, discussed in Chapter 4. In recognition of the potential dangers that exist for officers during roadside encounters, the Court has allowed officers to take reasonable steps to ensure that the driver and the passengers of the vehicle are not armed and dangerous. Accordingly, the officer has the right to order the driver and all of the passengers to exit the vehicle. *Pennsylvania v. Mimms*, 434 U.S. 106 (1977); *Maryland v. Wilson*, 519 U.S. 408 (1997). If the officer has reasonable, articulable suspicion that the driver or any passenger is armed, the officer is also permitted to frisk the occupants and seize any weapons that could be used against the officer. *Arizona v. Johnson*, 129 S. Ct. 781 (2009).

A. *Terry* Automobile Searches

During a lawful traffic stop, police officers can conduct a limited search for weapons in the interior passenger compartment of the car if the officer has reasonable suspicion that the suspect poses a danger to an officer's safety due to the presence of weapons in the vehicle. In *Michigan v. Long*, 463 U.S. 1032 (1983), after the defendant's car swerved into a ditch, the officers asked the defendant for his vehicle registration. When the defendant walked towards his car, the officer shined a flashlight inside the car to check for weapons and saw a hunting knife on the floor near the driver's seat. The officer then observed a pouch protruding under the armrest. The officer retrieved both items and a subsequent search of the pouch revealed marijuana. In response to the defendant's motion to suppress the drugs, the Court recognized that "roadside encounters between police and suspects are especially hazardous, and that danger may arise from the possible presence of weapons in the area surrounding a suspect." The Court then stated that "the search of the passenger compartment of an automobile, limited to those areas in which a weapon may be placed or hidden, is permissible" if the police officer possesses reasonable, articulable suspicion that the suspect is dangerous and may gain immediate control of a weapon.

The Court was careful to note that in order to engage in a *Terry* area search of a vehicle, the officer must have a reasonable belief that the motorist will arm himself if permitted to reenter the vehicle. Also, the *Terry* area search must be narrowly tailored to include only a search for weapons and not the discovery or preservation of incriminating evidence. *See United States v. Diaz*, 519 F.3d 56 (1st Cir. 2008) (*Long* search proper where car involved in a shooting earlier in the evening); *United States v. Christian*, 187 F.3d 663 (D.C. Cir. 1999) (*Long* search permissible where officers saw a dagger in the car and reasoned that there might be additional weapons). The Court acknowledged, however, that officers are permitted to seize contraband or other incriminating evidence they see in plain view during the course of a lawful weapons search of the passenger compartment of the vehicle. (See Chapter 10.)

B. Investigating Unrelated Criminal Activity

During a lawful traffic stop, police officers also have the limited authority to investigate criminal activity that is completely unrelated to the traffic violation. Even without reasonable suspicion, the officer can have a narcotics detection dog sniff the exterior of the car to determine whether drugs are inside. *Illinois v. Caballes*, 543 U.S. 405 (2005) (see Chapter 2). The officer can also pose incriminating questions to the occupants of the vehicle without informing them of their *Miranda* rights, because they are not in custody during a routine traffic stop. *Berkemer v. McCarty*, 468 U.S. 420 (1984). If any of these investigative activities extend the duration of the traffic stop, however, the seizure becomes unreasonable and all evidence recovered during this extended period of time is subject to suppression under the exclusionary rule. Also, as discussed in Chapter 8, the officer can ask the motorists for consent to conduct a "full blown" search of the entire car. In so doing, the officer need not first inform the motorists that they are free to leave or that they have the right to refuse to consent to the search of their vehicle. *Ohio v. Robinette*, 519 U.S. 33 (1996).

C. Pretextual Traffic Stops and Racial Profiling

Given the volume of traffic laws in each jurisdiction that must be obeyed by motorists, police officers have very broad authority to stop cars in order to enforce these laws and protect public safety. While police officers regularly stop cars for speeding and other more serious safety violations, police officers also may conduct lawful traffic stops for extremely minor civil infractions (*i.e.*, broken taillight, seatbelt violations, failure to use a turn signal). As has been observed by legal scholars and others, if police officers follow any car long enough, eventually they can justify stopping the driver for violating one of the many traffic laws. Thus, the authority to enforce traffic laws also vests police officers with the power to use the traffic laws to stop cars and investigate unrelated criminal activity. In jurisdictions across the country, police departments have abused this power by engaging in race-based traffic stops, commonly referred to as "racial profiling." There have been numerous civil lawsuits filed by racial profiling victims across the country. In addition, there have been several local and national studies of traffic stops which demonstrate that in many jurisdictions minority motorists are pulled over by police at a significantly higher rate than their white counterparts.

In *Whren v. United States*, 517 U.S. 806 (1996), the Court had the opportunity to curtail the power of police officers to stop motorists under the pretext of issuing a citation for an extremely minor traffic infraction and then use the traffic stop to conduct a more intrusive, unrelated criminal investigation. In *Whren*, officers observed young African-American occupants in a dark-colored truck with temporary license plates. The officers became suspicious when the car remained at the stop sign for "an unusually long time—more than 20 seconds." After the police executed a U-turn to stop the car and give the driver an oral warning, the driver made a sudden turn without using a turn signal and drove off at an "unreasonable" speed. The officers then stopped the car to give the driver a warning, and, incredibly, observed a large quantity of drugs in the driver's hands in plain view.

The defendant argued that, at best, the police officers' decision to stop the car for such a minor traffic violation was a pretext to conduct an unrelated warrantless search for evidence, and, at worse, the officers were engaged in racial profiling. The Court held that "the constitutional basis for objecting to intentionally discriminatory application of laws is the Equal Protection Clause, not the Fourth Amendment." The Court rejected any constitutional analysis of the reasonableness of the seizure based on the ulterior motives or subjective intentions of the officers. The Court held that if police officers have probable cause to believe that any traffic laws are violated, the subsequent traffic stop is a reasonable seizure under the Fourth Amendment.

The Court's holding in *Whren* effectively placed the pervasive practice of racial profiling during traffic stops beyond the reach of the Fourth Amendment. Post-*Whren*, several states have passed legislation designed to redress racial profiling and, as discussed in Chapter 8, several states have placed significant restrictions on the authority of police officers to conduct "suspicionless" consent searches that commonly accompany race-based and other pretextual traffic stops.

III. Searches of Automobiles Incident to Custodial Arrest of Motorists

A. Overview

In *Chimel v. California*, 395 U.S. 752 (1969), the Court held that, incident to a lawful arrest of a person in their home, police officers are permitted to conduct a limited search of the area in the residence that is within the arrestee's immediate control in order to secure any weapons and prevent the destruction of evidence. (See Chapter 6) In *New York v. Belton*, 453 U.S. 454 (1981), the Court applied the *Chimel* search incident to arrest rule to searches of automobiles incident to the arrest of a motorist. The Court ruled that when an occupant of a car is arrested, the area "within the arrestee's immediate control" that can be searched incident to the arrest is limited to the interior passenger compartment of the car. In *Thornton v. United States*, 541 U.S. 615 (2004), the *Belton* search incident to arrest rule was extended to allow the search of cars upon the arrest of a "recent occupant" of the vehicle. More recently, in *Arizona v. Gant*, 129 S. Ct. 1710 (2009), the Court restricted warrantless searches of vehicles incident to the arrest of an occupant or recent occupant of the car to two scenarios: (1) when the arrestee is unsecured and could gain access to the car; and (2) when there is reason to believe that evidence related to the offense of arrest is contained in the car.

B. *New York v. Belton*

In *Belton*, a police officer observed a car driving at excessive speed and pulled the car over. The officer smelled burnt marijuana and saw an envelope on the floor of the car marked "Supergold" which the officer associated with marijuana. The officer then ordered the driver and the occupants to exit the vehicle and placed each of them under arrest for possession of marijuana. The officer then retrieved the envelope from the car and found marijuana inside. Though all occupants were at a safe distance outside of the car, the officer conducted a thorough search of the interior passenger compartment of the car, including a black jacket on the back seat that belonged to passenger Belton. The officer unzipped the jacket pocket and recovered a quantity of cocaine. The defendant moved to suppress the cocaine, arguing that the officer's search of the jacket was beyond the scope of a permissible search incident to arrest. In upholding the car search, the Court held that such searches are limited to the interior passenger compartment of the car and can include any locked containers located in the interior passenger compartment that could contain contraband or evidence, as well as any enclosed storage areas in the passenger compartment (*i.e.* glove box, armrest storage area). The *Belton* rule applies with equal force to the driver and any of the passengers who are placed under lawful custodial arrest.

C. *Thornton v. United States*

In *Thornton*, the Court extended the *Belton* rule to cases where the police officer first initiates contact with the arrestee after the arrestee has exited the car and has become, essentially, a pedestrian. In *Thornton*, the police officer noticed that petitioner was acting suspiciously and, upon running a check on the vehicle tags, learned that the tags on the car were registered to another car. Before the officer ordered the defendant to pull over, the defendant parked his car in a parking lot and exited the vehicle. The officer approached to request his driver's license and requested permission to search him. When the defendant agreed to a search, the officer recovered a large quantity of drugs from his pocket and placed him under arrest. The officer then searched the vehicle and found an illegal handgun under the driver's seat.

The *Thornton* Court rejected the defendant's contention that the search of the car was unlawful since the defendant was not arrested in the car and his arrest was not related to the car. The Court found that the *Belton* rule also extended to recent occupants of vehicles. The Court reasoned that "the arrest of a suspect who is next to a vehicle presents identical concerns regarding officer safety and the destruction of evidence as the arrest of one who is inside the vehicle." The Court held that while the police officer's authority to search the car does not turn on whether the arrestee was inside or outside of the car at the time of the arrest, in order to establish that an arrestee was a "recent occupant" of a vehicle, the government must show that the arrestee was in close proximity to the vehicle—both temporally and spatially—at the time of the arrest. *United States v. Booker*, 496 F.3d 717 (D.C. Cir. 2007) (*Thornton* spatial and temporal proximity requirements were met where the police were unable to catch up with defendant until after he parked his car and was walking away); *but see State v. Dean*, 76 P.3d 429 (Ariz. 2003) (no *Belton* search allowed where the defendant was arrested over two hours after he ignored officer's request to pull his car over, drove home, parked his car, ran inside, and hid in the attic); *Gauldin v. State*, 683 S.W.2d 411 (Tex. Crim. App. 1984) (search of the defendant's parked truck was not valid under *Belton/Thornton* rule where the defendant drove the truck to the bar less than hour before his arrest, was approached by the police while in the bar, and then arrested outside in parking lot).

D. *Arizona v. Gant*

Post-*Belton*, lower courts widely interpreted the holding in *Belton* as giving police officers an automatic entitlement to search the interior of every vehicle incident to the arrest of a motorist or recent occupant of the car, regardless of whether there was any possibility that the arrestee could access weapons or evidence in the car. In *Arizona v. Gant*, 129 S. Ct. 1710 (2009), the Supreme Court flatly rejected this broad interpretation of *Belton* and placed significant restrictions on car searches incident to a lawful arrest. In *Gant*, when police officers investigating a drug trafficking tip arrived at the targeted residence, they were met by Gant. Gant identified himself and informed the officers that the homeowner was not present. A subsequent records check on Gant revealed that his driver's license was suspended and that there was an outstanding warrant for his arrest for driving with a suspended license. Shortly after the officers returned to the residence, they arrested two other persons on the premises for minor offenses and placed each of them in handcuffs in patrol cars. Thereafter, Gant drove up to the residence and parked his car. The officers watched as Gant exited his vehicle, closed the car door, and began walking towards the house. When Gant was approximately 12 feet from the car, the officers arrested him for the driver's license violation, handcuffed him, and placed him in a police car. The officers then searched the interior passenger compartment of Gant's car and recovered a gun and a bag of cocaine. Gant moved to suppress the evidence and argued that the search of his car was unconstitutional because he was already handcuffed and secured inside the police car before the search was initiated.

The Supreme Court reaffirmed the holding in *Chimel* that the search incident to lawful arrest serves the dual goals of allowing police officers to seize weapons and secure destructible evidence located in close proximity to the arrestee. The Court stated, however, that "[i]f there is no possibility that an arrestee could reach into the area that law enforcement officers seek to search, both justifications for the search-incident-to-arrest exception are absent and the rule does not apply." Thus, the Court concluded that the holding in *Belton* did not allow car searches "when there is no realistic possibility that an arrestee could access his vehicle."

In arguing for the continuation of the broad interpretation of *Belton*, the government maintained that the automatic search rule that had been in place for 28 years was reasonable because it struck the correct balance between law enforcement interests and the arrestee's reduced expectation of privacy in the vehicle. The Court disagreed and stated:

> A rule that gives police the power to conduct such a search whenever an individual is caught committing a traffic offense, when there is no basis for believing evidence of the offense might be found in the vehicle, creates a serious and recurring threat to the privacy of countless individuals. Indeed, the character of that threat implicates the central concern underlying the Fourth Amendment—the concern about giving police officers unbridled discretion to rummage at will among a person's private effects.

The Court further noted that as a result of the broad interpretation of *Belton*, "[c]ountless individuals guilty of nothing more serious than a traffic violation have had their constitutional right to the security of their private effects violated." Therefore, the Court ruled that when an occupant or recent occupant of an automobile is arrested, the police can only conduct a search incident to arrest if: *(1)* "the arrestee is unsecured and within reaching distance of the passenger compartment at the time of the search;" or (2) "it is reasonable to believe evidence relevant to the crime of arrest might be found in the vehicle."

1. The "Unsecured" Arrestee and the "Possibility of Access" to the Vehicle

Even as the Court in *Gant* recognized the importance of allowing vehicle searches to prevent arrestees from accessing weapons concealed in the vehicle, the Court acknowledged that only in exceptional cases will an arrestee actually pose a genuine threat to officer safety. Specifically, the Court noted that "[b]ecause officers have many means of ensuring the safe arrest of vehicle occupants, it will be *the rare case* in which an officer is unable to fully effectuate an arrest so that a real possibility of access to the arrestee's vehicle remains." Thus, the Court stated that the threat to officer safety must exist "*at the time of the search*." While the Court did not elaborate on the range of circumstances that might constitute a valid threat to officer safety, the Court noted that in *Belton* the threat existed because that case involved "a single officer confronted with four unsecured arrestees." By contrast, *Gant* involved five officers on the scene with three suspects already handcuffed and placed in squad cars prior to the search.

2. A "Reason to Believe" Arrest-Related Evidence in Car

In addition to allowing *Belton* car searches when the unsecured arrestee has access to the vehicle at the time of the search, the *Gant* Court also stated that a *Belton* search is permissible if there is "*reason to believe*" that evidence related to the arrest is located in the vehicle. The Court stated that while "in many cases, as when a recent occupant is arrested for a traffic violation, there will be no reasonable basis to believe the vehicle contains relevant evidence," in other cases, "the offense of arrest will supply a basis for searching the passenger compartment of an arrestee's vehicle and any containers therein." The Court noted that in both *Belton* and *Thornton,* the officers had reason to believe that there was evidence related to the offense in the car because both cases involved arrests for drug possession. In *Belton* the officers saw the "Supergold" envelope on the floor of the car prior to the search, and in *Thornton,* the officer found drugs on the defendant's person prior to the search of the car. By contrast, in *Gant,* the police officers did not have a reasonable basis for believing that any additional evidence related to Gant's traffic offense would be located in the car.

3. Summary

The holding in *Gant* prohibits the police from automatically searching all vehicles whenever a motorist is placed under custodial arrest. Instead, *Gant* only allows such vehicle searches when an unsecured arrestee is in close proximity to the car or when, due to the nature of the offense of arrest, there is reason to believe that evidence related to the crime is contained in the car. For example, following a DUI arrest, police could justify searching the car for empty and partially consumed containers of alcohol. Likewise, if the defendant is arrested for any drug or theft-related offense, the officer may have reason to believe that proceeds of the crime are located in the car.

Though *Gant* significantly restricted the authority of the police to conduct vehicle searches incident to the arrest of the occupant of a vehicle, several key aspects of the search incident to arrest rule remain intact. First, the initial authority to conduct the automobile search incident to arrest remains contingent on probable cause to make a custodial arrest. If the police lack probable cause to arrest, any evidence uncovered during the search of the automobile is subject to suppression under the exclusionary rule. *But see Herring v. United States*, 129 S. Ct. 695 (2009) (the evidence uncovered during a search of the car incident to arrest is not excluded where the wrongful arrest was caused by an isolated and attenuated administrative error) (see Chapter 12). Also, *Belton* still mandates that the scope of the car search following arrest is strictly limited to the interior passenger compartment, and the spatial and temporal proximity restrictions imposed by *Thornton* still govern whether the vehicle of a recent occupant may be searched incident to arrest.

IV. The Automobile Exception

The automobile exception to the warrant requirement allows police officers to conduct warrantless searches of vehicles if the officer has probable cause to believe that contraband or other evidence related to criminal activity is located in the car. While the automobile exception excuses the police from obtaining a warrant from a magistrate, the exception only applies if the police have probable cause to believe that contraband is located within the car. Once the police have probable cause, the automobile exception is triggered and does not require any additional exigency or emergency circumstances. The automobile exception generally allows police to search anywhere in the car where the objects subject to seizure could be located, including the trunk, the glove compartment and any containers (*i.e.*, luggage, purses, boxes) located in the car.

A. The Automobile Exception versus Search Incident to Arrest

There are two significant differences between the permissible search of a car under the automobile exception and the scope of authority granted to police officers to search cars incident to the lawful arrest of a motorist. First, while the *Belton* rule requires the police to have probable cause to arrest an occupant of the car, the automobile exception is based solely on probable cause to believe there is contraband in the car and is not contingent on the arrest of any of the occupants of the car. Second, *Belton* searches give police the limited authority to search only the interior passenger compartment of the car, but the automobile exception potentially gives police the right to search the entire car (including the trunk) in order to locate seizable evidence.

B. A Reduced Expectation of Privacy

Since *Carroll v. United States*, 267 U.S. 132 (1925), where the Supreme Court articulated the automobile exception to the warrant requirement, the rationale for the automobile exception has evolved. This evolution has greatly expanded the scope of the exception. The original rationale for the automobile exception was the exigency created by the mobility of cars. Specifically, the Court recognized that a vehicle (and its seizable cargo) could be easily moved out of the jurisdiction before a search warrant is obtained. Thus, in *Carroll*, the Court reasoned that requiring the police to delay the search to obtain a warrant was both impracticable and a hindrance to effective law enforcement. This exigency-based rationale was widely criticized because simply authorizing the police to temporarily immobilize the vehicle until a warrant could be obtained would be a lesser intrusion on an individual's privacy and maintain the constitutional presumption in favor of magistrate-issued warrants.

In subsequent cases, the Court expanded the rationale for the automobile exception beyond mobility. In *California v. Carney*, 471 U.S. 386 (1985), the Court stated that the automobile exception was partly based on mobility and partly based on the fact that individuals have a reduced expectation of privacy in cars. The Court found the reduced privacy interest resulted from the fact that cars, unlike homes, are subject to "pervasive" government regulations, including licensing and registration requirements. Given the government's legitimate interest in detecting and prosecuting crime, the reduced privacy interest in cars is adequately protected by the probable cause requirement without the additional warrant requirement. The Court reasoned that this broader rationale justified the warrantless search of vehicles, even when police officers have ample time to secure a warrant and the vehicle is already immobilized prior to the search. *Chambers v. Maroney*, 399 U.S. 42 (1970).

C. The End of the "Container Rule"

Another evolution of the automobile exception is the elimination of the so-called "container rule." Borne out of the recognition that individuals have a much greater expectation of privacy in their personal items (*i.e.*, luggage, briefcases, and other containers) than they do in their cars, the "container rule" restricted the extent to which the police could open and examine the contents of personal containers during the course of conducting a search of a car under the automobile exception. The container rule allowed the police to seize enclosed containers without a warrant, but required the police to obtain a warrant before a search of the container would be permitted. This "cars vs. containers" clash lead to a great deal of confusion among lower courts over the distinction between "the search of an automobile that coincidentally turns up a container and the search of a container that coincidentally turns up in an automobile." *California v. Acevedo*, 500 US 565 (1991).

The container rule was eliminated in *United States v. Ross*, 456 U.S. 798 (1982). The Court held that "if probable cause justifies the search of a lawfully stopped vehicle, it justifies the search of every part of the vehicle and its contents that may conceal the object of the search." The Court noted that any continued vitality of the container rule threatened to nullify the automobile exception since, as a practical matter "[c]ontraband goods rarely are strewn across the trunk or floor of a car; since by their very nature such goods must be withheld from public view, they rarely can be placed in an automobile unless they are enclosed within some form of container." Later, in *California v. Acevedo*, 500 U.S. 565 (1991), the Court announced one clear standard to govern all automobile searches: if the police have probable cause to search a car, the police may search the entire car for the item(s) to be seized, including any containers capable of holding the seizable evidence.

D. Restrictions on the Automobile Exception

After *Ross* and *Acevedo*, there are still two restrictions on the automobile exception. First, if the police have probable cause to believe that evidence or contraband is located somewhere in the car, they can search anywhere in the car where the item could physically be located. If, however, the police have probable cause to believe that seizable evidence is located in a specific container in the car, they may only search that container and not the entire car. Thus, the Court in *Ross* stated: "probable cause to believe that undocumented aliens are being transported in a van will not justify a warrantless search of a suitcase." Likewise, the Court noted that "probable cause to believe that a container placed in the trunk of a taxi contains contraband does not justify a search of the entire cab." Moreover, the police cannot conduct a search of a car under the automobile exception unless the police have lawful access to the car. If the police, without consent or a valid warrant, access the car by entering an area where an individual has a reasonable expectation of privacy (*i.e.*, enclosed garage connected to the home), the unauthorized search of the residence to locate the car will subject any evidence uncovered in the car to suppression under the exclusionary rule.

V. Inventory Searches of Impounded Vehicles

While a large portion of the work of police officers involves criminal investigations, police departments also have other administrative or "community caretaking" functions unrelated to collecting evidence and investigating crimes. One of these administrative duties is impounding automobiles. Police departments routinely impound cars with unpaid parking tickets, abandoned cars, and vehicles damaged in traffic accidents. The police also impound cars when the operator of the vehicle is placed under custodial arrest. Once a car has been impounded and towed, police departments routinely conduct an exhaustive inventory of the contents of the car, including the trunk, glove compartment and all containers in the car.

The Supreme Court has held that inventory searches are reasonable searches under the Fourth Amendment and require neither a warrant nor probable cause. *See Colorado v. Bertine*, 479 U.S. 367 (1987); *Illinois v. Lafayette*, 462 U.S. 640 (1983) (post-arrest inventory searches of arrestee's personal belongings permissible)(see Chapter 6). The Court has recognized that inventory searches are a non-investigative, purely administrative function. Therefore, the policies underlying the warrant requirement are inapplicable and the "benign noncriminal context of the intrusion" does not necessitate that police have probable cause prior to conducting the search. *South Dakota v. Opperman*, 428 U.S. 364 (1976). As discussed more fully below, even though the purpose of the inventory search is not to gather incriminating evidence, the government is permitted to use seizable evidence found during an inventory search to prosecute the motorist.

A. Purpose of Inventory Searches

The Court has recognized that inventory searches serve three important goals: (1) protecting the property of the motorist while in police custody; (2)

protecting the police against disputes arising over lost or stolen property from the vehicle; and (3) protecting the police and the public from potential danger resulting from items left in the car (*i.e.*, unsecured weapons, chemicals, explosives). Accordingly, the Court has stated that it would be unreasonable to prohibit the police from conducting an inventory of all of the property in impounded vehicles in order to advance these legitimate interests. The Court has also stated that the availability of less intrusive means to protect the interests of the government and prevent the intrusion into the privacy rights of the car owner does not determine Fourth Amendment reasonableness. Thus, the Fourth Amendment does not require the government to employ alternatives to impoundment, *i.e.*, the use of a secure impoundment lot, giving the motorist the opportunity to make alternative arrangements for the safekeeping of the vehicle, and/or allowing the motorist to remove the contents of the vehicle.

B. Requirements for a Valid Inventory Search

Although the Court has excused the probable cause and warrant requirements, inventory searches still constitute "searches" within the scope of the Fourth Amendment. Accordingly, inventory searches must be reasonable.

1. Standard Procedure

An inventory search must be conducted pursuant to standard police procedures that delineate the scope of the permissible search and establish clear boundaries on police discretion. These standards must be carefully tailored to ensure that the intrusion occasioned by the search will be "limited in scope to the extent necessary to carry out the caretaking function." Police procedures that provide no standardized criteria to guide police officers and leave the execution of inventory searches to the unbridled discretion of the individual officer will run afoul of the Fourth Amendment.

As the Court stated in *Florida v. Wells*, 495 U.S. 1 (1990), the individual police officer must not be allowed so much latitude that inventory searches become "a ruse for a general rummaging in order to discover incriminating evidence." In *Wells*, the defendant was stopped by police for speeding, and then arrested for DUI when they smelled alcohol on his breath. The defendant's car was impounded and a search of the vehicle at the impoundment facility uncovered, among other things, a locked suitcase in the trunk. When the suitcase was forced open to inventory the contents, a large quantity of marijuana was found. The Court ruled: "the Florida Highway Patrol had no policy whatever with respect to the opening of closed containers encountered during an inventory search. We hold that absent such a policy, the instant search was not sufficiently regulated to satisfy the Fourth Amendment and that the marijuana which was found in the suitcase, therefore, was properly suppressed."

2. Good Faith

The second requirement for valid inventory searches is that the search must be executed in good faith to advance the administrative goals of inventory searches. The policy or practice governing inventory searches should be designed to actually produce an inventory of the contents of the vehicle. *Florida v. Wells*, 495 U.S. 1 (1990). Automobile searches that appear to be a "subterfuge for criminal investigations" fall outside the scope of a valid inventory search and are not reasonable searches. *Fields v. State*, 382 So. 2d 1098 (Miss. 1980) (vacuuming the car to gather particles located on the carpet was beyond the scope of a valid inventory search).

3. Limited Scope

The police department regulations governing inventory searches must be sufficiently limited in scope to carry out the administrative functions for a valid inventory search. Regulations that permit the police to routinely rip open seat cushions and dismantle components of the car will likely exceed the non-investigative goals of protecting property and ensuring public safety. However, the Court in *South Dakota v. Opperman*, 428 U.S. 364 (1976), made clear that inventory searches can legitimately include securing items that are not in plain view and opening locked compartments. *See Johnson v. State*, 137 P.3d 903 (Wyo. 2006) (opening luggage permitted by police department inventory procedures); *United States v. Richardson*, 515 F.3d 74 (1st Cir. 2008) (lifting floor mats in the car during an inventory search was permissible where such searches were included in police department standard procedures).

Checkpoints

- Police officers do not need a warrant or probable cause to look inside a parked car to see any items visible to passersby or to monitor the movement of a car using either visual surveillance or tracking devices. Such non-intrusive investigative techniques do not invade an individual's reasonable expectation of privacy and, therefore, do not constitute a Fourth Amendment "search."

Checkpoints *continued*

- During a routine, non-custodial ("citation only") traffic stop, a police officer can order all occupants out of the car, but the officer can only frisk an occupant of the vehicle if the officer has reasonable, articulable suspicion that the individual is armed. Likewise, the officer is only allowed to search the interior passenger compartment of the vehicle if the officer has reasonable suspicion that the occupants have access to weapons inside the car. The "weapons only" search is limited to the interior passenger compartment of the vehicle.

- During a routine traffic stop when the occupants of a car are lawfully detained, police officers can conduct unrelated "suspicionless" investigations, including questioning the occupants of the vehicle and conducting narcotics dog sniffs on the exterior of the car.

- The invidious police practice of targeting specific motorists based on race ("racial profiling"), or engaging in other pretextual traffic stops, does not violate the Fourth Amendment prohibition against unreasonable searches and seizures, as long as the police have probable cause to stop the car for a traffic infraction. The officer's ulterior motives or subjective intentions are irrelevant to the reasonableness analysis of the Fourth Amendment.

- The warrantless search of a car incident to arrest is constitutionally permissible only if: (1) there is probable cause to arrest an occupant or recent occupant of the vehicle; (2) the arrestee is unsecured "at the time of the search" or the officer has "reason to believe" that evidence related to the arrest offense is in the vehicle; and (3) the search is confined to the interior passenger compartment of the car (including all containers and locked compartments).

- If police officers have probable cause to believe that seizable evidence is located somewhere in an automobile, due to the reduced expectation of privacy in cars, police officers can conduct a warrantless search of the vehicle under the automobile exception. The search extends to every part of the vehicle that could contain the seizable evidence, including the trunk and any containers.

- Acting pursuant to detailed departmental regulations, police officers are permitted to conduct searches of impounded vehicles in order to create an inventory of all of the contents of the car. The regulations must delineate the permissible scope of the inventory search and must provide appropriate restrictions on the exercise of discretionary authority by the officer performing the search. Because these administrative searches are not initiated to further any criminal investigation or gather incriminating evidence, police officers are not required to have probable cause or a warrant. Any incriminating evidence discovered during the course of a lawful inventory search, however, is properly admissible in a criminal proceeding.

Chapter 8

Consent Searches

Roadmap

- Consent as an exception to the warrant requirement
- The "totality of the circumstances" test for determining validity of consent
- Actual authority to consent to searches of homes and personal property
- Reasonable reliance on apparent authority
- Simultaneous, conflicting grants of authority to search
- Relationship between consent searches and racial profiling

I. Overview

In order for the government to engage in investigative conduct that would amount to a search (intruding into an area where an individual has a reasonable expectation of privacy) or a seizure (interfering with a possessory interest in property or restricting freedom of movement), the government must have a warrant or agents must act pursuant to a recognized exception to the warrant requirement. Otherwise, any government search or seizure is unreasonable and violates the Fourth Amendment. Most exceptions to the warrant requirement excuse the government from obtaining a warrant, but still require the government to have probable cause prior to conducting the warrantless search, see Chapter 6 (search incident to arrest), Chapter 7 (automobile searches), Chapter 9 (exigent circumstances), and Chapter 10 (plain view). By contrast, police officers are authorized to conduct consent searches when they have neither a warrant nor probable cause. With valid consent, police officers have the authority to search even when they have no cause whatsoever to believe that the individual has contraband or is in possession of any evidence related to criminal activity.

The rationale behind the consent search exception is based, in part, on a desire to encourage citizens to voluntarily assist law enforcement in investigating criminal activity based on a sense of "civic duty." In *United States v. Drayton*, 536 U.S. 194 (2002), the Court stated:

> In a society based on law, the concept of agreement and consent should be given a weight and dignity of its own. Police officers act in full accord with the law when they ask citizens for consent. It reinforces the rule of law for the citizen to advise the police of his or her wishes and for the police to act in reliance on that understanding. When this exchange takes place, it dispels inferences of coercion.

In addition, because an individual can consent to a police search at times when the police have neither probable cause to arrest nor reasonable suspicion to investigate, consent searches afford the government access to critical evidence that might not otherwise be discovered. Accordingly, the Supreme Court grants police officers wide discretion and imposes few restrictions on the authority of police officers to conduct consent searches of individuals, homes, cars, and other personal belongings.

II. The Scope of a Consent Search

Consent searches are not subject to the prohibition against general exploratory searches or "fishing expeditions" for incriminating evidence that restrain searches conducted pursuant to other exceptions to the warrant requirement. When the police act pursuant to valid consent, they are neither required to specify what they are looking for, state where they expect to find it, nor give any reason why they believe a particular individual is in possession of incriminating evidence. Whether out of fear or in an effort to deflect suspicion, individuals rarely refuse to consent or impose restrictions on the scope of their consent. As a result, under a broad, open-ended grant of authority (*i.e.*, "*Go right ahead and search wherever you want*"), there are no constitutional restrictions imposed on the geographical scope of a consent search. Police officers can search every container in every room of an entire house, open every compartment and search every container in a car, and conduct extensive searches (e.g., strip searches, body cavity searches) of any pedestrian that agrees to a search of his person. If an individual does allow only restricted access—a little known and rarely exercised power—any warrantless search outside of the scope of consent is unreasonable and violates the Fourth Amendment. Likewise, a consent search must cease immediately if an individual revokes consent.

III. Objective Reasonableness

In *Florida v. Jimeno*, 500 U.S. 248 (1991), the Court held that "the standard for measuring the scope of a suspect's consent under the Fourth Amendment is that of "objective reasonableness," or what the reasonable person would have understood the scope of consent to be under the circumstances. In *Jimeno*, the police stopped the defendant's car for a traffic violation and issued a citation. The officer also informed the defendant of his suspicion that Jimeno was transporting narcotics in the car and asked for consent to search. Upon receiving consent, the officer retrieved a brown paper bag on the floor of the car, opened it, and found cocaine. The defendant argued that the scope of his consent was limited to a generalized search of the interior of the car, and if the officer wanted to search individual containers in a car, he needed specific consent to search each container. The Court concluded that while the defendant could have limited the scope of his consent, the officer's conduct in opening the bag was reasonable. The Court reasoned that the officer told the defendant in advance that he wanted to search for narcotics, and narcotics are usually enclosed in some form of container.

Applying the objective reasonableness standard articulated in *Jimeno*, lower courts have held that it is unreasonable for an officer to believe that the scope of a general consent to search includes actions that cause property destruction or entail opening, locked or sealed containers in the geographical area of the search. *United States v. Strickland*, 902 F.2d 937 (11th Cir. 1990) (consent to search car did not include slashing open spare tire); *Cross v. State*, 560 So. 2d 228 (Fla. 1990) (consent to search tote bag did not include permission to break open sealed containers inside); *State v. Wells*, 539 So. 2d 464 (Fla. 1989) (unreasonable to believe scope of consent to search trunk extended to breaking open locked briefcase in trunk).

IV. What Is Valid Consent?

Valid consent to a search exists when an individual, without any form of official coercion, "freely and voluntarily" allows police officers to search a private area where there is a reasonable expectation of privacy (*i.e.*, inside a car, a dwelling, a personal container). Generally, there must be some affirmative assent to the intrusion before courts will find that the person consented. Mere acquiescence in the absence of protest or silence in the face of a request to search generally will not suffice to establish valid consent. Once the person has affirmatively agreed to allow the police to conduct a search, the threshold questions that must be resolved in order to determine the validity of consent are: (1) whether consent was voluntary; and (2) whether the consenting party had the authority to give consent.

A. Voluntariness and the "Totality of the Circumstances" Test

In order for consent to be valid, it must be voluntarily given. If the police coerce or induce a person to give consent through express or implied pressure, consent will be deemed involuntary, and any subsequent search will be unreasonable. The starting point for the analysis of the voluntariness requirement is *Schneckloth v. Bustamonte*, 412 U.S. 218 (1973). In *Schneckloth*, the Court held that the failure of the police to advise the defendant of his right to refuse the requested search did not, per se, render his consent involuntary. The Court found that the failure to inform the defendant of his right to refuse to give consent is but one factor in the "totality of the circumstances" that must be taken into account in determining voluntariness.

In addition to announcing the "totality of the circumstances" standard, the *Schneckloth* Court also specifically rejected the notion that, like the *Miranda* warnings required during custodial interrogation (see Chapter 14), police should be required to obtain informed consent before a consent search is deemed constitutionally valid. The Court reasoned that while *Miranda*-type warnings are mandated because of concerns regarding overbearing police tactics during incommunicado interrogations, consent searches normally occur "on a person's own familiar territory." The Court also flatly rejected the contention that voluntary consent is akin to a waiver of constitutional rights, which requires "an intentional relinquishment or abandonment of a known right or privilege." The Court reasoned that the "knowing and intelligent" waiver standard is limited to trial rights (e.g., waiver of the right to counsel, waiver of trial for guilty plea). Accordingly, no *Miranda*-style warnings—indeed, no warnings of any kind—are necessary to render consent to search voluntary. If an officer chooses to inform a suspect that he has the right to refuse consent, however, such disclosure would favor a finding that consent was voluntary.

Under the *Schneckloth* "totality of the circumstances" test, the Court balances several factors to determine whether the person has voluntarily (albeit unwittingly) consented to a warrantless search. While the Court has repeatedly refused to find that any single factor will *per se* render consent involuntary, some factors have had a more significant impact on the voluntariness analysis.

1. Degree of Police Coerciveness

The Supreme Court has stated that "[c]onsent that is the product of official intimidation or harassment is not consent at all." *Florida v. Bostick*, 501 U.S. 429 (1991). Notwithstanding, in *United States v. Drayton*, 536 U.S. 194 (2002), the Court found that voluntary consent can occur even when several police officers approach passengers in the cramped confines of a crowded bus and request permission to search them and their belongings for drugs. In *Drayton*, the defendant moved to suppress the packets of drugs found during a consent search of his person, arguing that his consent was not voluntary because the officer never informed him of his right to refuse to cooperate. The Court re-affirmed its ruling in *Schneckloth*, stating that there is no "presumption of invalidity" if a citizen consents to a search without explicit notification that he or she was free to refuse to cooperate with the police investigation. In applying the "totality of the circumstances" analysis, the Court noted that the officers asked for (but did not demand) permission to search, and spoke to the defendant in a polite, conversational tone. The Court also noted that the officers did not brandish a weapon, make intimidating statements, or block the defendant's path to prevent him from leaving the bus. Relying heavily on the absence of police coercion, the *Drayton* Court found that the defendant's consent was voluntarily given.

Post-*Drayton*, Supreme Court cases suggest that the use of coercive police action is the lynchpin of the voluntariness determination. While other factors remain relevant in the "totality of the circumstances" analysis, recent cases seem to imply that, absent coercive police action, the Court is inclined to find that the defendant acted voluntarily. Accordingly, the non-exhaustive list of police conduct that courts have found to create an atmosphere of coercion antithetical to voluntarily consent includes: (1) physical violence and/or the use of any form of physical restraint; (2) the use of threats and intimidation; or (3) a show of force, including brandishing a gun. In addition, courts have found consent involuntary when consent was given only after the police threatened to get a warrant (when they knew they lacked probable cause), or when police officers falsely stated that they already had a warrant. *See Bumper v. North Carolina*, 391 U.S. 543 (1968).

2. Custodial Status

The fact that a person is lawfully seized, in custody, or is being detained at the time consent is requested and given does not automatically render consent involuntary. Custodial status is but one factor in the totality of the circumstances to be considered in determining voluntariness. Thus, the fact that the police ask for consent after a lawful traffic stop, but before telling the motorist he is free to leave, does not render the subsequent consent to search involuntary. *Ohio v. Robinette*, 519 U.S. 33 (1996) (finding it "unrealistic" to mandate that police officers always inform detainees that they are free to go before their consent to a search is deemed voluntary). Likewise, the fact that a person is under arrest at the time consent is given does not make consent involuntary. In *United States v. Watson*, 423 U.S. 411 (1976), the Court ruled that "the fact of custody alone has never been enough in itself to demonstrate a coerced confession or consent to search." The *Watson* Court stated that absent an "overt act or threat of force" or an "indication of more subtle forms of coercion that might flaw his judgment," consent was voluntary and the subsequent warrantless search was valid.

3. Characteristics of the Suspect

Facts tending to suggest that the defendant is particularly vulnerable and susceptible to manipulation are another component in the voluntariness analysis. Included among the factors that can tilt the balance towards a finding of involuntariness are: (1) educational or intelligence deficiencies; (2) mental illness or impairment; and (3) the defendant's actions prior to giving consent, including prior refusals to give consent and prior assertions of the right to counsel. The Court has stated that consent secured under these circumstances must be "carefully scrutinized to determine whether it was in fact voluntarily given." *Schneckloth v. Bustamonte*, 412 U.S. 218 (1973).

In sum, the "totality of the circumstances" test for determining voluntariness of consent requires both coercive government action and a determination that the coercive tactics actually induced the individual suspect to consent. Coercive tactics alone will not suffice to establish that consent was involuntary because the same police action that would induce a particularly vulnerable individual to consent might not be sufficient to overbear the will of a stronger, more savvy individual.

B. Authority to Consent

In addition to the voluntariness requirement, consent is invalid if the consenting party did not have the authority to give consent. This issue usually arises when a third party gives the police consent to search an area where the defendant has a reasonable expectation of privacy and the police uncover incriminating evidence against the defendant. Third party consent is commonly litigated in the context of a co-tenant who grants the police permission to search a residence shared with others. In determining whether a third party can give valid consent to a search of shared property, the Court looks to the nature of the defendant's relationship with the third party and the nature of the third party's relationship to the property. The Court has held that third party consent searches are not unreasonable if the third party had actual or apparent authority to consent to the search of the location.

1. Actual Authority

In *United States v. Matlock*, 415 U.S. 164 (1974), after the defendant was arrested on the front lawn of the home he shared with his girlfriend, police officers asked his girlfriend for permission to search the home for evidence related to the crime. The Court held that "where two persons have equal rights to the use or occupation of premises, either may give consent to a search, and the evidence thus disclosed can be used against either." The third party consent rule has also been extended to shared personal belongings. *See Frasier v. Cupp*, 394 U.S. 731 (1969) (by sharing the duffel bag with his cousin, the defendant "assumed the risk" that cousin would consent to a search of the bag). Courts have not extended consent authority to third parties who merely have a business relationship to the searched property. *See Stoner v. California*, 376 U.S. 483 (1964) (hotel clerk could not consent to search of defendant's hotel room); *Chapman v. United States*, 365 U.S. 610 (1961) (landlord could not validly consent to the search of a house rented to another).

In *Georgia v. Randolph*, 547 U.S. 103 (2006), the Court restricted the third party consent rule. The Court held that when co-occupants are present when the police request permission to search their shared dwelling and one of the occupants expressly objects to the search, the police do not have the authority to conduct a warrantless search and use incriminating evidence against the non-consenting party. The Court reasoned that co-tenants have equal (not hierarchical) rights to the premises. As such, one person cannot overrule the property interest of the other, at least where refusal to consent is expressed. The *Randolph* Court did place a very critical limitation on the "conflicting consent" rule. The rule only applies when the non-consenting party is physically present and expressly voices an objection to the search. Where opposition to the requested search is unexpressed by a co-occupant at the time of the search, the Court has held that it is reasonable for the police to initiate a search based solely on the consent received from the occupant who was present.

The narrow holding of *Randolph* creates two troubling scenarios. First, if the police have probable cause to arrest a defendant at his home, the officer could remove the arrestee who has a "self-interest in objecting" from the premises and then request permission from the co-occupant to search the dwelling. Second, even if the defendant is physically present on the premises when the police arrive, but not standing at the front door when police request consent, the Court stated in *Randolph* that "the potential objector, nearby but not invited to take part in the threshold colloquy, loses out." It is also important to note that *Randolph* only restricts the government's use of evidence against the objecting party; any evidence recovered on the premises could still be used against the co-occupant who consented to the search. Finally, the holding in *Randolph* does not prohibit a co-occupant, acting on his or her own, from retrieving evidence from the home and delivering it to the police or voluntarily supplying the police with information on the existence and location of contraband in the residence to facilitate the police obtaining a search warrant for the premises. As discussed in Chapter 2, these "private searches" are beyond the scope of the Fourth Amendment because they do not involve "government action."

2. Apparent Authority

Valid consent to search can also be obtained from persons who do not have actual authority over the premises, but reasonably appear to possess such authority. In *Illinois v. Rodriguez*, 497 U.S. 177 (1990), the Court held that police searches conducted pursuant to permission granted by a person with "apparent authority" are valid. In *Rodriguez*, the defendant's former live-in girlfriend used her key to the defendant's apartment to open the door for the police to enter and arrest the defendant for assaulting her. When the police entered, they discovered drugs and drug paraphernalia in plain view. The defendant moved to suppress the evidence on the grounds that his former girlfriend did not have the authority to consent to a search of his home because she no longer resided there, did not pay rent, and was not a leaseholder. While the Court acknowledged that the ex-girlfriend did not have actual authority over the premises, the Court stated that the determination of consent must be judged against the objective standard of whether the facts available to the officer at the moment "would warrant a man of reasonable caution in the belief that the consenting party had authority over the premises." In an effort to restrict the scope of the apparent authority rule, the Court stated that a police officer cannot rely on apparent authority to justify warrantless searches each time a person claims to reside at the premises if "the surrounding circumstances could conceivably be such that a reasonable person would doubt its truth and not act upon it without further inquiry."

Post-*Rodriguez*, lower courts have used apparent authority to uphold third party consent given in a wide range of scenarios, *e.g.*, *United States v. Freeman*, 482 F.3d 829 (5th Cir. 2007) (apparent authority to search a backpack located in private train compartment found where the sole occupant consented to a search and told the police that all of the bags in the compartment belonged to him);

People v. Hopkins, 870 P.2d 478 (Colo. 1994) (apparent authority to search "fanny pack" where consenting party was wearing the bag around his waist and never stated that it was not his property).

V. Problems with Consent Searches

The broad scope and minimal constitutional restrictions on consent searches have led some to question whether the power to conduct consent searches has resulted in abuses by law enforcement officers. One issue that frequently arises in consent search cases is whether the suspect actually consented. In many cases, suspects dispute the officer's claim that consent was ever given. These denials are bolstered by facts which cause many to wonder why any person would voluntarily consent to a search when they know they have drugs or other contraband that will be discovered. *See Florida v. Bostick*, 501 U.S. 420 (1991) (rejecting the defendant's contention that "no reasonable person would freely consent to a search of luggage that he or she knows contains drugs"). Law enforcement officers can normally overcome this concern by simply asserting — truthfully or not — that consent was actually given.

Moreover, when police officers request a person's consent, often there are no other witnesses to the encounter. As a result, courts can either credit the account of the arresting officer who maintains that consent was given, or the court can believe the person found in possession of incriminating evidence who claims consent was never given. Overwhelmingly, the defendant does not prevail in this credibility contest. *See, e.g., United States v. Matlock*, 415 U.S. 164 (1974) (although the homeowner denied that consent was given, the trial court credited the police officer's testimony and upheld the search of the residence). Thus, although the government has the burden to show that it was acting pursuant to valid consent, *Bumper v. North Carolina*, 391 U.S. 543 (1968), that burden is often not a difficult one to bear.

Even assuming that consent was actually given, a second issue that arises with consent searches is whether an individual is truly able to exercise free choice when asked to consent to a search, or whether he or she simply submits to avoid adverse consequences, real or imagined. The cases seem to suggest that this self-imposed dilemma is not of constitutional magnitude if the police did not use coercive action to induce consent. While the request to search one's home is made while the resident is in comfortable surroundings, different considerations exist when police officers have a motorist lawfully detained on the side of the road during a routine traffic stop. During a traffic stop, the motorist (and all passengers) are seized for purposes of the Fourth Amendment and cannot opt to simply walk away and refuse to cooperate further with the officer's investigation. The detained motorist faces the very real possibility that a lack of cooperation could result in a custodial arrest and/or loss of their sole means of transportation. Yet, too often, courts find that consent given under these circumstances is entirely voluntarily.

Moreover, consent searches during traffic stops have been used by the police as a pretext to engage in the invidious practice of racial profiling. Because police officers are not required to have probable cause or reasonable suspicion that an individual is in possession of contraband prior to requesting consent, police officers can stop a car for any real or perceived traffic violation and then use the occasion of the lawful detention to request consent to conduct a "full-blown" warrantless search of the entire vehicle, all of the occupants, and all of their personal belongings. The Supreme Court has not restricted these suspicionless, pretextual searches of motorists and their vehicles. In fact, the Court has expressly stated that the reasonableness of a search or seizure is not based on the subjective intentions of the officer, but whether the action taken is supported by an objective finding of probable cause. For example, in *Whren v. United States*, 517 U.S. 806 (1996), the Court found that an officer's decision to make a traffic stop is reasonable under the Fourth Amendment if there is probable cause to believe the traffic laws have been violated, regardless of the "subjective intentions" of the officer. Thus, *Whren* and its progeny have given law enforcement officers very broad discretionary power to use the traffic laws to conduct completely unrelated investigative activity based on hunches, prejudices, or no reason at all.

VI. State Restrictions on Consent Searches

Several states have taken action to prevent the use of routine traffic stops to engage in exploratory, suspicionless consent searches unrelated to the traffic infraction. Noting the clear link between suspicionless consent searches and racial profiling, there have been judicial and legislative reforms to curb the use of consent searches unless: (1) there is a knowing waiver of the right to refuse consent; or (2) the police have reasonable, articulable suspicion prior to requesting that the motorist consent to a search of the vehicle. The state of Rhode Island has enacted the Racial Profiling Prevention Act, which provides:

> No operator or owner-passenger of a motor vehicle shall be requested to consent to a search by a law enforcement officer of his or her motor vehicle which is stopped solely for a traffic violation, unless there exists reasonable suspicion or probable cause of criminal activity.

R.I. GEN. LAWS §31-21.2-5(b) (2008). Also, in *State v. Fort*, 660 N.W.2d 415 (Minn. 2003), the Minnesota Supreme Court found, that under the state constitution, officers must have reasonable, articulable suspicion before expanding the scope of a traffic stop and seeking consent to search motorists regarding completely unrelated criminal activity. *See also State v. Carty*, 790 A.2d 903 (N.J. 2002) (the New Jersey constitution mandates that "for a consent search to be valid, the police must have a reasonable and articulable suspicion that a criminal offense is being or has been committed prior to requesting consent to search"). Other state and local restrictions on consent searches including a 2001 moratorium on the use of consent searches conducted by the California Highway Patrol and the use of a "Consent to Search" form in Austin, Texas that requires police officers to obtain a signed waiver as a prerequisite to conducting a consent search.

Checkpoints

- Valid consent searches can be conducted without either a warrant or probable cause.

- Consent searches apply to searches of one's person, personal belongings, residence, and automobile.

- Consent searches are only constitutionally valid if consent was voluntarily given.

- Consent can be voluntary even if the individual did not know (and was not told) of their right to refuse to consent to the search.

- In determining whether consent was voluntary, the Court looks at the "totality of the circumstances" to determine, among other things, whether (and to what extent) the police engaged in coercive action to induce the individual to consent to the search.

- An individual has actual authority to consent to a search of any property that they jointly own, jointly occupy, or have joint use of.

- Even in the absence of actual authority, a consent search may be valid if conducted pursuant to the apparent authority of one who reasonably appears to have the authority to consent to the search.

- The link between consent searches and racial profiling has led several jurisdictions to place restrictions on the ability of police officers to seek consent to search automobiles during routine traffic stops.

Chapter 9

Exigent Circumstances

Roadmap

- The probable cause requirement
- The requirement of a serious, imminent emergency
- The hot pursuit exception
- The public safety exception
- Destruction of evidence

I. Introduction

The exigent circumstances exception to the Fourth Amendment's warrant requirement is based on the acknowledgement that in the often dangerous and fast-paced work of apprehending criminals and protecting public safety, emergencies arise that require immediate action to protect public safety. In these emergency situations, the individual's expectation of privacy must yield to the government's superior interest in abating the emergency and the practical reality that securing a warrant will result in delay that could jeopardize the public. Accordingly, the exigent circumstances doctrine allows the police to make a forcible, warrantless entry into an area where an individual has a reasonable expectation of privacy—usually a home—in order to arrest a fleeing felon, address a threat to public safety, or prevent the imminent destruction of vital evidence. In determining whether the government's conduct falls within the scope of the exigency circumstances exception, the critical questions to ask are whether prior to entering the premises: (1) the police had sufficient information to establish probable cause; and (2) the police had reason to believe that an emergency of sufficient gravity warranted immediate action.

II. Requirements for the Exigent Circumstances Exception

A. Probable Cause

Even if there is an emergency that excuses the police from obtaining a warrant before conducting a search or seizure, the police must still demonstrate that they had probable cause to believe evidence or contraband was located in the space searched or that a person on the premises was subject to arrest for committing a serious crime. The exigent circumstances exception does not allow the police to enter a dwelling based merely on reasonable suspicion of criminal activity. If the police, faced with exigent circumstances, conduct searches and seizures without a warrant and without probable cause, their actions will fall outside of the exigent circumstances exception and any evidence obtained would be subject to suppression by the court under the exclusionary rule. (See Chapter 12).

B. Scope of Authority

Even if the police have probable cause, once they enter the premises pursuant to the exigent circumstances exception, the scope of their authority is limited by the nature of the emergency. Police officers cannot use the warrantless entry to conduct an exhaustive search of the entire premises. In *Warden v. Hayden*, 387 U.S. 294 (1967), eyewitnesses helped police track an armed robber to a private home. Within minutes of the crime, the police entered the defendant's home to search for the defendant and seize weapons used during the crime. In holding that the warrantless entry into the defendant's dwelling fell within the scope of the exigent circumstances exception, the Court noted that: "[s]peed here was essential, and only a thorough search of the house for persons and weapons could have insured that [the defendant] was the only man present and that the police had control of all weapons which could be used against them or to effect an escape." In rejecting the defendant's contention that the police exceeded the scope of the exigent circumstances exception in retrieving bloody clothes from the washing machine, the Court found that the discovery of the incriminating evidence occurred during the officers' lawful search of the premises for weapons used during the crime.

There are also limits on the duration of a search initiated under exigent circumstances. When police have abated the emergency that justified the initial intrusion, they are no longer authorized to continue searching for other evidence without a warrant. In *Michigan v. Tyler*, 436 U.S. 499 (1978), the Court held that "[a] burning building clearly presents an exigency of sufficient proportions to render a warrantless entry 'reasonable.'" However, the Court found that the government's re-entry onto the building the following day to determine the cause of the fire and the government's subsequent warrantless inspections of the premises weeks after the fire were "clearly detached from the initial exigency" and required a search warrant. *See also Michigan v. Clifford*, 464 U.S. 287 (1984) (warrantless re-entry and inspection of entire fire-damaged residence hours after fire extinguished unreasonable where there was no longer an exigency).

C. Obtaining Warrant Impractical

The exigent circumstances exception also requires some showing that the nature of the emergency made it impractical for the officers to delay a search or seizure to apply for a warrant. If, notwithstanding the emergency, the officers could have obtained a warrant without risk to public safety, their failure to do so will not be excused by the exigency. Courts have placed the burden on the government to demonstrate that the nature of the emergency made the delay to secure a warrant impractical. *See Thompson v. Louisiana*, 469 U.S. 17 (1984) (investigators testified that they had time to secure a warrant before commencing the search); *Dorman v. United States*, 435 F.2d 385 (D.C. Cir. 1970) (noting the lack of evidence by the government on why "the short delay inherent in the making of any application for a warrant" would have been intolerable).

D. When Circumstances Are Exigent

Not every real or perceived emergency that police encounter in trying to capture criminals or secure evidence will qualify as an exigent circumstance. The Court recognized that an exigency is not created simply because there is probable cause to believe a serious crime has been committed. The police must show an "urgent need" to justify warrantless searches or arrests. Although the finding of an exigency is a fact-based determination made on a case-by-case basis, the gravity of the underlying offense is an important factor. The Court has stated that it would be "difficult to conceive" of the application of the exigent circumstances exception when the underlying offense was "extremely minor." *Welsh v. Wisconsin*, 466 U.S. 740 (1984).

Cases where courts have found that the government's warrantless intrusion was justified by exigent circumstances generally fall into three categories: the *hot pursuit* of a fleeing felon; imminent danger affecting *public safety*; and risk of *evidence destruction*.

1. Hot Pursuit

In *Payton v New York*, 445 U.S. 573 (1980), the Court held that "the Fourth Amendment has drawn a firm line at the entrance to the house. Absent exigent circumstances that threshold may not reasonably be crossed without a warrant." In *United States v. Watson*, 423 U.S. 411 (1976), however, the Court found that the police can make a warrantless public arrest based on probable cause. The hot pursuit rule addresses the intersection of these two bedrock Fourth Amendment principles. The Court held that "a suspect may not defeat an arrest which has been set in motion in a public place, and is therefore proper under *Watson*, by the expedient of escaping to a private place." *See United States v. Santana*, 427 U.S. 38 (1976) (exigent circumstances based on hot pursuit justified the warrantless arrest where the defendant was standing outside in the doorway of her home, but quickly retreated into her house when the police approached to arrest her).

Hot pursuit presents a very clear scenario where obtaining a warrant is both impractical and would present a great risk to public safety and order. Mandating that police stop the pursuit of a fleeing felon and obtain a warrant from a magistrate would significantly increase the likelihood that the criminal will elude capture and perhaps escalate the confrontation with law enforcement in order to escape (*i.e.*, engage in an armed confrontation with police, take hostages, destroy vital evidence, lead police on a dangerous high-speed chase through the public streets). The hot pursuit rule does not apply, however, when the suspect is unaware that the police are "hot on his trail." *See Welsh v. Wisconsin*, 466 U.S. 740 (1984) (warrantless arrest of a DUI suspect at his home shortly after the car accident did not fall under the hot pursuit rule where the suspect was found in bed and unaware that the police were en route). Absent the urgency created by the hot pursuit of a fleeing felon, the police must secure a warrant before entering a person's home to make an arrest.

2. Public Safety

Exigent circumstances also arise when the police learn of a dangerous condition or imminent threat to public safety on private property that could be averted if the police act swiftly. In *Brigham City v. Stuart*, 547 U.S. 398 (2006), the police arrived on the scene in response to a noise complaint and looked into the house through a screen door and window and saw a physical altercation between several adults and a juvenile. Once the officers observed a bloody exchange of blows, they entered the home without a warrant to halt the violence. The Court found that exigent circumstances justified the warrantless entry to aid the injured person, prevent further violence, and restore order. The Court stated that exigent circumstances exists when an officer has an "objectively reasonable basis" for believing that there is an urgent need to quell an on-going violent encounter. By contrast, in *Minnesota v. Olson*, 495 U.S. 91 (1990), the police learned that the defendant, the alleged getaway driver in a fatal armed robbery, was an overnight guest at the home of a friend. Police surrounded the home and requested that the defendant come outside. When he did not comply, the police entered and placed him under arrest. The Court found that no exigent circumstances justified the warrantless entry into the home because there was no reason to believe the suspect had a weapon or that others present in the home were in danger. The Court also noted that, with the building surrounded, the defendant was not likely to escape and could have been arrested when he exited the dwelling.

The public safety rationale has also been used to justify warrantless entry into residences to conduct searches. Lower courts have found exigent circumstances where the police entered the home to search for explosives, *United States v. Perez*, 440 F. Supp 272 (N.D. Ohio 1977), and to search for bound-and-gagged victims, *State v. McCleary*, 568 P.2d 1142 (Ariz. Ct. App. 1977). However, the Supreme Court has refused to automatically extend the exigent circumstances exception to all murder scene investigations. In *Mincey v. Arizona*, 437 U.S. 385 (1978), after the officers rendered emergency aid and removed the decedent and the other victims from the scene, they proceeded to conduct an "exhaustive" and "intrusive" four-day search of the dwelling to gather evidence. The Court stated that after rendering aid to the victims there was no further exigency. Thus, a warrant was required for the police to conduct any further investigation of the murder scene. *See also Thompson v. Louisiana*, 469 U.S. 17 (1984) (same).

3. Destruction of Evidence

The imminent destruction of vital evidence is another form of exigency that can justify a warrantless search or seizure. This concern most frequently arises in the context of drug cases where the police have probable cause to believe that drugs are located on the premises and reason to believe that the suspects will destroy the evidence if police do not quickly enter the premises. Generally, the risk of destruction of evidence creates an exigency when the police can articulate specific facts that give rise to the reasonable belief that the suspects have been alerted to the impending arrival of law enforcement and would resort to destruction to avoid being captured with the incriminating evidence. Courts are not likely to find exigent circumstances simply because evidence is perishable or if there is only the mere possibility that evidence could be destroyed.

The risk of imminent destruction of evidence may not justify a warrantless entry into a dwelling if the police can use a less intrusive means to prevent destruction. In *Illinois v. McArthur*, 531 U.S. 326 (2001), the defendant's estranged wife reported to police that she had just seen the defendant hide drugs inside the home. The police informed the husband, who was standing on the porch, that he would not be permitted to re-enter the home unescorted until a search warrant could be obtained. The Court found that the police "reasonably could have concluded" that the defendant, if given the chance to re-enter the house would destroy the drugs. The Court also found that resort to the far less intrusive method of impoundment of the premises to prevent evidence destruction was reasonable and avoided the necessity of a presumptively unreasonable warrantless entry into a home. *See Mincey v. Arizona*, 437 U.S. 385 (1978) (police guard at apartment door "minimized" the possibility "that evidence would be lost, destroyed, or removed during the time required to obtain a search warrant").

The destruction of evidence rationale has also been used when the government seeks to obtain bodily fluids from an arrestee based on the fact that the incriminating information contained in bodily fluids will quickly diminish. In *Schmerber v. California*, 384 U.S. 757 (1966), a police officer directed a hospital physician to extract a sample of blood from a DUI arrestee who still appeared heavily intoxicated two hours after crashing his car. The Court found that the "interests in human dignity and privacy" make "searches involving intrusions beyond the body's surface" too intrusive for the routine search incident to arrest. The Court recognized, however, that the natural absorption of alcohol by the human body in a relatively short period of time resulted in the imminent destruction of the evidence of blood-alcohol concentration level. The Court ruled that such intrusions into an individual's body must be based on a "clear indication that in fact such evidence will be found" and not "the mere chance that desired evidence might be obtained." *But see Welsh v. Wisconsin*, 466 U.S. 740 (1984) (rejecting the government's contention that the destruction of evidence of blood-alcohol level in a DUI case justified the warrantless entry into home where the defendant was only charged with an extremely minor "non-jailable" offense).

Checkpoints

- The exigent circumstances exception to the warrant requirement requires police to have: (1) probable cause prior to initiating a search; (2) an imminent emergency that makes obtaining a warrant impractical; and (3) an emergency of sufficient magnitude, measured, in part, by the gravity of the underlying offense.

- Hot pursuit of a fleeing felon is one recognized exigency, but the hot pursuit rule does not apply if the suspect is unaware that the police are en route or if the underlying crime is a relatively minor offense.

- An imminent threat to public safety falls under the exigent circumstances exception, but police only have the limited authority to enter the premises to resolve the emergency and cannot conduct a generalized search and investigation beyond the scope of the exigency.

- The imminent destruction of evidence can create an exigency of sufficient magnitude to justify the warrantless entry onto premises if the police have facts to establish a reasonable belief that destruction is imminent. Otherwise, the Court has given tacit approval to simply securing the premises until a warrant can be obtained.

- In drunk driving and other cases where the police have a "clear indication" that valuable evidence of culpability is contained in bodily fluids and such evidence will quickly diminish in a relatively short time, the exigent circumstances exception can be invoked to require the suspect to submit to the forced extraction of bodily fluids for analysis.

Chapter 10

Plain View

Roadmap

- The probable cause requirement
- The lawful access requirement
- The prohibition against conducting "searches" to identify contraband
- The elimination of the "inadvertence" requirement
- Other senses: "plain touch," and "plain smell"

I. Introduction

The plain view exception to the warrant requirement allows the government to seize incriminating evidence observed during the course of a lawful investigation. The critical questions to be asked in determining whether the seizure of evidence falls within the scope of the plain view exception to the warrant requirements are: (1) did the police have the lawful authority to be at the location where the seized items were found; and (2) did the officer have probable cause to believe the seized items were evidence related to criminal activity without performing any additional "search" of the item.

II. Scope of the Plain View Exception

In *Coolidge v. New Hampshire*, 403 U.S. 443 (1971), the Supreme Court stated:

It is well established that under certain circumstances the police may seize evidence in plain view without a warrant. But it is important to keep in mind that, in the vast majority of cases, any evidence seized by the police will be in plain view, at least at the moment of seizure. The problem with the 'plain view' doctrine has been to identify the circumstances in which plain view has legal significance rather than being simply the normal concomitant of any search, legal or illegal.

To address the concern regarding the potentially limitless scope of the plain view exception, the Court has placed clear boundaries on its application. The government may seize items observed on private property under the plain view exception to the warrant requirement if: (1) the agents had the lawful authority to be present at the location where the evidence was seen and the lawful authority to access the item; (2) there has been no Fourth Amendment "search" conducted to determine the incriminating character of the evidence; and (3) there is probable cause to believe the item is contraband or evidence connected to criminal activity.

A. Lawful Presence and Access

While the plain view exception can authorize the warrantless seizure of property, it does not authorize the warrantless entry on to private property to affect such seizures. Police officers must already be on the property lawfully at the time incriminating evidence is seen in plain view. Thus, the plain view exception is usually invoked when the police are legitimately on the premises executing an arrest warrant or conducting a lawful search for unrelated items pursuant to a search warrant or an exception to the warrant requirement. See *Horton v. California*, 496 U.S. 128 (1990) (while search warrant only authorized seizure of jewelry, police could also seize weapons that were in plain view during the search for jewelry); *United States v. Carter*, 378 F.3d 584 (6th Cir. 2004) (officer's entry into motel room pursuant to defendant's consent "had the latitude of a guest" and could walk over to a nearby table and observe drugs in plain view). The Supreme Court has stated that an individual has no reasonable expectation of privacy in those items that are left in the plain view of police officers who have the legal authority to be on the premises in the area where the item is located. *Arizona v. Hicks*, 480 U.S. 321 (1987).

B. Seizures, Not Searches

The plain view exception authorizes only the warrantless *seizure* of items that the police can identify as contraband based solely on a visual observation of the item. The police must be able to identify the item as contraband without resorting to investigative activity that would constitute a Fourth Amendment "search" of the item. If the police need to do more than make a visual observation of the object to determine the incriminating character of the item (e.g., open it, shake it, squeeze it, test it), seizure of the evidence cannot be justified under the plain view exception. Courts have applied the plain view exception to items that are "inherently unlawful" and, therefore, easily identifiable as contraband on sight, including drug paraphernalia, explosives, or prohibited weapons. *See United States v. Looney*, 481 F.2d 31 (5th Cir. 1973) (submachine gun was validly seized under the plain view exception); *but see Eisman v. Superior Court*, 98 Cal. Rptr. 342 (Cal. Ct. App. 1971) ("plain white pills" which were not clearly identifiable as contraband until subsequent chemical analysis could not be seized under the plain view exception).

In *Arizona v. Hicks*, 480 U.S. 321 (1987), a police officer lawfully entered the defendant's apartment to investigate a shooting and to search for weapons. Upon arrival, the officer's suspicion was aroused upon observing expensive stereo equipment that seemed incongruous with the "squalid and otherwise ill-appointed" apartment. To confirm his suspicion that the equipment was stolen, the officer "moved some of the components" in order to read and record the serial numbers. Upon confirming that the serial numbers matched police records of stolen property, the officers seized the equipment pursuant to the plain view exception. The Court ruled that the officer's action in moving the stereo equipment to determine the serial numbers constituted a "search." The Court reasoned that the "distinction between 'looking' at a suspicious object in plain view and 'moving' it even a few inches" is significant for purposes of the Fourth Amendment. Because the actual incriminating nature of the stereo equipment was not known by the police until they investigated further, the officer did not have a "plain view" of stolen goods at the time of the seizure. *See also Stanley v. Georgia*, 394 U.S. 557 (1969) (pornographic film was not in plain view where the officers had to play the film with a projector and screen to determine its content).

C. Probable Cause Standard

In *Coolidge*, the Supreme Court ruled that before the seizure of an item can be justified under the plain view exception, the nature of the item as contraband must be "immediately apparent." The Court did not, however, define "immediately apparent." Post-*Coolidge* state and federal courts differed on how certain the police officer had to be that the item was contraband before seizure could be made under the plain view rule. In *Hicks*, 480 U.S. at 321, the Court squarely addressed this question and ruled that "immediately apparent" means the officer must have probable cause to believe the item is contraband before a warrantless seizure is constitutionally permissible. The *Hicks* Court reasoned that, while the plain view exception allows the police to seize property without a warrant, there is no rational justification for allowing the police to make warrantless seizures of property on a lesser standard than would be required to obtain a warrant to seize the same property. Thus, in *Hicks,* where the officer had reasonable suspicion that the expensive-looking stereo equipment might be stolen, the officer did not have probable cause to believe the equipment was contraband based solely on the officer's immediate visual observation. His actions in engaging in a new search to obtain that probable cause went beyond the scope of the plain view exception.

III. No "Inadvertence" Requirement

In *Horton v. California*, 496 U.S. 128 (1990), the Court further refined the contours of the plain view doctrine by eliminating the requirement that evidence be inadvertently discovered — not purposely sought — by police in the course of a lawful investigation. The original justification for the inadvertence requirement was to prohibit officers from broadly expanding the scope of searches by purposely excluding from the warrant application items they expect to find on the premises but lack probable cause to legally seize. In *Horton,* the police officer applied for a warrant to seize both guns and jewelry located at the defendant's residence. The magistrate, however, only issued a warrant for the jewelry. The officer testified that while searching for the jewelry he was also interested in finding weapons and other evidence connecting the defendant to the crime. The Court upheld the seizure of the weapon under the plain view exception. In abandoning the inadvertence requirement, the Court stated that under modern Fourth Amendment jurisprudence, a police officer's subjective intentions do not govern the reasonableness of the officer's conduct. Rather, the officer's conduct is constitutionally permissible if it is objectively reasonable, regardless of the officer's personal motive or subjective intent. *See also, Whren v. United States*, 517 U.S. 806 (1996) (discussed in Chapter 7).

IV. Beyond Plain View:
Other "Plain" Sensory Perceptions

Though commonly called plain *view,* in *Minnesota v. Dickerson,* 508 U.S. 366 (1993), the Court stated that the rationale underlying the plain view exception applies with equal force to perceptions made using other senses. The Court articulated the "plain feel" exception as follows:

> If a police officer lawfully pats down a suspect's outer clothing and feels an object whose contour or mass makes its identity immediately apparent, there has been no invasion of the suspect's privacy ... [and the] warrantless seizure would be justified by the same practical considerations that inhere in the plain-view context.

In *Dickerson*, the police lawfully stopped the defendant based on reasonable suspicion that he was engaged in criminal activity. During the course of the *Terry* stop (see Chapter 4), the police had the lawful authority to conduct a limited pat down search of the defendant to determine whether he was armed. During the pat down search, the officer felt a small lump in the defendant's pocket that he suspected was cocaine. The officer testified that he began "squeezing, sliding and otherwise manipulating the contents of the defendant's pocket" to confirm his suspicion that the defendant possessed drugs. The Court found that because the officer had to engage in a "search" in order to ascertain the incriminating character of the evidence, the plain feel exception did not apply. *See Bond v. United States*, 529 U.S. 334 (2000) (police conduct a Fourth Amendment search by squeezing, prodding, or manipulating the outside of a closed duffel bag to determine contents).

Post-*Dickerson*, if the officer can use sensory perceptions (e.g., touch, smell, hearing) to detect the incriminating nature of an object without engaging in a search, the warrantless seizure of the evidence would likely be reasonable under the Fourth Amendment. *But see Commonwealth v. Hatcher*, 199 S.W.3d 124 (Ky. 2006) (pipe was in plain view, but was not immediately apparent as contraband until the officers picked it up and smelled marijuana).

Checkpoints

- The plain view exception requires that police have the lawful authority to be at the location where evidence is obtained. This usually requires that the police have a warrant or the lawful authority to conduct searches and seizures pursuant to an exception to the warrant requirement.

- The plain view exception requires that police have probable cause to believe that the item they plainly see is contraband or other seizable evidence.

- Tangible evidence cannot be seized under the plain view exception if the police are unable to discern the incriminating nature of item without conducting a "search" of the item (*i.e.*, moving, squeezing, manipulating).

- The plain view exception does not prohibit the police from seizing evidence that they expected or anticipated they would find during course of a lawful investigation. Discovery of an item in plain view does not have to be inadvertent to fall within the scope of this exception to the warrant requirement.

- The rationale underlying the plain view exception also applies to the detection of evidence using other senses, including "plain smell" and "plain touch" and "plain feel," as long as the incriminating nature of the item is obvious to the investigating officer without resort to a "search" of the item.

Chapter 11

Administrative Searches and Special Needs

Roadmap

- Warrants to conduct administrative searches.
- Warrantless searches of closely regulated businesses.
- Regulations authorizing warrantless searches.
- Searches at an international border and its equivalent.
- Brief detention for Customs questioning.
- "Special needs" searches without a warrant or probable cause.

I. Overview

A. Defining and Analyzing Administrative Search and Seizure Cases

"Administrative" or "special needs" searches or seizures are generally understood to mean those that are conducted for purposes other than criminal prosecution. However, the Supreme Court has extended this definition to include brief seizures ("stops") of potential eyewitnesses to determine the extent of their knowledge about a crime. *Illinois v. Lidster,* 540 U.S. 419 (2004). Whether they will further extend the definition is thus far unclear.

The term "special needs" usually refers to searches or seizures of persons or their property, while the term "administrative searches" is more likely to refer to searches or seizures occurring at businesses or other entities in the course of the government's enforcing non-criminal statutes or administrative regulations. Nevertheless, the tests for the constitutionality of searches or seizures in either category tend to be the same, so the two terms will be used interchangeably here.

A common example of a special needs search is a search of a junior high school student's pocket book on suspicion it contains cigarettes or other items that the school administration considers to be contraband. The purpose of the search is not to uncover evidence of crime but rather to protect school safety and student physical and emotional health. A common example of an administrative search would be a federal Occupational Safety and Health Inspector's examination of a business's premises to make sure that its operations comply with federal job safety mandates. Again, the inspectors' goal is not to prevent, uncover, or prosecute crime but to maintain worker safety.

Ordinary criminal investigation-related searches generally require individualized suspicion, either in the form of probable cause or reasonable suspicion (with probable cause being the supposed default). Moreover, such searches usually require a warrant or a well-recognized exception to the warrant requirement. But administrative or special needs searches involve no such presumption of a warrant, probable cause, or reasonable suspicion. Instead, the first time the Supreme Court confronts a particular category of administrative search or seizure, it balances state against individual interests to craft a rule to govern that future class of cases. That rule may creatively articulate entirely novel ways of protecting individuals' privacy, property, and locomotive rights.

Occasionally that balance comes out to require reasonable suspicion or to require a warrant that may be issued on grounds other than traditional probable cause. For example, the Court in fact confronted a case involving the search of a junior high school student's pocketbook in *New Jersey v. T.L.O.,* 469 U.S. 325 (1985). It concluded that such a search may be undertaken if the relevant school official merely has reasonable suspicion, not probable cause, to believe that contraband will be found. By contrast, the Court has held that fire marshals may conduct searches of premises damaged after a fire merely upon a showing of probable cause to believe that a fire occurred and that examining the premises may help to determine its cause. Probable cause that a crime occurred is not required. *Michigan v. Tyler,* 436 U.S. 49 (1978).

Most often, however, the balance in administrative search or seizure cases is found to favor suspicionless, warrantless searches or seizures. For example, roadblocks to search for drunk drivers posing an imminent danger to public safety require neither probable cause, reasonable suspicion, nor a warrant. Furthermore, the Court in such cases usually requires limits on state actors' discretion to take the place of the limits that would ordinarily be imposed by obtaining a warrant. In the case of roadblocks, this might mean that there must be police rules or regulations governing who will be stopped, for what purposes, for how long, and the manner in which the seizure and any subsequent searches will be conducted.

Administrative search or seizure problems thus require the following steps in the analysis:

- Is the governmental person or entity conducting the search or seizure doing so for a primary purpose other than gathering evidence of crime or to question witnesses briefly about their knowledge of a crime?
- If yes, the search or seizure is an administrative or special needs one, so a further question must be asked: Is the purpose one that places this search or seizure within an existing recognized rule for this class of administrative or special needs searches or seizures?
- If yes, simply apply that rule for the class of cases. For example, if the purpose of a search of a junior high school student's pocketbook is to uncover evidence of contraband to protect student and educational personnel's health, safety, or the effectiveness of the educational goals of the institution, reasonable suspicion that contraband is present but no warrant is required.
- If instead the administrative search or seizure is one that the Supreme Court has never addressed before, then balance individual against state interests to determine what rule should govern this new class of cases, then apply the rule to the facts. The new rule must address whether a warrant is required and, if so, on what grounds; whether probable cause, reasonable suspicion, or no suspicion will be required; and, if no warrant is required, whether and what mechanisms can be used to limit state officials' discretion in ways analogous to the ways that a warrant would do so.

This approach is not that different from how the Supreme Court analyzes ordinary criminal searches, except that: (1) an analysis of governmental purpose is required to determine in the first instance whether the search or seizure is, on the one hand, a traditional criminal investigation-related search or, on the other hand, an administrative or special needs search or seizure; and (2) balancing is undertaken without any supposed presumption, or tipping of the scales, in favor of individualized suspicion or a warrant.

B. Determining Governmental Purpose

The governmental purpose inquiry raises two problems: first, the objective nature of the inquiry; second, the problem of dual or multiple purposes. The Court has explicitly declared that the subjective purposes of the state actors are irrelevant. What matters are the "objective, programmatic purposes." The Court has never defined this term exactly, but on its face it seems to look to the structure of the search program designed by the government to divine what an objectively reasonable person (an ordinary person, not a police officer or other governmental actor) familiar with the program's nature would understand as its purpose.

The second problem arises because, even when viewed objectively, the government may be understood to have dual purposes, one administrative or special needs, the other the pursuit of criminals or evidence of criminal wrongdoing. In such instances, the Court asks what is the *primary* governmental purpose. Again, the Court has never explained how to distinguish among "primary," "secondary," or "equal" purposes, leading commentators to suggest a variety of approaches. All that the Court has made clear is that this primary versus secondary versus equal purpose inquiry is still an objective one.

Ferguson v. City of Charleston, 532 U.S. 67 (2001), illustrates both these problems. In *Ferguson,* the Court struck down a program at a local public hospital whose patients were primarily poor that engaged in drug screening of its maternity patients suspected of using cocaine. Those testing positive were informed that the case would be forwarded to the police for prosecution if they did not complete a drug treatment program. Police officers worked closely with the hospital to design the program, and the subjective purpose of the hospital employees and the police was to protect the safety and health of the mothers and their children. The state argued that its primary purpose concerned a special need—patient health and safety—not criminal prosecution. But the Court concluded otherwise, finding that the primary objective programmatic purpose was criminal prosecution. Four factors seemed to be particularly important in the Court's determination that program was unconstitutional: first, patients violating treatment rules were indeed prosecuted; second, law enforcement was "extensively involved" in the design and day-to-day administration of the policy; third, the written policy itself incorporated matters, such as protecting the chain of custody, of concern only to law enforcement and irrelevant to health and safety concerns; and fourth, the threat of criminal prosecution was used to deter drug use, a use hard to distinguish from the "general interest in crime control."

In contrast to *Ferguson,* in an earlier drunk-driving roadblock case, *Michigan Department of State Police v. Sitz,* 496 U.S. 444 (1990), the Court at least implicitly found that the state's primary programmatic purpose was special needs or administrative: to protect the safety of drivers, passengers, other persons, and property from serious harm. At first blush, this conclusion seems odd because someone found to be a drunk driver is by definition guilty of the crime of drunk driving and would be subject to immediate arrest and prosecution. Of course, one purpose of making it a crime to drive while under the influence of alcohol is to protect health and safety, so that was certainly true of the roadblock. But almost all crimes in this sense have a purpose unrelated to crime control. Accepting that argument could effectively turn most searches and seizures into special needs or administrative ones.

C. Balancing

Once the Court determines that a case involves an administrative or special needs purpose, and that purpose does not fit into an existing rule for that category of cases, the Court must create a new rule by balancing state versus individual interests. Three factors are of primary, though not sole, importance. First, the weight of the state's interest must be determined. Two other considerations guide the Court's inquiry in this area: (a) the effectiveness of the chosen means in achieving the state's goals; and (b) the availability of other, less restrictive (not necessarily the least restrictive) alternative means for pursuing those goals. For example, a blood-testing program for drugs that had an enormously high error rate and for which more effective testing means are available would establish a very small government interest in conducting these searches in the manner that it chose.

Second, the Court must gauge the degree of the individual's interest. Generally, searches and seizures of cars and businesses are viewed as less invasive of privacy, property, and free movement than are searches and seizures of homes and businesses. Additionally, individuals involved in "pervasively regulated industries" and heavily monitored people (children, for example) are considered to enjoy lower protections because a history of extensive government supervision has long exposed their activities to public view. Automobiles, and all aspects of the automobile repair, distribution, and sale business are, for example, heavily regulated, and this has been true for many decades.

Third, the Court will inquire whether the state has placed adequate limitations on the discretion of government actors involved in the search and seizure program. Although warrants ordinarily serve this purpose, in special needs cases there usually are strong government justifications for rejecting the traditional warrant requirement. But in its place there must be other adequate procedures designed to avoid abuse of governmental discretion. Clear rules in statutes, regulations, or internal administrative policies telling government actors when and how to conduct their searches may be one way to limit such discretion.

D. Scope of Administrative and Special Needs Searches

Although the Fourth Amendment's warrant and probable cause requirements appear to apply to all searches, the Supreme Court recognizes limitations on the scope of the constitutional protection in certain circumstances. Among the situations in which a lesser showing of probable cause is permitted are searches performed by authorities for non-penal purposes, such as regulatory inspections, those conducted at the border or its equivalent, and when there are "special needs." The Court has not required that searches in these contexts be based on a particularized suspicion of wrongdoing, and warrants, when they are required, need not be based on the usual probable cause determination. While the searches can be quite invasive, such as the taking of a urine sample, the Court permits them even though the targets are not viewed as being involved in criminal activity. Indeed, one element for these searches to be found permissible is the *lack* of any indication of the person's involvement in a crime, which otherwise should trigger the Fourth Amendment's protections. The standards applied by the Court assume that the searches are not for the usual law enforcement purpose, although in many cases the Fourth Amendment issue arises in a criminal prosecution based on the fruits of such a search.

II. Administrative Searches

A. Administrative Warrant Requirements

The Supreme Court's decisions in *Camara v. Municipal Court*, 387 U.S. 523 (1967), and *See v. City of Seattle*, 387 U.S. 541 (1967), are the foundation for the warrant requirement for inspections by public officials other than the police arising from the enforcement of civil and regulatory ordinances and rules. In *Camara*, the defendant was a lessee of a ground-floor apartment in San Francisco who refused to permit a public health inspector to enter the premises without a warrant to conduct an inspection for possible housing code violations. In finding a Fourth Amendment violation from the attempted inspection, the Court held that administrative searches "are significant intrusions" on the privacy interests of those searched, and therefore a warrant was required. Except for emergency situations, when a warrant is not necessary, the probable cause requirement for regulatory inspections is different than for a criminal investigation. *Camara* stated that the warrant may issue "if reasonable legislative or administrative standards for conducting an area inspection are satisfied with respect to a particular dwelling."

In *See*, the warrantless inspection was of a warehouse by a fire department employee for possible fire code violations. The Court began by noting that the privacy interests in a private dwelling considered in *Camara* were the same for a business: "The businessman, like the occupant of a residence, has a constitutional right to go about his business free from unreasonable official entries upon his private commercial property." The warrant requirement still applies to administrative searches, but an "agency's particular demand for access will of course be measured, in terms of probable cause to issue a warrant, against a *flexible standard of reasonableness* that takes into account the public need for effective enforcement of the particular regulation involved."

Camara and *See* upheld the warrant requirement for routine administrative inspections of both residences and businesses conducted for non-penal purposes, at least absent an emergency. Also, any occupant can consent to a search, which always obviates the need for a warrant and probable cause. The significant change in the analysis of administrative searches in *Camara* and *See* was the Court's relaxation of the probable cause requirement of the Fourth Amendment. The government need not have any specific suspicion that the location covered by the warrant is involved in wrongdoing, and the warrant itself may cover a wider area than the usual authorization for a search of a particular location.

In *Marshall v. Barlows, Inc.*, 436 U.S. 307 (1978), the Court rejected the argument that regulatory inspections by the Occupational Safety and Health Administration (OSHA) pursuant to administrative guidelines provided as much protection for a business's privacy interests as an administrative warrant. It found that OSHA's authorization for warrantless entries gave the agency unbridled discretion about when and were to search, while "[a] warrant, by contrast, would provide assurances from a neutral officer that the inspection is reasonable under the Constitution, is authorized by statute, and is pursuant to an administrative plan containing specific neutral criteria." Because obtaining a warrant would not place an undue burden on OSHA, the Court held that the requirements for an exception to the administrative warrant were not met.

Obtaining an administrative warrant for commercial premises is often based on evidence of an existing statutory or regulatory violation, but can also be issued as part of a reasonable plan for searches in the public interest. For example, after *Barlows, Inc.*, OSHA inspections are based on a complaint about possible workplace safety or health violations.

A search conducted pursuant to an administrative warrant must meet the Fourth Amendment requirement that it be reasonable in relation to the alleged violation or plan to protect the public interest. For example, a search of business's entire premises is reasonable if the alleged safety violation occurs throughout the premises, such as improper ventilation or hazardous fumes. However, information that the violation is limited to a particular location, such as a loading dock or tool shop, would not support a wall-to-wall search. Once the public official is present pursuant to execute an administrative warrant, or even for a permissible warrantless regulatory search (see below), then items in "plain view" (Chapter 10) may be seized and used in a subsequent criminal prosecution.

B. Warrantless Searches of Closely Regulated Businesses

In *Colonnade Catering Corp. v. United States*, 397 U.S. 72 (1970), the Supreme Court recognized an exception to the warrant requirement outlined in *Camara* and *See* for businesses subject to pervasive government regulation. In *Barlows, Inc.*, the Court explained the rationale for the exception, stating that "when an entrepreneur embarks upon such a business, he has voluntarily chosen to subject himself to a full arsenal of governmental regulation."

The company at issue in *Colonnade Catering* operated pursuant to a liquor license, and the Court found "the liquor industry long subject to close supervision and inspection." The statute making it a crime to refuse a warrantless entry to inspect was not unconstitutional because "Congress has broad authority to fashion standards of reasonableness for searches and seizures" in this area. Similarly, in *United States v. Biswell*, 406 U.S. 311 (1972), the Court upheld the warrantless search of a gun dealer's locked storeroom during business hours as part of an inspection procedure authorized by federal statute. While liquor regulation was a power long exercised by Congress, gun control was of more recent vintage, but that did not affect the analysis of the propriety of the search. The Court held that "Federal regulation of the interstate traffic in firearms is not as deeply rooted in history as is governmental control of the liquor industry, but close scrutiny of this traffic is undeniably of central importance to federal efforts to prevent violent crime and to assist the States in regulating the firearms traffic within their borders."

The conclusion that the search did not violate the Fourth Amendment was buttressed by the fact that "the possibilities of abuse and the threat to privacy are not of impressive dimensions." Although the inspections constituted searches, they were not in violation of the Fourth Amendment because the reasonableness determination was based on the nature of the business and the statutory authorization for the search, which were not directly related to criminal law enforcement. The owner's consent to the search was irrelevant, as the Court noted in *Biswell* that "[i]n the context of a regulatory inspection system of business premises that is carefully limited in time, place, and scope, the legality of the search depends not on consent but on the authority of a valid statute."

In both *Colonnade Catering* and *Biswell*, the defendants were convicted of crimes, although the inspections themselves were not part of a criminal investigation. These searches can result in the filing of criminal charges so long as the goal of the inspection is not to gather evidence of a criminal offense.

That distinction became clear in the Court's decision in *New York v. Burger*, 482 U.S. 691 (1987). The Court began with the proposition that the privacy interest in commercial premises of a closely regulated industry are lower than for a private home, so the government's heightened interest in regulating the business may permit warrantless searches if they are reasonable. The court set forth three criteria for determining whether a warrantless inspection of a closely regulated business is reasonable under the Fourth Amendment:

- There must be a *substantial government interest* that informs the regulatory scheme pursuant to which the inspection is made.
- The warrantless inspections must be *necessary to further the regulatory scheme.*
- The regulatory statute must perform the two basic functions of a warrant: it must *advise the owner* of the commercial premises that the search is being made pursuant to the law and has a properly defined scope, and it must *limit the discretion* of the inspecting officers.

In explaining these criteria, the Court stated that the regulatory scheme can be furthered in allowing warrantless inspections if requiring a warrant would alert the business owner to the impending inspection and allow it to be impeded. A valid regulatory scheme authorizing these entries without a warrant must give fair warning to commercial enterprises that the business is subject to extensive regulation, including inspections, and any entry into business property must be limited in time, place, and scope.

The business involved in *Burger* was an automobile junkyard, and the Court found that the state had a substantial interest in regulating such businesses because of the problem of auto theft. Even though the statute furthered a criminal law enforcement goal of deterring theft, and police officers conducted the inspection, the Court found that the warrantless entry met the reasonableness requirement of the Fourth Amendment and upheld the defendant's conviction for possession of stolen property found as part of the inspection. The Court focused on the statutory scheme and not the actual inspection at issue, concluding that it was not "designed to gather evidence to enable convictions under the penal laws." *Burger* has been criticized for pushing the limits of the closely regulated business exception to the administrative warrant requirement beyond what should be permissible under the Fourth Amendment's warrant requirement.

C. Other Administrative Searches

After *Burger*, the Supreme Court upheld warrantless inspections of mines in *Donovan v. Dewey*, 452 U.S. 594 (1981), on the ground that "the Mine Safety and Health Act applies to industrial activity with a notorious history of serious accidents and unhealthful working conditions." Other businesses the lower courts have held as pervasively regulated, and therefore subject to warrantless administrative inspections, include commercial trucking, nursing, fishing docks, and animal research facilities. Lower courts have also upheld airport screening of passengers and baggage as valid administrative searches because they are based on a statute and apply to all persons and items that enter the airport. *United States v. Aukai*, 497 F.3d 955 (9th Cir. 2007) (*en banc*).

In *Michigan v. Tyler*, 436 U.S. 439 (1978), the Court held that an entry to fight a fire required no warrant, and the officials may remain there for a reasonable time to investigate the cause of the blaze. Thereafter, however, any additional inquiries to investigate the fire's cause must be pursuant to the warrant procedures governing administrative searches. Other warrantless administrative searches found to be invalid under the Fourth Amendment by lower courts include inspections of race track dormitories because they were more like a house and a search of a hospital to ensure compliance with anti-discrimination laws.

D. Motor Vehicle Regulation and Checkpoints

In *Delaware v. Prouse*, 440 U.S. 648 (1979), the Supreme Court held that stopping a vehicle and detaining its driver to check his license and automobile registration was unreasonable under the Fourth Amendment. The Court rejected the state's argument that the Fourth Amendment's proscription on unreasonable seizures did not apply because its interest in discretionary spot checks of vehicles to ensure the safety of its roadways outweighed the resulting intrusion on the privacy and security of any drivers detained. *Prouse* noted that these random stops "interfere with freedom of movement, are inconvenient, and consume time" while also creating "substantial anxiety" for the drivers. Moreover, the officer had virtually unfettered discretion to stop a vehicle, and the "kind of standardless and unconstrained discretion [which] is the evil the Court has discerned when in previous cases it has insisted that the discretion of the official in the field be circumscribed, at least to some extent." The Court held that

> except in those situations in which there is at least articulable and reasonable suspicion that a motorist is unlicensed or that an automobile is not registered, or that either the vehicle or an occupant is otherwise subject to seizure for violation of law, stopping an automobile and detaining the driver in order to check his driver's license and the registration of the automobile are unreasonable under the Fourth Amendment.

The Court noted that states can pursue legitimate means of stopping vehicles aside from random stops of individual cars, and that its holding did not preclude governments "from developing methods for spot checks that involve less intrusion or that do not involve the unconstrained exercise of discretion. Questioning of all oncoming traffic at roadblock-type stops is one possible alternative." In *Michigan Dept. of State Police v. Sitz*, 496 U.S. 444 (1990), the Court upheld a sobriety checkpoint at which all drivers were stopped and briefly examined for signs of alcohol use. Distinguishing *Prouse*, the Court found that "the balance of the State's interest in preventing drunken driving, the extent to which this system can reasonably be said to advance that interest, and the degree of intrusion upon individual motorists who are briefly stopped, weighs in favor of the state program." In addition, unlike the random stops in *Prouse*, the operation of the checkpoint did not involve the exercise of any significant discretion by the officers on the scene, so there was less possibility that the intrusion would be based on unreviewable factors.

Lower courts have upheld similar checkpoints when it is clear that, *inter alia*, the purpose of the checkpoint is to protect public safety or further other important state interests, the officers on the scene do not exercise discretion regarding which vehicles to stop, that the selection of the location and the basis for stopping selected vehicles if all will not be detained is made based on neutral criteria, and the operation does not unduly alarm motorists. After the initial stop of a vehicle, any further investigation beyond the brief examination must be based on at least reasonable suspicion under the *Terry v. Ohio* standard (see Chapter 4).

In *City of Indianapolis v. Edmond*, 531 U.S. 32 (2000), the Court recognized that the state's interest in employing a vehicle checkpoint could not be justified solely on the ground that it aided general law enforcement. The local government used checkpoints on six different occasions to interdict illegal drugs in which the officer would view the interior of the vehicle for signs of drugs while drug-detection dogs would walk around the outside of the car. Distinguishing *Prouse* and *Sitz*, the Court stated that the roadblock was designed to facilitate the detection of crime, and that "[i]n none of these cases, however, did we indicate approval of a checkpoint program whose primary purpose was to detect evidence of ordinary criminal wrongdoing." The Court also mentioned an exigent circumstances exception to the prohibition on checkpoints primarily designed for crime control, stating that "the Fourth Amendment would almost certainly permit an appropriately tailored roadblock set up to thwart an imminent terrorist attack or to catch a dangerous criminal who is likely to flee by way of a particular route."

In *Illinois v. Lidster*, 540 U.S. 419 (2004), the Court found that a suspicionless motor vehicle checkpoint set up to stop drivers for fifteen to twenty seconds to ask them whether they had seen a recent hit-and-run accident and to hand them a flyer about the case was a constitutional search more akin to drunk driving roadblocks or pure public safety measures like crowd control than to traditional criminal searches requiring individualized suspicion. The Court did not explain why this was so, nor did it make much effort clearly to fit the case into the schema it had created for distinguishing special needs from traditional criminal searches. Nevertheless, the Court did find purpose significant, concluding, "The stop's primary law enforcement purpose was *not* to determine whether a vehicle's occupants were committing a crime, but to ask vehicle occupants, as members of the public, for their help in providing information about a crime in all likelihood committed by others."

E. Welfare Home Visits

Many welfare programs require an initial interview and home visit by a government worker to determine eligibility for benefits. In *Wayman v. James*, 400 U.S. 309 (1971), the Supreme Court found that such visits were not searches within the meaning of the Fourth Amendment because the visit is more rehabilitative than investigative, and the refusal to allow the home visit does not result in any criminal penalty, only the denial of benefits. The Court noted that even if the statutory requirement could be described as a search, it still would not violate the Fourth Amendment "because it does not descend to the level of unreasonableness." The public's interest in protecting children who receive aid and the nature of providing public charity, with a concomitant interest in ensuring taxpayer funds are spent properly, support finding that the minimal intrusion of a home visit was reasonable.

F. Airport Screening

The Aviation & Transportation Security Act, 49 U.S.C. § 44901, adopted after the September 11 attacks, authorizes the Transportation Security Administration to engage in the "screening of all passengers and property, including United States mail, cargo, carry-on and checked baggage, and other articles, that will be carried aboard a passenger aircraft operated by an air carrier or foreign air carrier in air transportation or intrastate air transportation." Because the initial screening of passengers and bags is limited to electronic scans of individuals and luggage, and the government's interest in protecting passengers and the airline system is significant, it is likely this provision would be upheld as reasonable under the Fourth Amendment. A subsequent search of a bag may raise Fourth Amendment issues, particularly related to consent

(Chapter 4) and whether taking control of the bag from a passenger is a seizure (Chapter 2).

III. Border Searches

A. International Borders

Searches at an international border, or an equivalent entry-point, such as an airport at which international flights land, are treated differently from other searches because they are not governed by the Fourth Amendment's probable cause or warrant requirements. In *United States v. Ramsey*, 431 U.S. 606 (1977), the Supreme Court described the plenary customs power of a nation, that "searches made at the border, pursuant to the long-standing right of the sovereign to protect itself by stopping and examining persons and property crossing into this country, are reasonable simply by virtue of the fact that they occur at the border." As such, these searches need not be supported by probable cause, or any level of suspicion that is required for other seizures.

The Court made that clear in *United States v. Flores-Montano*, 541 U.S. 149 (2004), in which it upheld a search at the border in which officers removed the gas tank from the defendant's car, revealing narcotics hidden beneath it in a compartment, even though there was no basis to suspect he was transporting drugs. Although the seizure and removal took nearly an hour, the Court reiterated that "[t]he Government's interest in preventing the entry of unwanted persons and effects is at its zenith at the international border."

B. Detention

In addition to searches of property, such as luggage, automobiles, and boats, the Fourth Amendment does not limit the government's authority to briefly detain a person for questioning at the border. For a longer detention beyond the initial interview, however, the government needs a reasonable suspicion of criminal activity.

In *United States v. Montoya de Hernandez*, 473 U.S. 531 (1985), agents suspected the defendant was smuggling narcotics by swallowing balloons containing the drugs, and she was held almost a full day waiting for her to expel the items naturally. In rejecting a Fourth Amendment challenge to the detention on the ground that the government did not have probable cause, the Court noted that "the Fourth Amendment balance between the interests of the Government and the privacy right of the individual is also struck much more favorably to the Government at the border." The balancing process means that "the detention of a traveler at the border, beyond the scope of a routine customs search and inspection, is justified at its inception if customs agents, considering all the facts surrounding the traveler and her trip, *reasonably suspect* that the traveler is smuggling contraband." The reasonable suspicion standard is the lowest threshold for a seizure or search, and in other contexts, such as *Terry* stops (Chapter 4), it only justifies a limited detention. At the border, however, the government can hold a person for a substantially greater period so long as the seizure is based on a reasonable suspicion.

C. Roving Border Patrols

Although an initial search at an international border need not be supported by probable cause or a reasonable suspicion, searches away from the border are treated under the traditional Fourth Amendment criteria for reasonableness. In *Almeida-Sanchez v. United States*, 413 U.S. 266 (1973), the Supreme Court held that the warrantless search of an automobile without probable cause or consent by a roving patrol of agents of the United States Border Patrol on a highway at least 20 miles north of the Mexican border was not a border search and therefore violated the Fourth Amendment. The Court rejected the government's argument that searches by the Border Patrol were the equivalent of inspections of highly regulated businesses upheld in *Camara* and *See*, noting that "businessmen engaged in such federally licensed and regulated enterprises accept the burdens as well as the benefits of their trade, whereas the petitioner here was not engaged in any regulated or licensed business."

While probable cause was required for the search in *Almeida-Sanchez*, the Court interpreted the Fourth Amendment to require only a reasonable suspicion for the Border Patrol to detain a vehicle stopped for brief questioning at a point away from the border about whether the occupants entered the country illegally. *United States v. Brignoni-Ponce*, 422 U.S. 873 (1975), identified the factors an agent can consider to support a reasonable suspicion that there are illegal aliens present, including the characteristics of the area in which Border Patrol agents observe the vehicle, its proximity to the border, traffic patterns on the particular road, previous experience with alien traffic, and information about recent illegal border crossings in the area. While the ethnic or racial appearance of the occupants can be one factor in forming reasonable suspicion, it is insufficient alone to authorize the stop. The Court stated, "The likelihood that any given person of Mexican ancestry is an alien is high enough to make Mexican appearance a relevant factor, but standing alone it does not justify stopping all Mexican-Americans to ask if they are aliens."

D. Fixed Checkpoints

The Court takes a different approach if an automobile is stopped at a fixed checkpoint away from the border. In *Almeida-Sanchez*, the Court noted that "searches at an established station near the border, at a point marking the confluence of two or more roads that extend from the border, might be functional equivalents of border searches."

That point was reached in *United States v. Martinez-Fuerte*, 428 U.S. 543 (1976), when the Court upheld the convictions of defendants for transporting illegal aliens after they were stopped and questioned at a checkpoint over sixty miles from the international border. After an initial viewing by Border Patrol agents, the defendants were directed to a secondary inspection area where agents questioned them about their citizenship. In balancing the government's interests in stopping illegal immigration with the privacy rights of the automobile occupants, the Court determined that "[w]hile the need to make routine checkpoint stops is great, the consequent intrusion on Fourth Amendment interests is quite limited." The interference with motorists at fixed checkpoints is minimal, the Court emphasized the limited discretion officers exercised in selecting the location of the checkpoint and the cars that would be stopped. It noted that "checkpoint operations both appear to and actually involve less discretionary enforcement activity. The regularized manner in which established checkpoints are operated is visible evidence, reassuring to law-abiding motorists, that the stops are duly authorized and believed to serve the public interest."

Likening a stop in this context to the search of a closely regulated business, the Court held that the seizures and questioning at a fixed checkpoint did not require any particularized suspicion of wrongdoing. Moreover, the Court distinguished its position in *Brignoni-Ponce* that the stop could not be based solely on the ethnicity or race of occupants. "We further believe that it is constitutional to refer motorists selectively to the secondary inspection area ... on the basis of criteria that would not sustain a roving-patrol stop. Thus, even if it be assumed that such referrals are made largely on the basis of apparent Mexican ancestry, we perceive no constitutional violation."

IV. Searches of Vessels

A ship is the equivalent of an automobile for the purpose of conducting a warrantless search if there is probable cause (see Chapter 7). Indeed, the automobile exception to the warrant requirement is based on the Supreme Court precedent in *Carroll v. United States*, 267 U.S. 132 (1925), that authorized a warrantless search of a ship because it can be quickly moved out of the jurisdiction before a warrant can be obtained.

Statutes authorize the Coast Guard to board a vessel on the high seas or in the territorial waters of the United States without a warrant or probable cause to conduct a safety and document inspection so long as the ship is subject to United States law. The search is limited to the vessel's public areas, including cargo holds and the engine room. Once on board, the Coast Guard can develop a reasonable suspicion of criminal conduct which will allow for a limited search of other areas of the vessel. If there is probable cause for a search, then a full "stem-to-stern" inspection is permitted.

Under another statute, Customs officials can conduct document and safety inspections of any vessel in the United States, within a customs-enforcement area, or in customs waters. In addition, a ship fleeing the customs waters can be detained so long as it was first hailed within customs waters. Pursuant to the Maritime Drug Law Enforcement Act, government officials can board a "vessel without nationality" to determine its identity, and if it is truly stateless then it is subject to United States jurisdiction and can be boarded for a document and safety search.

While random automobile stops to check the vehicle's registration were prohibited in *Prouse*, the Court took a different approach to the entry on a vessel on a waterway. *United States v. Villamonte-Marquez*, 462 U.S. 579 (1983), upheld the boarding of a sailboat by Customs officers to check its documentation, during which the officers smelled burning marijuana and subsequently found over two tons of it during a search. The Court held that boarding the boat pursuant to a federal statute authorizing entry on to any vessel to check its papers without probable cause or reasonable suspicion was permissible because "[t]he nature of the governmental interest in assuring compliance with documentation requirements, particularly in waters where the need to deter or apprehend smugglers is great, are substantial; the type of intrusion made in this case, while not minimal, is limited."

V. Special Needs Searches

The Supreme Court recognizes searches in a number of areas that are permissible even though conducted without a warrant or probable cause because of "special governmental needs" to gather information. The label "special needs" derives from a balancing analysis by the Court of the government's particular interest in the underlying activity as compared to the privacy interests of the individuals searched. The special need must be a current problem that is effectively addressed through the search, so that the determination is whether the search without a warrant or probable cause—and without a reasonable suspicion of criminal activity—meets the Fourth Amendment's reasonableness requirement. If it does, and courts have found most searches involving the special needs doctrine to be reasonable, then the search is permissible so long as its immediate objective is not "to generate evidence for law enforcement purposes." In most cases, law enforcement agents do not conduct the special needs search, and it is undertaken by other public officials, such as school principals and drug-testing services.

A. Public School Students

The language referencing the government's special needs as the basis for ascertaining the reasonableness of a search first appeared in Justice Blackmun's concurring opinion in *New Jersey v. T.L.O.*, 469 U.S. 325 (1985), which upheld a public school official's warrantless search of a high school student's purse that turned up evidence of marijuana sales. Justice Blackmun wrote, "The elementary and secondary school setting presents a *special need* for flexibility justifying a departure from the balance struck by the Framers" requiring probable cause and a warrant to conduct a search. The Court, in a majority opinion by Justice White, upheld the search on the ground that the balancing of the government's interest in the school setting outweighed the privacy interests of the student. It held that "the accommodation of the privacy interests of schoolchildren with the substantial need of teachers and administrators for freedom to maintain order in the schools does not require strict adherence to the requirement that searches be based on probable cause to believe that the subject of the search has violated or is violating the law." So long as the search is not "excessively intrusive," then it is permissible "when there are reasonable grounds for suspecting that the search will turn up evidence that the student has violated or is violating either the law or the rules of the school." The special need in *T.L.O.* was the maintenance of order and discipline in the school, including deterring drug use.

In *Safford Unified School District #1 v. Redding*, 129 S.Ct. 2633 (2009), the Court found that the strip search of a student was excessively intrusive under *T.L.O.* The student was suspected of possessing low-level prescription pain medication and over-the-counter pills, and the search was conducted pursuant to a school policy that prohibited the possession of such items without prior permission. The Court described the standard for a school search as "a moderate chance of finding evidence of wrongdoing," rather than the higher probable cause standard that there be a "fair probability" of finding the evidence.

While the suspicion of possession of the items was sufficient to justify a search of the student's backpack and outer clothing, the Court found that "the content of the suspicion failed to match the degree of the intrusion" when the student was required to almost completely undress. The Court held that "the *T.L.O.* concern to limit a school search to reasonable scope requires the support of reasonable suspicion of danger or of resort to underwear for hiding evidence of wrongdoing before a search can reasonably make the quantum leap from outer clothes and backpacks to exposure of intimate parts."

B. Public Employees

A plurality of the Court applied the special needs doctrine in *O'Connor v. Ortega*, 480 U.S. 709 (1987), to uphold the search of a public employee's office by a superior. The plurality opinion by Justice O'Connor noted that the workplace covers "those areas and items that are related to work and are generally within the employer's control," although "[t]he appropriate standard for a workplace search does not necessarily apply to a piece of closed personal luggage, a handbag or a briefcase that happens to be within the employer's business address." In weighing the government's justification for the search against the employee's privacy interest, the plurality determined that "[b]alanced against the substantial government interests in the efficient and proper operation of the workplace are the privacy interests of government employees in their place of work which, while not insubstantial, are far less than those found at home or in some other contexts."

Citing Justice Blackmun's concurring opinion in *T.L.O.*, the *O'Connor* plurality found that the presence of special needs "for legitimate work-related, noninvestigatory intrusions as well as investigations of work-related misconduct" meant that a warrant was not required to search a public employee's workplace. The conduct of the government officials must still meet the reasonableness requirement, that it be related in scope to the circumstances justifying the search at the inception.

C. Probationers and Parolees

The Supreme Court held in *Hudson v. Palmer*, 468 U.S. 517 (1984), that prison inmates have no reasonable expectation of privacy in their prison cells entitling them to the protections of the Fourth Amendment, so officers can search the cell at any time without a warrant or probable cause. Defendants serving a term of probation are also being punished by having certain conditions imposed on them, but they are not inmates in a prison and so have a greater privacy interest in their homes and property. However, probationers receive less protection than ordinary citizens under the Fourth Amendment from searches designed to ensure compliance with the requirements of the probation.

In *Griffin v. Wisconsin*, 483 U.S. 868 (1987), the search of the defendant's home by a probation officer was pursuant to a state statute authorizing the inspection if there were "reasonable grounds" to believe contraband was present on the premises. The Court found that the "State's operation of a probation system, like its operation of a school, government office or prison, or its supervision of a regulated industry, likewise presents 'special needs' beyond normal law enforcement that may justify departures from the usual warrant and probable-cause requirements." The search did not violate the Fourth Amendment even though the information about the defendant's possession of a weapon came from the police, who were present during the search. In finding the reasonable grounds standards sufficient to permit a warrantless search, the Court determined that "[i]n some cases—especially those involving drugs or illegal weapons—the probation agency must be able to act based upon a lesser degree of certainty than the Fourth Amendment would otherwise require in order to intervene before a probationer does damage to himself or society."

In *United States v. Knights*, 534 U.S. 112 (2001), the Court upheld a warrantless search by a police officer of a probationer's home based on reasonable suspicion, not probable cause. The defendant had agreed to a condition of probation for another crime that the government could search his home and property at any time without a warrant or even reasonable cause for the search. The Court declined to decide whether the probation condition constituted valid consent, concluding instead that the search met the Fourth Amendment's reasonableness requirement for searches of probationers under *Griffin*. The Court held that "[w]hen an officer has *reasonable suspicion* that a probationer subject to a search condition is engaged in criminal activity, there is enough likelihood that criminal conduct is occurring that an intrusion on the probationer's significantly diminished privacy interests is reasonable." Note that the search in *Knights* was conducted by the police for a law enforcement purpose, but the government's "interest in apprehending violators of the criminal law, thereby protecting potential victims of criminal enterprise, may therefore justifiably focus on probationers in a way that it does not on the ordinary citizen."

In *Samson v. California*, 547 U.S. 843 (2006), the Court applied its holding in *Knights* to the suspicionless search of a parolee that resulted in the discovery of illegal narcotics. A California statute required all parolees to agree "to be subject to search or seizure by a parole officer or other peace officer at any time of the day or night, with or without a search warrant and with or without cause." In upholding the search, and effectively the statute, the Court noted that it had "repeatedly acknowledged that a State's interests in reducing re-cidivism and thereby promoting reintegration and positive citizenship among probationers and parolees warrant privacy intrusions that would not other-wise be tolerated under the Fourth Amendment." In balancing the state's in-terest with that of the individual, *Samson* explained that parolees have an even lower expectation of privacy than probationers because parole is more akin to imprisonment than probation is.

VI. Drug Testing

A particular application of the special needs doctrine has been used to allow drug and alcohol testing programs that are not based on reasonable suspicion of use of these intoxicants nor is a warrant required. The Supreme Court has upheld random testing programs under the Fourth Amendment when the ob-jective is not for law enforcement purposes and the program involves a pervasively regulated industry or individuals with a reduced expectation of privacy. Like other types of administrative searches, the programs must be administered pursuant to regulations that limit the discretion of public officials in the selection and timing of the tests, and the goal for conducting the tests could not be achieved if a reasonable suspicion of drug or alcohol use would be effective in monitoring abuses. In conducting the Fourth Amendment balance, the Court has noted that these tests are quite invasive of the individual's personal pri-vacy, so the decisions upholding the programs emphasize the respect for per-sonal dignity.

A. Public Employees

In *Skinner v. Railway Labor Executives' Association*, 489 U.S. 602 (1989), and *National Treasury Employees Union v. Von Raab*, 489 U.S. 656 (1989), the Court upheld drug and alcohol testing programs for railway workers and U.S. Customs Service officers. In *Skinner*, the Federal Railroad Administration re-quired private rail companies to conduct blood and urine tests of certain em-ployees after a major train accident. Although the tests constituted searches under the Fourth Amendment, the Court found that requiring a warrant was unnecessary because "in light of the standardized nature of the tests and the minimal discretion vested in those charged with administering the program, there are virtually no facts for a neutral magistrate to evaluate." The focus on limited discretion was important because it obviated the need for the screen-ing that a warrant requirement would impose, and the Court noted that "the regulations contain various safeguards against any possibility that discretion will be abused." Moreover, there was a substantial risk that evidence of drug or alcohol use would be lost if a warrant were required before testing the workers because the substances are eliminated quickly from a person's body. The government's strong public safety interest outweighed the privacy rights of the workers, and the Court concluded that "imposing a warrant requirement in the present context would add little to the assurances of certainty and regularity already afforded by the regulations, while significantly hindering, and in many cases frustrating, the objectives of the Government's testing program."

Von Raab involved urinalysis tests of those Customs Service officers seeking a transfer or promotion into a position related to drug interdiction programs that involved carrying a weapon, or handling classified information. The Court noted that the drug testing was unrelated to any law enforcement purpose, and the special need to deter drug use by those in sensitive governmental positions "may justify departure from the ordinary warrant and probable-cause requirements." Although the invasion of personal privacy from collecting a urine sample "could be substantial in some circumstances," the Court found that Customs Service employees "who are directly involved in the interdiction of illegal drugs or who are required to carry firearms in the line of duty likewise have a diminished expectation of privacy in respect to the intrusions occasioned by a urine test." Balanced against the expectation of privacy was the fact that "[i]t is readily apparent that the Government has a compelling interest in ensuring that front-line interdiction personnel are physically fit, and have unimpeachable integrity and judgment." Therefore, the Court upheld the drug testing program for those employees who would be involved in drug interdiction programs or carry a gun, but it remanded the case for further consideration whether the designation of those who would handle classified documents, which included baggage clerks and messengers, was sufficiently narrow.

B. Public School Students

The Court extended its rationale for allowing drug testing to public school students in *Vernonia School District 47J v. Acton*, 515 U.S. 646 (1995). In response to a significant increase in drug usage and a "drug culture" led by athletes in its schools, the district instituted a program under which all participants in school sports programs would be subject to random drug tests through the collection of urine samples. The Court, relying on *T.L.O.*, noted that students have only a reduced expectation of privacy because "the subjects of the Policy are (1) children, who (2) have been committed to the temporary custody of the

State as schoolmaster," and for the drug testing policy at issue "[l]egitimate privacy expectations are even less with regard to student athletes." The collection of urine samples was respectful of the students, and "the privacy interests compromised by the process of obtaining the urine sample are in our view negligible." The Court clarified the nature of the government's interest that can permit a warrantless search for which there is no probable cause in the special needs context, describing it as "an interest that appears *important enough* to justify the particular search at hand, in light of other factors that show the search to be relatively intrusive upon a genuine expectation of privacy." In weighing the need to deter pervasive drug use in the district's schools, the Court found that there was an "immediate crisis of greater proportions than existed in *Skinner* ... [a]nd of much greater proportions than existed in *Von Raab*," thereby justifying the drug testing program in which there was no reasonable suspicion of individual drug use.

The Court applied the analysis in *Vernonia School District 47J* to a much broader student drug testing program in *Board of Education of Independent School District No. 92 of Pottawatomie County v. Earls*, 536 U.S. 822 (2002). In *Earls*, the school district required every middle or high school student participating in an extracurricular program, from athletics to the Future Farmers of America club, to take a drug test. In assessing the governmental interest in suspicionless drug testing, the Court extended its analysis by finding that "[t]he health and safety risks identified in *Vernonia School District 47J* apply with equal force to Tecumseh's children. Indeed, the nationwide drug epidemic makes the war against drugs a pressing concern in every school." Unlike the specific evidence in *Vernonia School District 47J* of increased drug usage and the role of athletes in a local drug culture, the Court in *Earls* upheld the drug testing program on the broader ground that drugs in general are a sufficient threat that the limited expectation of privacy that students have was outweighed." It is not clear whether the Court would uphold drug testing of *all* school students, regardless of their participation in an extracurricular activity, but *Earls* can be read as supporting such a conclusion.

C. Rejected Testing Programs

In two cases, *Chandler v. Miller*, 520 U.S. 305 (1997), and *Ferguson v. City of Charleston*, 532 U.S. 67 (2001), the Supreme Court rejected drug testing programs because they did not meet the requirements for a special needs exception to the warrant and probable cause requirements. The two decisions show that there are limits on the government's power to impose broad drug-testing programs, although the analysis is largely fact-specific so it is difficult to say at the outset whether other types of programs will pass muster under the Fourth Amendment.

In *Chandler*, the challenge was to a Georgia program under which candidates for certain elected state offices had to certify that they had taken and passed a drug test. Describing the requirements of the special needs doctrine as a "closely guarded category of constitutionally permissible suspicionless searches," the Court rejected the state's Tenth Amendment argument that its sovereign power to establish criteria for state offices affected the Fourth Amendment analysis of the warrantless search. "We are aware of no precedent suggesting that a State's power to establish qualifications for state offices — any more than its sovereign power to prosecute crime — diminishes the constraints on state action imposed by the Fourth Amendment." While the drug testing procedure was "relatively noninvasive," the Court found that the state's justification for the program was inadequate because "[a] demonstrated problem of drug abuse, while not in all cases necessary to the validity of a testing regime, would shore up an assertion of special need for a suspicionless general search program. Proof of unlawful drug use may help to clarify — and to substantiate — the precise hazards posed by such use." The program also did not meet the requirement of the special needs doctrine that it be an effective means to accomplish the stated goal, and the Court found that it "cannot work to ferret out lawbreakers, and respondents barely attempt to support the statute on that ground." In invalidating the candidate drug testing program, the Court concluded that "[t]he need revealed, in short, is symbolic, not 'special,' as that term draws meaning from our case law."

In *Ferguson*, the Court rejected a drug testing program for pregnant mothers who were suspected of drug use, under which positive test results were given to the police for prosecution as leverage to get the mothers into treatment programs. The Court found that the drug testing involved a significant invasion of privacy compared to other special needs searches because a "reasonable expectation of privacy enjoyed by the typical patient undergoing diagnostic tests in a hospital is that the results of those tests will not be shared with nonmedical personnel without her consent." In looking at the justification for the drug testing policy, the Court rejected the proffered basis that it was "protecting the health of both mother and child." Instead, it found that the warrantless search was for a general law enforcement purpose because the written policy "devotes its attention to the chain of custody, the range of possible criminal charges, and the logistics of police notification and arrests. Nowhere, however, does the document discuss different courses of medical treatment for either mother or infant, aside from treatment for the mother's addiction." Moreover, police and prosecutors were extensively involved in the day-to-day administration of the program, supporting the conclusion that "the immediate objective of the searches was to generate evidence for *law enforcement purposes.*"

Ferguson emphasized that although the motive for the drug testing program was benign, it still violated the Fourth Amendment "given the pervasive involvement of law enforcement with the development and application of the [hospital] policy." A dissenting opinion by Justice Scalia argued that the presence of a law enforcement purpose does not automatically vitiate the special needs doctrine "since the special-needs doctrine was developed, and is ordinarily employed, precisely to enable searches by law enforcement officials who, of course, ordinarily have a law enforcement objective." The dissent noted that *Griffin* involved a search by a probation officer with law enforcement officers present, yet the Court upheld the warrantless search there under the special needs doctrine.

D. Lower Court Decisions

Since *Skinner, Von Raab,* and *Vernonia School District 47J,* the lower federal courts have largely upheld drug testing programs for public employees and in schools under the special needs doctrine. Among the workplace programs that have met the requirements allowing warrantless testing are those for police officers, firefighters, probation and parole officers, and correctional facility officers.

In *Stigile v. Clinton,* 110 F.3d 801 (D.C. Cir. 1997), the court upheld a testing program for those working in the Office of Management and Budget because of their access to the work areas of the President and Vice President. In addition to drug testing of students involved in extracurricular activities, a program involving a metal detector and pat-down search of male students from the sixth to twelfth grades was upheld because of the special need to maintain safety and discipline in the school. If there is a reasonable suspicion that a student is involved in misconduct, then any subsequent search is reviewed to determine its reasonableness under *T.L.O.* and not under the special needs doctrine. Not every program passes muster under the special needs doctrine. For example, lower courts invalidated a program of drug testing for teachers injured on the job, and a program that tested government employees for syphilis, sickle cell, and pregnancy in addition to drug usage.

Checkpoints

- In analyzing administrative and special needs searches and seizures, a key consideration is whether the primary purpose is something other than gathering evidence of a crime or to question witnesses about an offense.

- Administrative search warrants can be issued without probable cause if reasonable legislative or regulatory standards for conducting an area inspection are satisfied.

- Owners of commercial property may have a lower expectation of privacy, especially if it is a closely regulated business.

- If the owner knows the business is closely regulated because there is a substantial government regulatory interest, then a warrant is not required for searches that are not primarily for a law enforcement purpose, even if evidence is obtained for subsequent use in a criminal prosecution.

- Warrantless business inspections must be pursuant to a regulatory scheme that limits the discretion of the public officials and advises the owner that the search is pursuant to law.

- Border searches, including those at the equivalent, such as an airport or fixed checkpoint, do not require probable cause or reasonable suspicion.

- An individual may be detained briefly at the border for questioning without probable cause, and a longer detention is permissible if there is reasonable suspicion of wrongdoing.

- Roving border patrols away from an international border must adhere to the Fourth Amendment to detain a person or automobile for questioning.

- Vessels on waterways and the high seas are subject to warrantless entry and limited searches, including inspection of registration and related documents.

- Special government needs may permit a warrantless search if the government's interest outweighs the privacy interest of those searched and the search is not designed to generate evidence for law enforcement purposes.

- Public school students, public employees, and probationers/parolees have a reduced expectation of privacy, and the government's special needs in dealing with each allow for warrantless searches.

- Drug-testing of public employees are permissible special needs searches so long as there is a strong government need to ensure health and safety, to protect the integrity of law enforcement, or to combat drug problems in schools. Drug tests are impermissible if the primary purpose is to gather evidence for law enforcement or when the program will not fulfill the stated governmental purpose.

Chapter 12

Remedies for Fourth Amendment Violations

Roadmap

- Exclusionary rule history and rationales
- Procedures for asserting the rule
- Exceptions and limitations
- Other remedies for Fourth Amendment violations

I. Introduction

The exclusionary rule prevents the introduction in criminal trials of evidence that was obtained by violating defendant's Fourth Amendment rights. This is the most powerful, and controversial, remedy for Fourth Amendment violations, because its application can hinder criminal prosecutions. It is also relatively easy for defendants to pursue, and cost-free for those represented by public defenders. In recent years, the exclusionary rule has been narrowed, and there are now a number of situations in which it is unavailable.

There are other remedies for Fourth Amendment wrongs, but these are more difficult to obtain. Victims of illegal searches and seizures may sue for damages, using common law tort theories and causes of action created by state and federal statutory law, although such lawsuits impose procedural burdens and attorneys' fees on those seeking relief. Administrative actions, such as police disciplinary proceedings, also may be available, but these do not result in tangible relief to the victims of the constitutional violation. Finally, in extreme cases, law enforcement officials may be prosecuted criminally for their unconstitutional actions; again, this kind of remedy does not benefit victims directly.

II. Development of the Exclusionary Rule

A. *Weeks*: The Exclusionary Rule in Federal Court

The Supreme Court articulated the Fourth Amendment exclusionary rule nearly one hundred years ago in *Weeks v. United States*, 232 U.S. 383 (1914). The criminal defendant in that case, Fremont Weeks, had been the subject of an illegal search conducted by a United States Marshal, who had entered and searched his home without a warrant. Based on evidence found there, the government charged Weeks with sending gambling materials through the mail. Weeks demanded that the evidence be excluded from his trial, and ultimately the Supreme Court agreed with him. The Court stated that, if the product of an unlawful search and seizure could be used in evidence, the Fourth Amendment "is of no value, and ... might as well be stricken from the Constitution." The Court observed, though, that the Fourth Amendment applied only to federal officials, and it hinted that it would not extend the exclusionary remedy to violations by state and local law enforcement officers.

B. *Mapp*: The Exclusionary Rule Extended to States

For many years after *Weeks*, the availability of an exclusionary remedy for improper searches and seizures by state and local officials continued to depend solely on state law. Some states created exclusionary remedies similar to the one announced in *Weeks*, and by the time the Supreme Court surveyed the state law landscape in 1949, sixteen states had implemented a *Weeks*-type exclusionary rule. But of those states that had expressly considered the matter, a greater number—thirty-one—had chosen not to do so.

During this period, while states were left to themselves to decide how best to provide relief for wrongful searches and seizures, justices of the Supreme Court were engaging in what was known as the "incorporation debate." At stake in a series of cases was whether the restrictions listed in the Bill of Rights' first eight Amendments applied to state and local officials. The Bill of Rights had been written as a limitation only upon federal power, but the post-Civil War amendments to the United States Constitution (particularly the Fourteenth Amendment) raised the question whether state and local actors also should be constrained. In the phrasing of the time, the task for the Court was deciding which of the Bill of Rights would be "incorporated" against the states by virtue of the Fourteenth Amendment's due process clause.

The Fourth Amendment incorporation question first came to the Court in *Wolf v. Colorado*, 338 U.S. 25 (1949). The case had two parts: first, whether the prohibition against unreasonable searches and seizures should be incorporated against the states through the Fourteenth Amendment; second, if so, whether the exclusionary remedy should be incorporated along with it. As to the first question, the Court quickly determined that the right against unreasonable searches and seizures was a "basic" one, "implicit in the concept of ordered liberty," and therefore incorporated through the Fourteenth Amendment. The second part of the question posed a more difficult issue. In order to decide whether the exclusionary remedy was a basic right, implicit in the concept of ordered liberty, the Court looked to state practices. Noting that a minority of states imposed rules of exclusion, the Court concluded that the remedy was not of bedrock importance. As a result, it held that the Fourteenth Amendment did not incorporate the exclusionary rule against the states.

That holding was short-lived. Twelve years later, in *Mapp v. Ohio*, 367 U.S. 643 (1961), the Court took a second look at the issue. The facts in the case were clear: Ohio police had entered Dollree Mapp's house illegally without a warrant and, searching through her effects, had found pornographic materials for which she later was criminally prosecuted. Overruling *Wolf*, the Court held that the materials could not be used in the criminal trial against Mapp. The Court gave several reasons for its holding. First, it declared that the Fourth Amendment's prohibitions implicitly contain remedial measures, noting that rights are meaningless without remedies. Its second major rationale was that of "judicial integrity": the judicial branch should have nothing to do with evidence tainted by law enforcement wrongdoing. Finally, and most importantly, the Court wished to remove an underlying incentive for many Fourth Amendment violations—the desire to discover and prosecute criminals—and was convinced that the exclusionary rule imposed a robust deterrent effect upon law enforcement misconduct.

Mapp stands for the proposition that courts must exclude evidence obtained through Fourth Amendment violations, and it remains good law today, although its application has been narrowed. It was part of the "criminal procedure revolution" lead by Chief Justice Earl Warren and the Court over which he presided. The Warren Court construed constitutional criminal procedure rights expansively and applied them equally to the actions of state and federal officials. This revolution was controversial at the time and has remained so. According to its supporters, the Warren Court finally gave the Bill of Rights an appropriate, bold interpretation that brought to fruition its promise of limited governmental powers and enhanced individual dignity; according to critics, it stretched the Constitution beyond its terms and reduced the effectiveness of the criminal justice system by causing defendants to be released on "technicalities." Critics continue to point to *Mapp*'s exclusionary rule as a leading example of Warren Court judicial activism. This controversy continues to play out in cases that narrow the reach of the exclusionary rule. See Part III below.

III. Standing and Procedures for Asserting the Exclusionary Rule

A. Who Can Assert the Exclusionary Rule: The "Standing" Doctrine

One of the fundamental principles of the American legal system is that a litigant must establish "standing" before asserting a claim for relief. Among other things, the standing requirement ensures that each litigant has a personal stake in the case and thereby an incentive to sharpen the issues for the court. Generally, standing involves two broad inquiries: first, whether the litigant suffered an "injury in fact," and second, whether the litigant is asserting his or her own legal rights, rather than basing the claim for relief on the rights of others. Fourth Amendment claims are no exception to the rule of standing: a person aggrieved by an unlawful search or seizure and seeking a remedy (including application of the exclusionary rule) must establish standing before a court will address the claim.

The principal case on the issue of standing for Fourth Amendment purposes is *Rakas v. Illinois,* 439 U.S. 128 (1978). In that case, the Court held that Fourth Amendment rights are "personal" ones that can be asserted only by the individual who suffered the unlawful search or seizure. A person whose rights were not violated by the search or seizure does not have standing. This is true even if the person was harmed by the search or seizure. For example, a criminal defendant implicated by evidence that was unlawfully seized from the person of another would not have standing to move for the exclusion of that evidence.

Rakas narrowed the class of litigants who would survive the standing test in unlawful search situations, because it disavowed an earlier test that granted standing to anyone "legitimately on the premises" where a search occurred. The Court in *Rakas* held that the earlier test created "too broad a gauge" for measuring Fourth Amendment rights.

In order to establish standing after *Rakas*, a person must prove that his or her personal rights were violated by a search or seizure. The test for determining whether a person's rights were violated by a search or seizure is: in the case of an unlawful search, whether the person had a legitimate expectation of privacy in the invaded place (see Chapter 2). In the case of an unlawful seizure of things or places, the test is whether the person had a possessory interest in the things or places seized. In the case of an unlawful seizure of a person, the test is whether the person's freedom of movement was affected in a substantial way (see Chapter 4). If a defendant can satisfy the particular test for the alleged violation, then he or she has standing to assert an exclusionary rule claim under the Fourth Amendment.

Although standing is sometimes considered a "threshold" issue that a court must decide before addressing the merits of the claim, the Court in *Rakas* pointed out that the exclusionary rule standing tests are subsumed within the substantive Fourth Amendment inquiry, which is this:

- did the defendant have a reasonable expectation of privacy in the place searched, or a possessory interest in the item or place seized, or a liberty interest in bodily movement; and
- if so, was the search or seizure unlawful?

Many courts continue to refer to the inquiry as a threshold one involving "standing," but in actuality they appear to use that term to refer to the first part of the two-part substantive Fourth Amendment inquiry.

B. How to Assert the Exclusionary Rule

A criminal defendant must assert the exclusionary rule by making a motion to suppress evidence. Usually this is a written document, filed pretrial, which asks the judge to rule specified evidence inadmissible at trial on the ground that it was the product of an illegal search or seizure. In the motion to suppress, the defendant must allege a prima facie claim for relief—in other words, a claim that, if true, would entitle the defendant to exclusion. Thus, the defendant must assert that he or she suffered an illegal search or seizure by a government actor, that the exclusionary rule applies, and that the particular evidence sought to be excluded was a product of that search or seizure. Typically the defendant will ask the court for a hearing on the motion to suppress, and the hearing will be granted if the defendant has articulated a prima facie claim.

The Supreme Court has articulated few rules about burdens of proof in exclusionary rule claims, and the instances in which it has are addressed in several other Chapters. For the most part, it has left the lower courts to determine these for themselves. The general pattern in the lower courts is this: most jurisdictions impose a burden of proof on the defendant to establish:

- whether the defendant has standing—in other words, whether his or her personal Fourth Amendment rights are at issue;

- whether there was government action that violated those rights;
- whether the evidence sought to be suppressed was a product of the government action.

Other than these issues, allocation of the burden of proof depends on the posture of the claim. Where the search or seizure was accompanied by a warrant, most courts make the defendant prove that the government lacked probable cause or that the warrant was insufficiently particular. Likewise, the Court has held that the defense has the burden of proving that a search or arrest warrant affidavit contains deliberate falsehoods or falsehoods in reckless disregard of the truth. See *Bumper v. North Carolina*, 391 U.S. 543 (1968). But the prosecution ordinarily has the burden if its actions were warrantless. For example, if the search or seizure was not accompanied by a warrant, the prosecution generally must prove that an exception to the warrant requirement applies. Similarly, if the suppression question turns on an exclusionary rule exception (see Part III below), the prosecution typically will be required to prove the exception's applicability. Regardless of who holds the burden of proof, it ordinarily is satisfied by a preponderance of evidence, although some courts impose a "clear and convincing" standard if the prosecution contends that a search was consensual or that seized property was voluntarily abandoned.

Burdens of proof can pose significant challenges to defendants, who often are the only witnesses (other than law enforcement officers) to the searches and seizures from which they seek relief. Because defendants rarely can satisfy their burden of proof through the testimony of others, they must take the stand themselves in order to establish their claims. The problem is that their testimony might incriminate them. For example, a defendant challenging the seizure of unregistered guns might have to admit to owning the guns. If left unprotected from the incriminating effects of their testimony, defendants often would forego the exclusionary remedy, and the public would lose the benefit of the remedy's powerful check on law enforcement misconduct. In order to ease the way for defendants to testify at suppression hearings, the Supreme Court has established a rule barring the government from using that testimony against them as substantive evidence. See *Simmons v. United States*, 390 U.S. 377 (1968). However, if a defendant later takes the stand at trial and testifies falsely or inconsistently, the government may impeach him or her with the prior suppression hearing testimony.

IV. Exclusionary Rule Limitations

A. Recent Narrowing of the Exclusionary Rule

After the Court decided *Mapp*, the exclusionary remedy appeared to be constitutionally required in all cases except those whose facts implicated an express, recognized exception or limitation, discussed below. But in more recent years, a bare majority of the Court has retreated from a rule of automatic applicability to a narrower remedy that applies only when law enforcement officers acted with culpability in violating Fourth Amendment rights, and, even then, only when exclusion would likely deter future violations. *Herring v. United States*, 129 S. Ct. 695 (2009). It remains unclear which approach will win the Court's long-term support—the automatic one, in which the exclusionary rule applies absent an explicit limitation, or the narrow one, in which the exclusionary rule applies only where it is likely to remedy culpable, deterrable law enforcement conduct. The choice of approach will turn largely on the composition of the Court, but lawyers nevertheless must be knowledgeable about the underlying rationales for both approaches.

B. Limitations on the Exclusionary Rule

1. The "Good Faith" Exception

The Court's narrowing trend is obvious in the companion cases of *United States v. Leon*, 468 U.S. 897 (1984), and *Massachusetts v. Sheppard*, 468 U.S. 981 (1984), in which the Court articulated what is known as the "good faith exception" to the exclusionary rule. In both cases, the Court upheld the admission of evidence that had been discovered through illegal searches and seizures. And in both, two factors were uppermost in the Court's reasoning: first, the police had not been at fault for the illegality of the searches and seizures; and second, they had acted reasonably ("in good faith") by relying on facially valid warrants.

In *Leon*, the illegality stemmed from the fact that, although law enforcement officials acted pursuant to a facially valid search warrant, courts later determined that the magistrate should not have issued the warrant because the information contained in the supporting affidavit was stale and insufficient. The warrant's invalidity rendered illegal the search and seizure of evidence. Nevertheless, the Court ruled that the exclusionary rule should not apply because its costs—preventing the use of probative evidence—outweighed its benefits in these circumstances. Those benefits, according to the Court, lie only in deterring government officials who might otherwise have incentives to violate Fourth Amendment rights. Under the circumstances present in *Leon*, the Court believed there were no deterrent benefits to be had with respect to either the magistrate, who issued the warrant, or the police, who executed it. As to the magistrate, the Court reasoned as follows:

> Judges and magistrates are not adjuncts to the law enforcement team; as neutral judicial officers, they have no stake in the outcome of particular criminal prosecutions. The threat of exclusion thus cannot be expected significantly to deter them. Imposition of the exclusionary sanction is not necessary meaningfully to inform judicial officers of their errors, and we cannot conclude that admitting evidence obtained pursuant to a warrant while at the same time declaring that the warrant was somehow defective will in any way reduce judicial officers' professional incentives to comply with the Fourth Amendment, encourage them to repeat their mistakes, or lead to the granting of all colorable warrant requests.

As to the police, the Court stated that application of the exclusionary rule would incur no benefits because the police had reasonably believed the warrant to be valid when they executed it:

> The deterrent purpose of the exclusionary rule necessarily assumes that the police have engaged in willful, or at the very least negligent, conduct which has deprived the defendant of some right. By refusing to admit evidence gained as a result of such conduct, the courts hope to instill in those particular investigating officers, or in their future counterparts, a greater degree of care toward the rights of an accused. Where the official action was pursued in complete good faith, however, the deterrence rationale loses much of its force.

The *Leon* Court also elaborated on what it meant by "good faith." The most important parts of the Court's explanation are these:

- The good faith inquiry is an objective one, turning on what the reasonable officer should have known and done, not what the individual officers subjectively understood or intended.
- The objective standard requires officers to "have a reasonable knowledge of what the law provides." This is meant to encourage law enforcement education.
- The good faith exception is meant to be available only in "borderline cases."
- There are four instances in which police action can never be considered to have been taken in good faith:

- Where the magistrate or judge issuing the warrant was misled by information in an affidavit that the affiant knew was false or that he would have so known had he not recklessly disregarded the truth;
- Where the magistrate or judge "wholly abandoned his judicial role," because in such circumstances "no reasonably well trained officer should rely on the warrant";
- Where the officer relied on an affidavit "so lacking in indicia of probable cause as to render official belief in its existence entirely unreasonable"; and
- Where the warrant was "so facially deficient—*i.e.*, in failing to particularize the place to be searched or the things to be seized"—that no reasonable officer would believe it to be valid.

The Court decided *Sheppard* on the same day as *Leon*. In that case, law enforcement officials involved in a murder investigation also had acted pursuant to a warrant later determined to be invalid. This time the problem lay not in the warrant's supporting affidavit, but in its form. The *Sheppard* warrant had been meant to authorize a search for evidence of murder, but it had been issued on a form warrant that authorized only a search for controlled substances. The error was the judge's, who had promised police that he would fix up the form but failed to do so. The Court held that because the police had acted with objective reasonableness when they relied on the warrant to search for—and seize—evidence of murder, application of the exclusionary rule was not likely to deter future police misconduct. Accordingly, the rule would not be applied.

The Court also has held the exclusionary rule inapplicable where police acted reasonably in relying on a statute that authorized warrantless searches, even though the statute was later held to be unconstitutional. In *Illinois v. Krull*, 480 U.S. 340 (1987), after police searched an automobile wrecking yard and found stolen cars, the owner of the wrecking yard was arrested and prosecuted. The police search had been authorized by an Illinois statute that then permitted warrantless searches of wrecking yards, but a day after the search, a federal court in a different case had invalidated the statute on Fourth Amendment grounds. The Court held that evidence from the search could be used against Krull, because at the time police engaged in the warrantless search, they were legislatively authorized to do so. Said the Court, "[i]f the statute is subsequently declared unconstitutional, excluding evidence obtained pursuant to it prior to such a judicial declaration will not deter future Fourth Amendment violations by an officer who has simply fulfilled his responsibility to enforce the statute as written."

In *Arizona v. Evans*, 514 U.S. 1 (1995), the Court held the exclusionary rule to be inapplicable where a court clerk had failed to remove an invalidated arrest warrant from law enforcement computers, causing Evans to be arrested illegally. Pursuant to his illegal arrest, he was searched and discovered to be in possession of a small quantity of marijuana, for which he was prosecuted. Noting that the error had been that of a court employee, rather than of someone in the police department, the Court found that police had engaged in the arrest and search in reasonable reliance on the apparently valid warrant, and it ruled that the marijuana could be used against Evans.

Bare majorities decided the latest two decisions in this line of cases, and they went in opposite directions. In *Groh v. Ramirez*, 540 U.S. 551 (2004), the Court held that where a federal law enforcement officer prepared an obviously invalid warrant, he could not later claim he acted reasonably in relying on it. The issue before the Court was not the applicability of the exclusionary rule, but the qualified immunity of the officer who had been sued for damages under 42 U.S.C. § 1983. The reasonableness inquiry, though, is the same for both, and the Court clearly was considering the exclusionary rule implications of its decision. The warrant in *Groh* failed to list a single item to be searched for and seized, and it neglected to incorporate those items by reference to the supporting application. A federal judge signed the warrant, apparently without noticing its defects, and the officer executed it. Holding that the officer's actions had not been reasonable, the Court noted not only that the warrant been obviously invalid on its face, but also that it had been prepared by the officer himself. Moreover, unlike the situation in *Sheppard*, there was neither an indication that the officer had apprised the issuing judge of the defect, nor evidence that the judge had promised to remedy that defect.

Four of the Justices in the *Groh* majority found themselves in the dissent in *Herring v. U.S.*, 129 S. Ct. 695 (2009), where a different five-Justice majority disavowed the applicability of the exclusionary rule in a situation in which police had not acted culpably despite the fact that they had arrested Herring on the basis of a law enforcement error. The error had been that of a county sheriff's employee, who had failed to update the sheriff's database to reflect the recall of a warrant for Herring's arrest. Five months later, a law enforcement officer from a neighboring county relied on that database to arrest Herring, and in doing so engaged in a search incident to arrest that revealed illegal objects for which he was prosecuted. The Court held that the exclusionary rule did not apply, and that the objects found during the search incident to arrest could properly be used against him, because the employee's error was a matter of "isolated negligence attenuated from the arrest." The Court stated that "[t]o trigger the exclusionary rule, police conduct must be sufficiently deliberate that exclusion can meaningfully deter it, and sufficiently culpable that such deterrence is worth the price paid by the justice system." It further explained:

The extent to which the exclusionary rule is justified by these deterrence principles varies with the culpability of the law enforcement conduct. As we said in *Leon,* "an assessment of the flagrancy of the police misconduct constitutes an important step in the calculus" of applying the exclusionary rule. Similarly, in *Krull,* we elaborated that "evidence should be suppressed 'only if it can be said that the law enforcement officer had knowledge, or may properly be charged with knowledge, that the search was unconstitutional under the Fourth Amendment.' "

The Court concluded that "the exclusionary rule serves to deter deliberate, reckless, or grossly negligent conduct, or in some circumstances recurring or systemic negligence," and that the error in *Herring* did not "rise to that level."

In at least one important aspect, *Herring* appears to contradict *Leon's* insistence on objective inquiries: it requires courts to inquire into the mental states of individual officers. On the other hand, *Herring's* mention of "systemic negligence" as a means of preventing application of the good faith exception is consistent with *Leon's* discussion of the importance of police training programs. In any event, *Herring* makes the good faith exception much more likely to apply. Now two facts must be present before the exclusionary rule will apply in situations involving warrants: first, the officer must have been culpable or the administration systemically negligent; second, applying the exclusionary rule must promise to meaningfully deter future police errors. This approach suggests, without explicitly stating, that good faith is presumptively available in searches based on warrants (whether actual or purported), putting the burden on the defendant to prove otherwise.

2. The "Knock and Announce" Exception

At the same that it has expanded the "good faith" exception to the exclusionary rule, the Court also has (again by a five Justice majority) identified another category of cases in which the exclusionary rule does not apply: those involving police failures to knock and announce their presence when executing residential search warrants. The knock and announce rule is a common law doctrine that the Court recognized as having constitutional magnitude in *Wilson v. Arkansas,* 514 U.S. 927 (1995). But in assuring the constitutional status of the knock and announce rule, the Court did not at first decide whether the exclusionary rule would apply to its violations. More than ten years later, it carved out an exclusionary rule exception for those violations in *Hudson v. Michigan,* 547 U.S. 586 (2006). There, the Court observed that applying the exclusionary rule would not further the underlying rationales of the knock and announce rule, which evolved in order to reduce the risk of fear and violence surrounding the execution of a residential warrant, rather than to prevent law enforcement officials from seeing or taking evidence of crime. The Court also weighed two factors in determining that the exclusionary rule should not apply: first, the relatively high social costs in terms of lost convictions that its application would impose; and second, the relatively low incremental deterrence its application would gain because police have only "minimal" incentives to violate the knock and announce rule, and they face other deterring influences that did not exist when *Mapp* was decided.

3. The "Independent Source" and "Inevitable Discovery" Exceptions

In the cases discussed above, the evidence sought to be suppressed was unquestionably a "but-for" product of an illegal search or seizure — in other words, it would not have been discovered in the absence of the illegality. There is a category of cases, however, in which the prosecution can break that causal link, and in those cases, the exclusionary rule will not apply.

One such situation is that involving an "independent source" for the evidence. For example, in *Segura v. United States*, 468 U.S. 796 (1984), federal agents unlawfully entered Segura's apartment and remained there until a search warrant was obtained. The search warrant itself was valid and "untainted" by the unlawful entry, because no information discovered during the unlawful search had been mentioned in the warrant affidavit. The admissibility of what the agents discovered while illegally in the apartment was not before the Court, but the Court held that the evidence found for the first time during the legal execution of the warrant was admissible because it was discovered pursuant to an "independent source" unconnected with the invalid entry. By permitting the admission of that evidence, the court would put investigators in the same, not a worse, position than they would have been in had the illegality not occurred. Putting them in a worse position would create too much deterrence, causing police to be too cautious in fighting crime.

What would have been the result if the agents had sought to use against Segura evidence discovered while they waited (illegally) in the apartment for the warrant? The opinion in *Segura* had left that question unanswered, but four years later, in *Murray v. United States*, 487 U.S. 533 (1988), the Court answered it. The evidence would be admissible, the Court said, so long as the products of the illegal search were not used to obtain the warrant. Again, the key issue was putting the government in the same position it would have been in without the illegality, so as not to over-deter.

The facts of *Murray* are difficult to reconcile with this rationale, however. After receiving tips from informants about drug trafficking, and after having engaged in legal investigations, federal agents illegally forced their way into a warehouse, where they saw a number of marijuana bales. They left without disturbing the bales and kept the warehouse under surveillance until they reentered with a search warrant. In applying for the warrant, the agents did not mention their illegal entry into the warehouse or the observations they had made during that entry; instead, only the informants' tips and the lawful pre-entry investigations were used to support the warrant application. The agents later admitted, however, that they had not begun to prepare a warrant affidavit, or even engaged in any discussions of obtaining a warrant, until after their illegal entry into the warehouse. Nevertheless, the Court permitted the prosecution to use the marijuana bales as evidence.

A closely related doctrine, the "inevitable discovery exception," was developed in *Nix v. Williams*, 467 U.S. 431 (1984). The constitutional right at issue in *Nix* was the Sixth Amendment right to counsel, which protects different interests than the Fourth Amendment right against unreasonable searches and seizures. But the key analysis focused on the rationales for excluding illegally obtained evidence, and as a result *Nix* has great relevance to the Fourth Amendment exclusionary rule. The evidence at issue in *Nix* was the body of a murder victim. Williams had been arrested and charged with the murder, and in response to illegal post-arrest questioning by Iowa police, he led them to the body. The location and condition of the body became important pieces of evidence against Williams, and on appeal, he contended that they should have been excluded as the products of illegal questioning.

Williams' case went to the Supreme Court twice—first on the issue of the illegal questioning (see Chapter 15), and second on the applicability of the exclusionary rule. Unquestionably, traditional exclusionary rule analysis would dictate that if the body (including its location and condition) was the product of an illegality, it should be excluded and the resulting conviction overturned. But the State of Iowa proved that, at the time Williams revealed the location of the body, police were engaged in an organized and thorough search and would have discovered it through those independent means had the illegal questioning not occurred. Under these circumstances, the Court held, the evidence should be admitted in order to keep the state in the same position it would have been in without the illegality.

4. The "Attenuated Taint" Doctrine

Evidence obtained through a search or seizure may be characterized as direct or derivative. A good example of direct evidence obtained through an illegal search would be drugs found during a search of an arrestee. An example of derivative evidence would be drugs found in a second location to which police were directed by a note found during the illegal search of the first location. The Court has held that the exclusionary rule does not operate where the derivative evidence is *too* indirect, *i.e.* attenuated.

The "attenuation" doctrine was developed in *Wong Sun v. United States*, 371 U.S. 471 (1963). The case involved a long string of facts that were important to the Court's analysis, beginning with federal agents' illegal entry into the home of James Toy. A tip about drug dealing had motivated their entry, and the agents questioned Toy at gunpoint about that. Toy denied having engaged in drug transactions but implicated "Johnny," who lived in a different house. The agents went to that house, entered, and questioned Johnny Yee, who surrendered heroin to them. Yee told the agents that Toy and "Sea Dog" had given him the heroin, but that he didn't know Sea Dog's real name. The agents then re-questioned Toy, who identified Sea Dog as Wong Sun and provided Wong Sun's address. Agents went to that address and arrested Wong Sun.

Federal prosecutors charged Toy, Yee, and Wong Sun with narcotics offenses and released them on their own recognizance. Several days later, the three men came voluntarily to federal offices to undergo questioning, in response to which they made statements. Toy and Wong Sun were tried and convicted on the basis of all of this evidence, and both appealed on the ground that the evidence should have been suppressed. The Court ruled the following with respect to Toy's exclusionary rule claim:

- Toy's arrest was illegal, because it was not supported by probable cause.
- Toy's statements at the time of the arrest were direct products of the illegality, rather than of any "purging" act of free will; as a result, the exclusionary rule applied to them.
- The heroin seized from Yee was a direct product of the illegal arrest of Toy because it was obtained by exploiting that illegality; as a result, the exclusionary rule applied to it.
- Toy's statements several days later did not have to be analyzed because, combined with other admissible evidence, they were not sufficient to convict him.

With respect to Wong Sun's exclusionary rule claim, the Court held:

- Wong Sun's arrest was illegal, because it was not supported by probable cause.
- Wong Sun's statements were not the direct product of his illegal arrest,
because he had been released and voluntarily returned several days later
to make the statements. This act of free will purged the statements of the
taint of the illegal arrest; hence, Wong Sun's statements were admissible
against him.
- The heroin seized from Yee was admissible against Wong Sun because
the illegality vis-à-vis Toy did not affect his (*i.e.*, Wong's) rights. [Note
that this is an application of the standing doctrine, discussed above.]

The attenuation doctrine often involves statements made after illegal arrests. Sometimes, suspects make such statements after they are given *Miranda*
warnings. Do *Miranda* warnings "purge" the taint of the illegal arrest, rendering them admissible? In *Brown v. Illinois*, 422 U.S. 590 (1975), the Court
said no—at least not as a per se matter. It explained that a per se "cure-all" would
provide government officials with an incentive to violate the Fourth Amendment. In *Brown*, the Court also articulated three factors that it considered relevant to attenuation in the context of post-arrest statements:

- The temporal proximity of the arrest and the confession;
- The presence of intervening circumstances;
- The purpose and flagrancy of the official misconduct.

5. The "Criminal Trial" Limitation

As part of its effort to confine the reach of the exclusionary rule to those
situations in which its deterrent effects outweigh its costs, the Court has declared that it applies only in criminal trials. It does not apply in ordinary civil
cases, administrative proceedings (such as deportation proceedings), or some
quasi-criminal proceedings, such as parole revocation hearings. According
to the Court, the rule is not justified in these contexts because it provides
only "minimal deterrence benefits" outside of traditional law enforcement
situations.

On the other hand, the exclusionary rule has been applied in a few quasi-
criminal cases, such as some civil tax proceedings and civil forfeiture cases.
Courts use the following factors in order to decide whether deterrence would
be served by application of the exclusionary rule in a particular proceeding:

- The nature of the civil proceeding.
- Whether the same agency or sovereign initiated both the illegal search
and the civil proceeding.

- An explicit understanding or sharing of information between the law enforcement body that conducted the illegal search and the one that initiated the civil proceeding.
- A statutory regime in which both the law enforcement body and the civil
agency share resources—particularly resources derived from the civil
proceeding.
- A strong relationship between the law enforcement interests of the searching agency and the civil proceeding at which the seized material is being
offered.

Even where the exclusionary rule applies, it requires the suppression of evidence from the trial itself, but not from other stages of the procedure. For example, grand juries are permitted to examine evidence that was illegally obtained,
and judges are permitted to consider illegally obtained evidence for sentencing purposes.

6. The Impeachment Exception

Within the criminal trial itself, evidence that was obtained through constitutional violations may be admitted for the limited purpose of impeaching a
testifying defendant. The rationale for the impeachment exception is that the
"shield" provided by the exclusionary rule "cannot be perverted into a license
to use perjury by way of a defense." *Harris v. New York*, 401 U.S. 222, 226
(1971). In other words, if a defendant takes the stand and says things that are
deceptive or untrue, the prosecutor is permitted to undermine the defendant's
credibility by demonstrating the falsity of the testimony, even if that means
using inadmissible evidence.

The impeachment exception has two important limitations. First, the impeachment must relate either to the defendant's testimony on direct examination or to questions asked by the prosecutor on cross-examination that are
"reasonably suggested" by the defendant's testimony on direct examination.
That is to say, the prosecution cannot manipulate cross-examination in order
to get inadmissible evidence before the jury. The second major limitation to the
impeachment exception is that it applies only to testifying defendants: other defense witnesses cannot be impeached with evidence suppressed by operation
of the exclusionary rule. See *James v. Illinois*, 493 U.S. 307 (1990).

7. Limitation on Federal Habeas Review

Pursuant to federal habeas corpus statutes, individuals in state or federal
custody may file petitions in federal court challenging the constitutionality of
judicial rulings that led to their imprisonment. For example, a person con-

victed of a crime may seek habeas relief on the ground that the trial court should have excluded an involuntary confession. However, the Supreme Court has restricted the availability of habeas relief for Fourth Amendment violations. In *Stone v. Powell*, 428 U.S. 465 (1976), it held that a Fourth Amendment exclusionary rule violation may not form the basis for habeas relief if the proceedings that resulted in the conviction provided a "full and fair" opportunity to litigate the Fourth Amendment claim. The Court's decision was based on a cost-benefit analysis in which it noted the high costs of the exclusionary rule and found, on the benefit side, "no reason to believe that the overall educative effect of the exclusionary rule would be appreciably diminished if search and seizure claims could not be raised in federal habeas corpus review."

V. Other Remedies for Fourth Amendment Violations

As the materials in this Chapter reveal, the Court has narrowed the scope of the exclusionary rule, leaving some criminal defendants without an exclusionary remedy for violations of their Fourth Amendment rights. Other victims of Fourth Amendment violations may be without an exclusionary remedy because the illegal law enforcement activity did not result in evidence of criminality. In light of these limitations, lawyers must be familiar with alternatives to the exclusionary rule. These are discussed below.

A. Section 1983 and *Bivens* Actions

The most common civil remedy against local officials is provided by 42 U.S.C. § 1983. Section 1983 creates a cause of action (which may be brought in state or federal court) for a person who is deprived under color of state law of any rights, privileges, or immunities secured by the United States Constitution. It provides:

> [e]very person who, under color of any statute, ordinance, regulation, custom, or usage, of any State or Territory or the District of Columbia, subjects, or causes to be subjected, any citizen of the United States or other person within the jurisdiction thereof to the deprivation of any rights, privileges, or immunities secured by the Constitution and laws, shall be liable to the party injured in an action at law, suit in equity, or other proper proceeding for redress.

Section 1983 authorizes monetary damages and equitable relief against local officials and, through them, municipalities. It does not apply, however, to states themselves, which are immune under the Eleventh Amendment, or to state officials acting in their official capacities.

In order to prevail in a § 1983 lawsuit, a plaintiff must establish that the allegedly illegal conduct: 1) was committed by a government official acting within the scope of that official's authority or misusing that authority; and 2) deprived the plaintiff of constitutional or other federal rights. The plaintiff need not prove that the defendant had a specific mental state, unless the constitutional right requires one. For instance, deprivations of equal protection require proof of discriminatory intent on the part of the government official; proof of Fourth Amendment claims generally do not.

Section 1983 lawsuits cannot be brought against federal officials, but for Fourth Amendment claims against such officials (and possibly claims involving other constitutional rights), plaintiffs enjoy a similar remedy that was created by the Court in *Bivens v. Six Unknown Named Agents of the Federal Bureau of Narcotics*, 403 U.S. 388 (1971). That judicially created remedy arose out of Bivens' claim that federal agents illegally entered his home without a warrant, handcuffed him in front of his wife and children (whom they also threatened to arrest), searched his apartment "from stem to stern," arrested him, and hauled him down to the federal courthouse, where he was interrogated and strip searched. Bivens sued the agents in federal court, seeking $15,000 from each. No statutory remedy was available to him, and the exclusionary rule did not apply because he was not charged with any crime. Given the lack of any other remedy, the Supreme Court held that the Fourth Amendment implied a private cause of action, and it permitted Bivens' lawsuit against the federal agents to proceed. The substantive analysis in a *Bivens* action mirrors that of a § 1983 claim.

In both *Bivens* and § 1983 actions, although plaintiffs may seek damages from government officials who allegedly violated their Fourth Amendment rights, defendants may be shielded from liability by a doctrine known as "qualified immunity," if their conduct did not violate clearly established statutory or constitutional rights of which a reasonable official would have known. And certain officials—such as legislators and judges—may have the benefit of absolute immunity from liability under *Bivens* or § 1983 if they were acting within the scope of their office.

An additional federal remedy exists under 42 U.S.C. § 1985, if the plaintiff can establish that government officials agreed among themselves or with other actors to violate his or her constitutional rights.

B. Common Law Tort Remedies

A person victimized by an unconstitutional search or seizure may file a common law tort claim against the government. Depending on the type of illegality involved, the claim might be for false arrest, false imprisonment, trespass to land, trespass to chattels, conversion, assault, battery, intentional infliction of emotional distress, negligent infliction of emotional distress, or invasion of privacy. The officials named in such a tort action have the defense that state or federal law, depending on the situation, authorized their actions. Only if a jury finds that authority to have been exceeded or lacking will the plaintiff's claim succeed.

These claims are difficult for other reasons. Aside from enormous practical hurdles such as the costs of funding complex and lengthy lawsuits, plaintiffs face significant procedural barriers, including the broad immunity of government actors, and tactical challenges such as the difficulty of finding witnesses who will testify against police. In addition, juries may be especially reluctant to rule against police, and even when they do, often award only nominal damages.

C. The Federal Tort Claims Act

Sovereigns can make themselves immune from lawsuits except to the extent that they have consented to suit by statute. The Federal Tort Claims Act (FTCA) is such a statute and serves as the exclusive remedy for tort claims against the United States government. The FTCA allows individuals to bring lawsuits against the federal government (as opposed to individual federal officials) for personal injuries and property damage "caused by the negligent or wrongful acts or omissions of ... employees of the Government while acting within the scope of [their] offices or employment." The FTCA creates an exclusive remedy, and a plaintiff who brings both a *Bivens* action against federal officials and an FTCA claim against the federal government may be precluded from enforcing both judgments.

D. RICO

In unusual situations involving widespread law enforcement misconduct, aggrieved individuals may be able to sue under the civil arm of the Racketeer Influenced and Corrupt Organizations Act ("Civil RICO"). In order to state a claim under Civil RICO, a plaintiff must allege pecuniary loss resulting from "(1) conduct (2) of an enterprise (3) through a pattern (4) of racketeering activity." Racketeering activity includes murder, kidnapping, bribery, and extortion, as well as obstruction of justice or criminal investigations, and tampering with or retaliating against witnesses, victims, or informants.

E. Injunctive Relief

Plaintiffs may seek injunctive relief against government officials in order to prevent future violations of Fourth Amendment rights. For example, in *City of Los Angeles v. Lyons*, 461 U.S. 95 (1983), Lyons sued the city and individual officers in order to bar police from using "chokeholds." The Court's holding makes it nearly impossible for such relief to be granted. First, the Court explained, a person in Lyons' position must establish standing by satisfying the "case or controversy" requirement of Article III of the United States Constitution. To do so, a plaintiff must show that he or she "has sustained or is immediately in danger of sustaining" a direct, real, and immediate injury as the result of the challenged conduct. That the plaintiff suffered injury in the past from the conduct is not enough. Second, even if the plaintiff can overcome the hurdle of standing, he or she faces the demanding standard for injunctive relief, which is awarded only upon a showing of real and immediate threat of irreparable injury.

F. Administrative Sanctions

Government officials may face administrative sanctions and other measures that deter them from violating Fourth Amendment rights. These can range from internal departmental systems that punish bad behavior and reward the good, to civilian review boards that investigate and publicize claims of misconduct.

G. Criminal Prosecutions

Government officials are not immune from criminal sanctions, and these sometimes are brought successfully in cases involving Fourth Amendment violations. In addition to common law crimes that may apply if a government official acted without sufficient justification, there are specific criminal statutes covering law enforcement conduct. For example, 18 U.S.C. §§ 2234–2236 criminalize malicious searches by federal officers. In that same title of the United States Code, § 241 creates criminal liability for federal officials who conspire to violate constitutional rights, and § 242 criminalizes the actions of state officials who deprive persons of their constitutional rights under color of state law. These federal criminal sanctions can be pursued only by federal prosecutors and require proof beyond a reasonable doubt.

The beating of Rodney King is an example of how challenging it is to use the criminal sanction to remedy illegal law enforcement activity. King was tasered, beaten, stomped on, and kicked by police officers after he resisted arrest for drunk driving. The barrage of force lasted for over a minute and a half, despite the fact that King had become incapacitated, and it caused multiple fractures to King's face and leg. The assault was captured on videotape, and the shocking footage enraged many in Los Angeles and elsewhere, particularly those in the local African-American community who had documented years of racial profiling and excessive force at the hands of the police.

The Los Angeles District Attorney's Office charged four of the officers with crimes under California law but a nearly all-white jury from the suburban Simi Valley community acquitted them. The acquittal sparked days of furious rioting. Ultimately, the federal government stepped in, charging the officers with violations of 18 U.S.C. § 242. After a trial presided over by a more diverse jury, two of the officers were convicted and sentenced to thirty months in prison. The other two were acquitted. King himself was awarded $3.8 million in damages from the City of Los Angeles.

VI. Review Problem

A. Problem

Police Officer Eastgate is working on an overtime shift in which her express assignment is to write tickets and make arrests. If she does not write enough tickets or make enough arrests, her department will not assign her in the future to work the lucrative overtime shift, which pays a particularly high hourly wage.

During Eastgate's shift, she drives past a pickup truck waiting at a red light and notices that the driver, Richard, is not wearing a seat belt — an offense in the jurisdiction. As Eastgate writes a ticket, she notices a large bulge in Richard's pocket, and in response to her questioning he explains that it is a handgun. He produces his handgun permit, which appears to be in order, but she wonders whether he has a prior felony conviction, which would render his possession illegal.

She radios a police employee at headquarters, who tells her that Richard has a prior conviction for possession of cocaine. Richard overhears this and explains that his prior conviction was for a misdemeanor, not a felony. When Eastgate asks the employee about this, she is told, "it looks like a felony but the strange thing is he got probation, so it may not be accurate." She then orders Richard out of his car and places him under arrest for being a felon in possession of a handgun. As she pats him down she feels a large object in his jacket pocket. He then begins to struggle with her and tries to flee, but she eventually is able to subdue him.

It turns out that the object in Richard's jacket is cocaine, and his prior conviction was a misdemeanor. The state charges him with possession of cocaine and for resisting arrest, and he files a motion to suppress the cocaine. Should the trial court grant the motion?

B. Analysis

Eastgate's decision to stop and ticket Richard for the seatbelt offense was lawful, because she observed him violating the seatbelt law. The handgun arrest, though, was unlawful, because Richard was not a "felon in possession." The tricky issue is whether the good faith exception to the exclusionary rule should apply to the cocaine found during the search incident to arrest. Under *Herring*, the question turns on whether the police employee's mistake about the prior conviction, and Eastgate's reliance on the information she received from that employee, were "so objectively culpable as to require exclusion," and in order to establish that level of culpability, Richard will have to produce evidence of recklessness or systemic negligence.

He may be able to do so. Although the problem does not indicate whether headquarters had a good record-keeping system, it is clear that the employee had doubts about the accuracy of the record. The employee's failure to investigate further arguably constitutes recklessness, because a reasonable police employee would know that important consequences turn on the distinction between felony convictions and misdemeanor ones. The employee may not have known that a "felon in possession" issue was at stake, but clearly the employee was aware of a substantial risk that a wrong decision could be made based on the dubious record. Even if the employee was not reckless in ignoring the dubious record, Eastgate surely was. The employee's comment informed her that the record was of questionable accuracy, and she did not ask for further investigation into the nature of the prior conviction. She also had an incentive to make the arrest without carefully checking the facts, because she wanted to earn overtime shift assignments in the future. Eastgate probably will be held not to have acted in good faith.

Richard has another argument on the good faith issue: the overtime policy of Eastgate's department increases the likelihood of constitutional errors. Consistent with the exclusionary rule goal of deterring police misconduct, the court should apply the rule here in order to deter her department (and others with similar practices) from offering financial incentives that encourage such misconduct.

One last point needs to be analyzed before deciding Richard's motion to suppress. The prosecution will argue that Richard's resistance and attempted flight "purged" the search of the taint from the improper arrest. Citing *Wong Sun*, the prosecution will point out that Richard made a choice to resist and flee, and that these intervening acts alleviated the illegality of the handgun arrest. The court's decision will turn on whether Eastgate discovered the cocaine by "exploiting" the illegal arrest, or instead whether Richard's acts had a causal connection to the discovery. Because Eastgate had initiated the search incident to arrest before Richard resisted, it is likely that the court will rule in his favor: the search was a direct product of the illegal arrest.

Checkpoints

- The exclusionary rule applies in state and federal criminal trials.

- Criminal defendants must have "standing" in order to claim the benefits of the exclusionary rule.

- The Court limits the exclusionary rule to situations in which it will deter future law enforcement misconduct. Recently, it has suggested that only "culpable" official action will be the subject of the exclusionary rule, and the rule does not apply to many illegal searches and seizures that were effectuated "in good faith."

- There are many other limitations on and exceptions to the exclusionary rule, where the Court has found its application unlikely to deter future illegal searches and seizures.

- Other remedies exist for Fourth Amendment violations, although these are more difficult to obtain.

Chapter 13

Due Process Voluntariness

Roadmap

- Totality of circumstances test
- Voluntariness as a fact-specific inquiry focusing on police conduct and susceptibilities of defendant
- Exclusionary rule applicability to involuntary statements

When criminal suspects confess to having committed crimes, prosecutions are much more likely to be successful. Statements to law enforcement officers also can be critical to ongoing criminal investigations. And a defendant's acknowledgement of guilt has long been viewed as an important part of the rehabilitative process. For all of these reasons, government officials in many situations seek to obtain statements that may implicate individuals in criminal activity. This Chapter explains how due process provisions in the Fifth and Fourteenth Amendments limit the means by which the government can obtain and use defendant's statements. Another powerful limitation has its source in the Fifth Amendment's privilege against self-incrimination. That constitutional provision, and its special application in *Miranda*, is covered in Chapter 14.

I. Due Process Voluntariness

The government may not coerce or compel an individual into making a statement and then use that statement against the person in a criminal case. According to the "voluntariness" doctrine, the due process guarantees of the Fifth and Fourteen Amendments require the government to establish that the defendant made the statement voluntarily—in other words, that his or her own free will was not overborne by government coercion. Courts have identified multiple goals that are furthered by the voluntariness rule, including reducing wrongful convictions by excluding questionable evidence, protecting the integrity of the judicial system from the taint of immoral interrogations techniques, deterring police misconduct, enhancing trust in and respect for government, and upholding individual dignity.

A. Development of the Doctrine

The United States Supreme Court first applied the voluntariness doctrine to the states in *Brown v. Mississippi*, 297 U.S. 278 (1936). The case arose at a time when white violence against African-Americans was rampant, especially in the states of the former Confederacy. The racially charged atmosphere is apparent in the speed with which the defendants, three African-American men, were tried and sentenced for the March 30, 1934 death of a white man: "They were indicted on April 4, 1934, and were then arraigned and pleaded not guilty. Counsel were appointed by the court to defend them. Trial was begun the next morning and was concluded on the following day, when they were found guilty and sentenced to death." The only evidence against the defendants consisted of their confessions, which had been obtained by gruesome torture after the men denied involvement in the crime. The Supreme Court, reviewing the case, was shocked by the treatment of the three defendants. But it was the fact that their convictions were based solely on their "spurious confessions" that offended the due process clause of the constitution. The Court explained that, although many of the guarantees in the Bill of Rights did not then apply to the states, the due process clause of the Fourteenth Amendment prohibited states from engaging in judicial processes that offended fundamental principles of justice: "It would be difficult to conceive of methods more revolting to the sense of justice than those taken to procure the confessions of these petitioners, and the use of the confessions thus obtained as the basis for conviction and sentence was a clear denial of due process."

Out of *Brown* arose what is known as the doctrine of "voluntariness," which forbids use of a defendant's statement in a criminal trial unless the prosecution proves that the defendant made the statement voluntarily.

B. Totality of the Circumstances Test

The test for voluntariness is whether, under the "totality of the circumstances," the statement was a product of free will rather than of government coercion. *Blackburn v. Alabama*, 361 U.S. 199 (1960). In practice, the test has two parts:

- whether government officials subjected the defendant to coercion; and, if so,

- whether the coercion was sufficient to overcome the defendant's will.

All facts and circumstances relevant to these questions are admissible: the inquiry is a very fact-specific, case-by-case one. Among other factors, the following are frequently involved in the voluntariness inquiry:

- Factors focusing on law enforcement:
  - Length of detention leading up to the confession;
  - Duration and intensity of questioning, including the number and behavior of the officers;
  - Use of force or the threat of force; and
  - Use of psychological techniques such as pressure, deception, and promises of leniency.
- Factors focusing on defendant:
  - Age, educational level, and native cognitive abilities;
  - Current mental and physical condition, including impairment from drugs or alcohol and access to food, water, restroom facilities, and sleep; and
  - Other factors, such as defendant's size, gender, race or ethnicity, and life experiences, that might affect his or her vulnerability under the circumstances.

C. Investigatory Techniques

The majority of voluntariness cases arise out of four types of law enforcement techniques: physical, psychological, use of lies and deception, and extending promises of leniency. Each of these will be discussed below.

1. Physical Techniques

As demonstrated by *Brown*, when the government uses force, it will fail to prove voluntariness, because force will be held to overcome the free will of a person undergoing questioning. Even the threat of force is impermissible. But closer to the line are law enforcement techniques that manipulate a suspect's fear of injury. If these are too overt, they will result in suppressed confessions.

For example, in *Arizona v. Fulminante,* 499 U.S. 279 (1991), the Supreme Court outlawed the use of a confession obtained after officials urged the defendant's fellow inmate to induce him through fear into confessing to a killing. The inmate was a former police officer, and he offered to protect Fulminante from violent inmates who, he intimated, would give Fulminante rough treatment because of rumors they had heard about the killing. In exchange for the protection, the inmate warned, "You have to tell me about it, you know. I mean, in other words, for me to give you any help." The Court ruled that Fulminante's subsequent statement to the inmate was inadmissible because there had been "a credible threat of physical violence" that overbore his will.

Other physical techniques include lengthy interrogations in which suspects become sleep deprived. Sometimes they may be interrogated without rest breaks and may be denied food and water. These factor into the voluntariness analysis. For example, the Court relied heavily on the fact that the defendant in *Payne v. Arkansas*, 356 U.S. 560 (1958), had been denied food for twenty-five hours in finding his confession involuntary.

2. Psychological Techniques

Police use psychological techniques much more frequently than force, and as a result the typical voluntariness case requires the court to decide whether those techniques overcame the will of the particular defendant. For example, in *Spano v. New York*, 360 U.S. 315 (1959), police obtained a confession through a combination of tactics that included:

- questioning by many officers and a skilled prosecutor, who used leading questions;
- interrogation for eight hours during the night without rest;
- refusal to respect Spano's request to remain silent or to call his lawyer [the case was decided before *Miranda*]; and
- enlisting Spano's friend into falsely inducing his sympathy for supposedly having gotten the friend into trouble.

Further weighing in the Court's decision were Spano's characteristics and experiences:

- he appeared to have been emotionally unstable;
- he had never been involved with the criminal justice system;
- he was foreign born; and
- he had completed only the 8th grade.

Considering all of these factors, the Court held the confession inadmissible.

Similarly, in *Leyra v. Denno*, 347 U.S. 556 (1954), the Court invalidated the use of a confession obtained after several days and nights of intensive questioning, which culminated in questioning by a state-employed psychiatrist who, posing as a physician, appeared to use hypnosis on the suspect. By the time of his confession, the suspect was dazed and confused.

3. Lies and Deception

These typically are not enough, alone, to produce a finding of involuntariness. In *Frazier v. Cupp*, 394 U.S. 731 (1969), the Court upheld the admissibility of a confession obtained after police falsely told the suspect that his accomplice had already confessed. Other circumstances included a relatively short period of questioning and the fact that the suspect was a mature adult of normal intelligence.

4. Promises of Leniency

These also tend not to cross the line into forbidden techniques unless they contain or imply a threat that the suspect will suffer adverse consequences by refusing to confess. The Supreme Court overturned a conviction where a young mother was told that she would not be prosecuted if she confessed to having sold marijuana; she also was warned that if she did not cooperate, she would be imprisoned and lose her parental rights. *Lynumn v. Illinois*, 372 U.S. 528 (1963).

II. The Exclusionary Rule for Involuntary Confessions

The exclusionary rule applies to involuntary statements in a particularly powerful way, rendering them inadmissible for all purposes, including impeachment. *Mincey v. Arizona*, 437 U.S. 335 (1978). Although the Court ruled in *Fulminante* that the harmless error rule applies to involuntary confessions that are erroneously admitted at trial, confessions are so persuasive to juries that it can be difficult for the prosecution to establish, beyond a reasonable doubt, that a wrongfully admitted confession did not contribute to the conviction.

The fruit of the poisonous tree doctrine sometimes applies to involuntary statements as well. If an initial confession was followed by one or more subsequent ones, and the first statement is held to be involuntary, the subsequent statements will be closely examined to determine if they were also a product of the coercion present during the first episode. In the *Leyra* case noted above, the Court found that the facts of the first confession "controlled the character" of the suspect's subsequent statements, and it excluded the subsequent statements. On the other hand, as the next Chapter will discuss, if the constitutional infirmity in the first episode was a failure to give *Miranda* warnings, as opposed to coercion resulting in an involuntary statement, then the fruit of the poisonous tree doctrine does not apply. *Oregon v. Elstad*, 470 U.S. 298 (1986).

III. Proving Voluntariness

Voluntariness only becomes an issue when the prosecution seeks to introduce a defendant's statement at trial, and as the proponent of that evidence, it bears the burden of proving voluntariness by a preponderance of the evidence. But the defendant may face a threshold burden, if it is not clear that government coercion produced the confession. Like any other constitutional right, the due process clause requires government action, and in voluntariness claims coercion must come from government officials or others acting on their behalf. Thus, where a suspect confessed out of the belief that the "voice of God" commanded it, rather than out of his own free will, the constitution does not require suppression. *Colorado v. Connelly*, 479 U.S. 157 (1986). There must be a link between "coercive activity of the State, on the one hand, and a resulting confession by a defendant, on the other."

The voluntariness inquiry, like any other question of admissibility of evidence, takes place outside of the presence of the jury. But if the trial court rules in favor of the prosecution, the defendant must be permitted to attack the accuracy and reliability of the confession in front of the jury, by introducing evidence about the circumstances in which it was made. *Crane v. Kentucky*, 476 U.S. 683 (1986). Some states go farther by permitting the defendant to seek a second voluntariness determination from the jury, but this is not constitutionally required.

IV. Review Problem

A. Problem

Armed with a warrant, police arrest Bartlett, a 34-year-old laborer, at work one morning at about 8:30. Bartlett is booked and placed in a holding cell, and at about 2 PM, a police employee provides with him a hamburger. Two detectives visit him at 7:30 that evening, informing him that he is under arrest for two murders. They further tell him, falsely, that eyewitnesses have linked him with the crime. The detectives interrogate Bartlett for an hour, during which he denies everything. Then one of the detectives tells him that they have searched the house where he lives with his mother and grandmother and found an unregistered handgun. This is a true statement. The detective also states, this time falsely, that Bartlett's grandmother got upset during the search and was rushed to the hospital, and that his mother "went nuts" and was arrested. Bartlett drops his head after hearing this information and is quiet for nearly ten minutes. Then he admits that he "did it," saying that he does not "want anyone else to get in trouble." The detectives insist that Bartlett give them all of the details of the crime, because a blanket confession will not convince them that he is telling the truth and "won't do anyone any good, including your mom and grandma." Bartlett then agrees to make a videotaped statement, which is completed at about 10:30 PM.

B. Analysis

If the prosecution wishes to use Bartlett's statements against him, it will have to prove that each of them was made voluntarily. The test for voluntariness is a fact-specific inquiry that focuses on the conduct of law enforcement and susceptibilities of defendant. The inquiry is (1) whether government officials subjected the defendant to coercion, and, if so, (2) whether the coercion was sufficient to overbear the defendant's will.

Examining the totality of the circumstances, although both the prosecution and Bartlett have facts in their favor, it is likely that Bartlett's confession will be admitted despite the falsehoods and physical deprivations that he experienced. The prosecution will point to the following facts in its favor:

- Bartlett was a mature adult.
- The fact that he held a job indicates that he did not have a substantial mental or psychological impairment, and there is no indication that he did not have a normal level of schooling.
- Bartlett was arrested in a public place, so he would not have been placed in fear that he was being held secretly. He was "booked"—in other words, the police invoked the regular processes of law enforcement—and this would have further reinforced his awareness of the regularity of process.
- There is no indication that Barlett was threatened with force or the fear of force.
- Barlett was fed in the middle of the day, and there is no indication he was not permitted to rest or use bathroom facilities during the period of time he was incarcerated.
- While the police falsely told Bartlett that he had been implicated in the murders, and that his mother and grandmother had been upset, these facts alone should not be enough to cause him to confess falsely to a double

murder, and under *Frazier v. Cupp* they are not enough to render his confessions involuntary.

On Barlett's side, these facts will be stressed:

- He was held for 14 hours without seeing his family, a friend, an attorney, or anyone who could have provided counsel to him.
- He was given food only once during 14 hours, and it is unknown whether he had breakfast.
- He was held for 11 hours before his arrest was explained to him.
- The falsehoods that the police told him, in his exhausted and hungry condition, would have led him to believe that there was no hope for him, and that the safety and well-being of his family depended on his confession. His frail physical and psychological condition are apparent from his reaction of dropping his head and being quiet for nearly ten minutes after hearing the information.
- The first involuntary statement produced the second, because it was a product of the same coercion plus the further psychological pressure about his "mom and grandma."

Checkpoints

- The due process clauses of the Fifth and Fourteenth Amendments require federal and state prosecutors seeking to use statements against criminal defendants to prove that those statements — voluntary — *i.e.*, that they were not the product of government coercion.

- The test for voluntariness is whether, examining the totality of circumstances, there was government coercion that overcame the defendant's will.

- The totality of circumstances test considers all relevant factors, including law enforcement conduct and the defendant's particular characteristics. Among factors relating to the defendant are his or her mental capacities, experience with the criminal justice system, and educational background.

- An involuntary confession must be excluded from the defendant's criminal trial, and cannot even be used to impeach the defendant. Its erroneous admission, however, is subject to the harmless error rule.

Chapter 14

Miranda and Confessions

Roadmap

- The *Miranda* warnings
- The definitions of "custodial" and "interrogations"
- The "core" Fifth Amendment privilege against self-incrimination versus "prophylactic" rules
- Compulsion versus coercion
- Knowing, voluntary, and intelligent waivers
- The right to silence versus the right to counsel
- *Miranda*'s Fifth Amendment right to counsel versus the Sixth Amendment right to counsel
- *Miranda* as not "offense-specific"
- "Incommunicado" interrogation in a "police-dominated" atmosphere
- Special waiver rules for when the suspect has already "invoked" his:
    - right to silence; the "scrupulously honored" test
    - right to counsel; the suspect-reinitiation test
- Special *Miranda* "fruit-of-the-poisonous-tree" doctrines for:
    - a later confession as fruits
    - physical evidence as fruits
- Impeachment
- *Miranda* Exceptions
- Scope of the Fifth Amendment outside *Miranda*

I. Background

The due process voluntariness test for the admissibility of confessions proved to be a paper tiger. The case-by-case nature of the test made it difficult to apply, led to inconsistent results, and failed to give police clear guid-

237

ance concerning proper interrogation procedures. Moreover, courts rarely suppressed confessions, so rarely indeed that critics suspected that confessions that many objective observers would label coerced were nevertheless escaping constitutional scrutiny. Concerns like these, as well as worries about the disparate racial impact of police interrogation practices, apparently led the Court to cast about for a better test. The one it ultimately settled upon, the *Miranda* rule, named after the case that originated it, *Miranda v. Arizona*, 384 U.S. 436 (1966), was rooted in the Fifth Amendment privilege against self-incrimination, and, in theory, supplemented, rather than replaced, the due process test.

The Fifth Amendment's privilege against self-incrimination declares that "no person ... shall be compelled in any criminal case to be a witness against himself." The history of the privilege is disputed, but it is often said to be based on a rejection of torture and forced testimony that were aspects of the early English justice system. During the early seventeenth century, the English Crown empowered ecclesiastical courts to investigate charges of religious heresy. Persons brought before these courts faced a "cruel trilemma": asked to swear an oath to testify truthfully, they had the choice of (1) refusing to take the oath, which constituted contempt and virtually guaranteed that the contemnors would be tortured in the infamous Court of Star Chamber; (2) taking the oath and telling the truth about their religious beliefs and practices, which were most likely considered heretical and punishable by death; or (3) taking the oath and lying about their religious beliefs and practices, which constituted perjury and was punishable by death and, perhaps more seriously for some, eternal damnation. The privilege helps to protect defendants from facing a similar trilemma by allowing them simply not to respond to questions posed.

The language and history of the privilege do not, at first blush, seem to be a good fit for regulating police interrogation. The privilege arose in the context of examination in court before a magistrate. Modern interrogation is usually conducted by the police and generally takes place in the isolation of a police station interrogation room rather than in a more public courtroom . Furthermore, the text of the privilege does not bar all questioning but only "compelled" testimony. Historically, the relevant compulsion came from the consequences of lying, admitting to wrongdoing, or refusing to answer under *oath*. But police interrogations do not occur under oath. Moreover, the text of the privilege speaks of being a "witness against himself," which may imply again a technical notion of the witness as one who "testifies" in court.

II. *Miranda*

The Supreme Court in *Miranda* was unfazed by these concerns. *Miranda* had several holdings:

- first, that the Fifth Amendment privilege or "right to silence" did indeed apply outside of court—indeed, during police investigation;
- second, that, although the privilege applies only when there is "compulsion," compulsion is inherent in a "custodial interrogation";
- third, that such compulsion may be overcome only by creating a Fifth Amendment right to counsel before and during questioning and by administering a set of warnings of the rights to counsel and silence (it is worth noting, however, that, as of this writing, the Supreme Court has accepted certiorari in *Florida v. Powell,* No. 08-1175, *cert. granted,* June 22, 2009, a case raising this question: "Do warnings given to criminal suspects pursuant to *Miranda v. Arizona,* 384 U.S. 436 (1966), that advise a suspect of the right to consult with counsel before and at any time during questioning, but that fail to inform the suspect unequivocally of the right to have counsel *present* at all times during custodial interrogation, fail to satisfy the Fifth Amendment?") ; and
- fourth, that the police may not engage in interrogation even after giving these warnings unless counsel is first provided, or if the defendant knowingly, voluntarily, and intelligently waived his right to silence and to counsel.

Each of these holdings and their justifications are examined in more detail below.

A. *Miranda*'s First Holding: The Privilege Applies outside the Courtroom

The *Miranda* Court addressed concerns that the privilege did not apply outside the courtroom in several ways. First, the privilege arose before the development of modern police forces. Today, interrogation is conducted by the police, not by magistrates, but the consequences of police questioning are much the same. A confession made to the police and read to the jury at trial will go a long way toward a conviction. Refusing to answer police questions, absent the protection of the privilege, would allow the prosecution to reveal to the jury the absence of the defendant's denying serious charges made about him by the police. That non-denial may be interpreted as an admission of guilt, thus leading to a conviction. If, on the other hand, the defendant speaks, but lies, those lies will likely be revealed to a jury, again raising the probability of conviction. Truth, lies, or silence may all thus lead to punishment, a consequence analogous to the classic cruel trilemma. The Court appreciated this practical equivalence. Moreover, the broad purpose of the privilege, said the Court, was to accord to its citizens "dignity and integrity." The privilege protected citizen dignity via a "complex of values," specifically:

> To maintain a fair state-individual balance, to require the government to shoulder the entire load, to respect the inviolability of the human personality, our accusatory system of criminal justice demands that the government seeking to punish an individual produce the evidence against him by its own independent labor, rather than by the cruel, simple expedient of compelling it from his own mouth. In sum, the privilege is fulfilled only when the person is guaranteed the right to remain silent unless he chooses to speak in the unfettered exercise of his own free will.

By stating the privilege's values at this high level of generality, the Court readily concluded that "all the principles embodied in the privilege apply to informal compulsion exerted by law-enforcement officers during in-custody questioning," for "[t]oday ... there can be no doubt that the Fifth Amendment privilege is available outside of criminal court proceedings and serves to protect persons in all settings in which freedom of action is curtailed in any significant way" from being compelled to incriminate themselves. We will soon see, however, that several Justices want to modify this view, describing a *Miranda* violation, though rooted in the Fifth Amendment privilege, as not actually occurring until a suspect's confession is admitted into evidence *at trial*.

B. *Miranda*'s Second Holding: Compulsion Is Inherent in "Custodial Interrogation"

Having decided that the privilege created a "right to silence" that *could apply* outside the courtroom, the Court next had to consider under what circumstances "compulsion" would in fact exist by police questioning. The Court's answer: whenever a person is subjected to interrogation "in custody" of the police, any questioning is *"inherently compelling,"* that is, always compelled. The Court reached this conclusion by a detailed examination of the manuals used to train the police in interrogation techniques. Those techniques rarely involve physical coercion or the "third degree," but they do involve psychological pressure, "for the blood of the accused is not the only hallmark of an unconstitutional inquisition." The manuals critically recommended interrogating suspects in isolation from family, friends, or advisors, while surrounded by, and made dependent upon, the police. They further suggested such methods as offering the suspect a legal excuse for his actions; playing "Mutt and Jeff" (one cop friendly, another hostile); placing the suspect in a phony lineup in which a supposed witness confidently identifies the suspect as the wrongdoer; counseling the suspect that silence might create an impression of guilt; giving him false legal advice; and tricking or cajoling him out of exercising his constitutional rights. The goal of such techniques is for the police to dominate the suspect, the "aura of confidence in his guilt under[mining] his will to resist" and his isolation being "essential to prevent distraction and to deprive him … of any outside support." Concluded the Court,

> It is obvious that such an interrogation environment is created for no other purpose than to subjugate the individual to the will of his examiner. This atmosphere carries its own badge of intimidation. To be sure, this is not physical intimidation, but it is equally destructive of human dignity. The current practice of incommunicado interrogation is at odds with one of our Nation's most cherished principles — that the individual may not be compelled to incriminate himself. Unless adequate protective devices are employed to dispel the compulsion inherent in custodial surroundings, no statement obtained from the defendant can truly be the product of his free choice.…

C. *Miranda*'s Third Holding: Overcoming Compulsion

1. *Prophylactic Rule*

But what "protective devices" were necessary to safeguard the privilege? The Court ultimately crafted three such devices: (1) a set of warnings to convey to the suspect the substance of his right to silence and of related rights; (2) the creation of a Fifth Amendment "right to counsel" during police questioning that appears nowhere in the text of that Amendment; and (3) the creation of a supposedly muscular standard of "knowing, voluntary, and intelligent" waiver as a *prerequisite* to any questioning. The idea of "devices" being used to "protect" the privilege later led the Court to describe *Miranda* as a "prophylactic rule," that is, one that serves to cover or shield the *core privilege* from harm. That characterization created fodder, however, for critics to argue that *Miranda* lacked constitutional authority because it applied even when the "core" or "real" privilege did not. *Miranda*'s supporters, by contrast, thought it was always within the Court's power under the Constitution to craft rules necessary to give practical protection to rights in the real world rather than being mere pretend or paper rights. Yet some supporters also came to see *Miranda* as too weak a protection: permitting questioning to proceed without a lawyer where there was a waiver, arguing instead that no waiver could truly be "knowing, voluntary, and intelligent" without a lawyer's advice.

2. Why Warnings Are Necessary

Warnings were required, the *Miranda* Court also said, to make those unaware of their rights cognizant of them — "the threshold requirement for an intelligent decision as to its exercise." But warnings were required as well even for those who knew their rights because "the warning will show the individual that his interrogators are prepared to recognize his privilege should he choose to exercise it." The Court also worried that inquiry in individual cases into whether the defendant was aware of his rights would "never be more than speculation." Accordingly, the Court created a per se rule: warnings must be given in *every case* before interrogation takes place, whether or not the suspect already knows his rights.

3. The Content of the Warnings

Of what were those warnings to consist? First, the suspect must be warned of his right to remain silent. Second, that warning must be accompanied by the explanation that "anything said can and will be used against the individual in court," for only then is he made aware of the consequences of waiving his rights, an essential prerequisite to an intelligent choice whether to do so. Furthermore, this explanation "may serve to make the individual more acutely aware that he is faced with a phase of the adversary system — that he is not in the presence of persons acting solely in his interest." Third, the suspect must be told that he has the right to consult counsel before and during any questioning and, fourth, that if he is indigent, counsel will be appointed and made available for consultation just as if he had been able to hire his own attorney because the "financial ability of the individual has no relationship to the scope of the rights involved here."

These last two warnings, both concerning the right to counsel, created an entirely new Fifth Amendment right never before recognized by the Court and distinct from the right to counsel expressly recited in the Sixth Amendment. The Court has interpreted the Sixth Amendment right to begin only after "formal adversarial proceedings have begun," generally meaning after a complaint has been filed or an indictment returned, though the Court did extend that right to an earlier stage in only one case; the Court has since limited that case, *Escobedo v. Illinois*, 378 U.S. 478 (1964), to its facts. (See Chapter 15). Absent the *Miranda* Fifth Amendment right to counsel, therefore, the suspect would be devoid of guaranteed access to counsel under the Sixth Amendment before or during interrogation. The Court thus created the counsel right as necessary to making the guarantees of the Fifth Amendment privilege real, for a "once-stated warning, delivered by those who will conduct the interrogation, cannot itself suffice" to "assure that the individual's right to choose between silence and speech remains unfettered throughout the interrogation process." Moreover, the

> presence of counsel at the interrogation may serve several significant subsidiary functions as well. If the accused decides to talk to his interrogators, the assistance of counsel can mitigate the dangers of untrustworthiness. With a lawyer present the likelihood that the police will practice coercion is reduced, and if coercion is nevertheless exercised the lawyer can testify to it in court. The presence of a lawyer can also help to guarantee that the accused gives a fully accurate statement to the police and that the statement is rightly reported by the prosecution at trial.

D. *Miranda*'s Fourth Holding: The Waiver Requirement

But even the giving of warnings and the guarantee of counsel where desired were insufficient, concluded the Court, to protect a privilege "so fundamental to our system of constitutional rule...." Thus questioning was still impermissible absent a *prior* knowing, voluntary, and intelligent waiver of the rights recited in the *Miranda* warnings. Moreover, once warnings have been given, if "the individual indicates in any manner, at any time prior to or during questioning, that he wishes to remain silent, the interrogation must cease" because he has then shown an intention to exercise that right so that any statement taken thereafter "cannot be other than the product of compulsion, subtle or otherwise." For similar reasons, once he requests an attorney, "the interrogation must cease until an attorney is present. At that time, the individual must have an opportunity to confer with an attorney and to have him present during any subsequent questioning."

None of these protections, emphasized the Court, were meant to render all confessions inadmissible. Nor does *Miranda* apply to "[g]eneral on-the-scene questioning as to facts surrounding a crime or other general questioning of citizens in the fact-finding process" because they do not occur in the inherently compelling atmosphere of in-custody police interrogation. Nor does *Miranda* apply to "[v]olunteered statements of any kind," for no "interrogation" is then involved.

Furthermore, the Court conceded that the safeguards it created might be replaced by legislative alternatives imposed by Congress or the states if those procedures "are at least as effective in apprising accused persons of their right of silence and a continuous opportunity to exercise it...." To hold otherwise, said the Court, would be to impose a "constitutional straightjacket which will handicap sound efforts at reform...." Until such legislative reforms come about, however, the Court declared, the protections it crafted must apply to *any* custodial interrogation, without reference to whether the statements later obtained were inculpatory or exculpatory, and must govern while the suspect is "in custody at the station or otherwise deprived of his freedom of action in any significant way."

The Court never explained, however, why, if it were true that counsel was necessary to overcome inherent compulsion, a waiver of that right, and of other *Miranda* rights, could be "knowing, voluntary, and intelligent" without counsel's advice. For this and other reasons, many commentators have viewed *Miranda* as an uneasy compromise between the rights of the individual and the needs of law enforcement.

III. *Dickerson v. United States*

Shortly after *Miranda* was decided, Congress adopted 18 U.S.C. § 3501, purporting to re-establish the due process voluntariness test as the primary constitutional standard governing the admissibility of interrogations. Under that statute, a confession obtained in violation of *Miranda* but that is still voluntary under the due process clauses would be heard by the jury. For many years, most prosecutors, judges, and defense attorneys alike ignored the statute, viewing it as blatantly unconstitutional. But activist opponents of *Miranda* argued that the decision had no constitutional basis, being a mere "prophylactic" safeguard of a true constitutional right, thus rendering the decision void.In any event, even if not void, *Miranda* could therefore readily be overturned by statute, an outcome invited by the Court itself and purportedly achieved by 18 U.S.C. § 3501.

These arguments were put to rest by *Dickerson v. United States*, 530 U.S. 428 (2000). There, the Court reaffirmed the *Miranda* rule. That rule, said the Court, was unquestionably a constitutionally based one, for the Court applied the rule to the states, something it lacked power to do unless the rule was of constitutional origin. The *Miranda* opinion itself was replete with language demonstrating that the Court there understood itself to be announcing a constitutional rule. Indeed, *Miranda*'s invitation to legislatures was to craft an *equally effective rule,* making clear that not just any legislation could replace *Miranda.* Again, for the Court's pronouncements to supersede legislation, those pronouncements required the force of the Constitution behind them. Likewise, explained the Court, its creation of exceptions to the *Miranda* rule in the post-*Miranda* world did not constitute an alteration of the immutable protections of the privilege but merely the "sort of modification ... as much a part of constitutional law as the original decision." Nor did the Court's statement in the post-*Miranda* decision in *Oregon v. Elstad,* 470 U.S. 298 (1986), that *Miranda*'s rule "serves the Fifth Amendment and sweeps more broadly than the Fifth Amendment" alter its constitutional status, even though *Elstad* itself limited the application of *Miranda*'s exclusionary rule in a way it had not done in its Fourth Amendment exclusionary rule jurisprudence. The *Dickerson* Court explained away this apparent inconsistency between this Fourth Amendment and Fifth Amendment precedent, simply noting that *Elstad*'s holding merely "recognize[d] the fact that unreasonable searches and seizures under the Fourth Amendment are different from unwarned interrogation under the Fifth Amendment."

Having established *Miranda*'s constitutional credentials, *Dickerson* rejected the argument that § 3501, when combined with the greater supposed modern availability of civil remedies for police abuses, constituted an adequate substitute for *Miranda.* Neither that provision nor the civil remedies provided any warnings, any way to assure the suspect that the exercise of his rights would be honored, or any other means provided for dispelling the inherently compelling atmosphere of in-custody police interrogation.

Additionally, concluded the Court, "[w]hether or not we would agree with *Miranda*'s reasoning and its resulting rule, were we addressing the issue in the first instance," the doctrine of *stare decisis* prohibited overruling well-established precedent absent some special justification. No such justification had been shown. Explained the Court:

> *Miranda* has become embedded in routine police practice to the point where the warnings have become part of our national culture. While we have overruled our precedents when subsequent cases have undermined their doctrinal underpinnings, we do not believe that this has happened to the *Miranda* decision. If anything, our subsequent cases have reduced the impact of the *Miranda* rule on legitimate law enforcement while reaffirming the decision's core ruling that unwarned statements may not be used as evidence in the prosecution's case in chief.

Finally, explained the *Dickerson* Court, although *Miranda* imposed on the state the cost of excluding even voluntary confessions by suspects aware of their rights from evidence if *Miranda*'s technical dictates were not met, the due process voluntariness totality of the circumstances test, while still a supplement to *Miranda*, was no replacement for *Miranda*. This is so, said the Court, because the voluntariness test is "more difficult than *Miranda* for law enforcement officers to conform to, and for courts to apply in a consistent manner."

IV. The *Miranda* Rules Summarized

Miranda is thus still good law, and its holding may be summarized as embracing a small set of rules. The following summary includes a few new details to be elaborated upon shortly:

Rule 1: The Fifth Amendment privilege is not limited to the courtroom but extends to informal interrogation by police of suspects who are not under oath.

Rule 2: *Miranda* applies only to "custodial" "interrogation," terms to be defined in more detail shortly but roughly respectively meaning incommunicado holding of a suspect in a police-dominated atmosphere ("custody") where he is subjected to questioning or its functional equivalent ("interrogation").

Rule 3: When *Miranda* applies, the suspect must be warned of his rights to:

- remain silent
- to consult with an attorney before and during questioning and given the explanations that:
- anything he says can and will be used against him in a court of law;
- if he cannot afford an attorney, one will be appointed for him to consult with before and during questioning.

Rule 4: *Miranda* created a Fifth Amendment right to counsel as an essential safeguard for protecting the privilege.

Rule 5: The *Miranda* warnings must be given to every suspect before custodial interrogation, regardless of whether the suspect already knows his rights.

Rule 6: Giving warnings is not enough. No interrogation may occur unless the defendant knowingly, voluntarily, and intelligently waived his *Miranda* rights.

Rule 7: If a defendant asserts his right to silence, interrogation must cease.

Rule 8: If a defendant asserts his right to counsel, questioning must cease until he is permitted to consult with an attorney.

These rules have been slightly modified and expanded by later case law.

V. *Miranda*'s Impact

There is a debate over *Miranda*'s impact on law enforcement. Some analysts argue that *Miranda*'s cost in terms of lost confessions has been negligible, while others argue that, in absolute numbers, the cost has been large. Yet, in terms of percentages, even the latter thinkers insist on but a 3.8% lost conviction rate for serious criminal cases. In a system as large as ours, they argue that this still means that many convictions that would otherwise be obtained are not. Value judgments ultimately determine whether you think this cost (if you accept the accuracy of this higher figure) is worth it. Nevertheless, even under this 3.8% loss figure, that means over 96% of cases that would have been won pre-*Miranda* are still won even post-*Miranda*. Indeed, in at least one study 80% of suspects waived their *Miranda* rights.

This high rate of waiver is probably partly the result of police questioning tactics. For example, detectives might deliver the warnings and request their waiver in a rapid, perfunctory fashion; might de-emphasize the warnings, describing them in a monotone voice as a "mere formality" or something "just like on TV"; might encourage waiver by stressing that it allows the suspect to "tell his side of the story"; or might convince the suspect that waiver is in his best interest, tactics that, if artfully used, will likely survive legal challenge. If the suspect does affirmatively assert his rights, refusing to waive them, police might just leave him alone in the hope that stewing on the matter will lead him to change his mind and *ask* to talk to them.

Police might also subtly try to get a suspect who asserts only his right to silence (as opposed to his right to a lawyer, two rights that, as we will soon see, are treated differently for purposes of waiver) to change his mind, a tactic discussed shortly, that can, under certain circumstances be legal. If this too fails, police will often question "outside *Miranda*," that is, knowingly violating *Miranda* rights. The resulting confession will be suppressed in the prosecutor's case-in-chief, but post-*Miranda* case law allows prosecutorial use of the suppressed confession for impeachment purposes. Thus, if the defendant chooses to testify at trial—his privilege against self-incrimination protecting him from being forced to do so—he can be questioned about any inconsistencies between his trial testimony and his confession. Police, knowing this, figure that they are better off getting a confession that may be used only to impeach than no confession at all.

Miranda also lacked devices to aid the suppression hearing judge in finding the facts relevant to a motion to suppress. *Miranda* requires neither videotaping the entire interrogation process (as opposed to taping just the confession but not the circumstances leading up to it, a tactic police often use, though not even this more selective form of videotaping is required by *Miranda*) nor even keeping accurate records of the length, location, and circumstances of interrogation. What happened is thus decided based upon the suspect's word against that of his police interrogators, which often works to the detriment of the suspect. Although videotaping technology was in its infancy at the time that the Court decided *Miranda*, modern critics of the decision argue that *Miranda as applied* is insufficient to protect suspect's constitutional rights under that decision without such technological aids to judicial factfinding. They argue that evolving technology mandates evolving constitutional rules to add meat to the bone of the original *Miranda* decision. Analogous arguments have occasionally gained some traction under state constitutions, and some states have by statute imposed videotaping requirements, but most thus far have not followed this path.

Miranda, as interpreted by later courts, arguably fails in one final way. Once a knowing, voluntary, and intelligent waiver of *Miranda* rights is found, courts almost routinely find that the confession was also voluntary for due process purposes—despite the *Miranda* opinion itself, in the view of many commentators, saying nothing to support such a rule. The result in practice, therefore, is that the questioning techniques used to conduct a pre-indictment interrogation after obtaining a *Miranda* waiver are left largely unregulated.

We say "largely" because, even if the *Miranda* waiver was uncoerced, if the police then beat the suspect into confessing because they disbelieved his initial post-waiver statement that he was innocent, the courts would likely depart from practice and find that the confession itself was involuntary, thus suppressible under the due process clauses, despite the *waiver's* being voluntary for *Miranda* purposes. But, nevertheless, absent physical force or its threat, constitutional regulation *in practice* often leaves the interrogation room after a valid *Miranda* waiver is obtained. This outcome troubles some commentators, who conclude, based upon empirical evidence, that some questioning techniques are so psychologically compelling under certain circumstances as to create a grave risk of innocents confessing. Accordingly, these analysts would flatly bar interrogation of the mentally handicapped, questioning anyone for more than six hours, inducing confessions by threats of punishment or promises of leniency, threatening adverse consequences to a friend or loved one, or misrepresenting the evidence against the suspect. Other critics argue, however, that such rigid, per se rules have no place in a flexible, case-specific inquiry whether a specific individual's confession was coerced or compelled, for each individual's character and circumstances are unique. Yet, others may note, this last position arguably ignores *Miranda*'s own adoption of per se rules, most notably this one: no use may be made of an un-*Mirandized* confession at trial, *even if* the individual defendant already knew his rights anyway.

None of these comments mean, however, that *Miranda* is useless. *Miranda* educates the general public as well as affected individuals about some of their core constitutional rights. *Miranda* reduces the *risk*, if not always the actuality, that a suspect will not freely choose to talk to the police rather than remain silent. *Miranda* does prompt significant absolute numbers of suspects feeling pressured to talk to instead assert their rights, refusing to follow government dictates. Furthermore, *Miranda* raises the likelihood that suspects who talk will do so with awareness of their rights, a perhaps misguided choice from the perspective of the suspect's self-interest, but a choice far less troubling than one made out of complete ignorance or from a ready assumption that police will ignore their rights entirely. Some of *Miranda*'s defenders also argue that the mere existence of the warnings requirement helps to professionalize police, making them attentive to constitutional rights and avoidant of the most coercive of interrogation tactics.

VI. Compulsion versus Coercion

It is important to emphasize that the Fifth Amendment privilege against self-incrimination, and thus *Miranda*, prohibits "compelled" statements while the due process clauses prohibit "coerced" ones. Unfortunately, the Court has never clearly defined the difference between compulsion and coercion. What the Court has done, however, is to make clear that compulsion is something less than coercion so that a voluntary confession might still be a compelled one. For *Miranda* purposes, the Court has also held that an "incommunicado" (relatively isolated) interrogation in a police-dominated atmosphere is *inherently compelling*, absent *Miranda* rights-warnings and waivers, even if the police do no more than ask questions. But simply asking questions is not so "coercive" as to "overbear the will" for due process purposes. More is required to constitute coercion.

Although that something more need not necessarily be actual or threatened physical harm or pain, due process is violated only if more aggressive psychological or physical pressures beyond questioning in a police-dominated atmosphere are used. If they are so used, whether they constitute coercion is a question to be determined under the "totality of the circumstances" due process test. *See generally* Mark Godsey, *Rethinking The Involuntary Confession Rule: Toward a Workable Test for Identifying Compelled Self-Incrimination*, 93 CAL.

L. REV. 465, 467–518 (2005) (synthesizing the relevant case law). Conversely, even an uncoerced, thus voluntary, confession is nevertheless considered "compelled" under *Miranda* if it was unwarned in an isolated, police-dominated atmosphere. The two inquiries are thus distinct, though well-known critics like the late Professor Joseph Grano have argued that they should not be, and some critics have worried that "loose language" in recent Supreme Court *Miranda* case law may signal to lower courts that the Court is implicitly, or is at least considering, eroding the distinction. *See* Joseph D. Grano, *Miranda's Constitutional Difficulties: A Reply to Professor Schulhofer*, 55 U. CHI. L. REV. 174, 185 (1988) (arguing that the voluntariness test is the same under both the due process and self-incrimination clauses); Godsey, *supra*, at 509 & nn. 246–47 (noting that, given the Court's "loose language," "many have undoubtedly assumed that the test under the self-incrimination clause is now identical to the due process involuntary confession rule and that both doctrines overlap and simultaneously prohibit the admission of involuntary confessions.").

Commentators wrestle with crafting a clearer definition of compulsion. Some thinkers argue that confessions made under undue pressure to speak violate the autonomy inherent in human dignity, thus making them compelled, even if the interrogation techniques are not so offensive as to violate American notions of fundamental fairness, notions protected by the due process clauses. But a dignity-protecting justification for the privilege does little to clarify compulsion's meaning. Professor Mark Godsey has recently sought to articulate a more specific "objective penalties" test to determine the baseline circumstances of the person being interrogated. "This baseline is a function of the environment in which the interrogation takes place and the rights the parties are generally allowed in this setting." For example, when officers are interrogating a person in her house, where the person has the right to smoke whenever she wants, the officers cannot tell her to stop smoking because that would take away one of her rights. Under Godsey's test, impermissible compulsion exists any time an interrogator alters a person's status quo by removing one of her rights as established by the baseline.

To date, we are aware of no courts that have taken up Godsey's invitation. Nevertheless, his argument remains a viable one worth defense counsel's consideration in arguing a suppression motion.

VII. Custody

Remember that *Miranda* applies in the first place only if the suspect is in "custody." If he is not, then *Miranda* warnings are not required. "Custody" is shorthand for the existence of the inherently compelling circumstances upon which the Court relied as necessitating the *Miranda* rule. Those circumstances, of course, are "incommunicado" interrogation in a "police-dominated" atmosphere.

A. Custody Is an Objective, Not a Subjective, Test

A person who has been formally arrested is in custody for *Miranda* purposes, a bright-line rule. Absent formal arrest, however, the Court applies an objective test, asking how "a reasonable man in the suspect's position would have understood the situation," that is, whether a reasonable man under the circumstances would have understood the interrogation as one done incommunicado in a police-dominated atmosphere. Subjective considerations are irrelevant. Thus an officer's "unarticulated plan [to arrest a suspect] has no bearing on the question whether a suspect was 'in custody' at a particular time." *Stansbury v. California*, 511 U.S. 318 (1994). Likewise, whether *this particular suspect* felt compelled does not matter. What matters is how the reasonable person would have understood the situation.

The Court underscored the irrelevance of the officers' subjective expectations in *Stansbury v. California*, 511 U.S. 318 (1994). There, Stansbury agreed to accompany police to a stationhouse for questioning. He was indeed questioned, albeit without *Miranda* warnings, and he admitted seeing the homicide victim that night. Only when he further admitted to having several prior felony convictions did the police *Mirandize* him (*i.e.*, administer his *Miranda* warnings), at which point he requested an attorney. The trial court denied Stansbury's motion to suppress his statements, concluding that he was not in "custody" when first questioned, even if the officers may have subjectively believed the contrary. The Supreme Court agreed, emphasizing the objective nature of the custody test in which *unspoken* police intentions, which are by definition unknown to the suspect, cannot contribute to a compelling atmosphere. "Save as they are communicated or otherwise manifested to the person being questioned," explained the Court, "an officer's evolving but unarticulated suspicion[s] do not affect the objective circumstances of an interrogation or interview, and thus cannot affect the *Miranda* custody inquiry." Because the police invited, rather than demanded, Stansbury to accompany them to the police station, and he readily agreed to do so, he could not reasonably have perceived the situation as police-dominated. Thus, the situation was not inherently compelling, so *Miranda* did not apply.

B. A Fourth Amendment Comparison

Miranda had said not only that it could be triggered by custody but also by otherwise depriving a person of his "freedom of action in any significant way."

This *sounds* similar to the Fourth Amendment test for seizure of a person: whether a reasonable person would have felt free to leave. But sound and content are different things. The two tests are emphatically not the same, for one can reasonably believe he is not free to leave, subjecting him to a Fourth Amendment seizure, yet still not have had his freedom of action "significantly" curtailed under *Miranda*. *Miranda*'s reference to restricting freedom of action is thus best understood not as an alternative trigger to custody but rather as a way of underscoring that "custody" need not mean formal custody, formal arrest, or even presence in a police station, but can encompass informal sets of circumstances that necessarily involve incommunicado interrogation and police domination.

Berkemer v. McCarty, 468 U.S. 318 (1994), illustrates the point. Berkemer involved unwarned police questioning during a routine traffic stop. The Court concluded that Berkemer was neither in custody nor had he had his freedom of action significantly curtailed by an ordinary traffic stop. Such stops are generally temporary and brief, the motorist expecting that, after his license and registration are checked, he will likely soon be on his way, even if only after receiving a traffic ticket. This situation is sharply distinct from, concluded the Court, "stationhouse interrogation, which frequently is prolonged, and in which the detainee often is aware that questioning will continue until he provides his interrogators the answers they seek." Furthermore, concluded the Court, a number of features offset the aura of authority surrounding the officer and the knowledge that he has discretion whether to issue a citation. Most importantly, the traffic stop is *public* so that passersby on foot or in cars can witness the transaction—an exposure to public view that reduces the chances that the officer will "use illegitimate means to elicit self-incriminating statements" and that the motorist will fear that "if he does not cooperate, he will be subjected to abuse." Additionally, the motorist usually is confronted by one, or at most two, officers. Accordingly, said the Court, this was not a situation in which a motorist "feels completely at the mercy of the police" and not the sort of "police dominated" atmosphere of which *Miranda* spoke.

Berkemer's logic suggests the Court did not necessarily declare *Miranda* inapplicable to *all* traffic stops but only to "typical" ones. For example, it might be argued that a stop at 3:00 a.m. by an officer on an empty road, off the beaten path, in which the officer is quickly accompanied by multiple backup officers and drug-sniffing dogs is an incommunicado circumstance in which the reasonable person would perceive himself to be dominated by the police. Note too that a traffic stop like that in *Berkemer* is unquestionably a Fourth Amendment "seizure" of the person, requiring reasonable suspicion, yet not, in the Court's view, "custody" under *Miranda*.

C. The Relevance of Location

Location is relevant but not determinative in answering the custody question. Questioning in a suspect's own home can sometimes constitute custody, just as questioning in a police station may sometimes not do so. Thus, in *Oregon v. Mathiason*, 429 U.S. 492 (1977), when a suspect voluntarily went to a police station for questioning, was informed that he was not under arrest, and then left the police station without any police resistance, he could not later argue that his statements should have been excluded from trial because he was not *Mirandized*. By contrast, in *Orozco v. Texas*, 394 U.S. 324 (1969), a suspect was held to be in custody after he was awakened at 4:00 a.m. and questioned by four officers who entered his bedroom at a boarding house.

A jailed or imprisoned suspect is also generally considered to be in custody, even if the questioning concerned a crime other than the one for which he had been incarcerated. Therefore, in *Mathis v. United States*, 391 U.S. 1 (1968), a defendant who was incarcerated on *state* charges successfully sought to exclude incriminating statements that he made after being questioned by a federal Internal Revenue Service investigator who failed to give him his *Miranda* warnings. But lower courts have not read *Mathis* to mean that all incarcerated persons must be *Mirandized* before questioning. The Ninth and Fourth Circuit Courts of Appeals instead require a showing that the questioning officer placed further limitations on the individual's freedom than were imposed by general prison conditions. The test in both circuits is whether the officer's conduct "would cause a reasonable person to believe his freedom of movement had been further diminished." *See Garcia v. Singleton*, 1 F. 3d 1487 (11th Cir. 1994); *United States v. Conley*, 779 F. 2d 970 (4th Cir. 1985), *cert. denied*, 479 U.S. 80 (1986).

Probationers generally agree as a condition of probation to meet with their probation officer when directed to do so and to truthfully answer his questions "in all matters." The probationer also knows that non-compliance with these requirements might lead to his probation's being revoked. In *Minnesota v. Murphy*, 465 U.S. 420 (1984), however, the Court concluded that such conditions did not alone mean that probation officer questioning of a probationer occurs in "custody." Reporting to a probation officer is neither a formal arrest nor a significant restraint on free movement. Nor did it matter to the Court that the probation officer *intended* to elicit incriminating responses, that Murphy did not expect questioning about criminal activity, and that he had not consulted with counsel prior to interrogation. There was, emphasized the Court, a lack of evidence suggesting that Murphy believed or reasonably could believe from the objective circumstances that his probation would be revoked if he terminated his meeting with the probation officer. Absent such evidence, the Court would not conclude that an objectively reasonable person would have felt subject to the sort of compulsion to speak contemplated by *Miranda*.

D. The Reasonable Person "Under the Circumstances"

Virtually all reasonable man or reasonable person tests judge what the reasonable person would think or do "under the circumstances." A decision all courts face, therefore, in using reasonable person tests is what circumstances count as those in which the reasonable person finds himself. In the case of the *Miranda* custody determination, were all the circumstances in fact facing the suspect to count as those facing the "reasonable person"—for example, including the suspect's personality, childhood experiences, educational history, and profession—the test would in practice become purely subjective, a test of what *this suspect* rather than the reasonable one would think or do. There is, therefore, always a spectrum from a more objective test (counting fewer circumstances) to a more subjective one (counting more circumstances). How many and what circumstances to count as those facing the reasonable man is thus ultimately a policy question, guided by the policies underlying the particular area of the law.

In *Yarborough v. Alvarado*, 541 U.S. 652 (2004), the Court for the first time confronted the question of what "circumstances" the reasonable person should be considered to face for purposes of the custody determination. A majority of a divided Court there held that a suspect's age is not necessarily a factor to be considered in the custody determination. Seventeen-year-old Michael Alvarado was brought by his parents to a California police station for questioning in connection with a homicide. His parents stayed in the police station lobby while a detective questioned Alvarado for about two hours without giving him *Miranda* warnings. Alvarado acknowledged some involvement in the killings. When the interview was over, the detective escorted Alvarado back to where his parents were waiting, and the three drove away. He was later arrested, charged, and convicted of second-degree murder. Although the trial court denied his motion to suppress his statements, finding that he had not been in custody, and two other courts (exercising habeas jurisdiction) agreed, the United States Court of Appeals for the Ninth Circuit reversed, holding that "the state court erred in failing to account for Alvarado's youth and inexperience when evaluating whether a reasonable person in his position would have felt free to leave."

The United States Supreme Court rejected the Ninth Circuit's judgment, based primarily on the deferential standard of review that federal courts in habeas corpus must apply to state court findings. But, in another portion of its opinion, the Court went further, distinguishing the objective *Miranda* custody question from the partly subjective due process overbearing-the-will question. Whether a suspect's will is overborne for due process voluntariness purposes turns on all the characteristics of the individual suspect, including his age, education, intelligence, and prior experience with law enforcement. But these subjective factors must be irrelevant, concluded the Court, in the purely *objective Miranda* custody inquiry, which is designed to give clear guidance to the police. A suspect's age, said the Court, was a purely subjective factor out of place in *Miranda*'s objective world. Furthermore, said the Court, officers often will not know a suspect's interrogation history and, if they do, the relationship between it and whether a reasonable suspect would feel free to leave is merely speculative. A suspect with criminal justice system experience might believe he is not free to leave, but he also might view "past as prologue," his release from prior interrogations suggesting that he would be released from this one as well. "We do not ask police officers," said the Court, "to consider these contingent psychological factors when deciding whether suspects should be advised of their *Miranda* rights." Neither the suspect's prior experience with police interrogation nor his age were relevant to the custody inquiry.

Justice O'Connor, a member of the five-Justice minority, wrote a concurring opinion stating that there may be cases in which the suspect's age is relevant, but Alvarado was almost 18, so it would not be reasonable to expect police to recognize his technically under-age status.

Justice Breyer, writing for a four Justice dissent, argued, however, that the majority fundamentally misunderstood the nature of objective "reasonable person" tests. Those tests often take some personal characteristics into account, in tort law as well as in criminal and constitutional law. What to take into account turns on the purposes of the relevant legal test in the particular area of law. Age, concluded Breyer, is an "objective circumstance" of which police should be aware if they are responsibly trying to avoid compelling circumstances. Moreover, the Court's analysis of the relevance of a suspect's history with law enforcement was "a bright red herring in the present context where Alvarado's youth (an objective fact) simply helps to show (with the help of a legal presumption) that his appearance at the police station was not voluntary." Concluded Breyer,

> Common sense and an understanding of the law's basic purpose in this area are enough to make clear that Alvarado's age—an objective, widely shared characteristic about which the police plainly knew—is also relevant to the inquiry. Unless one is prepared to pretend that Alvarado is someone he is not, a middle-aged gentleman, well versed in police practices, it seems to me clear that the California courts made a serious mistake.

VIII. Interrogation

Remember that *Miranda* applies only when the police engage in "interrogation." A person who runs into police headquarters screaming, "I killed Mary Smith last night; I did it with a cleaver!" has not been interrogated. The police need not close their ears to what he has said. On the other end of the spectrum, a detective who expressly asks a suspect, "Didn't you kill Mary Smith last night with a cleaver?" is clearly engaging in interrogation. But there is a whole range of fuzzier situations lying between the boundaries of spontaneous blurt-outs and express questioning about a crime.

A. The Objective, Reasonable Police Officer Test

For those circumstances, the Court uses a standard it first articulated in *Rhode Island v. Innis*, 446 U.S. 291 (1980), which applies an objective test for whether the words or actions of a police officer constitute the "functional equivalent" of express questioning. Here is the test: *Should* the police officer know that his words or actions are "reasonably likely to elicit an incriminating response"? In answering this question, however, courts may take into account "any knowledge the police may have had concerning the susceptibility of a defendant to a particular form of persuasion," for that "might be an important factor" in the analysis.

Note that this objective test is judged from the perspective of the police, *not* the suspect. The inquiry, therefore, concerns what the reasonable police officer should have known would be the effect of his actions, not what the actual effect was upon this particular suspect. Nor is any inquiry made into the reasonableness of the *suspect's* beliefs. But what the reasonable officer should have known turns on what information *these individual officers* had or lacked at the time. Thus, if the officers knew that the suspect was an alcoholic and only gave him alcohol when he made inculpatory statements, the officers' awareness of the alcohol problem is relevant to deciding whether a reasonable police officer should have known that conditional provision of alcohol to the suspect was reasonably likely to elicit incriminating information.

1. A Significant Probability of Eliciting a Confession Is Required

Although this test might seem to cast a broad net, in practice it does not. The Court has used at least two techniques to limit the scope of the *Innis* test. The first technique involves interpreting the "reasonable likelihood" portion of the test to refer to a fairly significant probability of eliciting a confession. A related approach is for the Court to be deferential to lower court findings of fact on questions relevant to answering the reasonable likelihood inquiry.

Both techniques were on display in *Arizona v. Mauro*, 481 U.S. 520 (1987), in which police attended and tape-recorded a meeting between a woman and her husband, who had been taken into custody for suspicion of killing their son. The Court rejected any characterization of the police's arranging the meeting as a "psychological ploy" intended by the officers to elicit Mauro's confession. Remarkably, without expressly overruling or modifying the *Innis* test, the Court engaged in little independent analysis of the objective question whether the officers should have known that these arrangements would elicit incriminating statements from Mauro. Instead, the Court majority focused on the Arizona Supreme Court's finding that the officers were subjectively aware of a "possibility" that Mauro would incriminate himself during the meeting. But, said the Court, subjective awareness of a mere "possibility" of incrimination does not indicate "a sufficient likelihood of incrimination to satisfy the legal standard articulated in ... *Rhode Island v. Innis.*"

Mauro's holding might mean that the Court has abandoned an objective test in favor of an entirely subjective one based upon the officers' actual intentions, expectations, and goals. Given that the Court did not overrule the *Innis* test, the better reading of *Mauro* is that awareness of facts sufficient to make a reasonable officer aware of a "possibility" of incrimination is insufficient to show that the officer was or should have been aware of a "reasonable likelihood" of incrimination, the word "likelihood" implying more of a probability of harm than does a mere "possibility."

2. Mere "On the Scene" Questioning Distinguished

The Court's second technique for narrowing the *Innis* test is to characterize brief interactions as "on the scene questioning," which *Miranda* permits, rather than custodial "interrogation," which *Miranda* regulates. *Pennsylvania v. Muniz*, 496 U.S. 582 (1990), is illustrative. There, an officer performed a "field sobriety test" to establish probable cause that a suspect was driving under the influence of alcohol. In doing so, the arresting officer explained to the arrestee how the field sobriety tests would be administered. During that process, the arrestee made incriminating statements. The Court held that the officer's statements were "not likely to be perceived as calling for any verbal response." By contrast, however, the Court recognized that a request that the arrestee compute the date of his fourth birthday did constitute interrogation, rendering inadmissible the arrestee's inept response.

Drunk driving cases raise another potential *Miranda* problem. Many states have enacted "informed consent" laws requiring drivers to submit to sobriety tests (which include breathalyzer tests, physical coordination tests, and mental ability tests) or risk losing their driving privileges. If an officer warns a suspect that she may, under these laws, lose her license or have it suspended, and she is shortly thereafter given the *Miranda* warnings and questioned, does that make any such questioning "compelled" interrogation, perhaps invalidating any waiver of rights as "involuntary," or is the point at which the informed consent warning is given merely general "on-the-scene questioning" before any actual interrogation has been done? There is no clear answer to these questions, but at least one court has suggested that informed consent warnings preceding *Miranda* warnings violate that case's rules unless there is a "clear break" between the field sobriety warnings and the *Miranda* rights-reading. Sufficient time must elapse between the two types of warnings so that it is reasonable to believe that the compulsion created by the field sobriety warnings has been dispelled. *See State v. Scott*, 826 P.2d 71 (Or. App. 1992). Here is a typical field sobriety warning, which may give you a sense of the strength of the position of courts like those in *Scott*:

> You are about to be asked to take a breath test to determine the alcohol content of your blood. Driving under the influence of intoxicants is a crime. You are subject to criminal penalties if the test or other evidence shows you are under the influence of intoxicants. If you refuse or fail the test, evidence of the refusal or failure may be offered against you. If you refuse or fail the test, your driving privileges will be suspended.

B. When Is an Officer's Request That a Suspect Identify Himself "Interrogation"?: The *Hiibel* Case

1. The Hiibel *Majority*

In *Hiibel v. Sixth Judicial District Court of Nevada Humboldt County*, 542 U.S. 177 (2004), the Court also faced a related but somewhat different sort of question. More specifically, it addressed whether information sought by the police pursuant to a statutory command to respond to the police request was an "incriminating" "testimonial communication." If it was, then police questioning about it should constitute "interrogation" under *Miranda*. In *Hiibel*, an officer responding to a tip asked a man on the scene for identification. The officer made eleven unsuccessful requests to elicit the man's name, then warning the man that he would be arrested if he persisted in refusing to identify himself. When that refusal continued, the officer arrested the man, later identified as Larry Dudley Hiibel.

Hiibel was charged with, and convicted for, obstructing a public officer's discharge of his duties. That charge was based on a statute requiring persons detained by an officer on reasonable suspicion of a crime to identify themselves by name, though the statute prohibited compelling answers to any other inquiry. Hiibel challenged his conviction partly on the ground that he was compelled to incriminate himself by being required to give his name, thus violating his constitutional privilege against self-incrimination. The Court affirmed the conviction, rejecting the Fifth Amendment claim.

Specifically, the Court concluded that Hiibel's giving his name under these circumstances would not "incriminate" him because it would not "furnish a link in the chain of evidence needed to prosecute him." Said the Court, "As best we can tell, petitioner refused to identify himself only because he thought his name was none of the officer's business. Even today, petitioner does not explain how the disclosure of his name could have been used against him in a criminal case." The Court further noted that all persons have names, and disclosing one's name "is likely to be so insignificant in the scheme of things as to be incriminating only in unusual circumstances." Although that unusual case might arise in the future, explained the Court, Hiibel's situation did not fit that bill.

2. Stevens's Dissent

Justice Stevens dissented. First, he concluded that Hiibel's revelation of his name was "testimonial," for a "testimonial communication" is "the extortion of information from the accused," the attempt to force him "to disclose the contents of his own mind." Questioning during a *Terry* stop, argued Justice Stevens, unquestionably qualifies as interrogation, so a compelled response to such questions, because they result from extorting information from the suspect, are therefore also testimonial in nature.

Nor would Justice Stevens accept the majority's core argument that Hiibel's compelled disclosure of his name would not have been "incriminating," for in Stevens' view, one's name can readily provide the necessary link to inculpatory evidence. "[W]hy else," Stevens asked, "would the Nevada legislature require its disclosure only when circumstances 'reasonably indicate that the person has committed, is committing, or is about to commit a crime?'" Indeed, insisted Stevens, a name can be the key to accessing a "broad array of information about the person, particularly in the hands of a police officer with access to a range of law enforcement databases"—information that can be highly useful in a criminal prosecution.

Under the majority's approach, would an officer's request to see an automobile insurance or registration card, or a national identity card (if one were created), be "incriminating," if answered, under the Fifth Amendment? The majority's only guidance came in this *dictum*:

Respondents urge us to hold that the statements ... [that the statute] requires are nontestimonial, and so outside the Clause's scope. We decline to resolve the case on that basis. "[T]o be testimonial, an accused's communication must itself, explicitly or implicitly, relate a factual assertion or disclose information." ... Stating one's name may qualify as an assertion of fact relating to identity. Production of identity documents might meet the definition as well. As we noted in *Hubbell*, acts of production may yield testimony establishing the "existence, authenticity, and custody of items [the police seek]."

IX. Waiver versus Invocation of Rights

A. Components of a Valid Waiver

Even if a suspect has been properly warned of his *Miranda* rights, he may not be interrogated unless he knowingly, intelligently, and voluntarily waived *each* of those rights. The Supreme Court explained in *Miranda* itself that, if the suspect "indicates in any manner and at any stage of the process that he wishes to consult with an attorney before speaking there can be no questioning." Nor may the police question him if he indicates in any manner that he does not want to be questioned. Furthermore, explained the Court, the suspect's merely answering some questions or volunteering some information on his own *does not* deprive him of his right to refrain from answering further questions until he has consulted with a lawyer and subsequently thereafter consented to questioning. Additionally, the burden of showing a valid waiver is a "heavy one" resting on the state. Because the state is responsible for creating the circumstances of isolation in which the interrogation occurs, and the state is best able to make available corroborated evidence of warnings, that burden rightly rests "on its shoulders."

The *Miranda* Court elaborated further on the meaning of waiver, noting that a valid waiver could occur when the suspect indicates his willingness to speak without an attorney, followed closely by a statement. But, stressed the Court, "a valid waiver will not be presumed simply from the silence of the accused after warnings were given or simply from the fact that a confession was in fact eventually obtained...." Instead, the "record must show, or there must be an allegation and evidence which show, that an accused was offered counsel but intelligently and understandingly rejected the offer. Anything less is not waiver." The Court also noted that lengthy interrogation or lengthy incommunicado incarceration before making a statement are strong evidence that a waiver was *not* valid. Likewise, "any evidence that the accused was threatened, tricked, or cajoled into a waiver will, of course, show that the defendant did not voluntarily waive his privilege." Concluded the Court, the requirements of warnings and waiver are "fundamental with respect to the Fifth Amendment privilege and not simply a preliminary ritual to existing methods of interrogation."

Despite the Court's emphasis on the prosecution's "heavy burden" of persuasion with regard to waiver, it later held that the prosecution "need prove waiver only by a preponderance of the evidence." *See Colorado v. Connelly*, 479 U.S. 157, 168 (1986). The Court reasoned that since the voluntariness of a confession can be established by a mere preponderance, "then a waiver of the auxiliary protections established in *Miranda* should require no higher burden."

1. Implied Waiver

Waiver, as the *Miranda* Court explained, may not be implied from silence after being warned, nor may it be presumed simply from the fact that the suspect eventually answered questions. However, an express verbal waiver of each of the rights is not necessary either. Waiver can sometimes be implied from conduct falling short of an express relinquishment of all the rights. For example, in *North Carolina v. Butler*, 441 U.S. 369 (1979), Butler had been arrested for armed robbery. The arresting FBI agents determined that he had "an 11th grade education and was literate." He was given an "Advise of Rights" form to read and, when asked if he understood those rights, stated that he did. But, when asked to sign the waiver at the bottom of the form, he refused, stating, "I will talk to you, but I am not signing any form." He then made damaging statements. The Court upheld the admission of those statements, emphasizing that the question of waiver "is not one of form, but rather whether the defendant in fact knowingly and voluntarily waived" his *Miranda* rights. At least in some cases, the Court explained, "waiver can be clearly inferred from the actions and words of the person interrogated." A per se rule mandating express waiver of each right was therefore inappropriate. From a prosecuting lawyer's perspective, however, such a waiver would certainly be preferable, strengthening the case that the waiver was knowing, voluntary, and intelligent.

2. Voluntariness

The voluntariness inquiry is similar to that under the due process clauses: whether the totality of the circumstances show the waiver was the product of a free and deliberate choice. *Connelly*; *Moran v. Burbine*, 475 U.S. 412 (1986). The focus of the question to be answered differs somewhat, however. The due process question is whether the confession itself was voluntarily made. The *Mi-*

randa question is whether the suspect's *waivers of his rights to silence and to counsel* were voluntarily made. Furthermore, certain factors may weigh more heavily in the *Miranda* than in the due process context. For example, a long delay between being Mirandized and rights waiver might suggest that the waiver was derived by overcoming the suspect's will to invoke his *Miranda* rights.

3. Knowing and Intelligent

The questions whether the waiver was knowing and intelligent "likewise turn on the particular case facts, including the background, experience, and conduct of the accused." Such factors matter because the waiver question is a purely subjective one of what was happening in the mind of the accused. The accused's intellectual ability to understand the warnings or his inadequate appreciation of the consequences of waiver might thus be relevant factors suggesting that the waiver was neither knowing nor voluntary, though in application the Court seems to avoid any stringent requirement that the suspect fully understand every conceivable limit on the scope of *Miranda* rights or every facet of every consequence of waiver.

Notably, in *Connecticut v. Barrett*, 479 U.S. 523 (1987), defendant Barrett had been advised of his *Miranda* rights and signed a card stating that he understood those rights. Barrett then made oral admissions to having committed sexual assault, though insisting that he would not give a written statement unless his attorney were present. That insistence might suggest that Barrett believed that a purely oral statement could not be used against him, or at least that it would not prove as damaging to his case as would be a written one. At a minimum, some may argue, it seems counterintuitive to agree to give an uncounseled oral statement but not a written one because either can potentially be used against the suspect at trial. The Court considered the "illogical" nature of Barrett's choice to be unimportant in the waiver analysis, refusing to conclude that it demonstrated an unknowing, unintelligent waiver because it indicated that Barrett had failed to understand that oral statements could and would be as damaging as written ones. Said the Court, "[w]e have never embraced the theory that a defendant's ignorance of the full consequences of his decisions vitiates their voluntariness."

Barrett is instructive for another purpose: it illustrates that a waiver can be limited in scope. Barrett obviously invoked his right to counsel for the purposes of making a written statement, but he waived that right, and his right to remain silent, as to his oral statements. Police honored the scope of his waiver, so his statements were admissible.

B. Invocation and Its Consequences

Without a valid (*i.e.*, knowing, intelligent, and voluntary) waiver, a suspect may not be subjected to custodial interrogation. If he is, his statement will be suppressed, even if he never invoked his rights, for example, never asking for an attorney or saying that he wanted to remain silent. But what if he does invoke his rights—does that make a valid waiver, and thus interrogation, forever impossible? The answer to that question differs based upon *which right* the suspect invoked—the right to silence *or* the right to counsel. Before understanding the differences between these two situations, however, it is first necessary to explore what constitutes an invocation of a right. How clear must a suspect be that he is affirmatively asserting his rights?

1. What Constitutes Invocation?

In *Davis v. United States*, 512 U.S. 452 (1994), the Court put the burden of clarity of invocation on the suspect, at least concerning invocation of the right to counsel. Davis had been arrested on suspicion of beating a sailor to death with a pool cue. Navy investigators read him his *Miranda* rights, and he signed a form waiving them. He agreed to speak to the investigators, but, after about an hour of interrogation, said, "Maybe I should talk to a lawyer." The investigators stopped questioning him and sought to clarify whether he was in fact asking to speak to counsel before continuing being questioned. Davis now said that he did not want to speak to a lawyer and made incriminating statements. About an hour later, he said that he thought he wanted a lawyer before saying anything more. At his murder trial, the court admitted all the statements between his first, tentative expression of interest in consulting counsel and his ultimate somewhat clearer statement that he now really did want a lawyer. The Supreme Court agreed with the trial court's ruling. Justice O'Connor, writing for a five-member majority, stated that requiring questioning to cease upon an ambiguous invocation of the right to counsel would impose unreasonable obstacles to legitimate law enforcement activity. Instead, the majority concluded, an appropriate balance is struck by requiring a suspect to "articulate his desire to have counsel present sufficiently clearly that a reasonable police officer in the circumstances would understand the statement to be a request for an attorney."

Four concurring justices disagreed, arguing that the majority's rule created too great a risk that Fifth Amendment safeguards would be meaningless in the "real world." Suspects making statements that they believe express a desire for counsel might be deterred from reiterating that desire if law enforcement officers are permitted to brush off their remarks and continue questioning. A better rule, argued the dissenters, would require police to cease questioning and to ask questions that would clarify whether the suspect wishes to talk to counsel before interrogating further.

2. Resumption of Questioning after Rights Are Invoked

a. The Right to Silence

Even if a suspect has unquestionably invoked his rights, we must determine which right he has invoked. If he has invoked his right to silence (but *not* his right to counsel), questioning must immediately cease but can later resume if either one of two sets of circumstances exists: (a) the suspect re-initiates contact with the police about the circumstances underlying the offense of his own accord, rather than at the instigation of the police, and, before actual questioning takes place, an initial (if it has not happened before) or a new (if it has happened before) knowing, voluntary, and intelligent waiver of *Miranda* rights is obtained, or, (b) the police "scrupulously honor" the suspect's right to silence. Although the facts might be ambiguous in a particular case or require resolving credibility questions as to whether the suspect in fact re-initiated contact, the legal rule for re-initiation (option (a) above) is clear: Did the *suspect* express a desire to talk to the police without their prompting and, if so, did the officers get a valid waiver before resuming questioning? But the legal rule is itself ambiguous when reliance is instead placed on the "scrupulously honored," option (b) above.

The Court never defines what it means by the term but uses it in a way consistent with this meaning: the police "scrupulously honor" a suspect's right to silence when they behave in such a way as to convey to him that they will respect his wishes, take his rights seriously, and question him again later *only* after: (1) inquiring whether he has changed his mind about not talking and, (2) if he has, still not interrogate him without obtaining a valid waiver. The Supreme Court has addressed the scrupulously honored test in only one case, *Michigan v. Mosley*, 432 U.S. 96 (1975), so we only know with confidence that police have met the test if they behave in ways substantially identical to that of the police in *Mosley*.

The defendant in *Mosley* had been arrested for robberies and *Mirandized* (given his *Miranda* warnings). When he refused to talk, he was left alone. Two hours later, a different detective again *Mirandized* Mosley and questioned him only about an unrelated murder after obtaining a knowing, voluntary, and intelligent waiver of rights. Mosley then made incriminating statements about the murder. The Supreme Court found no *Miranda* violation, reasoning that among *Miranda*'s main purposes were ensuring that defendants be informed of their right to silence and that police will scrupulously honor that right's exercise so as to dispel the inherently coercive atmosphere present during custodial interrogation.

Trying to make a "reasonable and faithful" interpretation of *Miranda*, the Court held that the "admissibility of statements obtained after the person in custody has decided to remain silent depends under *Miranda* on whether his right to cut off questioning was scrupulously honored." Several factors suggested that Mosley's rights were so honored: (1) he was advised of his *Miranda* rights; (2) then immediately left alone when he asserted his right to silence; (3) later only questioned by a different detective; (4) after having been reminded of his right to remain silent and having been given an opportunity to exercise that right, and (5) questioned by that detective about a crime unrelated to the one on which he had originally asserted his right to silence. Under those circumstances, concluded the Court, the police could not be said to have undercut Mosley's previous decision not to speak. Accordingly, the statements regarding the murder were not rendered inadmissible by the police interrogating Mosley after invocation of his right to silence during a previous interrogation on another offense.

b. Cautionary Notes Concerning Waiver of the Right to Silence

Several cautionary notes must be sounded concerning waiver of the right to silence:

(1) If police have "scrupulously honored" a suspect's right to silence, that only permits them to seek a valid waiver from him. If he does not then knowingly, voluntarily, and intelligently waive his *Miranda* rights—all of them—his statements will be inadmissible.

(2) It remains unclear under what circumstances other than those in *Mosley* will the Court find subsequent police questioning to have "scrupulously honored" the right to remain silent.

(3) *Miranda Rights Are Not Offense-Specific:* Do not confuse the *Mosley* scrupulously honored rule with the following rule: *Miranda* rights are not offense-specific. What this latter rule means is this: once *Miranda* rights have been successfully invoked, the police may not resume questioning as to *any* crime unless the invocation of rights complies with: (a) the *Mosley* rule or (b) the invocation of the right to counsel complies with the *Edwards* rule, to which we turn shortly.

For example, if a suspect is arrested on a robbery charge and says he wants to remain silent, and if the police *do not* "scrupulously honor" that request as outlined in *Mosley*, then the police cannot, of course, interrogate Mosley further about that specific robbery. But they also may not interrogate him about different robberies, or about a murder, arson, forgery, or any other crime whatsoever. Absent scrupulously honoring his right to silence, or his re-initiating police contact about his crimes (followed by a valid waiver), his invocation of a right to silence in one case constitutes an invocation for any and *all* other cases. The result differed in *Mosley* only because the police questioned Mosley about another offense *only after* scrupulously honoring his right to silence.

Correspondingly, if the same suspect arrested on a robbery charge says, "I want a lawyer," he has invoked his right to counsel and may not be questioned about the robbery *or any other offense* unless he re-initiates police contact on his own, and they thereafter get a valid waiver. There is no "scrupulously honored" test concerning the right to counsel. Absent suspect re-initiation, invocation of the counsel right for one offense is invocation as to all offenses.

In Chapter 15, the Sixth Amendment right to counsel during interrogations will be discussed. That right is narrower than the *Miranda* right to counsel, because the Sixth Amendment right applies only *after* initiation of formal adversarial proceedings (usually meaning after a complaint or indictment has been filed, whichever comes first), rather than during all custodial interrogations. Indeed, whether the defendant is "in custody" is not necessary to trigger the Sixth Amendment right, though it is necessary to trigger the *Miranda* right. Moreover, the Sixth Amendment right is *not* offense-specific. Invoking the Sixth Amendment right to counsel as to a robbery thus bars, absent a valid later waiver, further questioning without counsel about that particular robbery. But the police may, unlike with *Miranda*, still attempt to question the suspect concerning other robberies, murders, assaults, rapes, indeed any other offense whatsoever.

c. The *Miranda* Right to Counsel

As hinted at above, invocation of the Fifth Amendment *Miranda* right to counsel activates a simpler, clearer bright-line rule than does invocation of the right to silence. That rule, first articulated in *Edwards v. Arizona*, 451 U.S. 477 (1981), is as follows: *all* government questioning must cease once a suspect exercises the *Miranda* right to counsel. The *only* exception to this bar is if the suspect re-initiates contact with the police about an offense, without police prompting (in effect, a suspect change of heart), and the police next obtain a knowing, voluntary, and intelligent waiver of *Miranda* rights.

In *Edwards*, police gave defendant his *Miranda* rights, leaving him alone when he responded by saying that he wanted to speak with an attorney. The next morning the officers re-approached Edwards in his jail cell and read him his *Miranda* rights again. Edwards said he was willing to talk and made incriminating statements that he subsequently sought to suppress. The Court held that the later questioning violated his right to the assistance of counsel. The Court recited its rule thus:

[A]lthough we have held that after initially being advised of his *Miranda* rights, the accused may himself validly waive his rights and respond to interrogation, the Court has strongly indicated that additional safeguards are necessary when the accused asks for counsel; and we now hold that when an accused has invoked his right to have counsel present during custodial interrogation, a valid waiver of that right cannot be established by showing only that he responded to further police-initiated custodial interrogation even if he has been advised of his rights. We further hold that an accused, such as Edwards, having expressed his desire to deal with the police only through counsel, is not subject to further interrogation by the authorities until counsel has been made available to him, unless the accused himself initiates further communication, exchanges, or conversations with the police.

Note how the Court seems to elevate the right to counsel over the right to silence. The *Miranda* right to counsel protects the suspect "by the prophylaxis of having an attorney present to counteract the inherent pressures of custodial interrogation which arise from the fact of such interrogation and exist regardless of the number of crimes under investigation or whether those crimes have resulted in formal charges." *Arizona v. Roberson*, 486 U.S. 675, 685 (1988). The Court presumes that a suspect invoking his *Miranda* right to counsel considers himself unable to deal with the pressures of custodial interrogation without counsel's assistance. That presumption does not disappear just because officials have approached the suspect about a separate investigation. The presumption vanishes *only* when custody ends.

d. Another Sixth Amendment Comparison Concerning the Right to Counsel

The Sixth Amendment right to counsel, you will soon see, though narrower than *Miranda* in several respects, is broader in one respect: it applies after formal adversarial proceedings have begun even if the suspect is not in "custody" (as defined in *Miranda*) when questioned. For example, assume that a robbery complaint is filed against a suspect, but he is released on his own recognizance after his preliminary arraignment to await trial. He is visited at his home several days later by a single, plainclothes, unarmed police officer. The officer arrives around noon, asks if he can come in for a moment; the suspect, who is surrounded by his wife and three adult children, agrees. The officer asks a single question: "I just want to know whether you are willing to talk to me about the robbery with which you are charged." A court is unlikely to find these circumstances to involve "incommunicado" questioning in a "police-dominated atmosphere," thus not constituting "custody" for *Miranda* purposes. The *Miranda* right to counsel is thus inapplicable. But because a complaint has been filed in the robbery case, the Sixth Amendment right to counsel still applies. Accordingly, the suspect may not be questioned about the robbery without counsel unless the officer obtains a knowing, voluntary, and intelligent waiver of the suspect's Sixth Amendment rights. (See Chapter 15)

One final point of comparison, again to be discussed in more detail in Chapter 15, is this: a suspect's invocation of his Sixth Amendment right to counsel, until recently, barred further questioning as to that offense, or even further police efforts to obtain a Sixth Amendment rights waiver, absent the suspect's re-initiation of discussion of the matter—a rule in the Sixth Amendment context analogous to the *Edwards* rule in the Fifth Amendment, *Miranda* context. But, in *Montejo v. Louisiana*, 129 S.Ct. 2079 (2009), the Court reversed itself, ending the per se rule's application under the Sixth Amendment. Thus, even when a suspect has invoked his Sixth Amendment rights, the police may continue to try to obtain a valid waiver of those rights and, if successful, can question him without violating that Amendment. Excluding the confession would thus turn on whether other doctrines, such as *Miranda* or due process, bar its use at trial.

e. Suspect Re-Initiation Redux

That a suspect asks for a drink of water or to use the telephone does not constitute re-initiation of police contact on his part. Rather, the defendant must make statements or inquiries that can reasonably be interpreted as evincing "a willingness and a desire for a generalized discussion about the investigation" at hand. Only after that occurs can the police seek a knowing, voluntary, and intelligent waiver of *Miranda* rights from a suspect who previously invoked one of them if the police want to rely on suspect re-initiation as a ground for justifying their interrogation.

Oregon v. Bradshaw, 462 U.S. 1039, 1045 (1983), illustrates the operation of these principles. Bradshaw had been arrested and booked after a car wreck caused one person's death. The police read him his *Miranda* rights and rearrested him for furnishing liquor to the minor who was killed in the crash. After these warnings, he asked for a lawyer. Upon arriving at the jail, however, he asked a police officer, "Well, what is going to happen to me now?" The officer responded that Bradshaw did not have to talk, the officer was not trying to get him to talk, and if he wanted to anyway, he had to do so of his own free will. Bradshaw said that he "knew" all this and made incriminating statements during a continuing conversation with the officer. The Court held that the defendant's inquiry, "Well, what is going to happen to me now?," initiated further conversation and that *Edwards* did not bar the officer from questioning Bradshaw at that point.

Remember, however, that the defendant's re-initiation of conversation does not alone validate the confession. The state still must prove that the defendant then validly waived his *Miranda* rights. Re-initiation gets you past the *Mosley* (for silence) and *Edwards* (for counsel) *per se* rules but does not eliminate the requirement that a knowing, voluntary, and intelligent waiver of rights be made prior to the actual interrogation.

f. Fruit of the Poisonous Tree

Before *Dickerson* reaffirmed *Miranda*'s constitutional status, the Court decided *Oregon v. Elstad*, 470 U.S. 298 (1985), which applied a much more limited version of the exclusionary rule to *Miranda* violations than to Fourth Amendment violations. The *Elstad* rule seemed to suggest that only the direct but not the "indirect" fruits of a *Miranda* rule violation need be suppressed.

Elstad involved a suspect in custody who made an incriminating statement before police officers warned him. That statement, the direct fruit of the failure to warn, was inadmissible, but the police never explained that point to the suspect. Instead, they read him his *Miranda* rights, and he made another confession. Under ordinary Fourth Amendment-like exclusionary rule analysis, discussed in Chapter 12, that second confession would also have been excluded as the indirect fruit of the first, unwarned confession, which had caused the suspect to believe that the "cat was out of the bag." But Justice O'Connor, in her opinion for the majority, held that the second statement could be admitted so long as the first one was voluntarily made. For O'Connor, "the dictates of *Miranda* and the goals of the Fifth Amendment proscription against self-incrimination are fully satisfied in the circumstances of this case by barring use of the unwarned statement in the case in chief. No further purpose is served by imputing 'taint' to subsequent statements obtained pursuant to a voluntary and knowing waiver."

Justice O'Connor's opinion seemed, at least implicitly, to accept the argument that, given the Court's description of *Miranda* as a mere "prophylactic" rule designed to protect true or core Fifth Amendment rights, *Miranda* was not constitutionally based. But if *Miranda* is itself non-constitutional, then it merits lesser protection than true constitutional rights. Accordingly, in weighing costs and benefits—the Court's general approach to deciding the scope and meaning of the exclusionary rule in various circumstances—the balance required less vigorous fruits protection in the Fifth than in the Fourth Amendment context. The minimal additional deterrent value of excluding indirect fruits of an initial *Miranda* violation thus did not seem worth the candle. For apparently similar reasons indeed, the Court had previously held that if police acquire a potential witness's name from a *Miranda*-violative interrogation, the testimony of that witness will not necessarily be excluded, even though the suspect's statements themselves will be. *Michigan v. Tucker*, 417 U.S. 433 (1974).

But if this analysis were correct, *Dickerson*'s declaration that *Miranda* is in fact a constitutionally based rule should have implicitly overruled *Elstad*, requiring *Miranda* fruits analysis to track that under the Fourth Amendment. That does not, however, appear to be the case. In two post-*Dickerson* cases, *United States v. Patane*, 542 U.S. 630 (2004), and *Missouri v. Seibert*, 542 U.S. 600 (2004), a majority of the Court seemed to accept a less-vigorous approach to *Miranda* fruits than Fourth Amendment fruits, though no majority coalesced around any single clear rule, and the rules seemed to differ based upon whether the indirect fruits consisted of physical evidence or another confession.

In *Patane*, a bare majority agreed that physical evidence obtained from an unwarned confession need not be excluded. Samuel Patane had violated a restraining order by attempting to contact his ex-girlfriend, and the officers who arrested him also wanted to question him about his illegal possession of a firearm. After his arrest, the officers tried to *Mirandize* him, but he said that he knew his rights, and they did not have to complete the warnings. He made inculpatory statements about the firearm, including instructions about where to find it, leading to his being charged with unlawful possession. The government conceded that the statements were inadmissible but argued that the firearm itself should not be excluded. The Tenth Circuit disagreed, holding that *Elstad*'s embrace of a less vigorous fruits doctrine in the *Miranda* context did not survive *Dickerson*. Applying ordinary fruits analysis, that court concluded that the firearm should have been excluded.

But, in the Supreme Court, five justices held to the contrary, though no majority agreed on a governing rationale. A plurality consisting of Justices Thomas and Scalia and Chief Justice Rehnquist believed that there had been no constitutional violation whatsoever, either of *Miranda* or of the core privilege against self-incrimination. Justice Thomas, the author of the plurality opinion, wrote that the "core protection afforded by the Self-Incrimination Clause is a prohibition on compelling a criminal defendant to testify against himself at trial." This core protection "cannot be violated by the introduction of *nontestimonial* evidence obtained as a result of voluntary statements." Thomas continued: "a mere failure to give *Miranda* warnings does not, by itself, violate a suspect's constitutional rights or even the *Miranda* rule" because violations of the right and the rule take place *only when unwarned statements are admitted at trial.*" Further, "because police cannot violate the Self-Incrimination Clause by taking unwarned though voluntary statements, an exclusionary rule cannot be justified by reference to a deterrence effect on law enforcement" because there is nothing unconstitutional to deter.

The remaining two justices supporting the firearm's admissibility, Justices Kennedy and O'Connor, urged narrower grounds for decision. Justice Kennedy based the concurrence on a "recognition that the concerns underlying [the *Miranda* rule] must be accommodated to other objectives of the criminal justice system," specifically, truth-seeking. Explained Kennedy, "[i]n light of the important probative value of reliable physical evidence, it is doubtful that exclusion can be justified by a deterrence rationale." But he believed it unnecessary to decide whether the plurality was right in saying there was "nothing to deter" or whether, instead, the failure to give *Miranda* warnings in itself constituted a *Miranda* violation.

Four Justices dissented, seeing the law enforcement incentives created by the plurality as perverse. Said Justice Souter, "[t]here is no way to read this case except as an invitation to law enforcement officers to float *Miranda* warnings when there may be physical evidence to be gained." Justice Breyer, in his separate dissent, said he would favor a rule requiring exclusion of physical evidence obtained as a result of unwarned questioning "unless the failure to provide *Miranda* warnings was in good faith."

Justice Breyer's "good faith" test had also been proposed by him in *Seibert*. There, as in *Elstad*, police first obtained an unwarned confession, then a warned one "covering the same ground." But, unlike *Elstad*, in which the police wrongly believed that the defendant was not in custody, the successive interrogation technique in *Seibert* was intentional, done pursuant to a police protocol in which officers had been taught to "question first, then give the warnings, and then repeat the question 'until I get the answer that she's already provided once.'" This "question-first" technique, insisted Justice Souter in a four-justice plurality opinion, was designed to undermine *Miranda* and should be treated as such:

> ... [W]hen *Miranda* warnings are inserted in the midst of coordinated and continuing interrogation, they are likely to mislead and deprive a defendant of knowledge essential to his ability to understand the nature of his rights and the consequences of abandoning them. By the same token, it would ordinarily be unrealistic to treat two spates of integrated and proximately conducted questioning as independent interrogations subject to independent evaluation simply because *Miranda* warnings formally punctuate them in the middle.

According to the plurality, the "question-first" technique used on Seibert thwarted *Miranda*'s effectiveness, and his post-warning statements, induced through use of that technique, had to be excluded. The plurality offered this explanation for how courts in future cases can distinguish between the permissible *Elstad* situation and the prohibited *Seibert* one:

> The contrast between *Elstad* and this case reveals a series of relevant facts that bear on whether *Miranda* warnings delivered midstream could be effective enough to accomplish their object: the completeness and detail of the questions and answers in the first round of interrogation, the overlapping content of the two statements, the timing and setting of the first and the second, the continuity of police personnel, and the degree to which the interrogator's questions treated the second round as continuous with the first.

The plurality thus created a multiple-factor objective approach designed to determine whether *Miranda* warnings were likely effective from the suspect's perspective, although one of the plurality's members, Justice Breyer, wrote separately to provide a different method of distinguishing *Elstad* from *Seibert*. He would create a rule that would require exclusion of "the 'fruits' of the initial unwarned questioning unless the failure to warn was in good faith," and it was this intent-of-the-officer approach that he repeated in *Patane*.

The plurality's renunciation of the "question-first" technique employed in *Seibert* was bolstered by a separate concurrence by Justice Kennedy, whose opinion can fairly be characterized as a fifth vote for prohibiting that technique and a second vote for applying an intent-based test:

> The technique used in this case distorts the meaning of *Miranda* and furthers no legitimate countervailing interest. The *Miranda* rule would be frustrated were we to allow police to undermine its meaning and effect.... When an interrogator uses this deliberate, two-step strategy, predicated upon violating *Miranda* during an extended interview, postwarnings statements that are related to the substance of prewarning statements must be excluded absent specific, curative steps.

In a dissent written for four justices, Justice O'Connor reiterated her position in *Elstad* that, because the fruit of the poisonous tree doctrine does not apply to *Miranda* violations, the only appropriate analysis is the voluntariness of the first and second statements.

So where do all these conflicting opinions leave the fruit of the poisonous tree rule in *Miranda* cases? First, it seems highly likely that physical fruits obtained from a *Miranda*-violative confession need not be suppressed, though the Court has not agreed on any single rationale.

Second, later confessions resulting from an initial *Miranda*-violative confession may, under some circumstances, be excluded but not under other circumstances, though the Justices cannot agree on what circumstances matter. Three of the four Justices signing onto the *Seibert* plurality opinion would apply a multi-factor, case-specific weighing test to determine whether under the specific facts of a particular case the later confession should be suppressed. These factors include whether the same officers conducting the first interrogation also conducted the second, the degree to which the officers treated the second interrogation as really a continuation of the first one, the degree to which the content of the two statements overlapped, and how complete and detailed the questioning was during the first interrogation. This non-exhaustive list of factors are weighed to answer this question, as the *Seibert* plurality posed it: "Could ... [the warnings] reasonably convey to [the suspect] that he could choose to stop talking even if he talked earlier?" Thus the strongest case for excluding a second confession as fruit of the first would be one where the same officers conducted both interrogations, treating both as really part of a single continuous questioning process, with the first interrogation, however, having been lengthy and detailed, and the second confession substantially overlapping in content with the first. The weakest case for exclusion would be where the contrary of each of these factors existed, with intermediate cases being subject to far more debate.

Two other Justices, however, would have applied some variant of an intent-based test, essentially excluding the later confession if the police intentionally violated *Miranda* during the initial interrogation precisely for the purpose of then obtaining a second confession in which the suspect was "formally" *Mirandized*. What all this means is that no majority of Justices has agreed on a single test for suppressing confessions as fruits, but a majority do agree that the test varies with circumstances, the only question being whether the relevant circumstances are those identified in the *Seibert* plurality's multi-factor test or a narrower inquiry into circumstances demonstrating the ill intentions of the questioning officers.

Another complication to keep in mind, however, is that Justices O'Connor and Rehnquist, whose votes were central to excluding physical fruits in *Patane,* and Justice Souter, who authored the *Seibert* plurality opinion, are no longer on the Court. Further clarification or further confusion of the fruits doctrine may thus be in the offing whenever the new lineup of Justices has an opportunity to re-visit the issue. Thus far, however, one thing seems clear: the Court applies a different, more ambiguous, and arguably less suspect-protective approach to *Miranda* fruits issues than to those arising under the Fourth Amendment.

X. Impeachment

Although a confession obtained in violation of *Miranda* is inadmissible in the prosecutor's case-in-chief, it may be used to impeach the defendant, provided the usual trustworthiness standards are met, if he chooses to take the stand. The principle justifying this rule was embraced by the Court long before *Miranda*:

> It is one thing to say that the Government cannot make an affirmative use of evidence unlawfully obtained. It is quite another to say that the defendant can turn the illegal method by which evidence in the Government's possession was obtained to his own advantage, and provide himself with a shield against contradiction of his own untruths....
>
> [T]here is hardly justification for letting the defendant affirmatively resort to perjurious testimony in reliance on the Government's disability to challenge his credibility.

Walder v. United States, 347 U.S. 62 (1954).

Although the state may thus impeach a defendant with his own statement, for example, showing contradictions between that statement and his trial testimony, even if the statement was obtained in violation of *Miranda*, a defendant may nevertheless *not* be impeached based upon his *very exercise* of his right to remain silent. Thus the Court held in *Doyle v. Ohio*, 462 U.S. 610 (1976), that a prosecutor cannot comment on a defendant's post-arrest silence *after* he has been Mirandized. However, the prosecutor may comment on a defendant's post-arrest silence where he has not been warned. This is so because "the *Miranda* warnings contain an 'implicit assurance' that silence will carry no penalty." Accordingly, "it does not comport with due process to permit the prosecution during trial to call attention to [the defendant's] silence at the time of arrest and to insist that because he did not speak about the facts of the case at that time, as he was told he need not do, an unfavorable inference might be drawn to the truth of his trial testimony."

For this reason, explained the Court in *Greer v. Miller*, 483 U.S. 756, (1987), "the use for impeachment purposes of ... [a suspect's] silence at the time of arrest and after receiving *Miranda* warnings [violates] the Due Process Clause of the Fourteenth Amendment." Correspondingly, "absent some sort of affirmative assurances embodied in the *Miranda* warnings, the Constitution does not prohibit the use of a defendant's post-arrest silence to impeach him." In such a case, *no governmental action* induced the silence, so suppression is unnecessary. Similar logic renders a defendant's pre-arrest silence—for example, not denying his guilt in the face of such an accusation by his best friend — admissible to impeach him.

XI. *Miranda*'s Exceptions

The Court has recognized two primary exceptions to the *Miranda* rule: (1) routine booking practices; and (2) public safety. The Court recognized the first of these exceptions in *Pennsylvania v. Muniz*, 496 U.S. 582 (1990). Police arrested *Muniz* on drunk driving charges and asked him questions as they routinely did in processing DUI (driving under the influence of alcohol) suspects. The police queries focused on Muniz's name, address, weight, eye color, date of birth, and age, all of which, said the Court, were "reasonably related" to police administrative concerns. Accordingly, his slurred responses could be used against him at trial, despite his not being Mirandized before making these statements.

In *New York v. Quarles*, 467 U.S. 649 (1984), the Court created the public safety exception to *Miranda*. Police had responded to a midnight report that a woman had been raped at gunpoint. Officers had information indicating that the assailant had fled into an all-night grocery store. Officers entering the store spotted Quarles, who had run to the store's rear. In frisking Quarles, the officers found an empty shoulder holster, leading one of the officers to ask the handcuffed Quarles where the gun was located. Quarles replied, "the gun is over here." The Court held this unwarned statement to be admissible, reasoning that custodial interrogation occurred in circumstances posing a danger to the public. That danger was an interest that outweighed Quarles's interest in being warned of his rights. Without such an exception, concluded the Court, the gun might have become a dangerous weapon in an accomplice's hands or might be found by a store employee or customer.

The Court has rejected a "minor offenses" exception. In *Berkemer v. McCarty*, 468 U.S. 420 (1984), a motorist stopped for a misdemeanor traffic offense made incriminating remarks when questioned by police during a roadside stop. Although the motorist had not first been Mirandized, the Court held that *Miranda* did not apply because the motorist was never "in custody." A routine traffic stop by a lone police officer on a busy road subject to ready observation by others simply did not, in the Court's view, constitute the sort of "incommunicado" activity or police "domination" at which *Miranda* aimed. Yet the Court emphasized that *if* the suspect had been in custody, the *Miranda* interests would have been applicable and warnings required. Any "minor offenses" exception would leave law enforcement officers unsure in many circumstances whether the offense being investigated was "serious" or not.

XII. Undercover Activities

Illinois v. Perkins, 496 U.S. 292 (1990), specifically addressed the question whether *Miranda* is violated when a "suspect is unaware that he is speaking to a law enforcement officer and giving a voluntary statement." Police placed an undercover agent in a cell with Perkins, who had been incarcerated on battery charges but whom police also suspected of murder. The agent asked Perkins whether "he had ever 'done' anybody." Perkins responded with a lengthy description of precisely the murder of which he was suspected. The trial court suppressed these statements, and state appellate courts affirmed. But the Supreme Court reversed, finding no *Miranda* violation because "[c]onversations between suspects and undercover agents do not implicate the concerns underlying *Miranda*." A suspect who does not know he is in the presence of a police agent cannot, the Court explained, face the "inherently compelling pressures" generated by a police-dominated atmosphere.

XIII. Privilege against Self-Incrimination outside *Miranda*

The Fifth Amendment privilege against self-incrimination can be invoked in other situations as well. It may become an issue when the government subpoenas evidence in a criminal case, and it can also be raised in civil cases. The remaining part of this Chapter will focus on non-*Miranda* self-incrimination issues that arise in criminal cases.

A. Thresholds: Compulsion, Incrimination, Testimony

A defendant advancing the contention that the government violated his or her privilege against self-incrimination must satisfy a three-part showing, because the right is implicated only by communications that are (1) compelled, (2) incriminating, and (3) testimonial. Each of these will be discussed below. It is the third characteristic—the requirement that a communication be "testimonial"—that most frequently presents defendants with difficulties.

1. Compulsion

The Court has held that, "[a]bsent some officially coerced self-accusation, the Fifth Amendment privilege is not violated by even the most damning admissions." *United States v. Washington*, 431 U.S. 181 (1977). Government coercion can take several forms. It may come at the hands of police engaging in custodial interrogation, as this Chapter discussed with respect to the *Miranda* doctrine. It may take the form of a subpoena to testify or produce documents before a grand jury. It may arise from a statute or court rule that requires the defendant to provide advance notice if he or she intends to rely on an alibi defense at trial. In any situation in which a government actor forces the defendant to say, or do, anything, compulsion exists sufficient to satisfy this part of the inquiry.

2. Incrimination

The privilege can be asserted so long as there is a "substantial and real" hazard that the defendant's communication can be used in a criminal prosecution or can serve as a link in a chain leading to other evidence that can be used in a criminal prosecution. *Kastigar v. United States*, 406 U.S. 441 (1972). In reality, despite the "substantial and real" language, the Court interprets this test very broadly, making it relatively easy for a defendant to satisfy this part of the inquiry. Even exculpatory statements implicate the privilege, because they can conceivably be used against a person—for example, in a perjury prosecution.

3. Testimony

The Court has defined "testimony" as a "communicative act or writing." *Schmerber v. California*, 394 U.S. 757 (1966). Excluded from this definition are physical acts that do not reveal workings of the defendant's own mind, such as putting on an article of clothing for identification purposes, speaking particular words in a lineup, submitting samples of handwriting, and submitting to blood alcohol tests. Each of these situations has been presented to the Court, and in each the Court ruled the privilege inapplicable because the compelled acts were simply physical movements, rather than acts that revealed the defendant's thought processes. See, respectively, *Holt v. United States*, 218 U.S. 245 (1910); *United States v. Wade*, 388 U.S. 218 (1967); *Gilbert v. California*, 388 U.S. 263 (1967); and *South Dakota v. Neville*, 459 U.S. 553 (1983). A memorable application of this limitation can be found in an Alabama robbery trial during which the court required the defendant to open his mouth and show his teeth to the jury after an eyewitness testified that the robber had "a bigger gap than mine" in his front teeth. *Huff v. State*, 452 So.2d 1352 (Ala. Crim. App. 1984). The defendant complained on appeal that the forcible showing violated his privilege against self-incrimination because he was, literally, "convicted out of his own mouth." Needless to say, his argument was unavailing. The testimony requirement becomes a challenge when it is applied to pre-existing documents, as discussed below.

B. Pre-Existing Documents

In some situations—particularly those involving white-collar crime—evidence of criminal activity is most likely to be found in documents, and prosecutors can use various procedural mechanisms (subpoenas, for example) to compel people to turn over documents. A recipient of such a subpoena, fearing prosecution, may want to resist giving over the documents and may file a motion to quash the subpoena on the basis of the privilege against self-incrimination. Applying the three-part analysis, the recipient's claim appears viable: the subpoena satisfies the compulsion prong; a "substantial and real" hazard of incrimination undoubtedly can be shown; and finally, according to the subpoena recipient, the documents constitute testimony because they are "communicative acts or writings." But the subpoena does not force the recipient to create the documents; instead, it compels only the production of documents that already exist. In this situation, where the government seeks the production of pre-existing documents, the privilege cannot be asserted on the basis of the documents' contents. *Fisher v. United States*, 425 U.S. 391 (1976).

Yet the privilege is not completely inoperable here. Although the contents of the documents cannot form the basis of a self-incrimination claim, the subpoena recipient can attempt to resist the subpoena on the ground that it compels a "communicative act"—a physical act that reveals the workings of his or her own mind. That act, or sequence of actions, begins when the recipient reads the subpoena, considers which documents the subpoena describes, and turns them over to the prosecution. When the recipient places the documents on the prosecutor's desk, he or she is communicating, in essence, "Documents corresponding to the description in the subpoena do, in fact, exist; I have them; and here they are." This information may be unremarkable, but at times it can be extremely incriminating. For example, police investigating a gambling suspect undoubtedly would like to know if the suspect possesses gambling records. Also, if such records exist, the police would like to have them. Clearly, an official cannot force the suspect to create records, because the privilege against self-incrimination would apply. On the other hand, if such records already exist, their contents were not the products of compulsion and cannot be shielded. Can the official simply issue a subpoena to the suspect for "all existing records of gambling"? Applying the three-step analysis, one would conclude (1) that compulsion is present; (2) that the suspect would be incriminated by acknowledging the existence and character of the records, as well as by the fact that he or she possesses gambling records; and (3) that the suspect's act of production is testimonial in that it contains an implicit communication about the records' existence, their character as "gambling records," and the fact that the suspect possesses them. In this situation, a court should grant the suspect's motion to quash the subpoena on self-incrimination grounds.

C. The "Required Records" Exception

There is an exception to the applicability of the privilege in the circumstances discussed above: where the government seeks statements or communicative acts in order to fulfill an "administrative purpose," as opposed to a law enforcement one, then the privilege will be held inapplicable. See *Grosso v. United States*, 390 U.S. 62 (1968). This is known as the "required records" exception to the privilege. For example, motor vehicle drivers are required by state statutes to identify themselves after they have been involved in accidents. Required self-identification undoubtedly is a compelled communicative act that is accompanied by a substantial likelihood of incrimination. Nevertheless, the primary purpose of identification statutes is to further the important function of regulating and licensing driving. See *California v. Byers*, 402 U.S. 424 (1971). In such a situation, when government articulates an important regulatory purpose, "[i]t is irrelevant that records kept for regulatory purposes may be useful to a criminal investigation." *In re Doe v. United States*, 801 F.2d 1164 (9th Cir. 1986).

When the government seeks the benefit of the required records exception to the privilege against self-incrimination, a three-part test applies. The government must establish:

- that the purpose of the record-keeping requirement is regulatory;
- that the records are of a kind that the party customarily maintains; and
- that the records have a "public aspect."

In addition to scrutinizing record-keeping requirements under the three-part test, courts may refuse to permit the government to impose record-keeping requirements on groups that it has obviously targeted for law enforcement purposes. For example, in *Marchetti v. United States*, 390 U.S. 39 (1968), the Supreme Court held unconstitutional under the fifth amendment a federal tax law requiring gamblers to file special "wagering" tax returns. According to the Court, the law was nothing more than a way of requiring gamblers to incriminate themselves.

D. Invoking and Waiving the Privilege

Only "natural persons" — *i.e.*, people, as opposed to entities — enjoy the privilege against self-incrimination. *Hale v. Henkel*, 201 U.S. 43 (1906). In *Bel-*

lis v. United States, 417 U.S. 85 (1974), the Supreme Court did state that "this might be a different case if it involved a small family partnership, or … if there were some other pre-existing relationship of confidentiality among the partners." Also, there is a standing requirement: the privilege may be asserted only by the person holding it, rather than by another person seeking to exclude damaging evidence. *Fisher v. United States*, 425 U.S. 391 (1976). Finally, as with most constitutional rights, only deprivations by government officials are actionable. See *Flagg Bros., Inc. v. Brooks*, 436 U.S. 149 (1978).

Checkpoints

- *Miranda* creates a Fifth Amendment right to counsel and to a set of warnings as pre-requisites to counteracting the "inherently compelling" atmosphere created by "custodial" "interrogation."

- But police giving the warnings is necessary but *not* sufficient to permit police to interrogate a suspect; the police must also first obtain a knowing, voluntary, and intelligent waiver from the suspect of his *Miranda* rights.

- The suspect must be warned of his rights to:

  - remain silent;

  - counsel before and during questioning;

  - the appointment of such counsel if he cannot afford to hire one on his own.

- The suspect must be warned that anything he says can and will be used against him in a court of law.

- A suspect is in "custody" if he is formally arrested *or* if "a reasonable man in the suspect's position would have understood the situation" as restricting his freedom of movement in a "significant way," meaning that the reasonable man would have understood himself to face "incommunicado" interrogation in a "police-dominated atmosphere."

- "Interrogation" occurs when the police engage in express questioning or its "functional equivalent"; "functional equivalency" occurs if a police officer should have known that his words or actions were "reasonably likely to elicit an incriminating response."

- "Spontaneous blurt-outs" are not "interrogation."

- If, instead of waiving his *Miranda* right to silence, the suspect invokes it, all questioning must immediately cease, later re-questioning being permissible only if (1) the suspect voluntarily re-initiates the conversation, and the interrogator next obtains a knowing, voluntary, and intelligent waiver *or* (2) the police "scrupulously honor" the suspect's right to silence, and the interrogator next obtains a knowing, voluntary, and intelligent waiver.

Checkpoints *continued*

- Although the Court has never defined the term "scrupulously honored," the Court has found the test to be met in at least the following set of circumstances: (1) the suspect was advised of his *Miranda* rights; (2) then immediately left alone when he invoked his right to silence; (3) later questioned only by a different detective; (4) after having been reminded of his right to remain silent and having been given an opportunity to exercise that right; and (5) questioned by that detective about a crime unrelated to the one on which he had originally asserted his right to silence.

- If, instead of waiving his *Miranda* right to counsel, the suspect invokes it, all questioning must immediately cease and may resume *only* if the suspect (1) voluntarily re-initiates the conversation, and (2) the suspect is re-warned and knowingly, voluntarily and intelligently waives his *Miranda* rights

- *Miranda* rights are *not* offense-specific, that is, if a suspect refuses to waive or invokes his *Miranda* rights, further questioning is barred as to *any* offense, not just the offense for which the suspect was taken into custody.

- The fruit-of-the-poisonous-tree doctrine is weaker in the *Miranda* context than in the Fourth Amendment context, though the precise scope of the differences is unclear.

- It is likely that the physical fruits of a confession obtained in violation of *Miranda* will nevertheless be admissible in evidence, though the confession itself will not be.

- At least under certain circumstances, however, a second, warned confession covering largely the same ground as an earlier un*warned* confession will be inadmissible in evidence, along with the inadmissibility of the earlier unwarned confession; there is no consensus among the Justices on whether a multi-factor balancing test or some sort of intent-based test governs.

- Although a confession obtained in violation of *Miranda* is inadmissible in the prosecutor's case-in-chief, it may be used to impeach the defendant, provided the usual evidentiary trustworthiness standards are met, should he take the stand.

- There are two recognized exceptions to *Miranda*: (1) statements made during "routine booking" and statements obtained at a time when delaying to recite the *Miranda* warnings and to obtain a valid waiver would endanger public safety.

Chapter 15

Interrogations and the Sixth Amendment

Roadmap

- Commencement of judicial proceedings triggers Sixth Amendment right to counsel.

- Prohibition on deliberate elicitation through interrogation and surreptitious questioning after defendant is charged.

- Waiving the Sixth Amendment right to counsel.

- Other trial uses for statements obtaining in violation of the Sixth Amendment.

I. Introduction

In addition to the voluntariness (Chapter 13) and *Miranda* (Chapter 14) requirements for confessions, the Sixth Amendment plays an important role in limiting how the government can obtain a statement from a defendant. The Sixth Amendment provides, "In all criminal prosecutions, the accused shall enjoy the right ... to have the Assistance of Counsel for his defence." The right to counsel, which was held applicable to the states in the landmark decision in *Gideon v. Wainwright*, 372 U.S. 335 (1963), requires that the government not elicit statements from a defendant without a lawyer present after the person has been charged with a crime unless the defendant knowingly, voluntarily, and intelligently waives the Sixth Amendment right. Unlike circumstances in which *Miranda* issues arise, however, the Sixth Amendment protection is not limited to police interrogations but also includes the use of undercover agents and cooperating witnesses acting at the government's behest in obtaining statements from a defendant.

II. Development of the Right: *Massiah* and *Escobedo*

A. *Massiah*

In *Massiah v. United States*, 377 U.S. 201 (1964), for the first time the Supreme Court applied the Sixth Amendment right to counsel outside of the courtroom and the direct judicial process. Massiah, a merchant seaman, was indicted for importation of cocaine. A short time later, the government obtained a superseding indictment that also named Colson as a co-defendant. After retaining counsel, Massiah entered a "not guilty" plea and was released from custody. Colson secretly agreed to cooperate, and he and Massiah "held a lengthy conversation while sitting in Colson's automobile, parked on a New York street. By prearrangement with Colson, and totally unbeknown to the petitioner, the agent Murphy sat in a car parked out of sight down the street and listened over the radio to the entire conversation. The petitioner made several incriminating statements during the course of this conversation." The government introduced Massiah's statements in its case-in-chief at trial, and the Supreme Court overturned the conviction for violating the Sixth Amendment because the government elicited the statements from Massiah without his counsel present.

The Court held "that the petitioner was denied the basic protections of that guarantee when there was used against him at his trial evidence of his own incriminating words, which federal agents had *deliberately elicited* from him after he had been indicted and in the absence of his counsel." The majority did not explain what it meant by "deliberately elicited," nor did it discuss how broadly the prohibition on government interrogation of a defendant charged with a crime might be. The Court explained its extension of the Sixth Amendment to governmental conduct outside the judicial process by quoting from its seminal decision in *Powell v. Alabama*, 287 U.S. 45 (1932), that "during perhaps the most critical period of the proceedings ... that is to say, from the time of their *arraignment until the beginning of their trial*, when consultation, thorough-going investigation and preparation (are) vitally important, the defendants [are] as much entitled to such aid [of counsel] during that period as at the trial itself."

In a dissenting opinion in *Massiah*, Justice White questioned the application of the Sixth Amendment to an otherwise voluntary statement that did not implicate the defendant's trial preparation. "Massiah was not prevented from consulting with counsel as often as he wished. No meetings with counsel were disturbed or spied upon. Preparation for trial was in no way obstructed. It is only a sterile syllogism — an unsound one, besides — to say that because Massiah had a right to counsel's aid before and during the trial, his out-of-court conversations and admissions must be excluded if obtained without counsel's consent or presence."

B. *Escobedo*

A few weeks after *Massiah*, the Court held in *Escobedo v. Illinois*, 378 U.S. 478 (1964), that the refusal by police to honor a person's request to consult with his lawyer during the course of an interrogation denied him "the Assistance of Counsel" guaranteed by the Sixth Amendment. Escobedo was arrested in connection with a murder investigation, but had not yet been charged. He repeatedly asked to speak with his retained counsel before continuing the interrogation, which the police refused by saying that his lawyer "didn't want to see him." In fact, Escobedo's lawyer was at the station house requesting to meet with him, which other officers refused to allow.

Unlike *Massiah*, which involved surreptitious recording of the indicted defendant's statements, *Escobedo* involved a police interrogation before charges were filed, when the right to counsel usually attaches. Nevertheless, the Court found that "in the context of this case, that fact should make *no difference*. When [Escobedo] requested, and was denied, an opportunity to consult with his lawyer, the investigation had ceased to be a general investigation of 'an unsolved crime.' [Escobedo] had become the accused, and the purpose of the interrogation was to 'get him' to confess his guilt despite his constitutional right not to do so." In that context, "the refusal by the police to honor petitioner's request to consult with his lawyer during the course of an interrogation constitutes a denial of 'the Assistance of Counsel.'"

Escobedo reflected the suspicion of some Justices of the government's methods for obtaining confessions that did not otherwise violate the due process norm of voluntariness. The Court stated, "We have learned the lesson of history, ancient and modern, that a system of criminal law enforcement which comes to depend on the 'confession' will, in the long run, be less reliable and more subject to abuses than a system which depends on extrinsic evidence independently secured through skillful investigation."

While some viewed *Escobedo* as the first step toward recognizing a broad, Sixth Amendment-based right to counsel in interrogations, the Supreme Court's decision two years later in *Miranda* instead applied the Fifth Amendment to police questioning, largely supplanting reliance on the right to counsel as the basis for limiting government tactics to obtain confessions. In *Kirby v. Illinois*,

406 U.S. 682 (1972), the Court stated that *Escobedo*'s holding had been limited "to its own facts," and the Sixth Amendment is generally viewed as inapplicable to *pre-charge* government conduct.

III. Deliberate Elicitation

A. Interrogation as "Elicitation"

After *Miranda*, the question was whether *Massiah* was largely a dead letter or did its holding retain a role in limiting police conduct in obtaining statements. In *Brewer v. Williams*, 430 U.S. 387 (1977), the Supreme Court reinvigorated *Massiah* by relying on the Sixth Amendment to overturn a conviction in which the police obtained information from a defendant after he had been charged with a crime.

The case involved the famed "Christian Burial Speech" given by an officer as he transported Williams 160 miles to another city after his arraignment on a kidnapping charge to be questioned about the disappearance of a young girl two days earlier. Although the police had assured defense counsel that they would not question him during the car ride about the girl's disappearance, the officer engaged in a discussion with Williams, a former mental patient who professed to be deeply religious, about religion. The officer then said,

> I feel that we could stop and locate the body, that the parents of this little girl should be entitled to a Christian burial for the little girl who was snatched away from them on Christmas [E]ve and murdered. And I feel we should stop and locate it on the way in rather than waiting until morning and trying to come back out after a snow storm and possibly not being able to find it at all.

A short time later, Williams directed the police to the girl's body, and was convicted of first-degree murder for her death.

The Supreme Court determined that it need not consider whether the defendant's statement regarding the location of the body was obtained in violation of *Miranda* or was involuntary, because "Williams was deprived of a different constitutional right, the right to the assistance of counsel." The Court found that the right to counsel attaches when "a person is entitled to the help of a lawyer at or after the time that *judicial proceedings have been initiated* against him 'whether by way of formal charge, preliminary hearing, indictment, information, or arraignment.'" Because Williams had been arraigned on another charge before the car ride, the Sixth Amendment applied, prohibiting interrogation outside the presence of counsel.

Having established the applicability of the right to counsel, the Court then found that the conduct of the officer "deliberately and designedly set out to *elicit information* from Williams just as surely as and perhaps more effectively than if he had formally interrogated him." *Massiah* controlled the outcome of the case, and the Court restated its rule: "once adversary proceedings have commenced against an individual, he has a right to legal representation when the government interrogates him." Further, it was "constitutionally irrelevant" to the application of the Sixth Amendment that the interrogation in *Williams* was by a police officer while in *Massiah* it was conducted surreptitiously by a cooperating codefendant.

The Court did not explain what it meant by "deliberately eliciting" a statement in *Massiah*, and *Williams* determined only that the "Christian Burial Speech" was the *functional equivalent* of an interrogation. As discussed in Chapter 14, whether or not the police are interrogating a person is crucial for the application of *Miranda*. The Sixth Amendment right covers a broader array of police conduct, and the meaning of "interrogation" is not the same as it is under the Fifth Amendment. In *Rhode Island v. Innis*, 446 U..S. 291 (1980), the Court stated that "[t]he definitions of 'interrogation' under the Fifth and Sixth Amendments, if indeed the term 'interrogation' is even apt in the Sixth Amendment context, are not necessarily interchangeable."

B. Deliberate

The term "deliberate" connotes intent on the part of the government to obtain information from a defendant. In contrast, *Miranda* interrogation issues center on whether it is reasonably foreseeable to the police that their conduct will elicit incriminating statements , even if the officers did not intend an interrogation. The *Miranda* test for "interrogation" is thus purely objective, purportedly ignoring what the individual officer in fact sought to accomplish. But the Sixth Amendment "deliberate elicitation" test is purely subjective, focusing only on what the officer wanted to do rather than on what he reasonably should have realized would occur. (See Chapter 14)

In *United States v. Henry*, 447 U.S. 264 (1980), the Court found that placing an informant, Nichols, in the same jail cell as Henry and eliciting statements from him about the crime violated the Sixth Amendment. *Henry* reached this conclusion even though a government agent told Nichols not to initiate a conversation with Henry about the charged offense, but to pay attention to what he said if the topic arose in conversation. The Court found that "Nichols was *not a passive listener*; rather, he had 'some conversations' with Mr. Henry while he was in jail and Henry's incriminatory statements were the product of this conversation. While affirmative interrogation, absent waiver, would certainly satisfy *Massiah*, we are not persuaded, as the Government contends, that *Brewer v. Williams* modified *Massiah*'s 'deliberately elicited' test."

The fact that the government uses a secret informant rather than an officer does not change the Sixth Amendment analysis because the issue is not whether the defendant's right against self-incrimination has been compromised, but whether information was obtained outside the presence of counsel. As *Henry* noted, "Conversation *stimulated* in such circumstances may elicit information that an accused would not intentionally reveal to persons known to be Government agents." Therefore, "[b]y *intentionally creating a situation* likely to induce Henry to make incriminating statements without the assistance of counsel, the Government violated Henry's Sixth Amendment right to counsel." This conclusion makes it clear that "deliberate" is not limited to actual questioning, but also includes creating a situation in which the defendant is likely to respond to overtures from a person acting on the government's behalf.

C. Elicitation

In *Maine v. Moulton*, 474 U.S. 159 (1985), the Court made it clear that the application of the Sixth Amendment does not depend on who instigated the conversation, so long as there is affirmative, rather than merely passive, government conduct involved. Moulton suggested to his co-defendant Colson, who was cooperating with the police, that they kill a witness in their pending theft case, and the government had a recording device installed on Colson's telephone. The government taped three calls from Moulton to Colson discussing the pending charges. During one call, Colson professed a lack of memory and asked Moulton to fill him in on the details of the theft. In reversing the conviction, the Court stated that "the prosecutor and police have an *affirmative obligation not to act in a manner that circumvents* and thereby dilutes the protection afforded by the right to counsel."

The Court rejected the state's argument that *Massiah* and *Henry* were distinguishable because the government did not set up the situation in which Moulton made incriminating statements. Instead, it found that "the identity of the party who instigated the meeting at which the Government obtained incriminating statements was not decisive or even important to our decisions in *Massiah* or *Henry*." The Sixth Amendment imposes an affirmative obligation on the government to avoid obtaining information from a defendant who is charged with a crime about the offense at issue, so that "*knowing exploita-*

tion by the State of an opportunity to confront the accused without counsel being present is as much a breach of the State's obligation not to circumvent the right to the assistance of counsel as is the intentional creation of such an opportunity."

Moulton did point out that "the Sixth Amendment is not violated whenever —by *luck or happenstance*—the State obtains incriminating statements from the accused after the right to counsel has attached." In *Kuhlman v. Wilson,* 477 U.S. 436 (1986), the Court held that the Sixth Amendment was not violated when an informant followed an officer's instruction to "only listen" to the defendant's "spontaneous" and "unsolicited" statements about the crime, and the only statement to the defendant was that his story "did not sound good." The Court held that a violation occurs only if "the police and their informant took some action, *beyond mere listening,* that was designed deliberately to elicit incriminating remarks."

The distinction between *Henry* and *Kuhlman* is based on whether the government created or exploited the situation in which the defendant made the incriminating statement, or merely placed an informant in a position to listen to a defendant's statements. For example, there would be no Sixth Amendment violation when the authorities tape a telephone call between a defendant and his girlfriend in which he made statements about the crime without any prompting. Similarly, if an informant was not acting on behalf of the government at the time of obtaining the information from the defendant, then there would be no violation of the right to counsel because the police did not create a situation designed to elicit a statement.

D. Jailhouse Snitches

The use of "jailhouse snitches" who provide information to the prosecution that is often important to obtaining a conviction has been the subject of substantial criticism. There have been a number of instances in which it has been revealed that informants fabricated testimony recounting statements made by other defendants while in jail, sometimes gleaning information about the case and then reporting to the authorities that the defendant voluntarily confessed to the crime. In *Kansas v. Ventris,* 129 S.Ct. 1841 (2009), the Supreme Court rejected the argument that jailhouse snitches were so inherently unreliable that their uncorroborated statements should always be excluded from trial. It noted that the criminal justice system "is built on the premise that it is the province of the jury to weigh the credibility of competing witnesses. . . ."

IV. Attachment of the Right to Counsel

A. Triggering the Right

The Sixth Amendment is triggered by the initiation of judicial proceedings, such as a formal charge, indictment, information, arraignment, or preliminary hearing. In *Rothgery v. Gillespie County*, 128 S.Ct. 2578 (2008), the Court explained that the right to counsel attaches

> by the time a defendant is brought before a judicial officer, is informed of a formally lodged accusation, and has restrictions imposed on his liberty in aid of the prosecution, the State's relationship with the defendant has become solidly adversarial. And that is just as true when the proceeding comes before the indictment (in the case of the initial arraignment on a formal complaint) as when it comes after it (at an arraignment on an indictment).

At that point, the defendant is entitled to be represented by counsel in the proceeding, and further interrogation outside the presence of counsel is generally prohibited. Even if the defendant has the right to counsel, however, the Supreme Court limited the scope of the protection by excluding statements only about the offense for which the right has attached. The police may interrogate a defendant or surreptitiously obtain information about a *different offense* than the one charged, even if it is related to the charged crime.

B. Other Charges

In *Maine v. Moulton*, 474 U.S. 159 (1985), the Court noted that while statements about the pending charge must be excluded from the government's case-in-chief, "to exclude evidence pertaining to charges as to which the Sixth Amendment right to counsel had not attached at the time the evidence was obtained, simply because other charges were pending at that time, would unnecessarily frustrate the public's interest in the investigation of criminal activities."

C. Offense Specific

In *McNeil v. Wisconsin*, 501 U.S. 171 (1991), the Court made it clear that the Sixth Amendment right is *offense specific* and not a broad prohibition on the government seeking information from the defendant about other crimes. Mc-

Neil was in jail on an armed robbery charge for which counsel had appeared for him at a bail hearing, and he later made incriminating statements to the police about a murder in another town. Although he waived his *Miranda* rights in the interrogation about the murder, McNeil argued that the Sixth Amendment right precluded all questioning outside the presence of his counsel on the armed robbery charge. The Court held that "[t]he Sixth Amendment right, however, is offense specific. *It cannot be invoked once for all future prosecutions*, for it does not attach until a prosecution is commenced...." *McNeil* distinguished the Sixth Amendment analysis from *Miranda*, which would prohibit further interrogation about other crimes once the defendant asserts the right to counsel under the Fifth Amendment.

D. Same Offense Test

Determining what constitutes the *same offense* for Sixth Amendment purposes requires reference to the Double Jeopardy Clause jurisprudence under the Fifth Amendment. The test adopted in *Blockburger v. United States,* 284 U.S. 299 (1932), prohibits a second prosecution for the same offense if the crime contains all of the same elements as that involved in the first proceeding. So long as the government must prove different "facts" for each crime, then a second prosecution would not be prohibited under double jeopardy. In *Texas v. Cobb*, 532 U.S. 162 (2001), the Court adopted *Blockburger*'s "same elements" test for determining the scope of the right to counsel: "We see no constitutional difference between the meaning of the term 'offense' in the contexts of double jeopardy and of the right to counsel. Accordingly, we hold that when the Sixth Amendment right to counsel attaches, it does encompass offenses that, even if not formally charged, would be considered the same offense under the *Blockburger* test."

Four justices dissented in *Cobb*, arguing that the proper test under the Sixth Amendment was to "define 'offense' in terms of the conduct that constitutes the crime that the offender committed on a particular occasion, including criminal acts that are 'closely related to' or 'inextricably intertwined with' the particular crime set forth in the charging instrument." No states have adopted the minority position in *Cobb* as the proper interpretation of under the state's constitution.

To determine whether two crimes are the "same offence" under *Cobb* and *Blockburger*, a court must look at the elements of each, and so long as *each crime* contains a *different element* than the other, they are not the same offense, and the police can interrogate a person about that different crime. For example, larceny is a lesser-included offense of armed robbery, so a defendant charged with larceny could not be questioned about whether the crime involved a weapon, which would elevate the crime to a robbery, once the right to counsel attaches to the larceny. On the other hand, a defendant could be questioned about the death of the victim of the larceny for a possible murder (or manslaughter) charge because the homicide and the larceny require proof of different elements, at least so long as the death was not the result of the larceny.

There is a split in the federal circuits whether the double jeopardy "dual sovereignty" doctrine that allows a second prosecution for the same offense by different sovereigns, such as different states or the federal government and a state, also applies to the Sixth Amendment right to counsel. In *United States v. Mills*, 412 F.3d 325 (2nd Cir. 2005), the Second Circuit stated, "The fact that *Cobb* appropriates the *Blockburger* test, applied initially in the double jeopardy context, does not demonstrate that *Cobb* incorporates the dual sovereignty doctrine." The Fourth Circuit took the opposite approach in *United States v. Alvarado*, 440 F.3d 191 (4th Cir. 2006), holding that because "defendant's state and federal offenses were inherently distinct under the dual sovereignty doctrine, they cannot be the same offense for purposes of the Sixth Amendment right to counsel." The First and Fifth Circuits also apply the dual sovereignty doctrine to Sixth Amendment right to counsel claims. United States v. Coker, 433 F.3d 39 (1st Cir. 2005); United States v. Avants, 278 F.3d 510 (5th Cir. 2002).

V. Waiver

A. Requirements

Like most individual constitutional protections, the right to counsel can be waived by a defendant, which allows the police to question the person without the presence of the lawyer. As with the *Miranda* rights, the waiver must meet the requirements of *Johnson v. Zerbst*, 304 U.S. 458 (1938), that it be knowing, intelligent, and voluntary. In the Sixth Amendment context, waiver can only take place when *the police* interrogate a person and not when there is a deliberate elicitation of information by a cooperating witness because the defendant would not know that the government was seeking information in the latter context. Waiver requires more than just a defendant responding to police interrogation, or its functional equivalent, without an explicit assertion of the right to counsel, particularly — although not only — if defendant has already requested representation by counsel. In *Brewer v. Williams*, 430 U.S. 387 (1977), the "Christian Burial Speech" case, the

Supreme Court stated that "waiver requires not merely comprehension but relinquishment, and Williams' consistent reliance upon the advice of counsel in dealing with the authorities refutes any suggestion that he waived that right."

B. Interrogation after Assertion of Right

An important question is whether the government can initiate questioning with a defendant after an assertion of the right to counsel in the case, even if the questioning is about another crime that would be the same offense under the *Blockburger* test. The Supreme Court has changed its approach to allow waiver of the Sixth Amendment right to counsel if it meets the requirement of being knowing, intelligent, and voluntary.

In *Michigan v. Jackson*, 475 U.S. 625 (1986), the Court held that a defendant's request to be represented by counsel means the defendant wants the lawyer's services at every critical stage of prosecution, including any subsequent interrogation. The Court adopted a prophylactic rule that any waiver of the right to counsel after a defendant asserts the right at an arraignment or similar proceeding is automatically invalid, unless the waiver followed the defendant's re-initiation of the conversation of his own accord. *Jackson* seemingly rested its holding on *Edwards v. Arizona*, 451 U.S. 477 (1981), which held that an assertion of the Fifth Amendment right to counsel under *Miranda* required the police to cease all questioning until the lawyer was present or the defendant re-initiated the conversation, followed by a knowing, voluntary, and intelligent waiver of his *Miranda* rights (see Chapter 14). The Court stated in *Jackson* that "the reasons for prohibiting the interrogation of an uncounseled prisoner who has asked for the help of a lawyer [in *Edwards*] are even stronger after he has been formally charged with an offense than before."

In *Montejo v. Louisiana*, 129 S.Ct. 2079 (2009), the Court overturned the *Jackson* presumption rendering invalid all waivers of the Sixth Amendment right to counsel after a defendant requests representation at an arraignment or other preliminary proceeding. In *Montejo*, the trial court appointed counsel for the defendant, who was indigent, for a murder charge in a proceeding in which he did not make an affirmative request for a lawyer. Later that day, he agreed to accompany two detectives to locate the weapon after receiving *Miranda* warnings, and while with the police he wrote an inculpatory letter of apology to the victim's widow. The government introduced the letter at trial, and the Louisiana Supreme Court upheld the conviction on the ground that *Jackson* did not apply because the defendant never actually requested a lawyer at the hearing; one was simply appointed without any inquiry or response.

The Supreme Court declined to read into *Jackson* a requirement that a defendant must make an affirmative request for legal representation before the Sixth Amendment protection from interrogation outside the presence of counsel applies. Because states have different rules for what must be done to secure the appointment of a lawyer, premising the Sixth Amendment right on whether a defendant actually asked for counsel "would lead either to an unworkable standard, or to arbitrary and anomalous distinctions between defendants in different States."

Rather than apply *Jackson*'s presumption to any case in which a defendant was represented by a lawyer, *Montejo* determined that a defendant can waive the Sixth Amendment right to counsel and allow further interrogation on the charged offense even after a request for representation. The Court explained that the prophylactic rule must have been based on the need to protect defendants from badgering by the police to give up their right to counsel, and that this "antibadgering rationale is the only way to make sense of *Jackson*'s repeated citations of *Edwards*, and the only way to reconcile the opinion with our waiver jurisprudence."

The Court determined that the proper protection from badgering was under *Miranda*, which requires a defendant to make a voluntary waiver of the Fifth Amendment rights before a custodial interrogation can take place. Finding that *Jackson* was "unworkable" and provided only "marginal benefits," the Court found that the prophylactic protection from waivers of the Sixth Amendment right was "simply superfluous" given the protections afforded by *Miranda* and *Edwards*. Thus, a voluntary waiver of the Fifth Amendment *Miranda* rights before a custodial interrogation may often also be sufficient to waive the Sixth Amendment right to counsel for a defendant questioned about the charged offense. In other words, *Montejo* substituted the analysis from *Miranda* (and its progeny) for *Jackson*'s prophylactic rule.

Miranda is limited to custodial interrogations, while the Sixth Amendment right to counsel is broader by applying also to noncustodial interrogations, such as day time questioning by a single officer at a defendant's home in the presence of his family members. The Court was untroubled by the possibility of police badgering circumstances in which *Miranda* rights need not be given, pointing out that "those uncovered situations are the *least* likely to pose a risk of coerced waivers." Whether that is in fact the case remains to be seen. Furthermore, under *McNeil*, the right to counsel is offense specific, so that a request for counsel on the charged offenses does not preclude a custodial interrogation about a different crime, where the only issue would be whether the waiver was valid under *Miranda* if there is a "custodial" interrogation, *i.e.*, questioning while the defendant is held "incommunicado" in a police-dominated atmosphere.

C. Interrogation with No Prior Assertion of Right

A different analysis applies if the defendant has been charged with a crime but has not requested the assistance of counsel. In *Patterson v. Illinois*, 487 U.S. 285 (1988), the defendant was in police custody and informed that he had been indicted for murder, but had not been arraigned on the charge or otherwise requested a lawyer. After indicating twice a willingness to talk about the crime, and waiving his *Miranda* rights, he made incriminating statements that the prosecution used against him at trial. The Court rejected the argument that the attachment of the right to counsel on the charge meant that no interrogation could take place without a lawyer. Instead, the Court found that the failure to assert the right to counsel was similar to *Edwards* and allowed for a determination of whether there was a valid waiver of the Sixth Amendment right. The *Patterson* Court held:

> Preserving the integrity of an accused's choice to communicate with police only through counsel is the essence of *Edwards* and its progeny —not barring an accused from making an initial election as to whether he will face the State's officers during questioning with the aid of counsel, or go it alone. If an accused "knowingly and intelligently" pursues the latter course, we see no reason why the uncounseled statements he then makes must be excluded at his trial.

The waiver was valid in *Patterson* because the *Miranda* warnings had informed him sufficiently of his right to counsel and to terminate the interrogation to consult with a lawyer. The Court held, "As a general matter, then, an accused who is admonished with the warnings prescribed by this Court in *Miranda* has been sufficiently apprised of the nature of his Sixth Amendment rights, and of the consequences of abandoning those rights, so that his waiver on this basis will be considered a knowing and intelligent one."

Patterson rejected the position that the Sixth Amendment right to counsel is somehow "superior" to the Fifth Amendment right in custodial interrogations. Therefore, like a person who has earlier asserted the *Miranda* right to silence and then seeks to resume questioning, a defendant can initiate contact with the police to discuss the pending charge and agree to waive the Sixth Amendment right to counsel without any special warnings beyond the standard *Miranda* warnings. "So long as the accused is made aware of the 'dangers and disadvantages of self-representation' during postindictment questioning, by use of the *Miranda* warnings, his waiver of his Sixth Amendment right to counsel at such questioning is 'knowing and intelligent.'"

It is important to stress, however, that police officers are *not* free to question a defendant post-charge simply because he has not affirmatively invoked the Sixth Amendment right to counsel. The police may not deliberately elicit a defendant's statement post-charge unless he *first* validly waived his right to counsel. Absent such waiver, police may not question him, even if he does not specifically ask for an attorney.

VI. Subsequent Use of the Statement

A. Impeachment

Like a violation of the Fourth Amendment's warrant requirements or *Miranda*, a violation of the Sixth Amendment right to counsel by interrogating a defendant or deliberately eliciting a statement outside the presence of counsel on the charged offense is subject to the exclusionary rule. Therefore, the prosecution cannot use the evidence in its case-in-chief. The statement can, however, be used to impeach the defendant if that person testifies inconsistently at trial. In *Michigan v. Harvey*, 494 U.S. 344 (1990), the Supreme Court held that a statement taken in violation of the subsequently overturned prophylactic rule of *Michigan v. Jackson* that prohibited further questioning after a defendant invoked his Sixth Amendment right could be used to impeach the defendant if he testified at trial inconsistently with the prior statement. Unlike introducing evidence obtained in violation of the right to counsel to prove the offense, the Court noted that "use of statements so obtained for impeachment purposes is a different matter," further noting that "[w]e have mandated the exclusion of reliable and probative evidence for *all* purposes only when it is derived from involuntary statements."

In *Kansas v. Ventris*, 129 S.Ct. 1841 (2009), the Court adopted the same approach to a statement deliberately elicited from a defendant by an informant planted in the jail cell to obtain information. The Court stated that "the *Massiah* right is a right to be free of uncounseled interrogation, and is infringed at the time of the interrogation." While the Sixth Amendment right to counsel is usually viewed as a trial right, in the interrogation context the violation occurs at the time of the interrogation or of deliberate elicitation of information from the defendant. The appropriate remedy is exclusion from the government's case-in-chief, but "[o]ur precedents make clear that the game of excluding tainted evidence for impeachment purposes is not worth the candle." Therefore, the prosecution can use a statement that was obtained in violation of the Sixth Amendment right to counsel in the pretrial phase to impeach the defendant because exclusion from any use at trial "would add little appreciable deterrence." This rule is consistent with the Court's position in other contexts that evidence subject to the exclusionary rule because of a violation of the Fourth or Fifth Amendment can be used to impeach the defendant (see Chapters 12 and 14).

B. Fruit of the Poisonous Tree

The Fourth Amendment "fruit of the poisonous tree" doctrine applies to a violation of the Sixth Amendment right to counsel. The government may not make use of the fruits of a statement taken in violation of the defendant's right to counsel to obtain further evidence, but the government can use it at trial if the limitations on that rule apply. To use evidence traceable to a statement taken in violation of the Sixth Amendment, the government must meet the requirements of the independent source, inevitable discovery, or attenuation rules.

In *Nix v. Williams*, 467 U.S. 431 (1984), a follow-up to the *Brewer v. Williams* "Christian Burial Speech" case, the Court held that the government proved that the discovery of the victim's body came within the inevitable discovery rule, and therefore the introduction of evidence from tests on it did not violate Williams' Sixth Amendment right even though his statement was excluded. Applying the same rationale as it does in Fourth Amendment cases, the Court stated that "suppression of the evidence would operate to undermine the adversary system by putting the State in a worse position than it would have occupied without any police misconduct."

VII. Review Problem

A. Problem

The police receive an anonymous tip that Derrek was one of the three men who robbed a liquor store, and he has one of the weapons used in the robbery. Derrek has an outstanding warrant for failure to pay child support. Officers arrest Derrek at his home, and he is charged with armed robbery. While Derrek is in a holding cell awaiting his arraignment the next day, Ivan, another prisoner, strikes up a conversation with him. After a brief discussion about the previous night's basketball playoff game, Ivan asked, "How'd they find you?" Derrek responds, "My old lady filed a complaint with the police because I'm behind on my child support. It's not like I've got lots of money, you know, to pay that stuff." Ivan says, "Is that all you're here for? You're lucky, they got me on a smack [heroin possession] charge." Derrek replies, "No, man, I'm here for robbing a store. I needed some money, you know, I was desperate." A short time later, Ivan is removed from the holding cell and reports on his conversation with Derrek to a police officer.

Ivan had agreed to cooperate with the police to obtain a reduced sentence and said he would strike up conversations with other prisoners about their charges. Officers had warned Ivan not to steer the conversation toward any particular crime, just to start talking and let the other prisoner lead the discussion of any criminal conduct. Prosecutors want to introduce Derrek's statement at trial in the government's case-in-chief. Defense counsel files a motion to suppress the statement to Ivan as a violation of the Sixth Amendment right to counsel. How will the court rule? Would it change the outcome if Derrek had only been charged with failure to pay child support at the time of the conversation with Ivan? If Derrek testifies at trial and denies any involvement in the robbery, can the government call Ivan to testify about what Derrek said while they were in jail?

B. Analysis

Because Derrek has been charged with the robbery, judicial proceedings have been initiated and the Sixth Amendment right to counsel attaches to the charge under *Massiah* and *Brewer*. The issue is whether Ivan's discussion with Derrek constitutes the *deliberate elicitation* of information from a defendant in violation of the right to counsel. *Henry* would control this case because Ivan was not a "passive listener" but actively sought information from Derrek. While Ivan did not specifically ask about the robbery, he did ask about the crime charged against Derrek, even though he did not know the exact nature of the offense. While the officer's instruction was not to steer the conversation toward any particular crime, the government intentionally created a situation that was likely to induce Derrek to make an incriminating statement in violation of the Sixth Amendment. Moreover, this is not the circumstance described in *Moulton* in which the statement came to prosecutors "by luck or happenstance." Therefore, the court should rule that the statement must be excluded from the government's case-in-chief. Note that if Derrek were to take the witness stand at trial and his testimony contradicted what he said to Ivan, then the prior statement could be admitted for impeachment under *Harvey*.

The crime charged is critically important, so the outcome would change if Derrek had been charged with only the child support violation while the police investigated his role in the liquor store robbery. In that instance, *Cobb* would apply and interrogation about an uncharged offense would be permissible so long as the statement was not involuntary. There is no issue of waiver of rights because the interrogation by Ivan is not being performed by an officer, so no *Miranda* warnings are required.

If Derrek testifies that he was not involved in the robbery, then Ivan can be called to testify about the jailhouse statement because it would be impeachment evidence. While the statement may be excluded from the government's case-in-chief, under *Kansas v. Ventris* it is admissible for impeachment purposes because the violation occurred at the time of the deliberate elicitation. There is no need to preclude all use of the evidence at trial because such a broad prohibition "would add little appreciable deterrence."

Checkpoints

- The Supreme Court recognized the Sixth Amendment right to counsel to limit interrogation of defendants and obtaining statements before *Miranda*.

- The right to counsel attaches at the commencement of judicial proceedings, whether by by indictment, information, arraignment, or preliminary hearing.

- Once the Sixth Amendment right attaches, the police may not deliberately elicit a statement from a defendant who has requested representation by counsel.

- Unlike *Miranda*, the right to counsel applies to both police interrogation and surreptitious questioning of a defendant.

- The government need not instigate the conversation with the defendant to violate the Sixth Amendment, but if an informant merely listens to a defendant's statements, or does not act at the government's behest, then there is no constitutional violation.

- The right to counsel only prohibits interrogating a defendant about the charged offense, and the *Blockburger* test for a Double Jeopardy violation also applies to determine whether the questioning concerned the same offense.

- The right to counsel can be waived, and the defendant need only receive the required *Miranda* warnings before the interrogation for a waiver to be valid.

- If a defendant has not requested counsel, then a defendant's decision to waive *Miranda* rights and respond to questioning is also a valid waiver of the Sixth Amendment right to counsel.

- The prosecution can use statements obtained in violation of the Sixth Amendment right to counsel through interrogation or by deliberate elicitation of information to impeach the defendant at trial.

- The "fruit-of-the-poisonous-tree" doctrine applies to violations of the right to counsel, and a statement obtained in violation of that right can be introduced to impeach the defendant.

Chapter 16

Eyewitness Identification

Roadmap

- Lineups, photospreads (also known as photo-arrays), show-ups, and other eye-witness identification procedures and their definitions
- Simultaneous versus sequential identification methods
- Double-blind identification procedures
- Lineup size and instructions
- The Sixth Amendment right to counsel as a ground for suppressing an eyewitness identification
- "Post-indictment" stage as triggering the right to counsel
- The test for suppressing an out-of-court versus an in-court identification as fruits of a Sixth Amendment right to counsel violation
- The Due Process Clauses as grounds for suppressing an eyewitness identification
- The test for suppressing an out-of-court versus an in-court eyewitness identification as the fruit of a due process violation
- The Fourth Amendment as a ground for suppressing an eyewitness identification

---

I. Introduction

In some criminal cases, there is no doubt about who did the crime. Instead, the dispute centers around whether the suspect acted with a wrongful mental state or deserves the benefit of an affirmative defense. For example, an alleged date rapist might admit to sexual intercourse but deny that he acted without consent, or at least deny that he knew or should have known of consent's absence. Alternatively, an alleged drug dealer might concede that he sold drugs but argue that he was entrapped, or an alleged assailant might admit to throwing a punch but insist that he did so in self-defense.

In many other criminal cases, however, there is no dispute that a crime took place, but the suspect denies that he was the wrongdoer. He need not, though

301

he may raise an alibi defense in which he offers witnesses placing him away from the scene at the time of the crime, for the burden of proving that he, and not someone else, sold the drugs, or punched an elderly man is always on the state to prove beyond a reasonable doubt. If the victim and the suspect knew each other well before the incident and the conditions for observation were good, this burden is usually not hard to meet. "That's the guy! He's been my next door neighbor for ten years, and we argued on the street for half an hour on a bright, sunny day" proves the point rather well, unless there is evidence to suggest that the witness had a motive to lie. But identifications in which the parties are strangers to one another are far more suspect, especially if the conditions for accurate observation and memory were not favorable, such as a midnight purse snatch on a dimly lit street in which the victim caught at most a fleeting glimpse of her assailant. Yet, so long as the victim expresses significant confidence in her identification, jurors are likely to give it substantial weight, failing adequately to appreciate the risks of error. Many of the proven wrongful convictions indeed have stemmed in significant part from mistaken eyewitness identifications.

There are two major points at which an eyewitness may be asked to make an identification: before trial and at trial. The procedures followed during pre-trial identifications can especially increase the risk of a mistake. Identifications can include show-ups (only one person, generally the suspect, is shown to the witness, usually close in space and near in time to the crime scene), lineups, (several persons are shown to the witness), and photospreads (also often called "photo arrays."). Suggestive means for implementing each of these procedures can worsen the risk of error. As one clear example, if a robber was a redhead and the suspect is the only redhead in a six-person lineup, that circumstance signals or "suggests" to the witness that he should pick the redhead. Fair identification methods seek to minimize such suggestion. Although these events occur outside of court, other pre-trial identifications, such as at a preliminary hearing, may occur in a courtroom.

Two constitutional provisions offer protection against mistaken identifications:the due process clauses require identification methods consistent with fundamental fairness, and the Sixth Amendment creates a right to counsel during "post-indictment" (a term of art to be defined shortly) identifications. Violation of these constitutional mandates may result in suppression of out-of-court identifications and many of their fruits, sometimes including later in-court identifications. If there is only one witness to a crime between strangers and an absence of any physical identification evidence (such as fingerprints or DNA), suppression of both pre and at-trial identifications likely means dismissal of the case. If there are other types of identifying evidence, suppression of even one eyewitness's testimony may nevertheless make conviction more difficult. Success on a motion to suppress eyewitness identifications is thus often an important goal of defense counsel. Increasingly, such success requires a strong substantive background in the latest scientific research on the factors affecting eyewitness accuracy.

II. The Science of Eyewitness Identifications

A. Sources of Error

Human memory operates more like a novelist trying to re-create a scene than like a camera. Observers attend only to certain features of their environment, and only some of what is observed makes itself into memory. Over time, memory of an event may be unconsciously altered to conform to later information about the event and may be altered by other, newer experiences and by a variety of biases. Both perception and memory can be skewed by environmental factors. For example, time can seem to slow during an anxiety-producing situation, such as a robbery, leading the victim to believe that he had more time to observe his assailant than was in fact the base. Poor or rapidly changing lighting conditions, great distance, and distracting noises may also distort perceptions. Even when perceptual conditions are poor, observers may revise their memories to fit their idea of what an object or face *should* look like rather than what it did. Cross-racial identifications also tend to be less reliable than intra-racial ones, articulating a description of an assailant may actually alter the witness's memory to conform to the description rather than the other way around, and leading questions can change memories to match those the questions imply. Memories may also fade as more time passes between crime and identification, though the witness may not appreciate this diminishing ability for accurate recollection of the events. The use of weapons during a crime also tends to shift the victim's focus from the assailant's face to his weapon, again an effect on witness attention about which the witness herself is likely unaware. The *gist* of a memory might survive, but its details may be reconstructions, not recordings, of the event, and details matter in selecting the right person.

Once a witness has made an identification, even if it is incorrect, later ones may result more from recollection of the earlier-identified face rather than the one observed at the time of the crime. The choice of words, or the absence of certain words, used by the detective or officer administering the identification procedure can also alter memory. Thus if a witness believes that the correct perpetrator is in the lineup or photospread, and especially if the witness further believes that the administering officer knows who did it, the witness will pick someone even if the true wrongdoer is in fact absent from the line or spread. The witness relies on comparative rather than absolute identification, that is, selecting from among the faces offered the one that looks *most like* that of the assailant rather than the one that truly matches him. An accurate witness should identify no one in a target-absent lineup in which the real wrongdoer is not present, yet many witnesses select the closest match to the target among the available choices, much like a student guessing among the options in a multiple choice test while ignoring the one declaring, "None of the above." The difference between the student guesser and the eyewitness guesser is that the former usually knows he is guessing while the latter does not. Moreover, once the witness has made even a tentative selection, feedback from the police officer suggesting to the witness that he "picked the right guy" my dramatically increase the witness's confidence in his choice. But juries may be most heavily swayed by the most confident witnesses, even where their confidence is misplaced.

B. Proposed Solutions

Social scientists have proposed a variety of reforms meant to reduce the chances of eyewitness error. A fairly thorough review of these reforms is necessary for several reasons: first, the science underlying them and their absence in any particular case may provide grounds for challenging a particular procedure as unduly suggestive, thus violating due process; second, that same science helps concerned prosecutors to press for reforms that improve both identification accuracy and the ability of the state's case to withstand a suppression motion; and third, some jurisdictions have already implemented these reforms, so familiarity with them is essential to any practitioner. Moreover, all the science underlying these reforms developed well after the now decades-old constitutional precedent concerning the admissibility of eyewitness identifications at trial; the logic of those constitutional rules, which we will shortly examine, suggests that there are strong arguments that at least some of these reforms are now constitutionally required. The basis for such an argument is straightforward: due process prohibits using identification procedures that unnecessarily create a very substantial likelihood of misidentification; procedures are "unnecessarily" suggestive if they fail to comply with readily available science that enable law enforcement to do better.

There is widespread scientific agreement about the wisdom of some variant of most of these reforms, and an increasing number of private think-tanks and public commissions have recommended at least voluntary governmental adoption of these changes. Many police departments have indeed embraced at least some of these improvements of their own accord, and in some states some of these measures have been mandated by the courts or the legislatures. Political support for change has been building partly because of reformers' emphasizing the public safety aspects of change: every wrongful conviction means that a guilty man goes free. But many other jurisdictions have resisted change or accepted it only slowly, reluctantly, and partially, fearing that new ways might protect the innocent but at the cost of increasing a different risk—that of freeing the guilty.

Here is a brief summary of some of the major proposals.

1. Use Double-Blind Lineups and Photospreads

"Double-blind" lineups occur when neither the witness nor the administering detective knows which, if any, of those in the lineup is the suspect. Even the most careful, well-intentioned officer can unconsciously convey cues to the witness about whom to select. A small smile, crossing the detective's face, a more encouraging tone of voice, or even widened or attentive eyes when the witness brings his attention to bear on, for example, lineup participant number 3, alerts the witness, again without his awareness, that number 3 is the suspect arrested by the police. Accordingly, it is number 3 whom the witness chooses. But if the detective has no idea whether or which suspect is in the lineup, this danger is eliminated.

2. Sequential versus Simultaneous Lineups

Traditionally, lineups are done in a simultaneous manner, meaning all the lineup participants are presented to the witness at the same time. Thus a witness may be shown six individuals standing in a line and asked whether he recognizes anyone. The same might be done with a photospread (six photos). The problem with this method is that it triggers the comparative process recounting above, leading a witness to assume that the true offender is indeed in the line, thus selecting the person who looks "most like" the witness's memory of the offender's face.

A newer, alternative method shows the witness each person or photo, one at a time. The witness is asked whether this one face is the guy. Because there are no other faces at that moment to which the witness can compare the observed face to other faces, comparative processes cannot work. In theory, therefore, a recognition process is triggered, the witness identifying a face only if it is the one that the witness indeed recognizes as being involved in the crime. However, pairing sequential methods with double-blind procedures is even more important than pairing the latter with simultaneous ones. Most sequential procedures stop showing faces when the witness positively identifies one of them. But if a detective aware of who is the suspect cues the witness to identify that suspect's face, the witness will not then be shown other faces that may be a better match or contain the "true" wrongdoer when the police are just wrong in their suspicion that a particular person committed the crime. The witness thus has no opportunity to "correct" his initial impressions, while with a simultaneous display of many faces, he may in theory be able to say, "No, I'm wrong; it's not number two but number four who mugged me."

There has been much empirical research seeking to test whether in practice sequential methods are better than simultaneous ones. Both laboratory and field experiments overwhelmingly confirm that, except in special circumstances that need not concern us here, sequential methods are better. Nevertheless, a smaller number of studies conclude that simultaneous methods are more accurate than the newer sequential ones, so the pro-sequential position cannot be said to be without controversy.

3. Lineup Size

Lineups generally consist of the suspect (who may or may not be the guy who really did the crime) and several "foils" (persons not suspected to have committed the crime). The larger the number of foils, the less the likelihood that a randomly guessing eyewitness will pick the suspect, thus the less the chance of error (a mere "guess" must be seen as an error, for it is based on speculation rather than recognition and informed choice). Thus a two-person lineup creates a 50% chance that the eyewitness will pick the suspect. Assume, for illustrative purposes, that the suspect is innocent. That means there is a very high chance —50%—that the witness will finger an innocent man. With five foils (six total participants), the chance of error by random guessing falls to 1/6, or about 16%. With nine foils (ten total participants), the chances of mistake fall to 10%. The bigger the lineup, the greater the time and labor costs of a lineup, for it is not easy to find many people who look enough alike (similar height, face, skin color, among other things) to avoid suggestion. Furthermore, the size of the risk of a mistake from simple guessing is to some degree a normative, not an empirical, question because it is always theoretically possible to have ever-bigger lineups. The line must be drawn somewhere. In the United States, historical practice has usually meant six-person lineups, but most researchers find that size of line too small to get the risk of error down to an "acceptable" level. They instead advocate routine use of ten-person lineups, which is the norm in England.

4. Lineup Instructions

Telling the witness that the perpetrator may or may not be in the lineup and that she need not identify anyone seems to reduce guessing. After an identification is made, the witness should be asked to recite in her own words the degree of confidence she has in her identification, and her answer should be recorded. Having her choose the words avoids inadvertent suggestion from the options being chosen by the detective. Recording the witness's answer is wise to guard against "confidence drift," the tendency of many witnesses to raise their confidence in their identification of the defendant as trial approaches. Witnesses seem at least subconsciously to reason, "Well if the police are trying this guy, they must be convinced he did it, so I must have picked the right guy." There is no necessary correlation between confidence level and accuracy. Some of the most confidenct witnesses can be wrong while some only moderately confident witnesses can be right. Yet juries give witness expressions of high confidence in their identification tremendous weight. Best practices require videotaping or digitally video recording the entire identification process so that the suppression judge and, if no suppression results, the jury can decide for themselves whether they believe suggestion was present.

5. Showups

Remember that a showup involves displaying only one person or photo to the witness. That procedure is necessarily suggestive because the witness has no other options from which to choose and because the witness may assume that, because he was given only one choice, the police must think that this is the guy. There is some dispute over whether these risks might be worth it if the identification is made very close to the time of the crime, for memories are freshest at that time. But there is no dispute that showups are a tremendously dangerous procedure, fraught with high risks of error, once a substantial amount of time has passed between the crime and the identification.

6. Sketches

Artist sketches, when no photos or bodies are available for identification, are also risky. The artist's questions can be suggestive, the artist's necessarily flawed efforts to depict the witness's description visually can themselves alter the witness's recollection as she views more sketches, and a later photo or in-person identification may in fact reflect the witness's memory of the sketch rather than true recognition of the face. Efforts are under way to resolve these problems technologically. For example, a massive computer database of potential facial features can be compiled, the witness being asked to construct his own sketch of the person by sitting at the computer and mixing-and-matching features until crafting a result that satisfies him.

III. The Right to Counsel

A. Overview

The Sixth Amendment to the United States Constitution guarantees an accused the assistance of counsel for his defense. But when does someone become an "accused"? The Court's answer: when formal adversarial proceedings have begun, for that is when the state has fully and firmly committed its resources to the defendant's conviction. In *Kirby v. Illinois*, 406 U.S. 682 (1972), the Court put it this way:

> The initiation of judicial criminal proceedings is far from a mere formalism. It is the starting point of our whole system of adversarial criminal justice. For it is only then that the government has committed itself to prosecute, and only then that the adverse positions of government and the defendant have solidified. It is then that a defendant finds himself faced with the prosecutorial forces of organized society, and immersed in the intricacies of substantive and procedural criminal law. It is this point, therefore, that marks the commencement of the "criminal prosecutions" to which alone the explicit guarantees of the Sixth Amendment are applicable.

The Court's description of when our justice system gears up sufficiently to create a real adversarial relationship between the state and the defendant may or may not be accurate, and some view *Miranda*'s creation of a Fifth Amendment right to counsel during custodial interrogation, even if before formal adversarial proceedings have begun, as belying this claim. But, as a growing number of wrongful convictions have shown, a skillful lawyer's presence at a pre-trial identification procedure, regardless of at what point it occurs in the criminal justice process, can help to improve flawed procedures by insisting on ones compliant with the science and, if his entreaties are ignored by the police, can build a record effectively to challenge weak procedures at trial. The formal proceedings starting place thus may relegate assisting in truth finding to a low or irrelevant role for counsel under the Sixth Amendment, replacing it with a more formal and symbolic mission, something contradicted by the Court's language in several cases to be discussed shortly.

Formal adversarial proceedings are generally held to have begun when a complaint is filed or an indictment or information returned, whichever occurs first. The shorthand term of art for events occurring after formal proceeding begin is "post-indictment." This term is routinely used by the courts even where no indictment procedure, but rather only a complaint (for misdemeanors) or a complaint followed by an information (for felonies) is used.

United States v. Wade, 388 U.S. 218 (1967), which in part addressed the value of counsel in preventing undue suggestion in identification procedures, is the seminal case concerning the right to counsel post-indictment.

B. *United States v. Wade* and Uncounseled Out-of-Court Identifications

Wade arose from a bank robbery done by a man with a small strip of tape on each side of his face, who had pointed a pistol at the female cashier and the vice president, the only persons then in the bank, forced them to fill a pillowcase with money, then drove off in a stolen car driven by an accomplice who had been waiting outside the bank.

Wade and two others were indicted for conspiring to rob the bank, while Wade himself was also indicted for the robbery itself. Counsel was appointed to represent Wade, and, fifteen days later, an FBI agent, without telling Wade's lawyer, arranged to have the two bank employees observe a lineup consisting of Wade and five or six other prisoners in a courtroom. Each person in the line wore strips of tape on their faces like those worn by the robber and, when so directed, spoke words allegedly uttered by the robber. Both employees identified Wade.

At trial, the two employees picked Wade out as the person who had robbed them, their prior lineup identifications being elicited from them as well on cross-examination. At the close of the prosecution's case, Wade's counsel moved for a judgment of acquittal or to strike the bank officials' courtroom identifications as stemming from a lineup conducted without counsel, in violation of his Fifth Amendment privilege against self-incrimination and Sixth Amendment right to counsel. The motion was denied, and Wade appealed his subsequent conviction.

The Court summarily rejected the Fifth Amendment challenge because Wade was compelled to display his person and the sound of his voice but not to divulge any knowledge he might have, thus not revealing any matter of "testimonial significance" protected by the privilege against self-incrimination. But the Court gave extended treatment to the Sixth Amendment right to counsel. In doing so, the Court seemed to craft a far broader role for counsel than the mere "spokesperson or advisor" version it adopted in *Ash*.

Indeed, the Court noted that the "Framers of the Bill of Rights envisaged a broader role for counsel than under the practice then prevailing in England of merely advising the client in 'matters of law,' and eschewing any responsibility for 'matters of fact.'" Moreover, said the Court, the Bill of Rights was adopted at a time when there were no organized police forces, the evidence being largely marshaled at the trial itself. But "today's law enforcement machinery involves critical confrontations of the accused by the prosecution at pretrial proceedings where the results might well settle the accused's fate and reduce the trial itself to a mere formality." Accordingly, the Court declared that the Sixth Amendment's text "encompasses counsel's assistance whenever necessary to assure a meaningful defense,'" quoted with approval its recognition in *Powell v. Alabama, 287* U.S. 45 (1932), that the period *from arraignment through trial* is "perhaps the most critical" one in which the accused requires counsel's guiding hand.It emphasized that the accused "is guaranteed that he need not stand alone against the State at any stage of the prosecution, *formal or informal,* in court or out, where counsel's absence might derogate from the right to counsel. The Court additionally stressed the important link between the right to counsel and the right to effective cross-examination at trial. Moreover, emphasized the Court, the Sixth Amendment right was not merely to counsel's presence but to the *effective assistance* of counsel.

The Court rejected the state's claim that the lineup was not a critical stage. To the contrary, insisted the court, the "vagaries of eyewitness identification are well-known," the criminal law's history being rife with instances of mistaken identification, and the identification process being "peculiarly riddled with innumerable dangers and variable factors which might seriously ... derogate from a fair trial." These dangers included suggestion in the manner in which the procedure is administered; the likely refusal of a witness making an identification to back off from it; the risk that (absent other evidence), it will dictate the result at trial; and the likelihood that witnesses who are also victims will act with spite or vengeance stemming from understandable outrage rather than with emotional clarity. Yet lineups are done in relative secrecy, there (then) being only rarely a record of the participants and no usable record of just what transpired, making reconstruction of the event at trial difficult.

The Court gave a variety of examples of suggestion, such as the defendant being the only "oriental," the only black-haired person, the only tall one, or the only young one in the lineup. Other examples included the defendant's being the only person in the line previously known to the witness. Counsel's presence, the Court explained, was essential effectively to address such suggestion:

> [N]either witnesses nor lineup participants are apt to be alert for conditions prejudicial to the suspect. And if they were, it would likely be of scant benefit to the suspect since neither witnesses nor lineup participants are likely to be schooled in the detection of suggestive influences. Improper influences may go undetected by a suspect, guilty or not, who experiences the emotional tension which we might expect in

one being confronted with potential accusers. Even when he does observe abuse, if he has a criminal record he may be reluctant to take the stand and open up the admission of prior convictions.

Furthermore, explained the Court, "any protestations by the suspect of the fairness of the lineup made at trial are likely to be in vain" because the jury is more likely to believe the officers' version of the facts and inferences therefrom than the unsupported testimony of the accused. Without counsel's presence, therefore, the Court continued, the accused would be unable "effectively to reconstruct at trial any unfairness that occurred at the lineup," thus "depriving him of his only opportunity meaningfully to attack the credibility of the witness's courtroom identification."

Counsel's absence in the *Wade* case itself, noted the Court, created just this set of problems, for the bank Vice-President testified that he saw someone (likely Wade) in an FBI agent's custody in the hall outside the courtroom where the identifications were to be made just *before the lineup itself.* The cashier likewise testified on cross that she saw from her courtroom seat Wade standing in the outside hallway within sight of an FBI agent, with the other prisoners to participate in the lineup appearing in the hall only later.

Even worse, noted the Court, in the companion case of *Gilbert v. California*, lineups were conducted in an auditorium in which 100 witnesses to alleged robberies made "wholesale identifications of Gilbert as the robber in each other's presence." "It is hard to imagine a situation," said the Court, "more clearly conveying the suggestion to the witness that the one presented is believed guilty by the police."

That the suggestion may have been inadvertent, moreover, was irrelevant. Furthermore, the Court rejected the state's argument that the lineup was not a critical stage because any flaws could be repaired upon cross-examination:

> Insofar as the accused's conviction may rest on a courtroom identification in fact the fruit of a suspect pre-trial identification which the accused is helpless to subject to effective scrutiny at trial, the accused is deprived of that right of cross-examination which is an essential safeguard to his right to confront the witnesses against him. And even though cross-examination is a precious safeguard to a fair trial, it cannot be viewed as an absolute assurance of accuracy and reliability. Thus in the present context, where so many variables and pitfalls exist, the first line of defense must be *the prevention of unfairness* and the lessening of the hazards of eyewitness identification at the lineup itself. The trial which might determine the accused's fate may well not be that in the courtroom but that at the pre-trial confrontation, with the state

aligned against the accused, the witness the sole jury, and the accused unprotected against the over-reaching, intentional or unintentional, and with little or no effective appeal from the judgment there rendered by the witness — "that's the man."

C. The In-Court Identification in *Wade*

Having found that the pre-trial lineup identification in *Wade* violated his right to the assistance of counsel during that procedure, the Court faced the question of what remedy to provide. Suppression of any mention of the out-of-court identification by the prosecution at trial, the Court suggested, would ordinarily be part of any remedy. But that remedy would be meaningless in Wade's case because the prosecutor never elicited testimony about the lineup. The prosecutor merely asked the witnesses whether they recognized anyone in court at the trial as the robber, at which time they each respectively pointed at Wade. It was *defense counsel* who brought out the lineup details at trial in the hope of discrediting the in-court identifications as irretrievably tainted by the suggestive out-of-court ones. Counsel, said the Court, faced the predicament of deciding whether to leave the in-court identification to stand without placing it in the context of the earlier suggestion or to bring out the lineup's weaknesses but at the risk of "bolstering the government witness's courtroom identification by bringing out and dwelling upon his prior identification." Had counsel been present at the lineup in the first place, however, he would have been better equipped to attack not only the lineup but the courtroom identification too. Suppressing prosecution mention of the lineup identification at trial may thus, implied the Court, be an incomplete remedy in many cases without also suppressing any later resulting in-court identification, the latter remedy being the sole one available, and thus a particularly important one, in *Wade*.

This observation did not mean, however, that in-court identifications must always be suppressed as the fruit of uncounseled pre-trial ones. Rather, the government must have the opportunity to prove by clear and convincing evidence that the in-court identification stemmed from the witness's observations during the crime rather than from the tainted pre-trial identification. The Court articulated a series of factors for the trial court to weigh in deciding whether this test for excluding evidence obtained by exploitation of the primary illegality was met or whether instead the in-court evidence was "sufficiently distinguishable to be purged of the primary taint." Explained the Court:

> Application of this test in the present context requires consideration of various factors; for example, the prior opportunity to observe the

alleged criminal act, the existence of any discrepancy between any pre-lineup description, and the defendant's actual description, any identification prior to the lineup of another person, the identification by picture of the defendant prior to the lineup, failure to identify the defendant on a prior occasion, and the lapse of time between the alleged act and the lineup identification. It is also relevant to consider those facts which, despite the absence of counsel, are disclosed concerning the conduct of the lineup.

Accordingly, the Court vacated the Court of Appeals' judgment, remanding it to that court with an instruction that it vacate the conviction and further remand the case to the district court to offer the prosecution the opportunity to prove that the in-court identifications were purged from the taint of the uncounseled lineups.

D. *Wade*'s Modern Implications

Wade may have contained the seeds of its own destruction. As in *Miranda*, the *Wade* Court intimated that legislative or other regulations eliminating the risks of abuse and suggestion and removing impediments to meaningful confrontation at trial may render lineups no longer "critical." However, neither Congress nor the federal authorities had crafted such effective alternatives to the *Wade* rule. Yet the advance of science and technology may do just that.

The *Wade* Court itself distinguished lineups from scientific analyses of fingerprints, blood samples, or hair, the latter not constituting "critical stages," thus not requiring counsel's presence, because "[k]nowledge of the techniques of science and technology is sufficiently available, and the variables in techniques few enough, that the accused has the opportunity for a meaningful confrontation of the Government's case at trial through the ordinary processes of cross-examination of the Government's expert witnesses and the presentation of his own experts." Scientific knowledge about human perception and memory processes involved in pre-trial and at-trial identifications have arguably now advanced so far that a talented lawyer afforded a broad scope in cross-examining fact-witnesses and permitted to call his own expert witness on the psychology of identification may be capable of effectively casting doubt on a particular identification's accuracy. The case for effective cross-examination is strengthened still further if lineups are required to be videotaped and the judge permitted and receptive to cautionary jury instructions warning of the dangers of poorly administered lineups. Should these safeguards still be insufficient, a legislature might by statute, or a police department by regulation, require adoption of just those procedures dictated by science to reduce the risk of error.

The *Wade* Court also articulated an expansive role for counsel, apparently both in preventing error by suggesting alternative procedures *before the lineup is administered* to avoid suggestion in the first place and by better preparing for cross by being a close observer and recorder of lineup events at trial. Although the Court later more narrowly described counsel's role as a spokesperson or advisor, that role might include advising *on what lineup procedures the defendant should insist upon* and acting as a spokesperson or advocate for their implementation. But, if this is so, the *Ash* holding that counsel's presence is not critical at photospreads because the accused is not present makes little sense. A lawyer's role as "spokesperson" may be most sorely needed exactly when the accused does not even have a theoretical chance to speak on his own behalf. A lawyer's presence might help to avert suggestion at the photospread in the first place, a matter *Wade* seemed to deem important for pre-trial identification procedures.

Wade suggests ethical lessons for both prosecutors and defense counsel as well. There are sometimes long delays between a crime and a trial. A prosecutor must be careful not to point out the defendant to the witness before she testifies as a way of pre-emptively refreshing the witness's memory. Absent counsel's assistance, such an action would constitute an invasion of the defendant's Sixth Amendment right to counsel at a critical stage. Correspondingly, today neither prosecutors nor defense counsel can competently do their jobs without knowledge and use of the current and advancing state of the science on identification witness psychology.

Ultimately, *Wade's* limitation to post-indictment identification procedures renders it of little value in the run-of-the-mill case. Most lineups, showups, and other identification procedures occur *pre*-indictment. Moreover, *Wade's* protections were further limited by the Court's declaring that, even post-indictment, counsel must be provided only at a "critical stage" of the prosecution. In common sense terms, a critical stage is one where the presence of counsel is seriously needed. In the abstract, every post-indictment stage might seem to be critical because defense counsel can seek to correct police errors before they cause harm, deter errors by his mere presence, record errors to improve case-strategizing and the effectiveness of trial cross-examination, immediately investigate leads and question witnesses revealed by each investigative process, and be clued in early to pre-trial motions and necessary legal research. But in *United States v. Ash*, 413 US 300 (1973), the Court narrowed defense counsel's role during pre-trial police or prosecutor investigation to that of a "spokesperson or advisor" to help the accused cope with the intricacies of the law and the inequality inherent in "trial-like" confrontations. Accordingly, the Court held that photographic identifications are not "critical stages" of the prosecution because no defendant is present in-person to be advised by counsel, nor is it a "trial-like" confrontation requiring counsel learned in the law. The *Ash* Court did not in its opinion address the psychological research studies even then available on suggestive identifications.

Given these limitations of *Wade*, the due process safeguards against suggestive identifications, which apply to *any* identification, whenever it occurs, are of far more practical importance.

IV. Due Process

A. Overview

Despite its greater practical importance, the due process test is much easier to explain. The Court has interpreted fundamental fairness under the due process clauses as requiring the suppression of any out-of-court identification that, based upon the totality of the circumstances, was so unnecessarily suggestive as to create a very substantial likelihood of misidentification. *See Neil v. Biggers*, 409 U.S. 188, 198 (1972); *accord Manson v. Braithwaite*, 433 U.S. 98 (1977) (reaffirming the *Biggers* analysis). If suppression of the out-of-court identification is required, a court must next decide whether the in-court identification must also be suppressed as the fruit of the unnecessarily suggestive pre-trial identification. The answer to this latter question is decided using the same test for whether to suppress the pre-trial identification but with one modification: the word "irreparable" is inserted before the word "misidentification." The Court has never clearly explained how the addition of the world "irreparable" changes the test. Presumably, the word is one of emphasis and degree, suggesting that the risk of error for excluding the at-trial identification must be significantly greater than that required to exclude the pre-trial identification.

B. Defining "Unnecessary Suggestiveness"

What constitutes suggestion is not hard to explain: any significant differences in appearance that draw attention to the suspect, making him stand out from the foils, or any actions by the police intentionally or inadvertently directing the witness's attention to the suspect or intimating that "he's the guy." The *Wade* case, in asserting that lawyers were needed at lineups in part to prevent, record, or expose suggestion, gave numerous examples of this phenomenon. Being the only redhead in the line, having multiple witnesses' watch as each identifies the suspect, police suggesting or flatly stating that the perpetrator is indeed in the line are but some of the ways that suggestion can be created. But not every difference constitutes suggestion. Were the line but one of clones, there would be no way for the witness to distinguish the true wrongdoer from others, so too much similarity can itself be misleading. In reality, some differences are unavoidable, and it's a good thing too. Due process requires only a "reasonable effort to harmonize the lineup," not perfect identity of lineup participants' appearance.

Yet suggestion alone does not violate the constitution. The suggestion must also be "unnecessary." *Stovall v. Denno*, 388 U.S. 293 (1967), illustrates the point. There, a black male was handcuffed to one of five white police officers, all of whom entered the hospital room of a woman who was an eyewitness to the stabbing-murder of her husband and a victim of a stabbing herself. The woman had just undergone potentially life-saving surgery. While there clearly was suggestion inherent in this procedure, the Court found the suggestion to be "necessary." No one knew how long the victim might live. There was thus a need for immediate action, and the victim was in no condition to visit the jail for a lineup. Under these emergency circumstances, the suggestive one-person showup was the "only feasible procedure" and, therefore, the due process clause was not violated.

While the *Stovall* Court seemed to treat "necessity" as akin to "urgency," less dire circumstances may also justify suggestive procedures. For example, in *Simmons v. United States*, 390 U.S. 377 (1968), the Court concluded that using photo arrays, instead of some other less suggestive identification procedure, one day after a gunpoint robbery, was necessary. The Court reasoned that:

> [a] serious felony had been committed. The perpetrators were still at large. The inconclusive clues which law enforcement officials possessed led to Andrews and Simmons. It was essential for the FBI agents swiftly to determine whether they were on the right track, so that they could properly deploy their forces in Chicago and, if necessary, alert officials in other cities.

The scope of the *Simmons* notion that suggestion may be necessary to determine whether the police are "on the right track" is uncertain. It is important to note, however, that the Court's discussion of necessity was directed to using the particular type of identification procedure — a photo array instead of a lineup. But the Court emphasized that each photo array, while not perfect, involved at least six photographs, with each witness being alone while viewing the photographs, and with no evidence that the FBI suggested which persons were under suspicion. The pressing need to conduct identifications by photo arrays did not in turn make it "necessary" that those photo arrays be conducted in a suggestive manner. Thus, the Court might have held there was unnecessary suggestiveness if the police had been sloppy or careless in the manner in which they conducted the arrays, for example, by using only one or two photographs or declaring that "the perpetrators are probably in those photos."

These points are especially important because there is reason to believe that photospreads are rapidly replacing lineups. Photospreads are easier and cheaper to administer. It may be hard to find enough persons with similar faces to the accused's on short notice. But it is far more workable to build up over time an ever-expanding database of photos for comparison purposes. New facial identification programs and other computer technologies can make identifying similar photos for an array a fast, accurate process. Indeed, software is now available for this very purpose and can and has been installed and tested on personal digital assistants (PDAs). If this technology becomes widespread, there may be less excuse for on-scene showups because a photo of the suspect can be taken and a photo array quickly compiled to show the witness on the officer's PDA.

Post-*Simmons*, however, the Court has indeed made it clear that police are expected to make reasonable efforts to render lineups fair and that the technical difficulty of organizing fair lineups does not make the resulting suggestion "necessary." For example, in *Neil v. Biggers*, 409 U.S. 188 (1972), the Court held that a showup was unnecessarily suggestive, despite the police finding no one at either the city jail or the juvenile home on the date of the identification procedure who fit a physical description comparable to the defendant's. The Court cited with approval the district court's opinion on the point: "In this case it appears to the Court that a lineup, which both sides admit is generally more reliable than a showup, could have been arranged. The fact that this was not done tended needlessly to decrease the fairness of the identification process to which petitioner was subjected." *Simmons's* holding may have contributed to the apparent growing flight from lineups to photospreads and, when combined with new PDA technology, may create growing pressure to render even on-the-scene showups a rarity, although such showups are currently quite common.

Although the due process test is designed primarily to minimize the risk of mistakenly convicting the innocent, that is not the sole goal. The necessity requirement seems to embody an assessment by the Court that the risk of error must be weighed against law enforcement need for the evidence and the degree of availability of less restrictive alternative identification measures. A jurisprudence focused more fervently on protecting the innocent would be concerned solely with whether there was suggestion raising an unacceptable chance of convicting the wrong person. Such a jurisprudence would also weight public safety more heavily, for catching the wrong person means that the right one is free to prey on the public once again. In effect, the Court's current doctrine suggests an implicit embrace of the idea that suppression is a form of punishment for the police as much as it as a protection for the innocent, and the police must engage in conduct that is in some sense wrongful if they are to "deserve" punishment. Where the police had no practical alternatives to the technique that they used, they cannot be said to be morally culpable and thus do not merit public chastisement.

C. The Likelihood of Misidentification

Even if an identification procedure was administered in an unnecessarily suggestive manner, the resulting pre-trial identification will be admissible if the court is convinced that the witness had a reliable independent basis for that identification. Thus a witness who observed a robber in bright light for twenty minutes and who gave an excellent detailed description of the robber to the police probably had a reliable independent basis for selecting the defendant from a visual lineup that was conducted one day after the crime, even if there was some unnecessary suggestion that he do so. In other words, the identification remains admissible if it is reliable despite the unnecessary suggestion. Reliability is thus the "linchpin" of the analysis.

In *Manson v. Brathwaite*, 432 U.S. 98 (1977), the Court articulated some of the factors to be considered in determining whether an unnecessarily suggestive identification was in fact reliable:

> the opportunity of the witness to view the criminal at the time of the crime, the witness' degree of attention, the accuracy of his prior description of the criminal, and the level of certainty demonstrated at the confrontation, and the time between the crime and the confrontation. Against these factors must be weighed the corrupting effect of the suggestive identification itself.

These same factors should be considered in determining the reliability of an in-court identification that is alleged to be the fruit of an unnecessarily suggestive out-of-court identification and are similar to the factors articulated by the Court as relevant in determined whether an in-court identification should be suppressed as the fruit of an uncounseled pre-trial identification obtained in violation of the Sixth Amendment. Some of these factors seem inconsistent with modern science. For example, the level of a witness's certainty in her identification generally has little, if any, correlation with accuracy. The list is also incomplete, excluding many factors that modern science deems important. But the list was never intended to be exhaustive and was likely illustrative. Modifying or updating the list thus does not seem inconsistent with the underlying legal test, which focuses on reliability, and may even be mandated by it.

V. Other Constitutional Issues

A. Fifth Amendment

Remember that the Fifth Amendment declares that "[n]o person shall be compelled in any criminal case to be a witness against himself...." Are you a witness against yourself if you are forced to appear in a lineup? The answer is no. The amendment "does not protect a suspect from being compelled by the State to provide real or physical evidence." *Pennsylvania v. Muniz*, 496 U.S. 582, 589 (1990). The reason for this is that the amendment extends solely to a suspect's being compelled to testify against himself or otherwise provide the State with evidence of a "testimonial or communicative nature." Placing yourself in a lineup is not of a testimonial or communicative nature because it does not compel you "to disclose any knowledge ... [you] might have." *United States v. Wade.*

B. Fourth Amendment

Can you be picked up on the street on suspicion of a crime, taken down to a police station, and forced to stand in a lineup? Such an action is unquestionably a seizure within the meaning of the Fourth Amendment because a reasonable person would not feel that he was free to leave. There are, of course, different types of seizures, as discussed earlier in this text, and this type—a full-blown arrest (an extended, highly intrusive seizure of the person)—generally requires probable cause. Consequently, logic suggests that such action on suspicion, indeed on any level of belief in guilt short of probable cause, should be unconstitutional. Nevertheless, the Court has suggested that forced participation in a lineup on reasonable suspicion may be acceptable if the police first obtain judicial authorization in the form of a court order or a special type of warrant. *See, e.g., Davis v. Mississippi*, 394 U.S. 721 (1969) (holding that officers acted improperly in rounding up and fingerprinting numerous black youths after a report of a rape victim who could offer little in way of description of her attacker; nevertheless, the Court left open the possibility that a court might authorize an identification procedure on something less than probable cause).

A related question is whether an out-of-court and subsequent in-court eyewitness identification obtained as a result of an illegal arrest can be suppressed as the fruit of the illegal arrest. The Supreme Court addressed this question in *United States v. Crews*, 445 U.S. 463 (1980). There, Crews was detained at police headquarters, but not then formally arrested, on suspicion of a series of robberies. That detention, which a suppression court would later find was a de facto arrest without probable cause, permitted police to photograph Crews, thereafter obtaining a photo-identification of him by two victims, followed by his being detained again and placed in a lineup, where he was once again identified. The trial court excluded the photographic and lineup identifications from trial as fruits of the illegal detention but permitted in-court identifications on the ground that they were based on independent recollections of the incident. Crews was thereafter convicted, his appeal ultimately reaching the Supreme Court.

The Court agreed that the in-court identification need not be suppressed. Justice Brennan delivered the opinion of the Court on most grounds. Brennan explained that there are three elements of a victim's in-court identification: (1) the victim's presence in court to identify the defendant; (2) the victim's knowledge of the crime itself that enables her to identify the defendant; and (3) the defendant's physical presence in the courtroom to be identified. As to the first of these elements, the robbery victim's presence at trial was not due to any police misconduct, for she had immediately reported the crime to the police, given them a full description of her assailant, and cooperated with them in every way, explained Brennan. As to the second element, Brennan explained that the suppression court had found that the victim's knowledge of the crime was so strong that it did not taint her in-court identification, and ample evidence supported this finding. As to the third element, Brennan explained that the defendant himself cannot be a suppressible fruit; however, Brennan and two other Justices reserved the question whether defendant's presence at a lineup made his body and face into "fruit" for that single purpose. But, in two concurring opinions, five Justices—a majority—took the position that a defendant's presence at trial and thus the availability of his face to be identified at that time can never be suppressed as the fruit of an illegal arrest. As Justice White put it in his concurrence, "A holding that a defendant's face can be considered evidence suppressible for no reason than other than the defendant's presence in the courtroom is the fruit of an illegal arrest would be tantamount to holding that an illegal arrest effectively insulates one from conviction for any crime where an in-court identification is essential." White unequivocally rejected such a holding as inconsistent with precedent and sound policy.

Crews does not foreclose the possibility of suppressing the out-of-court identifications where they were obtained as the result of an illegal arrest. Indeed, the trial court did just that on the facts before it. Nor does *Crews* prevent excluding physical evidence of the defendant's person other than eyewitness identification, such as, for example, obtaining fingerprints by violating the Fourth Amendment, as occurred in *Davis*, discussed above. But *Crews* does arguably stand for the proposition that an in-court identification by an eyewitness of a defendant's face may never be suppressed as the result of an illegal arrest or other seizure of the person in violation of the Fourth Amendment.

Checkpoints

- One ground for suppressing an out-of-court identification, such as during a lineup, photo-array, or show-up, is that it was obtained in violation of the Sixth Amendment right to counsel.

- That right guarantees the presence of a criminal defense lawyer at every "post-indictment" "critical stage" of a criminal prosecution, absent a knowing, voluntary, and intelligent waiver of that right.

- The term "post-indictment" is a term of art meaning after the start of formal adversarial proceedings, which in turn generally means after a complaint or an indictment has been filed, whichever comes first.

- The term "critical stage" means any stage of the criminal process at which a lawyer is needed to act as the defendant's "spokesperson or advisor" and includes post-indictment lineups and show-ups but does not include photo-arrays, so there is no right to counsel at such arrays.

- If counsel is not provided at a post-indictment lineup or show-up, that lineup or show-up may not be mentioned at trial, but the eyewitness will also be barred from appearing at trial and identifying the defendant as the criminal wrongdoer if that later in-court identification is the fruit of the uncounseled out-of-court identification.

- The in-court identification will be considered fruit of the tainted out-of-court identification unless the prosecution proves by clear and convincing evidence that the in-court identification stemmed from the witness's observations during the crime rather than from remembering identifying the defendant at the earlier, uncounseled out-of-court identification procedure.

- Under the "*Wade* test," so-named because it was first articulated in *United States v. Wade*, the trial court decides the fruits question by considering the following non-exhaustive factors:

    - the prior opportunity of the witness to observe the criminal act;

    - the existence of any discrepancy between any pre-lineup description given to the police by the witness and the defendant's actual description;

Checkpoints *continued*

- • any identification by that witness of a person other than the defendant prior to the lineup or showup involving that witness;

- • any identification of the defendant by the eyewitness by photograph prior to the physical lineup or show-up;

- • any failure of the witness to identify the defendant on a prior occasion;

- • the lapse of time between the crime and the identification.

- Another ground for suppressing an out-of-court identification is that it violated the due process clauses.

- The test for whether an out-of-court identification violated the due process clauses is this: Was the identification so unnecessarily suggestive as to create a very substantial likelihood of misidentification?

- Thus suggestion that risks error does not violate due process if the suggestion was "necessary," for example, if the witness was hospitalized and potentially facing death so that there was not more time to design a better procedure.

- Although the Supreme Court has never addressed the question, some commentators argue, and advocates may try to argue, that any procedure failing to comply with widely available scientific teachings on how to design non-suggestive identification procedures is "unnecessarily" suggestive. These teachings include:

  - • using a "double-blind" procedure in which even the detective administering the lineup has no idea which person in the line is the suspect;

  - • using a lineup of adequate size so that there is little chance that the witness chose the suspect simply by guessing rather than by recognition;

  - • instructing the witness not to assume that the suspect or the actual criminal is in the lineup.

- If the out-of-court identification was indeed unnecessarily suggestive, then the next step is to determine whether, despite the suggestion, the identification was sufficiently "reliable," or, instead, created a very substantial likelihood of misidentification.

- The non-exhaustive factors entering into this reliability determination for suppressing the out-of-court identification on due process grounds are apparently the same factors identified by the Supreme Court in the *Wade* test for suppressing an in-court identification on right to counsel grounds, and two additional factors not mentioned in *Wade*: (1) the witness's degree of attention at the time of the crime; and (2) the level of certainty the witness demonstrated in the identification he made at the time that he made it.

Checkpoints *continued*

- If the out-of-court identification is suppressed as violative of due process, then the witness may also be barred from identifying the defendant as the criminal in-court, primarily meaning at trial, if the following *test* is met: Was the procedure used so unnecessarily suggestive as to create a very substantial likelihood of *irreparable* misidentification?

- If an out-of-court eyewitness identification occurred because of a Fourth Amendment violation, then that out-of-court eyewitness identification may be suppressed if warranted under ordinary Fourth Amendment princip*les;* however, the in-court eyewitness identification may probably never be suppressed as the fruit of the Fourth Amendment violation.

- The Court has suggested in *dicta* that it may be willing to approve court-ordered detentions solely for the purpose of conducting eyewitness identification procedures on less than probable cause, likely mere reasonable suspicion, the Court suggesting that a new sort of warrant or other Court order would be required.

Chapter 17

Entrapment

Roadmap

- What is entrapment
- The different contexts in which an entrapment defense can arise
- The subjective and objective approaches to entrapment
- The predisposition to commit the crime
- The burden of proving entrapment
- What is entrapment-by-estoppel
- What is sentencing entrapment
- What is "outrageous government conduct"

I. Introduction

Some consider entrapment exclusively a criminal law defense. Others see entrapment as a procedural safeguard against government misconduct in manufacturing criminal acts. In part the difference of substance and procedure results from two different views taken by jurisdictions: a subjective and objective approach. The subjective approach looks at the defendant's conduct and provides a criminal law defense when the accused did not have the predisposition to commit the criminal activity. In contrast, an objective approach looks at law enforcement conduct, examining whether the accused was enticed to commit the misconduct because of government misconduct. Many jurisdictions approach entrapment from a hybrid perspective, looking first at whether the accused had the predisposition to commit the act, and then examining whether the government crossed the line in enticing the accused to commit the criminal activity.

Many claims of entrapment come from cases involving "sting operations," where the police deliberately use trickery and deceit to stop criminal activity. Police routinely use undercover agents in drug buys and in other undercover investigations. The question arises whether the accused would have committed the crime but for the enticement by law enforcement to engage in the activity. Questions also can arise as to whether law enforcement deliberately targeted individuals for illegitimate reasons, such as politics, race, or sexual orientation.

Another context that may present an entrapment defense is when an accused individual relies on an official's statement of the law of the legality of certain conduct. This is called entrapment-by-estoppel. Entrapment may also arise as an issue in the sentencing phase of a trial.

Some states have codified an entrapment defense. For example, Connecticut provides that "it shall be a defense that the defendant engaged in the proscribed conduct because he was induced to do so by a public servant, or by a person acting in cooperation with a public servant, for the purpose of institution of criminal prosecution against the defendant, and that the defendant did not contemplate and would not otherwise have engaged in such conduct." *C.G.S.A. § 53a-15 (2007).* Other jurisdictions, like the federal system, rely upon caselaw for this defense.

In addition to entrapment, government misconduct may raise a defense of "outrageous government conduct." This defense uses an objective approach and is grounded in the Due Process Clauses of the Constitution.

II. Subjective Approach

One approach to entrapment is to examine whether the accused had the predisposition to commit the offense. This approach is followed by the majority of states and is also used in the federal system. It is not, however, the approach used in the Model Penal Code. A subjective approach looks at whether law enforcement "implant[ed] in the mind of an innocent person the disposition to commit the alleged offense and induce its commission in order that they may prosecute." *Sorrells v. United,* 287 U.S. 435 (1932). Thus, if the accused would not have purchased drugs but for the continued solicitation by an undercover police officer, entrapment can be used when the defendant is charged for the illegal purchase of the drugs. Merely affording opportunities to commit a crime, however, is not entrapment. As noted by Chief Justice Warren, "a line must be drawn between the trap for the unwary innocent and the trap for the unwary criminal." *Sherman v. United States,* 356 U.S. 369 (1958).

Courts use different factors in assessing predisposition. Some of these factors are:

(1) whether the defendant readily responded to the inducement offered; (2) the circumstances surrounding the illegal conduct; (3) the

state of mind of a defendant before the government agents make any suggestion that the defendant shall commit a crime; (4) whether the defendant was engaged in an existing course of conduct similar to the crime for which the defendant is charged; (5) whether the defendant had already formed the design to commit the crime for which the defendant is charged; (6) the defendant's reputation; (7) the conduct of the defendant during negotiations with the undercover agent; (8) whether the defendant has refused to commit similar acts on other occasions; (9) the nature of the crime charged; (10) the degree of coercion which the law officers contributed to instigating the transaction relative to the defendant's criminal background.

United States v. Dion, 762 F.2d 674 (8th Cir. 1985).

Federal jurisdictions are split on whether to look only at the "disposition," *i.e.*, the mental state of the defendant to commit the crime, or to also examine the accused's "position," that is "whether the defendant was able and likely, based upon experience, training, and contacts, to actually commit the crime." *United States v. Knox*, 112 F.3d 802 (5th Cir. 1997). In *United States v, Hollingsworth*, 27 F.3d 1197 (7th Cir. 1994), the Seventh Circuit en banc reversed money laundering convictions of a dentist and farmer who lacked the "underworld contacts, financial acumen or assets, access to foreign banks or bankers, or other assets" to get into the international money-laundering business.

In the leading Supreme Court entrapment decision, *Jacobsen v. United States*, 503 U.S. 540 (1992), government agents spent twenty-six months repeatedly trying to get a Nebraska farmer to order sexually explicit photographs of children through the mail, in violation of the Child Protection Act of 1984. Two government agencies using "five fictitious organizations and a bogus pen pal" repeatedly attempted to get the defendant to engaged in illegal conduct. The Supreme Court, in a five to four opinion, held that "[w]here the Government has induced the individual to break the law and the defense of entrapment is at issue, ... the prosecution must prove beyond a reasonable doubt that the defendant was disposed to commit the criminal act prior to first being approached by Government agents." The Court reversed the conviction finding that as a "matter of law" the prosecution failed to prove" that petitioner was predisposed, independent of the Government's acts and beyond a reasonable doubt, to violate the law by receiving child pornography through the mails."

Although *Jacobsen* held that there was entrapment as a matter of law, courts often allow the trier of fact to determine if the government induced the defendant to violate the law. Some courts treat entrapment as an affirmative defense, requiring the accused to not only raise the issue but also to prove that the government engaged in misconduct and that the defendant did not have the predisposition to commit the crime. Other jurisdictions place the burden of production on the defendant, but then once presented by the defense, the burden of persuasion shifts to the prosecution to prove that the accused had the predisposition to violate the law.

The most obvious impediment to an accused presenting an entrapment defense is that it is difficult to present without admitting to the commission of the criminal act. After all, to argue that one was entrapped by the government to commit the crime usually necessitates that one first affirmatively acknowledge that he or she engaged in the criminal activity. The Supreme Court in *Mathews v. United States*, 485 U.S. 58 (1988), however, did hold "that even if the defendant denies one or more elements of the crime, he is entitled to an entrapment instruction whenever there is sufficient evidence from which a reasonable jury could find entrapment." The use of entrapment can also open the door to evidence of defendant's prior criminal activity. Thus, uncharged and charged conduct may be presented by the prosecution to show that the accused had the predisposition to commit the charged crime. Such evidence can be prejudicial to the defendant's claim of entrapment.

III. Objective Approach

Entrapment from an objective approach focuses on the government conduct as opposed to the accused's predisposition to commit the crime. It permits an entrapment defense to deter government misconduct. An example of conduct that warrants an entrapment defense would be when law enforcement guarantees that the conduct will go undetected or when police make an "offer of exorbitant consideration." *People v. Barraza*, 591 P.2d 947 (Cal. 1979).

The Model Code deliberately adopted this approach to allow for the full deterrent effect of the government misconduct. The drafters stated that a defendant "should not go to jail simply because he has been convicted before and is said to have a criminal disposition." The drafters of the Model Penal Code also were concerned that use of a subjective approach would diminish the importance of focusing on "discourag[ing] unsavory police tactics." *Model Penal Code § 2.13, Commentary.* Those endorsing a subjective approach respond that a guilty defendant should not be allowed to go free because of individual police misconduct.

The subjective and objective tests sometimes blend together because even a jurisdiction using an objective approach may examine the conduct of the police and those using an objective approach may include some evidence pertaining to the individual defendant. Some states provide a hybrid approach that examines the predisposition of the accused in addition to the police conduct in enticing the individual to commit the crime.

IV. Entrapment-by-Estoppel

Entrapment-by-estoppel can be used when the accused believes that his or her conduct is legal because of reliance on an official's statement of the law. It differs from what has been called a public-authority defense where the "defendant engages in conduct at the request of a government official that the defendant knows to be otherwise illegal." *United States v. Strahan*, 565 F.3d 1047 (7th Cir. 2009). In the case of entrapment by estoppel, the accused does not know of the illegality of the conduct.

Entrapment by estoppel applies "when an official assures a defendant that certain conduct is legal, and the defendant reasonably relies on that advice and continues or initiates the conduct." *United States v. Achter*, 52 F.3d 753 (8th Cir. 1995). It is grounded on being a violation of the Due Process Clause of the United States Constitution. Thus, a defendant who reasonably relies on a government announcement that a sales promotion program is legal, and then is unfairly prosecuted for participation in that program, can offer entrapment by estoppel as a defense.

V. Sentencing Entrapment

Entrapment is not solely an issue for the guilt-innocence phase of the trial. It can also arise as an issue in sentencing a defendant. Sentencing entrapment, sometimes called sentencing manipulation or sentencing escalation, occurs when "a defendant, although predisposed to commit a minor or lesser offense, is entrapped in committing a greater offense subject to greater punishment." *United States v. Stuart*, 923 F.2d 607 (8th Cir. 1991). For example, law enforcement may deliberately entice an individual to make multiple drug buys for the purpose of increasing the sentence or allowing for a mandatory-minimum sentence to apply.

Unlike a typical entrapment defense, sentencing entrapment does not necessitate a reversal of a conviction or serve as a basis for not prosecuting the accused. Rather, a successful claim of sentencing entrapment calls for a downward departure in the defendant's sentence. Some courts, however, reject sentencing entrapment when the defendant had the predisposition to commit the offense.

VI. Outrageous Government Conduct

Outrageous government conduct is considered a separate defense, although the arguments are similar to those used for entrapment under an objective approach. Premised upon a violation of the Due Process Clause of the U.S. Constitution, defendants claiming outrageous government conduct argue that the "conduct of law enforcement agents is so outrageous that due process principles would absolutely bar the government from invoking judicial process to obtain a conviction." *United States v. Russell*, 411 U.S. 423 (1973).

The defense of outrageous government conduct is seldom successful for a defendant and the Supreme Court approved its existence with a splintered vote. In *Hampton v. United States*, 435 U.S. 484 (1976), then-Justice Rehnquist writing for the plurality stated "that absent a violation of some protected right of the defendant, the Due Process Clause cannot be invoked to overturn a conviction because of government misconduct." *United States v. Gamble*, 737 F.2d 853 (Kan. 1984). This defense, however, survived because two concurrences and three dissenters in the *Hampton* case supported a defense of outrageous government conduct even when the accused might be predisposed to commit the crime.

The rare example of when outrageous government conduct can be successful is when law enforcement encourages the manufacturing of an illegal substance, provides the necessary ingredients and supplies for its production, and then offers technical assistance such as finding solutions when the defendant encounters difficulties in the production. In such cases, the government's extensive conduct in the criminal activity reaches a "demonstrable level of outrageousness." *United States v. Twigg*, 588 F.2d 373 (3d Cir. 1978).

Checkpoints

- Entrapment can be approached either subjectively or objectively, or using a hybrid of these two approaches.

- A subjective approach to entrapment is used by the majority of jurisdictions including the federal system.

- A subjective approach to entrapment looks at the defendant's predisposition to commit the crime.

- An objective approach, used in the Model Penal Code, examines whether law enforcement engaged in misconduct in enticing the accused to commit the crime.

- Jurisdictions vary on who has the burden of proving an entrapment defense with some jurisdictions having it as an affirmative defense.

- Reasonable reliance on an official's statement of the law when the accused believes that his or her conduct is legal provides a claim of entrapment by estoppel.

- Entrapment can be a basis for a sentence reduction when law enforcement deliberately manipulates the accused into criminal activity that will increase the sentence.

- It can be a due process violation when law enforcement engages in outrageous government conduct.

Mastering Criminal Procedure, Volume 1: The Investigative Stage Master Checklist

Scope of the Fourth Amendment
- ❏ Restrains government actors only
- ❏ Requires "search" or "seizure"
- ❏ Search requires a reasonable expectation of privacy in place searched
- ❏ No search if police access things exposed to public view or access, including a person's voice, handwriting exemplar, exterior of a car, open fields, garbage on curb
- ❏ "Seizure" is a restriction on a person's freedom of movement or interference with possessory interest in property
- ❏ Standing required

Warrants
- ❏ Probable cause needed
- ❏ Viewed by totality of the circumstances
- ❏ Credibility of informant and adequacy of basis for knowledge
- ❏ Particularity needed of place to be searched and items to be seized
- ❏ Neutral and detached magistrate must issue
- ❏ Executed within a reasonable period of time after issuance
- ❏ Officers executing must knock and announce their purpose unless emergency justification
- ❏ Analyze electronic surveillance under Fourth Amendment and applicable federal statutes

Arrests and Seizures of the Person
- ❏ Warrantless arrest in public if probable cause of commission by person of felony offense or any other violation of the criminal laws if state law gives police arrest authority
- ❏ Absent emergency, arrest warrant needed for a home

❏ Officers may not use deadly force unless an imminent threat to officers or others

❏ *Gerstein* hearing required if arrest without a warrant

❏ Seizure - when reasonable person feels not free to leave

❏ "Terry" stop - brief, relatively non-intrusive seizure of person

❏ Reasonable suspicion criminal activity afoot required for *Terry* stop, not probable cause

❏ Stopping vehicle allowed if probable cause to believe a traffic infraction

Warrantless Searches

❏ Incident to arrest

❏ Includes "grab-reach" area where evidence can be destroyed or weapons possible

❏ Includes entire passenger compartment of auto if unrestrained arrestee has access to the vehicle or if police have reason to believe evidence in passenger compartment

❏ "Protective sweeps" allowed in home for area immediately adjacent to arrest location

❏ Search allowed in home if officers have reasonable suspicion of possible danger to officers

❏ Inventory searches of car permitted after arrest

❏ Warrantless search permitted under "automobile exception" if probable cause to believe seizable evidence in car, including any package or bag that could contain the item

❏ Consent searches allowed if consent not coerced

❏ Police not required to inform that consent can be refused

❏ If police announce warrant present, consent to search not voluntary

❏ Consent only valid if individual had actual or apparent authority to consent to a search of the area

❏ If co-occupants, either can consent unless one co-occupant is present and objects to search

❏ "Pat down" (*Terry*) "frisk" for weapons allowed with reasonable suspicion suspect armed

❏ "Plain feel" seizure of contraband allowed when discovered during frisk

❏ *Reasonable* suspicion that motorist is armed permits limited search of passenger compartment

❏ Warrantless search allowed if hot pursuit of a fleeing felon or imminent threat to public safety

❏ No general exigency exception for murder crime scene

❏ Items can be seized if in plain view if police lawfully present, no additional search required, and immediate probable cause to believe contraband, etc.

❏ Warrant required to use sense-enhancing devices not in widespread use (e.g. thermal imaging) and directed at the home

❏ Administrative and special needs searches balance government's interest and reasonable expectation of privacy and require an objective programmatic purpose other than the general interest in crime control

❏ No Fourth Amendment violation for some suspicionless searches of probationers or parolees

❏ Brief stops for motor vehicle checkpoints allowed

❏ Border searches do not require probable cause

❏ Searches of public school students' persons allowed based on reasonable suspicion

The Exclusionary Rule

❏ Remedy for violations of the 4th Amendment, *Miranda* (5th Amendment) rights, and Sixth Amendment right to counsel

❏ Remedy imposed to deter police misconduct

❏ Not applicable to grand jury proceedings, civil proceedings, parole hearings, license revocations, violations of the knock-and-announce rule

❏ Good faith exception when reasonable reliance on judicial opinion later reversed; statute or ordinance later declared unconstitutional

❏ Reasonable reliance on a computer error that is not gross negligence or attributable to the police

❏ Not reasonable good faith reliance on a warrant when affidavit so lacking in probable cause, warrant invalid on its face, or police officer lied to obtain the warrant or acted in reckless disregard of the truth, or magistrate did not act in "neutral and detached manner"

❏ Exclusionary rule not applicable to impeachment of defendant

❏ "Fruit of the poisonous tree" doctrine suppresses evidence derived from the excluded evidence

❏ Exceptions to exclusionary rule include evidence obtained from an independent source, inevitable discovery evidence, intervening circumstances so "attenuated the taint" to void policy goals underlying exclusionary rule

Interrogation: Due Process, *Miranda* and the Sixth Amendment

❏ Due process requires voluntary statements

❏ Look at the totality of the circumstances

❏ *Miranda* applies when defendant in custody and being interrogated by the government

❏ *Miranda* requires informing (a) the right to silence and (b) the right to counsel prior to interrogation

❏ Waivers must be knowing, intelligent, and voluntary

❏ Silence not a waiver

❏ Custodial interrogation requires valid waiver

❏ Waiver not presumed merely because *Miranda* rights read

❏ Custody = not free to leave

❏ "Free to leave" different in *Miranda* and Fourth Amendment seizure

❏ *Miranda* does not apply to probation interviews

❏ Words or conduct likely to elicit response from person in custody constitutes interrogation

❏ *Miranda* does not apply to spontaneous statements and routine booking questions

❏ Fifth Amendment issue when *Miranda* warnings are given after inculpatory statements

❏ Terminating interrogation after *Miranda* warnings, police may later re-initiate questioning only if "scrupulously honor" right to remain silent

❏ Scrupulously honor when (a) suspect immediately left alone when asserting right to silence; (b) questioned by different detectives after the interrogation break; (c) questioning was for different offense; and, (d) questioning occurred after re-*Mirandized* and *knowingly, voluntarily,* and *intelligently* waived *Miranda rights*

❏ Unambiguous request for counsel,then all questioning must cease without counsel present

❏ *Miranda* rights extend to any other offenses, unless suspect re-initiates contact and validly waives rights or scrupulously honored rule met

❏ Statements taken in violation of *Miranda* can be used to impeach the defendant on cross-examination

❏ "Fruit of the poisonous tree" doctrine does not generally apply to *Miranda* violations and, if applicable, does not apply in the same way as it does to other constitutional violations

❏ Defendant can knowingly, voluntarily, and intelligently waive the right to counsel

❏ Sixth Amendment right to counsel is "offense-specific"

❏ Attempts to deliberately elicit information from person charged with crime violates the Sixth Amendment

❏ Same test for waiver of right to counsel for Fifth Amendment *Miranda* right and Sixth Amendment

Identifications

❏ Sixth Amendment right to attorney at post-charge line-up or show-up

❏ No Sixth Amendment right to attorney at pre-charge line-up or at photo identification

❏ Improper if unnecessarily suggestive process creates a very substantial likelihood of misidentification by the witness

❏ Can use if independent source for the in-court identification

Entrapment

❏ Two tests: subjective and objective

❏ Majority view is subjective test that focuses on predisposition

❏ Minority view is objective test that focuses on police conduct

❏ Outrageous government conduct = due process violation

Index

Page numbers refer to the first page of the entry.